A HISTORY OF THE
WEIMAR REPUBLIC

VOLUME I

*From the Collapse of the Empire
to Hindenburg's Election*

A HISTORY OF THE
WEIMAR REPUBLIC

By

Erich Eyck

Translated by

Harlan P. Hanson and Robert G. L. Waite

43

HARVARD UNIVERSITY PRESS

Cambridge, Massachusetts

1 9 6 7

Distributed in Great Britain by Oxford University Press, London

Library of Congress Catalog Card Number: 62–17219

Printed in the United States of America

To two friends who never failed me:
THEODOR HEUSS
on his seventieth birthday
and
GEORGE GOOCH
on his eightieth birthday

TRANSLATORS' FOREWORD

Erich Eyck needs little introduction to American historians. Yet the facts of his life are so peculiarly relevant to this, his most recent work, as to warrant brief summary here.

Born in Berlin in 1878 and educated there and in Freiburg im Breisgau, he took his degree in law and later studied taxation and administrative law under Dr. Hugo Preuss, the "Father of the Weimar Constitution." In 1904 he received his doctorate in history at the University of Berlin with a dissertation on the German labor movement. He practiced law from 1906 to 1937. As a journalist he contributed to Friedrich Naumann's *Hilfe*. Here he met Dr. Theodor Heuss and established a friendship that has lasted through the years. From 1915 to 1933 he was contributing editor of juridical matters for the *Vossische Zeitung*. He was active in the Democratic Party and was a member of the City Council of Berlin. Thus he served his community as attorney, journalist, and legislator.

When Hitler's regime denied him the possibility of continuing his active career in Germany, Dr. Eyck used his enforced leisure to study and, in his sixtieth year, to begin the writing of history. And it is as a historian that he is best known in America. His *Gladstone* (1938), *Pitt versus Fox: Father and Son* (1950), and *Bismarck and the German Empire* (1950) have previously appeared in English.* The last of these three books, which has been translated also into Italian and Swedish, is a condensation of his extended study *Bismarck: Leben und Werk* (Zurich, 1941–1944). Among Dr. Eyck's major histories, only his multivolume *Bismarck* and his *Das persönliche Regiment Wilhelms II* (Zurich, 1948) now remain to be translated into English. The history of the Weimar Republic, when coupled with his studies of Bismarck and William II, fulfills Dr. Eyck's ambition to write a political history of Germany which would span the years from 1815 (the birth of Bismarck) to 1933. The German edition of the present volumes appeared in 1954 and 1956.

It is, therefore, as a reflective man of affairs that Erich Eyck wrote this history of the German Republic. He combines the dispassionate judgment of a jurist, the flair of a journalist, and the perspective of a versatile and experienced historian with the informed insights of an active participant. Candidly confessing his

* The German editions of the first two works appeared as follows: *Gladstone* (Zurich, 1938) and *Die Pitt und die Fox, Väter und Söhne* (Zurich, 1948).

own point of view — which is that of a judicious moderate — he has given the modern reader and the future historian this account by one man who both participated in and pondered what was going on.

This double nature of the author's role is mirrored in his prose, which combines, or, to be more precise, alternates, the elegant periods of a Macaulay or Churchill with the acerbic candor of a Truman. The texture created by the interweaving of these two styles constitutes one of the striking values of the original German text. It has been our conscious endeavor to duplicate this fabric as best we could while, at the same time, staying as close as possible to what Erich Eyck actually wrote.

We have used the second (revised) edition of volume one (1957) and the first (sole) edition of volume two (1956). We have tried to translate this original as accurately as the two languages and the author's distinctive style allow. But we have sometimes found it necessary to expand sentences when the exact pattern of German grammar could not be brought over into English or where the literal meaning of a German phrase might not be clear to an English-speaking reader. We have at times altered the structure of sentences and broken up long paragraphs in the interest of clarity. The one major addition to the German text which appears in this translation — an addition made at Dr. Eyck's request — is clearly noted. Quotations from German poetry were translated especially for this occasion.

In this second printing we have made several emendations in our translation and occasional corrections of Dr. Eyck's text.

We are greatly indebted to Mr. John F. Naylor who prepared the endnotes for this edition and undertook the difficult task of supplying missing bibliographical data. Wherever possible he has also cited American and British editions of German books used by Dr. Eyck. Whatever stylistic merit is to be found in our translation derives in great part from our colleague Professor Fred H. Stocking, who kindly read our manuscript. The shortcomings of our work are, of course, our own. Indeed, if the fabric we have woven here serves, like other veils, to make the observer wish to see the corpus it partially reveals, we shall have achieved one of our principal goals.

H. P. H.
R. G. L. W.

Williamstown, Massachusetts

AUTHOR'S PREFACE

After writing my books on Bismarck and William II, which treat
the political history of Germany during the period approximately
from the Revolution of 1848 to the outbreak of the First World War,
I had thought of continuing my study of German history by including
the period of the Weimar Republic. But the shocking and lamentable
denouement of the Republic casts such a melancholy shadow over
its entire history that the retrospective historian needs firm resolve
and self-control if he is to persevere in his task. Moreover, if that
historian took part in the political life of the Republic, even in
minor roles, and if the collapse of the Republic meant for him the
loss of his homeland, then he cannot but sense constantly the "unspeakably painful torment of the old wound" as he examines the fate
of the Weimar Republic in detail.

But two considerations helped relieve me of my doubts. Knowledge and understanding of the immediate past is essential to both
a comprehension and a solution of the problems which Germany
and its former enemies face today. Furthermore, I experienced
these events personally and knew, or at least saw, a majority of the
political figures involved. As a student I sat in Helfferich's first class;
as a graduate assistant I met Radbruch in Liszt's seminar on criminal
law; as a young attorney I collaborated with Rudolph Breitscheid
in the organization of liberal meetings; and as an alderman in Berlin
I aroused the wrath of William Pieck. Perhaps, as a result of my own
personal experiences, I can give a more vivid picture of those times
than some later historian who will have to reconstruct them all
from documents, books, and newspapers.

Such personal intimacy with the period means, of course, that
the historian sees and reports the events only from one particular
point of view, no matter how earnestly he may try to "show how it
really was." But this seems to me to be not a great disadvantage —
if any — as long as the historian does not attempt to mask his personal viewpoint. I believe the reader of this book will at no time
doubt that it was written from the standpoint of a man who was a
liberal and a democratic supporter of the Republic. I was never,
however, a doctrinaire republican. (I find the British monarchy quite
comfortable.) It was simply that the course of events had made a
republic the indispensable and necessary form of government for
Germany. I hardly need add that today, after a study of the docu-

ments, and at some distance both in space and time, many of these events look different to me than they did at the time we lived through them.

Printed materials which I use are quoted and described as fully as seems necessary for any critical investigation of my text. To these sources I was able to add the fruits of conversations with men who had been active in the Weimar Republic. The observations of Dr. Otto Gessler, former minister of defense, and Dr. Hans Schäffer, former state secretary in the national Finance Ministry, were particularly valuable to me. I wish to express here my sincere thanks to both of these gentlemen.

ERICH EYCK

London, N.W. 3
December 1953

CONTENTS

From the Collapse of the Empire
to Hindenburg's Election

I

THE COLLAPSE OF THE MONARCHY

THE history of the Weimar Republic begins with the collapse of the German Empire, and this collapse, in turn, begins with the dismissal — which was extorted from the Emperor — of Bethmann-Hollweg on July 12, 1917.

The position and the task of the Chancellor had become more difficult with every month ever since the victorious advance of the German armies had come to a halt on the Marne in September 1914. Bethmann-Hollweg had comforted himself at the beginning of hostilities with the thought that a few powerful blows could bring the war to a quick end. When this hope was destroyed, he realized more quickly than did others what grave dangers a prolongation of the war would mean for Germany. This realization was a result not only of his better knowledge of the facts, but also of his personal temperament. He was simply not the sort of man to let himself be blinded to these dangers by military successes which, no matter how impressive, were nowhere decisive. And he soon came to recognize, better than others, the weaknesses of the German nation. As early as March 1915 he had written, in a confidential letter to von Valentini, the chief of the imperial civil cabinet: "In the course of the last 25 years, the soul of our people has been poisoned by jingoism to such an extent that our people would probably become cowards if deprived of such arrogant self-praise." [1]

This kind of skepticism made him rather unpopular among those who had managed to convince themselves that the enormous sacrifices and achievements of the German people and of the German armies would necessarily lead to success. In all likelihood his unpopularity would have been still greater if the optimists had known that he struggled with an inner suspicion that Germany was perhaps not completely without responsibility for the catastrophe that had overwhelmed Europe. Indeed, Bethmann-Hollweg had been bitterly reproached for the unpardonable words he had uttered on August 4, 1914, concerning the injustice done Belgium. And Belgium continued to be the center of attention for all those patriots who assumed that a victorious Germany would gain some territorial profit from its mighty endeavor. The voice of these people became ever louder and the government's opposition to a public discussion of war aims ever weaker and less successful.

Bethmann opposed such discussion because he realized that it would only evoke sharp, perhaps irreconcilable, divisions of opinion among the Germans. The ore deposits of Longwy and Briey might well seem indispensable to the iron and coal magnates, but what did they mean to the ordinary men lying in the trenches, or to the women waiting for their husbands and their sons? The united spirit of the German people was Bethmann's chief concern. He was proud of having created this unity at the beginning of the war, when even the Social Democrats had joined the "national front" and had voted for the war credits. He knew that this attitude had been possible for the Social Democrats only because they had, at that time, joined the overwhelming majority of the 'Germans in believing that Germany was fighting a defensive war. Bethmann knew that this unanimous support for the war effort would be withdrawn if the people thought that the war had been converted into a war of conquest. The noisy nationalists may have believed that such considerations were unnecessary in time of war, when the national government gathers all forms of power firmly into its own hands. But Bethmann knew the decisive importance of moral issues even in wars between whole nations. He knew that a political party which had won four million votes in the last election and to which millions of fighting soldiers belonged was no negligible factor even in wartime. He observed with concern the opposition which party leaders found in their own ranks, an opposition which in one case led to the splitting off of the Independent Socialists. He also knew that a war which made such extraordinary demands upon each individual would necessarily have a democratic effect upon German society — whether one welcomed the prospect or deplored it.

Now it was only natural that the German generals and admirals should see all this in quite a different light. They had grown up believing in a victorious Germany which in its last three wars, those of 1864, 1866, and 1870, had proved unconquerable. They were, to be sure, nonpolitical according to both tradition and specific orders, but that hardly meant they were without political opinion. It was understandable that the officers of the Imperial Army and the Imperial Navy would remain loyal to the Emperor (*Kaisertreu*). But this term must be understood in a rather special way. One can, for instance, understand why Social Democrats were excluded from the officer's corps, for their party was dedicated to a republican form of government. But the socialists were not the only Germans whose political beliefs prejudiced their chances for professional military careers. Only a Conservative was considered really *Kaisertreu*. To be sure, Catholic officers were acceptable even though they generally considered themselves Centrists; and a National Liberal scion of a Rhenish industrial or mercantile family could at least expect toleration. But a Progressive was beyond the pale. This was as true of reserve officers as of those on active service. The Hamburg attorney, Carl Petersen, was a member of one of the most respectable student corporations, his family had once provided Hamburg with a mayor, and he was later to be mayor himself. Nevertheless, on two separate occasions Petersen was called before the local military commandant and required to justify the fact that he had sheltered Friedrich Naumann * in his house. Another mayor of Hamburg presented his son-in-law, the attorney and reserve officer Dr. Semler, to the Emperor with the remark that he was also a member of the Reichstag. The Emperor, inquiring which party he belonged to and receiving the reply "the National Liberals," observed: "Well, that's acceptable — but only just." ² Colonel Schwertfeger was quite correct when he stated before the Investigating Committee of the Reichstag that the German officers stood politically to the Right.

This solid conservative bias could not, of course, be maintained throughout the war because the need for officers became so tremendous that the restrictions of peacetime had to be somewhat relaxed. From among the 33,000 active officers with whom the German Army had marched to war, a majority of the captains and lieutenants were killed within the first few months.³ But even without these losses, the old corps could not have begun to fill the need for officers. At the start of the offensive of March 1918 there were in service over 176,000 officers, a force which the authorities had been able to

---

* Friedrich Naumann (1860–1919) was a German Protestant theologian, publicist, and champion of dynamic, patriotic liberalism. Both in his book *Demokratie und Kaisertum* (1900) and in his periodicals, *Die Hilfe* and *Die Zeit*, he sought to combine parliamentary institutions with a popular monarchy and nationalism with socialism. He founded the short-lived National Socialist League (*Nationalsozialer Verein*, 1896–1903) and was a member of the Reichstag from 1907 to 1912 and 1913 to 1918. He was increasingly critical of Emperor William II, but his patriotism and imperialism are reflected in his highly influential book *Mitteleuropa* (1915) which called on Germany to assume the leadership of a great Central European empire. Before his death in 1919 he was one of the founders of the Democratic Party and a member of the Weimar National Assembly. TRANSLATORS.

assemble only by ignoring the ancient Code and by accepting instead every man who seemed, on the strength of his training and performance, fit to be an officer. Even the exclusion of Jews could no longer be strictly maintained. But the force of tradition and the old prejudices remained so great that at the end of 1917 an order of von Mackensen's Army Group found it necessary to complain that the form for recommending officer candidates continued to contain the question "concerning the political opinions of the candidate's family." [4] The great number of independent-minded young officers, however, did not alter the general attitude of the officer corps with respect to practical politics. For those who spoke for the corps, who spoke loudly and with emphasis, were generals and other high officers who, overwhelmingly, had belonged to the active professional "old Army." And the vast majority of them still stood to the Right.

On the Right, moreover, were also those who wished to make use of the war for conquests and annexations. The Conservatives and a good number of the National Liberals comprised, for the most part, the annexationist group. In the parties of the Middle, the Centrists and the Progressive People's Party, there were, along with persistent believers in a defensive war, many whose war aims waxed and waned with the armies' fortunes. The Social Democrats clung tenaciously to the concept of a defensive war and differed among themselves principally over the question of how this goal was to be reached. It was only natural that an officers' corps whose leading members inclined to the Right should adopt the annexationist tendencies of that wing. And this tendency was strengthened by purely military considerations. The generals believed that Germany's borders had to be extended both east and west for better protection in a future war. Put into political terms, this meant that Belgium would have to remain "under firm German control" and that Russia would have to cede vast areas in Poland.

Now, these desires of the generals and the admirals would have had little effect upon the political conduct of the war if the supremacy of civilian political leadership over the military had been established as firmly in the Wilhelminian Empire as in the parliamentary governments of the West. Georges Clemenceau could well say in his pungent manner, "War is much too important to be left to the generals." But a German imperial chancellor who even harbored such a thought would very soon have become politically incapacitated. This predominance of the military is rooted in the development of the Empire out of the military state of Prussia. Bismarck, to be sure, had been able to oppose the generals with success. But he could do so only because of the extraordinary power of his unique personality. He was domineering and could even be brutal if the occasion demanded. No nation can expect to be favored with such a personage more than once each century. And did not even this man have to fight desperately, at Nikolsburg, for example, for the primacy of statesmanship over military policy? In 1871 did he not yield on the question of annexing Metz, against his better judgment, to a king who preferred to lean on military advisers and who won popular endorsement in doing so? In later years did not even Bismarck find it expedient to shore up his political power by forming an alliance with von Albedyll, the chief of the military cabinet? Moreover, not only the power but also the authority of the generals had been growing steadily since that time.

This equilibrium between military and political factors was bound to shift to the disadvantage of the political leadership once the supreme military command came into the hands of two generals of unequaled popularity. The first chief of the General Staff during World War I, von Moltke, had been unable to rebel against civilian leadership because he had failed to achieve notable military success. His successor, General von Falkenhayn, had respected the Chancellor's authority. But after he had committed the critical error of the fruitless and unspeakably sanguinary attacks on Verdun, none other than the Imperial Chancellor von Bethmann-Hollweg insisted that von Falkenhayn be replaced by the two commanders who alone had won undying military fame and therewith the unquestioning confidence of the German people: Field Marshal von Hindenburg and General Ludendorff.

It is only natural at all times and among all nations that a victorious hero should be honored and loved by his people. Thousands of Germans who had been gripped by fear at the enemy's attack breathed freer with the news of victory, and they were slow to forget that hour of glorious relief. No one can be surprised that in a nation under such duress everyone, or nearly everyone, said: "Hindenburg will take care of everything!" But such popular sentiment can become hazardous if a nation entrusts to its military hero decisions which are beyond both his training and his temperament. And in Germany people were all too ready to ignore this truth. In every local tavern and in many editorial offices the words of the old warrior Blücher about the pen that spoiled what the sword had won were mechanically repeated. Simple minds understand the simple language of the victorious sword much more easily than they can grasp the cautious word with which the pen slowly binds together the results of claim and counterclaim, of compromise and concession. And simple minds are always in the majority. Furthermore, popular opinion blamed the professional German diplomats for having embroiled Germany in the war in the first place, though few Germans knew what really had happened and scarcely anyone knew what should have been done instead. As was to be expected, the "big navy" advocates, who by their aggressive naval policy had done so much to destroy the diplomats' freedom of action, studiously avoided any discussion of responsibility. Their voices were, of course, busiest and loudest on the Right.

According to the constitution, political and military authority were supposed to meet in the person of the Emperor. He was not only the monarch; he was also the Supreme War Lord. And this latter aspect of his office had been expanding, seemingly without limit, ever since the victory of the Prussian monarch and the military over the Prussian parliament in the constitutional conflict of the 1860's. In this respect, the Emperor enjoyed absolute rule, thanks to his private military and navy cabinets, which had gradually freed themselves of the last remnants of parliamentary control. As early as 1861 [5] Twesten had recognized this development and had called General Edwin von Manteuffel, the chief of the military cabinet, "a dangerous man in a dangerous position" — words which in those days required a duel.* Fifty years later, however, the ascendancy of the military was accepted with fatalistic equanimity.

It is scarcely astonishing that this union of all powers in the person of the emperor should give the German military effort its own peculiar flavor. Even before the war, William II, by a thousand loud and emphatic declarations, had accustomed not only Germany, but indeed the entire world, to the notion that he was the one and only arbiter of Germany's fate. "I," "I," and ever "I" echoed in endless oratory. "I am leading you toward wonderful days." Frederick the Great was the model to which he constantly referred and to which he privately likened himself. But when this comparison was put to test, it became shamefully apparent how little there was behind all these fine phrases and imperial gestures, how incapable he was of filling the critical place that history had allotted him. He even failed by far to match the example that William I had set for him. The grandson was certainly superior to his grandfather in intelligence and in quickness of mind. But to the same degree he fell

* Carl Twesten was an obscure city councilor who in the spring of 1861 had written a pamphlet entitled, "Was uns noch retten kann." In it he accused the Prussian military cabinet and General Manteuffel personally of attempting to dominate civilian life and politics. Manteuffel immediately took umbrage and gave Twesten his choice between retracting his views and fighting a duel. When Twesten chose the latter alternative, Manteuffel shot him through the arm. TRANSLATORS.

short in power of will, firmness of decision, toughness of nerve, sense of reality — briefly put, in character. For William I, in spite of all his limitations, had been a true king, before whom wiser and greater men were proud to bow. But William II merely *played* the role which fate had given him, and all his oratory and all his self-dramatization had only one result: there were times when even his most devoted admirers simply could not take His Majesty very seriously. His generals knew that he was no commander; his ministers, that he was no statesman. He was, it is true, intelligent enough to be able to decide, frequently and aptly, between opposing opinions. But he was too weak to stick by one of these decisions if it encountered the determined opposition of a willful man, even when such opposition extended far beyond its constitutional bounds. For, unlike William I, he had failed to learn how much power and influence the crown gains by requiring advisers to respect the limits of their authority. A vacuum thus developed at the very spot where power should have been concentrated.

The dangers in such a confusion of authority had already become clear in the decision concerning unlimited submarine warfare. The state secretary of the navy, Admiral von Tirpitz, had hurled this apple of discord into the midst of the German people in conscious opposition to the wishes of the Chancellor. Behind Bethmann's back, in an interview granted to the American journalist Karl von Wiegand on November 21, 1914, Tirpitz spoke glowingly of submarine warfare as the certain way "to force England to her knees." [6] He knew that Bethmann as well as the Emperor opposed this idea, and he therefore took pains to have the interview published in America without the knowledge of the Chancellor, his superior. Bethmann, to be sure, was able to deal with this naval revolt: Tirpitz was dismissed on March 15, 1915. But no sooner had the Chancellor helped Hindenburg and Ludendorff into the Supreme Command (August 29, 1916) than he discovered that he had thereby created opponents who would recognize the prerogatives of the Chancellor even less than had Tirpitz — and who, moreover, were more powerful than himself. As early as the end of 1916 he felt obliged to complain about the obstructions that "these two genial gentlemen continually place in the path of cooperation" and about their persistent efforts "to militarize the whole of political life." [7]

The initiative with regard to unrestricted submarine warfare, it is true, came not from the generals, but from one of the Reichstag parties. On October 2, 1916, the Centrist delegates adopted a resolution accepting in advance a declaration of unlimited submarine warfare in the event that the Supreme Command should wish to adopt such a policy.[8] Though this resolution did not formally limit the Chancellor's constitutional powers, it did in fact place the real power of decision in the hands of the military command. In the circumstances this action strengthened Ludendorff's hand and weakened the position of the Chancellor, who could no longer count on a majority in the Reichstag.

Bethmann and State Secretary Karl Helfferich had opposed with all their might the adventurous notion of an all-out submarine campaign because they were absolutely certain that such a step would be answered by an American declaration of war. To be sure, the admirals had solemnly promised to force England to sue for peace before the Americans would be able to join in the battle. But the ministers did not trust the admirals' calculations, calculations which Helfferich had painstakingly refuted.[9] Count Bernstorff, the German ambassador in Washington, emphatically warned the Chancellor against a war with the United States. And Austria-Hungary, Germany's ally, was equally skeptical. Count Czernin, the foreign minister of the Hapsburg monarchy, declined to be convinced even by the personal assurance of the commander of naval forces, Admiral von Holtzendorff, that he would *guarantee* success.[10]

Initially the Chancellor was able to obtain the Emperor's support. But in December 1916 first Ludendorff and then Hindenburg confronted the Foreign Office and the Chancellor with the insistent demand that they declare unrestricted submarine warfare as soon as possible. The field marshal supported his demand by alluding, as he would repeatedly during the war, to the morale of the army, whose fighting spirit, if not satisfied, might dissolve.[11] Bethmann-Hollweg, in a telegram of December 23, pointed out to him that unrestricted submarine warfare immediately affected German relations with neutral countries since it would be directed against neutral as well as enemy ships. It therefore constituted "an expression of foreign policy for which I have to bear the sole responsibility, a responsibility which is constitutional and can not be delegated." Hindenburg wired back brusquely: "I have received with regret Your Excellency's telegram . . . I shall be obliged to announce, in defense of the attitude of the Supreme Command of the Army, that Your Excellency claims, it is true, the final responsibility as Imperial Chancellor, but that I shall, very naturally, to the extent of my power and with the feeling of complete responsibility for the successful outcome of the war, insist that those military measures be taken which I consider appropriate for that purpose.[12]

In other words, the military command had formally declared war on the political leaders of Germany, and had won. On the morning of January 9, 1917, when the Chancellor arrived at General Headquarters at Pless, the decision, as he puts it in his memoirs, "had already *de facto* been made." [13] William II had, in short, yielded before the united attack of the generals and admirals. He had weakened once again. On that day he issued the order "that starting February 1, unrestricted submarine warfare was to be waged with total effort." The crisis took its course: the United States declared war on Germany and the submarine campaign brought Germany, as Bethmann later put it, what the Sicilian expedition had won for Athens.[14]

At this point Theobald von Bethmann-Hollweg committed the gravest error of his political career: he did not resign. He tried to justify this decision by arguing that it was his duty not to sabotage a decision which he had been unable to prevent. He wished, as he later wrote, to conserve that "fund of confidence" which he still possessed in certain German circles. He might also have argued, as later developments were to show, that there was no fit successor in sight. But all this does not alter the principle that a statesman commits professional suicide if, at a critical point, he executes a policy which he knows will be disastrous. "Every independent personality in harmony with itself is right; error comes only from inner contradiction." This responsible statesman had been taking extreme care to avoid a breach in Germany's relations with the United States. Therefore, when he suddenly altered his policy to one which would necessarily incur such a breach, a neutral observer could only conclude that either the German Chancellor or the German constitution (or perhaps both) had ceased to make sense. The new policy, whether wise or foolish, should have been executed by a new Chancellor. Only by resigning could Bethmann have defended the principle that political responsibility rested exclusively with the Imperial Chancellor. Only six months later Bethmann had to pay with his resignation for his abandonment of this principle. This resignation was, furthermore, the result of a confusion which demonstrated all too well how inefficient and obsolete the German political system had become.

In one respect, however, Bethmann's few remaining months in office were not without value. For some months he had been aware of the effect which a prolongation of the war would have on the German people. The demands on the populace had already been great; if even further sacrifices were exacted, the German people would soon agitate for political concessions. This fact was most obvious with respect to Prussian suffrage laws, the undiluted plutocratic character of which had stood for two generations in violent contradiction to the demands of the times. Perhaps Bethmann concerned himself with this question all the more because he could not morally rid himself of the charge of having earlier failed to press hard enough for a solution when he had had the opportunity. Admittedly his opposition on this issue should not be underestimated. The Conservatives, who enjoyed a practically unassailable majority in the Prussian Diet, still clung obstinately to their aristocratic attitude even in the midst of this national war. As late as 1916 their powerful leader, von Heydebrand, could still bring himself to declare to the lower house of the Prussian legislature that, "aside from a few inconsequential blemishes, the nature of our lower house meets the requirements of Prussia in an almost ideal fashion." [15] And when, on March 14, 1917, Bethmann offered this house the hardly revolutionary opinion that "Germany's very future requires political rights for the general population, in order that the just and joyous political collaboration of the masses may be obtained," he was met by icy silence on the Right.

But on the afternoon of this same March day the first reports of the Russian Revolution reached Germany; now many people, with the exception of those on the extreme Right, were obliged to realize that everything could not remain the same — even in Germany. Even William II knew it now. But there remained the real controversy over whether the Reichstag ballot with its "universal male, equal and secret" vote would be introduced into Prussia, as not only the Social Democrats but also the definitely liberal elements had been demanding for years. Bethmann, Helfferich, and several other ministers agreed to this proposition. But on April 2, when the Chancellor wished to present his ideas on suffrage reform to the Emperor at Homburg, the latter interrupted him brusquely with "But not the Reichstag ballot again!" Instead of opposing the Emperor explicitly on this point, Bethmann was satisfied with obtaining his sovereign's approval of and signature to the Easter Message. This announced, to be sure, the intent of the Emperor and King to carry out basic political reforms and even promised the abolition of balloting by social classes; but with respect to the new franchise the message offered only the prospect of direct and secret election of representatives. And there was a gaping hole in this Easter Message: there was no mention of equality of each man's vote.

But this omission could not erase the general impression that the Chancellor had now placed himself publicly and unambiguously with the Left. Hence the Right worked all the more sedulously to bring about his fall. In this connection the Right included the Supreme Military Command — or General Ludendorff at any rate.

In the presence of Under-Secretary Wahnschaffe the general called the Easter Message simply a "kow-tow to the Russian Revolution." [16] In a later letter (of December 8, 1917) to the Prussian minister of interior he was to declare boldly that he had greeted Bethmann-Hollweg's "departure from office as an act of liberation" because of the latter's "soft attitude toward the Left." [17] This will amaze no one who goes on in this same letter to read Ludendorff's political credo: "In my opinion the war has given us no grounds for democratization or republicanization . . . On the contrary I consider such a policy of yielding to the spirit of the age extraordinarily dangerous. Its consequences will inevitably lead us to disaster."

In late 1916 and early 1917 the German people had had to suffer through a frightful winter of austerity and of food shortages that had verged on famine. The thought of having to live through another such winter was truly dreadful. Was there no hope that peace might intervene? For a while they had clung to the promise which the navy men had made with such apodictic certainty: within six months the submarines would bring England to her knees. There was indeed real concern in England, where shipping losses had produced a very serious situation. But there was no sign of English surrender; and the further the summer progressed, the more likely it appeared that British determination would survive even this test.

This was the situation when, at the beginning of July, the Reichstag met in Berlin. The atmosphere was already charged, for all could see that something had to change, that neither at the front nor at home were affairs progressing satisfactorily. This excitement reached its peak in a speech delivered by the Centrist Matthias Erzberger before an executive session of the Reichstag's Committee on Naval Affairs. In this extraordinarily biting but thoroughly documented address, Erzberger demonstrated not only that the results of the submarine warfare had completely failed to fulfill the navy's promises but that the promises themselves had been empty from the very beginning. He stated flatly that he no longer had confidence in Admiral von Capelle, von Tirpitz' successor as state secretary of the navy. He declared further that a solid majority of the Reichstag should unite in proclaiming a purely defensive war, denying and declining any thought of conquest.[18]

Erzberger had sat in the Reichstag since 1903, when he had been its youngest member. His tireless industry and his ability to get things done had immediately brought him to the fore. In no wise popular among the older leaders of his party — men like Spahn and Gröber — he failed to make any meaningful impression when speaking in the Chamber. But his bustling energy could not fail to create for him a considerable sphere of influence. And his influence ranged beyond the limits of his own party, since members of the imperial government, fearful of his criticism, sought to engage and retain his favor.

From the beginning of the war the government had sought to make use of Erzberger's capacity for work as well as his excellent connections — particularly with the Vatican. At Rome, in the spring of 1915, he had come to know rather intimately Prince Bülow, the former chancellor, who was then engaged in an unsuccessful attempt to keep Italy from joining the Entente. Although in the past they had often differed sharply, Erzberger believed he had found in Bülow the man whom Germany needed in this decisive hour. It is no criticism of the former Swabian school teacher to suspect that he fell prey to the studied charms and the flattering manners of the prince. And one can well imagine how Erzberger felt when he heard Bülow speak patronizingly of his own successor as "poor old Bethmann."

Erzberger's great capacity for action was not combined with the ability to direct his activity along any consistent path. He was too "flexible" for that and too subject to his various, fleeting impressions. And so he wavered in his war aims, too. Thus when in July he stood firmly on the platform of a compromise peace, he stood there under the spell of certain influences. Shortly before his speech he had visited the chief of staff for the eastern front, Max Hoffmann. That sober, wise general, outlining the situation with complete candor, had convinced him that the war simply had to be brought to a close as soon as possible because of the military situation. A subsequent conversation with Ludendorff persuaded him that even Ludendorff did not regard things very differently. In addition, the condition of Germany's chief ally, Austria, had made a very deep impression on him. The young Emperor Charles had given Erzberger a report from his minister, Count Czernin, which depicted these conditions with ruthless pessimism and which even said: "The pressures upon our people are simply unbearable; the bow is so far bent that a break can be expected any day." [19]

All these things convinced Erzberger that Germany had to do something without delay to pave the way for peace, and he believed that there was one specific reason why such a step at this time could lead to success. He knew how eager the Pope was to mediate a peace that would end the frightful slaughter. He was probably not ignorant of the fact that on June 26 the papal nuncio in Germany, Monsignor Pacelli, later Pope Pius XII, had given the Chancellor a letter from the Pope to the Emperor, in which the former offered his services in a search for peace. In the course of his conversation with Bethmann, Pacelli had made perfectly clear that the Vatican considered the restoration of Belgium's independence and neutrality the indispensable prelude to any serious negotiations. Bethmann seemed basically to agree, though he had tried to twist the point to mean that Belgium should not come under the domination of England or France. Although Erzberger can hardly have known the details of this conversation, he did not have to be particularly gifted to guess that it must have chiefly concerned Belgium.[20]

Even before Erzberger's sensational speech the nonannexationist parties of the Middle and the Left had voiced the desire to make some joint statement. The Reichstag members of the Progressive People's Party had adopted a resolution — proposed by Friedrich Naumann and amended by Conrad Haussmann — calling for interparty consultations. The leader of their delegation, Friedrich Payer, who commanded great respect as a wise, calm, and reliable man, was selected chairman of the interparty committee at the first meeting of the group, shortly after Erzberger's speech. The committee consisted, apart from the Progressives, of representatives of the Social Democrats (Ebert, Scheidemann, David), the Centrists (Spahn, Erzberger, Fehrenbach), and the National Liberals (Stresemann, Schiffer, Richthofen, Junck).

The collaboration of the National Liberals added more confusion than clarity to the situation. While the other interested parties laid greatest stress upon a declaration of war aims, the National Liberals, partly because they were in no way unanimous on this point, sought to put the accent on a transition to parliamentary government. Of course the Social Democrats and the Progressives, and probably a majority of the Centrists, agreed with the National Liberals on this issue. And the Chancellor himself had learned enough from the experiences of war not to oppose the principle of parliamentary responsibility. But the other parties were quite right in pointing out to the National Liberals that the issue they emphasized was intimately connected with the time factor: the issue of war aims simply could not wait; it necessitated both an immediate and a common stand. Something else lay behind the position of the National Liberals. To many of their leaders a change to parliamentary government would mean principally a change in government, that is, Bethmann's dismissal. In particular, that was the view of Dr. Gustav Stresemann, who soon became the leader of his party's delegation.

Stresemann was without doubt a man of greater competence and scope than was Erzberger. He was educated in many fields, widely experienced, and an orator with a command of every register from biting sarcasm to engaging pathos. But, like Erzberger, he had not maintained a consistent position through all the political exigencies of war. Originally he was an outspoken annexationist and an early proponent of unlimited submarine warfare. If at this moment he was inclined toward a more moderate view, this was a result of the present military situation.

Stresemann considered that at this juncture there was something more important than the clarification of war aims — the dismissal of Bethmann-Hollweg. For he felt that the Chancellor was too weak to pursue steadfastly a policy that would bring peace. He attacked Bethmann during an executive session with an especially sharp speech of cutting frigidity.[21] Bülow was Stresemann's candidate.[22] He had hopes that Bülow could push through a parliamentary government. One can well believe that the former chancellor made extremely broad promises to Stresemann along these lines. He could point out, after all, that by resigning in 1909 after the Reichstag had denied his proposals for financial reforms he had taken a first step toward the recognition of ministerial responsibility.

And so the National Liberals finally declined to join in signing the resolution which one of their representatives had helped write. For this reason they had to leave the interparty committee, to the evident displeasure of their outvoted minority. The heart of the resolution, which was adopted by the Centrists, Progressives, and Social Democrats, and which suffered subsequent textual revisions, was a bare repetition of the original statement of August 4, 1914: "Ours is not a war of conquest." In harmony with this the resolution asked for a negotiated peace. "Forced cessions and political, economic, and financial extortions are incompatible with such a peace!" Here was a clear and obvious denial of a policy of conquest.

Neither Bethmann nor Helfferich could bring himself to an expression of support for this resolution. One can well understand why the Chancellor was displeased at Erzberger's sudden move, the details of which had not been shared with him.[23] But two important facts remained: the resolution stated a policy which reflected Bethmann's personal feelings, and a sturdy majority of the Reichstag had offered itself as a base upon which this policy might be constructed. His conversations with Payer and the leaders of the other parties must have convinced Bethmann of that support. Yet he feared the possible consequences of such a "soft" resolution on foreign affairs.[24]

In the course of a confidential discussion with the Social Democrat party leaders he evidently realized it was high time for him to yield to their demand that the Reichstag ballot be extended to Prussian elections as well. He therefore requested the Emperor, who happened to be in Berlin just then, to issue a supplementary message, one which would complete the Easter Message with the promise of *equal* franchise. William called a meeting of the Crown Council; it sat on Monday, July 9, and accepted the Chancellor's recommendation, six to five. Even this bare majority had been achieved only by virtue of the fact that imperial ministers, like Helfferich, were permitted to vote on this Prussian matter. The Emperor preferred to withhold his final decision until after consultations with his son, explaining that in a matter so important to the dynasty he owed the crown prince an opportunity to form and express an opinion. This was the first time that William had ever showed such consideration for the opinion of his son, since the Emperor quite correctly generally considered his son's political judgment of negligible value. One must therefore suspect that court whisperings were at work; not those of von Valentini, chief of his civil cabinet, who collaborated with the Chancellor most loyally, but rather those of the Emperor's personal entourage.

Once more the Supreme Military Command was showing signs of wishing to seize political leadership. No sooner were the first reports of the intended Peace Resolution made public than Hindenburg and Ludendorff came to Berlin and, without telling the Chancellor, requested an immediate audience with the Emperor "with respect to their reaction, from the military point of view, to Erzberger's proposal." But Bethmann succeeded in seeing the Emperor first. Consequently, when Ludendorff attempted the transition from military to political affairs, the Emperor terminated the general's remarks with the observation that the military command had no obligation to concern itself with political matters, which were the responsibility of the Chancellor. The generals had no alternative but to return, on the evening of July 7, to their headquarters in Kreuznach. This was, however, not actually a retreat, for Ludendorff had left behind him in Berlin a tool with which, even from a distance, he could still undermine the Chancellor's position.

This tool was an officer of the General Staff, a certain Colonel Bauer, who yielded to his superior neither in his dislike for Bethmann nor in his penchant for dabbling in politics. Bauer revealed the quality of his mind in a memorandum of March 1917 on the political situation. He was so proud of this miserable analysis that he actually saw fit to reveal it to an astonished public in one of his books.[25] Here, in this single memorandum, are collected all those phrases which were later to have such a pernicious effect on any healthy political development in Germany — including the cant about "Jewish liberalism." If Ludendorff had read only the sentence quoted here, he would have been confident that he could rely on this man. For Bauer interpreted the stricture against officers meddling in politics in a manner that is revealed by the following subtle and sophisticated sentence: "The monarchic-conservative parties have . . . dissociated themselves from the Chancellor to the extent that he has made himself a *weak-willed* agent (*willenlosen Werkzeug*) of the Left." Germans liked to talk about their Army's "professional honesty." But here one can see again that this honesty did not preclude military intrigue. Bauer consulted with Erzberger and Stresemann about the steps necessary to effect the Chancellor's fall. He was certainly primarily responsible for the Reichstag rumor that Ludendorff considered the war as good as lost if Bethmann remained Chancellor. Bauer himself tells us: "I wired the crown prince that he should come, while arranging simultaneously that he be invited."

The crown prince came. He declared himself content with the idea of equal suffrage in Prussia (though this declaration did not keep him from ranting against the proposal immediately thereafter). He then asked his father to dismiss Bethmann, just as Bauer had instructed him to do; he was met, however, by only a smooth change of the subject. But Bauer's store of tricks was not yet exhausted. Upon Bauer's advice, the crown prince summoned the party leaders to a meeting on July 11 in order that he might hear their opinions concerning a change of chancellors. Naturally Bauer arranged that from every party delegation only those gentlemen were invited whom he could trust to serve his ends: from the National Liberals, Stresemann; from the Centrists, Erzberger; and from the Social Democrats, Dr. David, who was more critical of Bethmann than was either Ebert or Scheidemann. Indeed, only Payer, as representative of the Progressives, spoke up unconditionally for the retention of Bethmann. The faithful Bauer sat hidden behind a curtain jotting down the statesmen's words in shorthand.

However much this maneuver may have favored Ludendorff's purpose, it did not lead directly to his goal. The Emperor had just given Bethmann another testimony of his confidence by signing the decree granting equal suffrage. Furthermore, in the conversation of the afternoon of July 12, he gave no sign of wishing to dispense with his Chancellor's services. Then suddenly a telephone message from Kreuznach arrived: Hindenburg and Ludendorff had requested to be relieved of their duties on the grounds that they could no longer collaborate with Bethmann. And lest their meaning be misunderstood, Ludendorff had taken pains to send another message: this time he would not weaken, but rather would insist upon his will or else resign.

Now it was up to William II to show what he conceived his office to be, the office which was his, as he had announced so often and so vociferously, by divine right. How did Wallenstein depict his great opponent, fallen on the battlefield at Lützen?

> What made this Gustaf
> Irresistible, unconquered here on earth?
> This: that he stood a king before his army!
> And a king, moreover, who is truly regal
> Was never conquered yet save by another.

But William II had never been a "truly regal" king. Had he been such a king he would have let the generals know immediately and in no uncertain terms that he would not put up with the insubordination — to use no stronger word — which they had shown. He would have let them know that no soldier, from private on up, could break his military oath to his king, and that the commanding generals in the field were no more free to leave their commands because the policy of their Supreme War Lord displeased them than was Private Schultz free to desert his post in the trenches merely because he did not wish to die for the annexation of Longwy and Briey. One can well imagine the reaction of Frederick the Great if one of his generals had resigned for such reasons! Hans Delbrück, who was not only Germany's greatest military historian but also a loyal German and Prussian through and through, told the Reichstag's Investigating Committee in loud and clear tones: "If the supreme military commander had had General Ludendorff brought to military trial for mutiny in July 1917, we would have been saved." [26]

But William II yielded, just as he had yielded so often during his reign whenever he saw someone bare his teeth. He accepted the letter of resignation that Bethmann had immediately offered him. With this act, the German Empire, as it had previously been known, came to an end. For up to now its fundamental principle had been that the Chancellor of the German Empire and Prime Minister of the Prussian Crown depended upon the confidence of the Emperor and King. So long as he enjoyed this confidence he could not be removed from his office, not even by vote of parliament. This was the basic axiom of the German constitutional system, as envisaged by Stahl and executed by Bismarck, the *differentia specifica* which distinguished it from the parliamentary systems of Western Europe.

There can be no doubt that Bethmann continued to enjoy the Emperor's confidence. Nevertheless, William sacrificed his Chancellor to a power unknown to the constitutions, either written or unwritten, of the Empire and of Prussia. Politically the situation would have been quite different if the force that overthrew Bethmann had been the German Reichstag. For that would have been a step toward a parliamentary form of government, which in the opinion of all informed people, including Bethmann, was bound to come sooner or later. But such action would have required that a majority of the Reichstag oppose the Chancellor in open session. Nothing of the kind took place. Instead, Ludendorff's confidant, the political dilettante Colonel Bauer, contrived to have a few carefully selected members of the Reichstag express personal opinions in their attacks on the Chancellor. Such action was a constitutional and political mockery of the way true parliaments express lack of confidence in a first minister. It was simply an intrigue against the constitutional system, whether one is thinking in terms of the traditional "German constitutionalism" or in terms of a genuinely parliamentary system of government. Furthermore, if a Reichstag majority had unseated the Chancellor in open parliamentary battle, they most certainly would have given some indication of the man they proposed as his successor.

But on this issue of succession the victors over Bethmann now demonstrated with shocking clarity their confusion and their uncertainty. Erzberger and Stresemann at least had a candidate: Bülow. But one could not approach the Emperor with this suggestion for His Imperial Majesty had considered Bülow a traitor ever since the *Daily Telegraph* affair. It was common knowledge that William had referred to him in extremely coarse language. Furthermore the Austrian ally had the gravest doubts about the man who, in 1915, had felt free to dispose of parts of the Austrian Empire. Ludendorff had obviously never once troubled himself with the question of who was to be the next Chancellor. In his memoirs he naïvely confessed his surprise at learning "that the responsible authorities did not always have a replacement for the Chancellor in readiness." [27] Amateur statesmanship cannot show itself more culpable than this.

And so it came to pass that on July 17, 1917, the German nation learned, to its astonishment, that a certain Herr Michaelis was to be its new Imperial Chancellor. Even well-informed political figures knew only that he was an assistant state secretary in some Prussian ministry and that, as a man responsible for keeping the populace properly fed, he had once opposed sharply a move on the

part of the agrarian interests. But no one, least of all Michaelis himself, could say that he had ever practised the art of politics. He was
neither more nor less than one of the thousands of Germany's able,
loyal bureaucrats. The thought of entrusting the German ship of
state, amid such storms, to this man would have been merely a joke
in poor taste were the situation not, most unfortunately, so very
serious. But then, after all, Herr Michaelis did enjoy the confidence
of the Supreme Military Command. William had taken care to ask
Hindenburg whom he wanted as Chancellor. And before formally
appointing Michaelis he had asked the field marshal if he approved.
William himself later told Kühlmann that Hindenburg had praised
Michaelis as a "decent, God-fearing man," and that he had thereupon "accepted him in God's name." [28] William II no longer had the
courage to ask Bethmann whom he wished to recommend as his
successor or whether he thought Michaelis up to the task. Such was
the state of "the strong monarchy," whose advantages over a parliamentary system in Germany had become a dogma of the ruling
classes!

Members of the Reichstag were, of course, bitterly disappointed
by this absurd handling of the crisis. Haussmann, who lamented
Bethmann's fall, told Erzberger that he feared the next Chancellor
would prove only a temporary replacement; to this Erzberger, with
his Swabian directness, replied, "He'll die in the cradle." [29] But the
majority parties were united on one point: whoever was to assume
leadership of German politics would have to subscribe to the Peace
Resolution and build his policies upon that base. Michaelis agreed.
Hindenburg and Ludendorff had returned to Berlin for a conference
with party leaders in the presence of Michaelis and Helfferich in
the garden of the Imperial Ministry of Interior; at this meeting the
generals also agreed. But neither the Chancellor nor the generals
were honest in their consent. Michaelis immediately destroyed the
effect of the Peace Resolution with the fateful words, "as I understand it"; and there can be no doubt but that he did this with
deliberate cunning. In a letter of July 25 to the crown prince, for
instance, he wrote of the "fatal resolution" and triumphantly added
that he had rid it of most of its danger through his "interpretation"! [30] The Supreme Military Command regarded the resolution
simply as one more scrap of paper. Under these circumstances, it is
completely understandable that Germany's enemies should be
totally unimpressed with this peace resolution. They had long since
become inclined to regard the Reichstag as a piece of political
decoration with neither power nor influence; and now this opinion
was given still further credence. The military agitators, however,

cited the resolution's ineffectiveness (for which they were to blame) as additional evidence of the futility of the Reichstag's policies.

Nevertheless, in their efforts to pass a peace resolution, members of the Reichstag had tried for the first time in German history to seize the political initiative and to defend it with a firm majority. Germany might have succeeded here in taking a significant step in the direction of parliamentary government if only such grievous errors in choosing parliamentary leaders had not been made. The whole incident shows the bitter consequence of a constitutional system that made it extraordinarily difficult for the parliament to develop effective political leadership.

From this point on the Supreme Military Command was the only decisive political power. The Emperor counted too, but only in a formal way. His self-confidence was so shattered that, upon Ludendorff's bidding, he even dismissed von Valentini, the chief of his civil cabinet, and replaced him (in January 1918) with von Berg, who was strictly conservative and approved by the general. Chancellor Michaelis had had no greater desire than to keep the favor of the mighty Supreme Command. His successor (since November 2, 1917), Count George Hertling, though an experienced parliamentarian and an accomplished politician, was much too old to summon up the energy necessary to do more than maintain formal defense of his powers against theirs. State Secretary von Kühlmann, who had assumed the direction of the Foreign Office upon Bethmann's resignation, was to be virtually chased from this post by Ludendorff. The Reichstag majority had neither the unanimity nor the forceful self-confidence necessary for the creation and execution of consistent policy.

It was particularly unfortunate that the Supreme Military Command made full use of its powerful position to render impossible any kind of negotiated peace. The note which Pope Benedict XV had sent to the leaders of all the warring nations on August 1, 1917, could have served as the basis of such a peace.[31] The task of replying to it devolved upon Michaelis and Kühlmann. As was to be expected after Pacelli's conversation with Bethmann, the Pope's note clearly placed the principal emphasis upon the restoration of Belgium's independence. This demand was consonant with the Reichstag's Peace Resolution; for a peace without annexations would, by definition, leave Belgium independent and untouched. It was therefore in the interest of those parties which had voted for the resolution to ensure that the Pope's inquiry on this issue received an affirmative reply. A committee of seven representatives was formed, and Michaelis, who had every reason to regain the Reichstag's confidence, declared his willingness to discuss his reply with this committee before sending it to Rome. Five of the seven members belonged to the parties which had backed the Peace Resolution.

State Secretary von Kühlmann firmly subscribed to this same proposition.[32] He was too wise, and he knew British interests and history too well, to let himself believe that England would ever conclude a peace which did not involve Belgium's restoration unless the island really had been "brought to its knees." And he knew better than the others how unlikely this had become since America's declaration of war. But he wished to introduce the issue of the restitution of Belgium at the close, not at the beginning, of the negotiations.[33] He cherished the idea that Germany would be playing its most important trump too early if it granted Belgian independence first. Despite Hans Delbrück's efforts to convince him of the error of this position, von Kühlmann put all his considerable powers of argument and influence to work on the members of the Reichstag in an effort to keep them from explicitly backing Belgian independence and to make them content instead with a reference to the Peace Resolution in the reply to the Pope. With the exception of the two Social Democrats, Ebert and Scheidemann, the committee was persuaded to accept this solution.

But the story does not end here. The decisive meeting of the Committee of Seven took place on September 10. On the next day, September 11, the Emperor held a meeting of the Crown Council at Bellevue Palace, a meeting in which Hindenburg and Ludendorff took part. Ludendorff delivered a political harangue which, in the passages extending beyond strictly military affairs, can reasonably be described as neither informed nor sophisticated.[34] With respect to Belgium, for instance, his minimal demands consisted of economic union with Germany, an extended German occupation, German possession of Liège, and the division of Belgium into its French- and Flemish-speaking parts. The Emperor proposed a program which was somewhat more modest but rather unclear and declared especially that the King of the Belgians could return to his throne. But this proved to have little effect on further developments, for Chancellor Michaelis took his lead from the generals rather than from the Emperor. The day after the Crown Council met he wrote a long letter to the field marshal, promising to include the demands of the Supreme Command "in our strategy of negotiations." [35] He did, to be sure, try to soften these demands a bit by noting that Liège was to be required "as a kind of temporary security." This was the least he dared say if he was to preserve even the external appearance of operating in accord with the Reichstag resolution, which he had, of course, cited in his reply to Rome and which disclaimed any and all desires for annexation.

But the Supreme Command was not content to leave Michaelis even this fig leaf behind which to hide. On September 15, Hindenburg, in a letter that betrayed Ludendorff's hand, answered: "We shall be able to carry out the required military and civil measures only if we are *and remain* sovereign masters of Liège." [36] A second sentence in this letter should be quoted here to illustrate the attitude of the men who actually ruled Germany and determined its future path. The letter refuted an argument of the Chancellor, and declared: "The mutual understanding that our neighbors will bear the costs of damages we have caused [in other words a decision of the Allies' not to claim reparations] will hardly strike anyone as a gain of consequence for us." And the mad extravagance of the annexationists becomes apparent in the sentence: "In so far as I know our nation's spirit, I am forced to doubt that, if we stop someplace short of our aims, Germans will find any consolation in the thought that the negotiating enemy had wished — and failed — to destroy us." This was Hindenburg's answer to the Chancellor's request that the generals employ such arguments in hopes of inducing moderation in those of "one-sided annexationist tendencies" who might visit their headquarters. For the good, honest Chancellor had long since stopped trying to satisfy the political parties whose wishes he had officially made his own. His only hope now was to win the favor of their annexationist opponents.

To make matters worse, the Chancellor carried on this correspondence with Hindenburg behind the back of the official responsible for foreign affairs. Kühlmann later stated in sworn testimony before the Investigating Committee that he was astonished, and not pleasantly so, when he learned about these letters through the press.[37] Thus by failing to take action, he had unwittingly helped Michaelis' dishonest game. Furthermore Michaelis was less than fully candid in his relations with the Reichstag. For before replying formally to Rome, he had secretly imparted his answer to the papal nuncio, who, after consulting with the Vatican in late August, had stated in clear and certain terms that the proposed reply "would mean the absolute end of the entire papal effort towards peace." [38] The nuncio also reported the answer which the British ambassador to the Holy See had given in regard to the papal note: a clear German acceptance of the restoration of Belgium was an absolute prerequisite to any peace negotiations.[39] And the nuncio himself, in his letter of enclosure of August 30, placed special emphasis upon the fact that the Pope considered such a German declaration a *sine qua non.* To this Michaelis replied in a letter, of September 24, 1917, prepared under von Kühlmann's direction.[40] This letter defended the German refusal to make an unambiguous statement about Belgium with the argument that various preconditions necessary for such a step did not yet seem certain enough to the imperial government. The reader of the letter could gather what all this was intended to mean from the following sentence, in which Michaelis expressed the hope of being able "in the none too distant future" to advise the Pope in greater detail concerning the *expectations and demands of the imperial government, with particular reference to Belgium.* If the German language still makes sense, this meant that, with respect to Belgium, the German government still had other demands in mind; in other words, it was not prepared to set Belgium *unconditionally* free. This private answer, therefore, not only denied the Pope's request but also disavowed the reference made in the official reply to the Reichstag's Peace Resolution.

The Committee of Seven was told neither that the Vatican had found utterly unacceptable the official reply prepared with the committee's advice, nor that the Chancellor had followed this official reply with letter which explicitly contradicted the reply on the very point which the committee had considered particularly important. With respect to the facts of the matter, it is clear that Michaelis defrauded the Reichstag. With respect to his motives, one can certainly say that Michaelis was inclined more toward the annexationism of the Supreme Command than toward the negotiation hopes of the majority parties, and that his attempt to conceal the difference between the parties and himself lest his chancellorship be put in jeopardy was quite consistent with his usual tactics. The cause of candor was well served when, shortly thereafter, in the Reichstag session of October 9, 1917, his own phenomenal clumsiness brought about his fall. Kühlmann tried, completely unsuccessfully to excuse his own role in the affair by referring to diplomatic considerations. (He probably had in mind his scheme of sounding out the British government through a neutral diplomat, the Spanish Ambassador Villobar at Brussels.) Perhaps of greater historical importance was Kühlmann's further explanation that he was concerned lest an open conflict break out with the Supreme Command. Indeed he went so far as to tell the Investigating Committee that "we narrowly escaped dictatorship." [41] "Any conscientious statesman was obliged to take into account a force which was as strong as the Supreme Command and which was supported by a very large, indeed a preponderant segment, of public opinion."

No man can say an acceptance of the papal proposals, as a

majority of the Reichstag had desired, would have brought peace closer. But one can and must observe that the generals did all they could to keep it safely out of reach.

The members of the Reichstag had learned enough in the process of Michaelis' accession to office to demand, upon his fall, that his successor not be named without their consent. As a matter of fact, Count George Hertling consulted with them before accepting the office of chancellor. This constituted, without question, a step toward parliamentary government.

At the same time, however, the fatal effects of the old system manifested themselves in the fact that the Reichstag had no one in its own ranks whom it could propose for the post. Hertling had not been a member for several years and came immediately from the presidency of the Bavarian Ministry of State. To a certain extent this gap between the Chancellor and the Reichstag was filled by the appointment as vice-chancellor of Friedrich von Payer, the chairman of the Progressive People's Party. He was without doubt a wise man, with decades of rich political experience behind him. But he was, even if somewhat younger than Hertling, nonetheless more than seventy years old, an age at which one can no longer learn to master completely new tasks. Although he solved many difficulties and gave much wise advice, he did not influence the general course of events. But at least he did preserve a more critical and independent position vis-à-vis the Supreme Command than did the generals' pawn, Count Hertling. And one can say the same for von Kühlmann, who kept the Foreign Office through the change.

In the field of internal politics the new government had the task of executing Bethmann's last agreement, his promise to extend the Reichstag ballot to Prussia. This understanding had been an essential element of the support the majority parties gave to Hertling, who, in addition to the office of imperial chancellor, had assumed that of Prussian premier. In this latter role he invoked the assistance of that experienced parliamentarian Dr. Friedberg, the leader of the National Liberals in the Prussian Landtag. The Prussian Ministry of Interior was entrusted to Dr. Drews, a sincere supporter of this reform. And so the new government laid a suffrage law before the Landtag. But a reactionary majority of the legislators insisted upon substituting a watered-down version of the existing plutocratic system of multiple votes in lieu of the proposed equality of franchise. Thus, up to the last possible moment, the Prussian Junkers demonstrated that they had learned nothing and that they were deaf to the march of history, whose threatening steps already echoed in the ears of every reasonably sensitive man. The Junkers therefore became principally responsible for the radical nature of the German Revolution.

But again the military leaders must share the responsibility. In the light of available evidence there can be no doubt about the Supreme Command's opposition to this reform. And there can be just as little doubt that the conservative opponents of the reform knew the generals' feelings on this matter, and that this knowledge strengthened their will to resist. For they could rest assured that the government would not employ its one truly useful means of breaking their resistance — namely, the dissolution of the Landtag — for the simple but overwhelming reason that the Supreme Command would not tolerate such a step. Stresemann pointed this out clearly to General Ludendorff in a detailed letter of April 29, 1918, the only fruits of which were six lines of reply, in which Ludendorff declined to make any public statement, saying that he preferred to allude openly to matters of domestic politics only "when in my opinion they might otherwise affect our ultimate victory." The inability to realize that the franchise issue "might affect the ultimate victory" is a further example of the general's political amateurism. No less revealing is the fact that he made this reply at a time when he could not avoid admitting to himself that his great spring offensive was a strategic failure.

The most important events in foreign affairs to occur in the months immediately following the change in chancellors were the two peace treaties on the eastern front: Brest-Litovsk (March 3) and Bucharest (May 7, 1918). These two treaties are of special relevance to our discussion in so far as they show the Supreme Command's further encroachment into the political sphere. At this point it is necessary to recall that the Bolshevik Revolution was made possible when Lenin, then living in Swiss exile, was granted permission to cross Germany by rail on his way to Russia, and that Ludendorff was principally, though perhaps not solely, responsible for this permission.[42] It would be unjust to blame Ludendorff for not foreseeing the monstrous consequences of the Bolshevik Revolution, although one might well expect the realization of his own shortsightedness in this respect to have tempered his later criticism of those who had to contend with these consequences. And one is certainly free to express astonishment at his failure to consider even the possibility of the debilitating effects which Bolshevism would have upon the morale of the German Army. In the winter of 1917–18, when the negotiations for peace were opened with the Bolshevists, General Ludendorff insisted that the Supreme Command be granted a voice in the discussions; this demand was granted by the

Emperor as early as December 18, 1917. That this decision contradicted the Bismarckian tradition is as certain as the fact that it met
with the approval of many — and, particularly, of many influential —
Germans. At this point the Chancellor, Count Hertling, was obliged
to fight a hard battle in defense of his constitutional responsibilities
and powers.[43] He gained a formal victory, in that the Emperor supported him in a decree of January 24, 1918. But at this very time an
incident took place which showed clearly where the actual power
in government lay: the Emperor gave in to the demands of the
generals, who were aided by the Empress and the crown prince,
and dismissed the chief of the civil cabinet, von Valentini.[44] It was
already clear which party would prevail.

In actual fact, Ludendorff succeeded in achieving most of his
aims in the peace negotiations. And he never forgave Kühlmann for
not joining him on all points. He had even less sympathy for Czernin,
the Austrian minister and negotiator, who could see the collapse of
the Dual Monarchy draw nearer with every day. Old Hindenburg
even prophesied that "the next war will be between Austria and
us." [45] The military rather than the political authorities are therefore to be blamed if Brest-Litovsk became a peace of annexation,
thus enabling Germany's later conquerors to fling a *tu quoque* in
the face of any criticism of their peace.

But even the Reichstag was unable to maintain a steady course.
All thoughtful parliamentarians — not just the Social Democrats —
realized that the Treaty of Brest-Litovsk contradicted the Peace
Resolution. On March 19 Conrad Haussmann wrote: "The eastern
peace, deadly as it was to all hopes of a just and lasting settlement,
has gone to the heads of the political dinosaurs"; and two days later:
"In our peace with Russia one can see how little profit lies in acts of
subjugation. The treaty has left us with a real hangover." [46] In any
event the Reichstag could hardly refuse to ratify this first sign of
peace, no matter how it looked, especially since the government was
linked to the majority parties through their man Payer. For that is
the other side of parliamentary responsibility. But it would have
been better if they had not left it up to the Social Democrats alone
to protest against this betrayal of the principles they all had openly
espoused. (Even among the Social Democrats, the Majority Socialists abstained from voting, leaving only the Independents to oppose
the ratification.) It cannot be denied that many men in the other
two coalition parties, the Centrists and the Progressive People's
Party, had weakened since the resolution passed. They knew that
the military command had moved most of the eastern divisions to
the western front, and, on the strength of the information they had

received, they could not doubt the generals' ability to mount and execute the planned offensive there. Indeed, on the very day the Reichstag voted, they heard that the offensive had begun with every sign of success. Nevertheless there was, particularly among the Progressive People's Party, a significant group of outstanding men like Naumann, Gothein, and Haussmann, whose principles did not melt away in the light of even the most auspicious military successes.

Ludendorff's spring offensive did indeed prove decisive. But it brought not the final victory that the great majority of Germans had confidently expected, but military defeat and, in consequence, political collapse. It is therefore quite understandable that thoughtful men have often asked themselves if this offensive was unavoidable, if it was really necessary to stake Germany's entire future on one throw of iron dice.

Now no one will wish to suspect a military expert with Ludendorff's reputation of having underestimated the importance and the risks of his move. He certainly knew as well as does any of his critics that even the best laid military plans can go awry, that they all contain an unavoidable element of uncertainty. But what were the predictable consequences of failure? Prince Max of Baden put this question to him on February 19, 1918, at his headquarters in Kreuznach. "Dann muss Deutschland eben zugrunde gehen!" * was the general's terrible reply. Was it then not his inescapable duty to seize every opportunity to spare Germany this dreadful alternative? Certainly the period just *before* the offensive (an offensive which the whole world expected and from which Germany's foes expected the worst) would have been a particularly appropriate time for negotiations. The enemy, knowing that little help would be forthcoming from America in the immediate future, would have been much more receptive to offers at this moment than later, when the Allies could count on millions of well-trained and superbly equipped American soldiers. Furthermore, President Wilson had proclaimed his Fourteen Points on January 8, 1918. One may think what one wishes of the Fourteen Points, but one must admit that they hardly implied the extinction of Germany that Ludendorff expected should his offensive fail.

These considerations were not presented to Ludendorff by Prince Max alone. On February 11, 1918, Frederick Naumann and others, including the most respected leaders of the German labor movement, handed Ludendorff a memorandum by Professor Alfred Weber and Dr. Kurt Hahn, in which the dangers of the situation

* "Then Germany will just have to suffer annihilation."

were most cogently presented.[47] They argued that the home front was no longer completely secure; that the great majority of the suffering populace regarded a fourth winter of war as unbearable; that the prospective bloodbath was monstrous; and that such a bloodbath would be accepted by the German people only if they "were convinced that the enemy had given us no alternative." For this very reason, they insisted, the planned attack should be preceded by a *diplomatic* offensive, the chief component of which would have to be "an unambiguous statement concerning *the future restoration of Belgian sovereignty and integrity.*"

Their argument was made with insight and detail. Ludendorff did favor them with a reply. But what was his response? He made a few trite remarks about the military position, but uttered not so much as one word about the memorandum's diplomatic proposal.[48] All of Ludendorff's statements under other circumstances give us every reason to take this answer not as an expression of a shy unwillingness to enter into nonmilitary affairs but rather as the negative expression of his firm intent to hang on to Belgium at all costs. Indeed, the Supreme Command now took the official position that even the barely reasonable statement of the Emperor to the Crown Council in September 1917 was no longer relevant since it had not led to peace within that year. A telegram of December 14, 1917, from the representative of the Foreign Office at the headquarters of the Supreme Command shows what the generals were really thinking as the year expired: "At the moment people here are feeling quite bullish and are full of projects for the foe's destruction!" [49] The Supreme Command even went so far as to demand of the Imperial Chancellor that he dissociate himself "in a public and positive fashion" from the Peace Resolution of July 19, 1917.[50] And not only the crown prince, but even the Emperor, joined in this demand.

Then, on March 21, 1918, the powerful German offensive broke forth upon the western front. Its first results were quite promising, more promising, indeed, than had been expected. The German people had every reason to believe that victory was assured when the Emperor, decorating Hindenburg and Ludendorff with highest honors, drew a clear parallel between the present defeat of the French and the defeat at Waterloo.[51] But great as was the tactical success, it failed to turn into strategic victory. At the beginning of April the attack had to be stopped, although its principal target, Amiens, had not been taken. To be sure, another attack at another point was undertaken on April 9; but this one could not be maintained beyond its initial advances either.

Whether this second offensive could possibly have achieved the desired strategic success is a question still debated by the experts [52] and one which therefore must rest unanswered here. But certainly at this point, after this second failure to achieve their goal, the Supreme Command must have realized that they could not smash the enemies' lines before the Americans would arrive, no matter at how many places along the front they tried. Furthermore, they knew that thousands of American soldiers were already deployed, and that the foe was growing stronger every month, while every month made it more difficult to replace the enormous German losses. When the Supreme Command reached these conclusions, it should have accepted the necessary consequence: the absolute necessity of straining every nerve to make peace as soon as possible. And since a peace of conquest was no longer possible, this would have to mean negotiated peace. The first step toward this end would have been to make a simple, flat statement to the German political authorities that the great operation had failed. But Ludendorff could not bring himself to do this.

Crown Prince Rupprecht of Bavaria, one of Ludendorff's subordinate commanders, wrote to the Chancellor as early as June 1, 1918, that the time had come to send out feelers for a negotiated peace since the prospect of delivering a decisive defeat to the foe had disappeared. He therefore recommended that Germany declare its willingness to preserve Belgium's absolute independence. He went on to say that even Ludendorff now realized that a decisive victory could not be had and was hoping instead "for the saving aid of some *deus ex machina.*" [53] But the Chancellor, completely under the spell of the Supreme Command, did not believe the prince.

A full month later the generals were still able to drive Secretary von Kühlmann from office for having dared to tell the Reichstag, on June 24, that "in view of the enormous size of this war of alliances . . . we can hardly expect to achieve peace through military means alone, without recourse to diplomatic negotiations." Ludendorff's conduct in this affair was particularly reprehensible since he must have known not only that what Kühlmann said was true, but also that the critical sentence was taken from a memorandum which he, Ludendorff, had forwarded to the Chancellor with his personal endorsement.[54] The memorandum had originated with Colonel von Haeften, director of the Military Division of the Foreign Office, whom Ludendorff had put in this post himself and whose political insight exceeded the general's by several orders of magnitude. But Ludendorff evidently regarded this thesis as an official secret, under no circumstances to be shared with the German nation. One can imagine what sort of impression the German people derived from seeing the generals chase the under-secretary out for having made this statement. They were *forced* to conclude that Kühlmann's statement was false, and that, therefore, its opposite was true, namely, that Hindenburg and Ludendorff, whom the nation still trusted, were convinced that they would win a final victory on the battlefield. Ludendorff must have been conscious of this effect. And since his words to Crown Prince Rupprecht and others show that he did not in fact believe that victory was possible, his behavior admits of only one conclusion: he found it more important to preserve his own prestige than to speak the truth.

Ludendorff's activities of the next month support this interpretation. In the conversations with the Chancellor at Spa in early July — in the course of which the Supreme Command extorted Kühlmann's dismissal — the generals made demands with respect to Belgium which could have been realized only if England had been utterly defeated. Admiral von Hintze, who had, with considerable reluctance, become the new state secretary for foreign affairs, records the following conversation he had with Ludendorff in mid-July. "I asked him directly whether he was *certain* of obtaining a final and decisive victory over the foe in his present offensive. Ludendorff repeated my question and replied (according to my memory) in these words: 'My response is a definite yes.'" [55] But just a few days later Foch opened his counteroffensive with a successful advance near Soissons. From this point on the German army was pushed more and more into a defensive posture. But did the Supreme Command now at last inform the political authorities that the situation had radically changed? On August 1, Under-Secretary von Radowitz reported from supreme headquarters to Vice-Chancellor von Payer: "The Supreme Command . . . is most confident . . . General Ludendorff . . . has expressed himself confidently . . . He hopes to be ready for new activities in the foreseeable future." But the "new activities" came from the other side. On August 8, the Australian Army Corps, under the command of General Monash, broke through the German front.[56] This was, to use Ludendorff's own later expression, "the black day of the German Army."

At this point Ludendorff finally told the Emperor enough of the truth to prompt the latter to say: "We can draw only one conclusion; we are at the limit of our capabilities. The war must be ended." [57] But Ludendorff kept up his old game of lies and tricks with the political leaders. On August 13, a discussion took place among Hindenburg, Ludendorff, Hertling, and Hintze. The generals went so far as to admit that there was no longer any possibility of a powerful German offensive, but they maintained that they did not, and in the future would not, have to restrict themselves to purely defensive activities. On the contrary, they would be able to mount local attacks from time to time. Most important of all, they claimed that by virtue of their defensive strategy they could break the spirit of the foe and thus *force him to terms of peace*.[58] Indeed, they went so far as to voice, as Hintze records, "the certainty of being able to attain this goal. By no word, by no syllable, by no hint did the field marshal or Ludendorff give us reason to realize or even guess that their professional estimate of the military situation had led them to conclude that diplomatic peace moves had become necessary. Their conversation was solely designed to reassure the Imperial Chancellor and myself in the face of their change in strategy; the goal, we were told, was still the same and was still within our reach."

Hintze's testimony is corroborated by the attitude toward war aims which the generals assumed in this conversation. They stuck by their former demands with no trace of softening. The same was true of their behavior in the Crown Council the next day. There Ludendorff discoursed on such topics as the necessity of imprisoning the former Ambassador Lichnowsky and the quality — or rather, the lack of quality — of the new recruits. While on this latter subject Ludendorff demanded, according to Hintze's notes, "a more vigorous conscription of the young Jews, hitherto left pretty much alone" and thus struck the demagogic chord of which he later was to make rich use.[59] But about the military situation, which the Crown Council had come to hear discussed, he said not one word! It was not the generals, it was Hintze, with his private, pessimistic estimate of the future, who concluded that "in making political decisions we can no longer ignore this turn of the war," or, in other words, that peace feelers had to be sent out, with more modest demands attached. But Hindenburg opposed him with arguments which Hintze in his minutes condensed to this sentence: "Hindenburg *hopes*, in spite of everything, that he will be able to stay on French soil and thus eventually impose our will upon the enemy." This was far too weak for Ludendorff! He crossed out the word "hopes" and wrote "*explains* that . . . he will be able." So intent was he to conceal the true gravity of the situation from even the most responsible authorities!

The Supreme Command held doggedly to this course for fully another six weeks, and all the time the situation, both military and political, became ever darker. Then suddenly, without warning, they put about and achieved — catastrophe.

On September 28, Hindenburg and Ludendorff concluded that the game was over, that the front could be pierced and rolled back at any moment, and that they required an immediate cessation of hostilities.[60] They requested the Chancellor to join them without delay. At the same time they suggested that he bring several influential leaders of the Reichstag into his government. The Supreme Command had heretofore stubbornly resisted such steps toward parliamentary rule.[61] Count Hertling, who was still ignorant of the military background behind this move, expressed astonishment at learning that the generals now favored what they formerly had opposed. Hertling himself remained an opponent of parliamentary responsibility and was determined to have no part in it. But in any event his time had run out. For not only had the coalition parties openly accepted the principle of parliamentary participation in the government — including even the Social Democrats — but they had also let Hertling know that they did not consider him, with his advanced age and tender health, fit for the enormously difficult task ahead. Hertling therefore went to Spa in order to hand his resignation to the Emperor. But when he arrived on September 29, he found the biggest surprise of all waiting for him.

Secretary von Hintze was already at Spa. He had gone there on his own initiative, having gathered from reports (not from the Supreme Command but from other sources) that the situation was becoming desperate. The diplomatic front was also collapsing. "Bulgaria lost; the loss of Austria-Hungary imminent; Turkey more a burden than a help." But on the morning of September 29, upon making this report to the Supreme Command, he was amazed to hear Ludendorff reply with the news that the military situation made an immediate armistice necessary lest catastrophe ensue. Hintze tried to make the general understand the effect that "such a sudden shift from fanfares of victory to the dirges of defeat would work upon the army, the nation, the monarchy, and the Empire." He sought to make clear to them "that along with the request for an armistice, indeed, prior to it, there must exist a readiness for peace." Ludendorff finally agreed that peace had to be made. But most important of all, he insisted, was the pressing necessity of an *immediate* armistice. At this point von Hindenburg made an observation which one could not believe if Hintze had not expressly testified to its truth: The state secretary must take care that the final peace include the German annexation of Longwy and Briey.[62] This is what was going on in the head of the man whom unnumbered Germans regarded as their nation's savior.

This request of the Supreme Command for an immediate armistice was astonishing not only to the Chancellor, but also to the Emperor. That Hertling now requested and received his relief from office needs no explanation. But even William himself had had no inkling of the truth before the generals spoke. And he, too, yielded to their demand without lengthy resistance, perhaps because he did not recognize its implications, or perhaps because he had lost the strength for independent thought. His lack of strength became evident in the selection of a new Chancellor: William, dropping the reins completely from his hands, was content to see others seize the initiative which he was no longer strong enough to hold.

In point of fact, the name of Prince Max of Baden was first mentioned by members of the Reichstag. Conrad Haussmann had been proposing him for some time now, having found in him a man who combined high moral character and humane sensitivity with sober political wisdom. He had every reason to believe that in Prince Max he had found just the right man for a situation which, even with respect to domestic politics, had become completely new. For on September 30 an imperial decree had stated that in the future "men enjoying the confidence of the people would partake to a greater (a typographical error read 'great') extent in the rights and duties of government." This decree even suggested the possibility that the Social Democrats might enter the government. And that was of crucial importance because only with their help could any regime hope to restrain the threatening flood. The Social Democrats had declined, for good reasons, to serve under Hertling. But they stood ready to assist Prince Max, however distasteful their share in his responsibilities must have been from a partisan point of view.

The prince arrived in Berlin on the afternoon of October 1. Colonel von Haeften briefed him quickly and reported the generals' demand for an immediate request for armistice. This news came as an utter surprise to the prince. His willingness to accept this thankless post was based on his assumption that as Chancellor he would be able to proclaim reasonable, realistic war aims, which could in turn lead to a negotiated peace. He realized immediately that a request for armistice not only would ruin such a program, but would turn a difficult situation into catastrophe. He declined to become Chancellor.[63]

A desperate struggle between Prince Max and the Supreme Command occupied the next few days. The generals needed a man to ask President Wilson for armistice and peace on the basis of his Fourteen Points, and to assume responsibility for this step in the eyes of Germany and the world. Hindenburg traveled to Berlin to get his man. The prince took pains to make clear to the field marshal what the expensive consequences of such a request would be, namely, that the acceptance of the Fourteen Points would, in all likelihood, mean the loss to Prussia of "Alsace-Lorraine and the purely Polish parts of the eastern provinces." Hindenburg's reply, in writing, is extremely characteristic: "The Supreme Military Command attaches no great value to the French-speaking parts of Alsace-Lorraine; a cession of German territory in the east is not contemplated here." As though after the publication of a German request for armistice and peace on the strength of Wilson's Fourteen Points it would be of the slightest consequence what had been "contemplated" by the German generals! One cannot avoid the conclusion that Hindenburg and Ludendorff had an utterly inadequate sense of the implications and effects of such a request. They spoke continually of the *respite* that their army needed; indeed, they even went so far as to say that, after the armistice expired, the army should be permitted to resume the battle, perhaps at the German border. At this same time it was perfectly obvious that the Allies would consider an armistice only under such conditions as would make a resumption of hostilities by the Germans quite impossible. Could a foe who now, after four years of war, felt victory in his hands — and a German request for armistice would give him every reason to feel it — act otherwise? Ludendorff had only to ask himself how he would have proceeded if the roles had been reversed. What miserable psychologists these German generals were!

They were also poor psychologists if they did not foresee that the morale of the soldiers would collapse in the face of the realization that the promised victory was forever lost; that the gaps in their own ranks could no longer be filled, while the Americans, whose influence Admiral Cappele had estimated at "exactly nothing," were bracing the ranks of the foe by hundreds of thousands. The generals were foolish too if they really thought that, after four war years of frightful suffering and severe austerity, the German people would pick up their weapons once they laid them down. But we shall have more to say on this point later.

First we must return to Prince Max's fight against a request for armistice. The pressure which the Supreme Command brought to bear on him was enormous; Ludendorff begged, in wires and calls too numerous to count, for the immediate dispatch of this request, threatening that otherwise he could not hold out even twenty-four hours longer. There was no one upon whom Prince Max could lean for support, for no one dared take issue with the military diagnosis of the two famous generals. Even the vice-chancellor declared that, if the prince refused to sign, he, Payer, would lend his good name to the army — and then resign. William was again an utter failure. At the Crown Council meeting of October 3, when Prince Max began a statement with the words "I oppose the request," the Emperor interrupted him with the words: "The Supreme Command requests it, and you have not been invited here to make difficulties for the Supreme Command!" [64] And thus the subjection of the commander-in-chief and the political authorities to the Supreme Command was expressed in one more way.

When the prince finally weakened and assumed the office of imperial chancellor under these frightful conditions, it was in the hope that his personal sacrifice would be beneficial to his fatherland. Prince Max knew that President Wilson had always directed his attacks against Germany's autocratic society and militaristic rulers, that he had always distinguished between these, his enemy, and the German people. The Chancellor realized that his personality and the parliamentary government which he would lead would have to demonstrate to the Allies that Germany had permanently rejected the old regime. Thus even the Social Democrats, in the person of Scheidemann, the new state secretary, were represented in his cabinet. But Prince Max did not realize that he was serving Ludendorff's end in this way. As long as the general had hoped for victory he had fought to keep final authority, political no less than military, concentrated in his own hands. But now, in defeat, he was more than happy to share disaster with others and particularly pleased to be able to include among them the Social Democrats, for whom he had previously shown nothing but hatred and scorn. It was, therefore, completely to Ludendorff's advantage that suddenly, on September 28, he announced his conversion to parliamentary government.

The details of the correspondence with President Wilson, which began with Prince Max's note of October 3, 1918, need not be recounted here. Most important was Wilson's note of October 23, in which he stated his intention to share the correspondence up to that point with his allies in order that they might come to a common decision about the armistice. But immediately he went on to say that he could propose to his allies only such an armistice as would make a resumption of hostilities by the Germans impossible. Any rational man could have predicted this requirement; it was answered, quite without the Chancellor's permission, by the Supreme Command with a general order which simply labeled Wilson's reply unacceptable. [65] To this act of insubordination Hindenburg and Ludendorff quickly added another by going to Berlin, although the Chancellor had given them to understand that they were to remain in Spa. The Chancellor was now obliged to ask the Emperor for Ludendorff's dismissal, though requesting at the same time that Hindenburg be retained. [66] Both wishes were granted: Ludendorff was relieved of his duties on October 26; Hindenburg, separating himself from his colleague, remained at his post.

In his memoirs Prince Max explains this step with the statement that he had lost confidence in Ludendorff. He had every reason to have lost it. Events at the front had demonstrated that Ludendorff had misjudged the situation of September 29, and that the postponement of the request for armistice, for which the prince had so vigorously fought and begged, might safely have been granted him. But still worse was the fact that the general was now bending every effort to call off the armistice upon which he had previously insisted. But the step he had taken was irrevocable. He could no more call off the armistice than he could summon back a shell that had been fired. He was experiencing the truth of Goethe's line: "The first step makes us free; the second makes us slaves."

On October 17, there was a meeting of the war cabinet, to which Generals Ludendorff and Hoffmann (the commanders in the east) had also been invited, in order that they might aid in determining what "Germany's military situation required." The stenographic minutes of this meeting show that Ludendorff was feeling his way completely in the dark. He said he would be able to hold the front if he received replacements. But he had no idea where enough replacements might be found. Various members of the cabinet pointed out to him that conscription was encountering ever increasing difficulties. He did not pretend to know how the million soldiers, presently living off the Ukraine and other occupied areas in the East, were to be fed if transported to the West. He left it up to the politicians to raise the nation's morale. "Capture the imagination of the people; lift up their hearts! Cannot Herr Ebert do that?" But then he had to listen while Scheidemann explained: "We have no more meat. We cannot provide potatoes, for we are short four thousand freight cars every day. We have no more fats at all. The emergency is so pressing that one is confronted by a complete mystery when one wonders what keeps the poorer parts of Berlin alive. So long as we cannot solve this mystery, we cannot hope to boost morale." The Chancellor asked Ludendorff directly: Would a continuation of the war lead to an improvement of the situation? Was there any assurance that the war could be brought to a close under more favorable conditions next year? Ludendorff's only answer was the empty observation: "Every exertion we make now improves our position." [67]

With this he abandoned his entire argument. For his thesis was tenable only if he could achieve significant military successes. Prince Max was completely correct when he said that every exertion which did not lead to better terms of peace amounted to a waste of resources, in other words, that all the blood such battles would cost through the winter and even, perhaps, the spring would prove in the end to have been an utterly useless and a senseless waste. No one can say flatly that the German army would have been able to avoid military catastrophe by maintaining its discipline and morale as it fell steadily backwards. On the other hand, it is quite possible to argue that Foch was probably not prepared to demand that his troops make a superhuman effort to win a final military decision during the remainder of 1918. But if it was certain that the decisive battle was to be fought within a few more months, what possible advantage could the Germans win by delay? Within those ensuing months a million or so American soldiers would arrive, the Allies' store of artillery and tanks would be vastly increased, and every Allied soldier would become more confident in the thought: "Now we've got them; this time victory is absolutely sure." And in the meantime would not the surrenders of Bulgaria, Turkey, and Austria-Hungary have wrought their effects? Would not divisions upon divisions of the foe be streaming up the Danube into undefended and indefensible South Germany? The Chancellor and the new state secretary for foreign affairs, Dr. Solf, were quite right in regarding Ludendorff's declarations with the greatest skepticism. And, indeed, there were few in Germany at that time, either in the Army or among civilians, who mourned the fall of the once so honored general. For he was generally considered the protagonist and embodiment of that policy of egregious annexation and massive slaughter which had so obviously failed, and of that ruthless militarism of which, after four years of war and siege, Germans had had more than enough. He was now considered the one, last obstacle on the road to peace, the goal of soldier and civilian alike.

Wilson's note of October 23 not only caused Ludendorff's fall; it also threatened the position of a much more lofty personage. "If it [the government of the United States] must deal with the military masters and the monarchical autocrats of Germany now," so read the note, "or if it is likely to have to deal with them later in regard to the international obligations of the German Empire, it must demand, not peace negotiations, but surrender." In Germany as in other countries this was taken to mean that Wilson did not wish to negotiate with William II. And if Wilson took this position, the attitudes of England and France were in all likelihood still more severe. On the other hand one could gather from the note that the conditions of Germany's surrender would be less rigorous if it first rid itself of the Emperor. "The note is not so bad at all; if the Emperor goes, we'll get a decent peace," were the words of Herr Noske, Social

Democratic representative, to Secretary Solf, when the latter's face grew ever more serious while reading the note. In a Reichstag address on October 24, before the contents of the note had been released, Noske stated that "only a unique, grand gesture on the part of the Crown" could relieve millions of this pressure. These words had all the more effect since Noske had shown himself throughout the war to be a German patriot.

And so the question of the Emperor's abdication was formally placed upon the legislative calendar. Prince Max sought to avoid this dilemma, so particularly embarrassing for him, by pressing for quick acceptance of those laws which were supposed to define permanently the new parliamentary form of government and the reciprocal limitations upon the imperial prerogative. In this way he hoped to deprive Wilson of the argument "that the determining initiative still remains with those who have hitherto been the masters of Germany." And, in fact, these basic laws were quickly passed and signed by the Emperor. But they altered nothing in the chain of events.

For Noske had described the atmosphere all too well; and this attitude was in no way restricted to the Socialist workers. The entire German people, so royalist a few short years before, had become completely disillusioned by its monarch. The first official document suggesting that imperial abdication was at hand is a telegram of October 25 to the Chancellor from the Prussian ambassador at Munich. The telegram makes it clear that the Bavarian prime minister and minister of war were both of this opinion.[68] This was not just the voice of Bavarian particularism; the word was to be heard throughout the land. One not only read it in the newspapers, one also heard it in every conversation on the sidewalk or in the streetcar; not just among close friends, but also among strangers who thus exchanged the burdens of their hearts. To be sure, an old Democrat like Haussmann could still tell Prince Max: "The German people will not reject its Emperor at the enemy's behest." But the man in the street did not agree. He had experienced too much; he could not and would not suffer any more. Let it be over as soon as possible! That was his single desire. If the Emperor stood in the way, then he had to be removed. Simple men think simply as a rule. In the Emperor they saw the man who had led them into this war, who had declared it. The enterprise had failed, and now he had to suffer the consequences. Today we know that things had not happened as simply as that. Yet whose fault was it but William's if the whole world thought that he had unleashed this war? He had certainly said and done everything possible to encourage the belief that everything that occurred in Germany was his doing and that the German sword lay restless in its sheath. And would not the glory have been his if he had won and marched as victor through the Brandenburg Gate?

These thoughts were shared not only by people at home but also by those at the front; not only by the troops, but also by the officers. During the war, whenever the generals stated with their usual bland assurance that "the Army" was of this or that opinion, they were, in fact, speaking only for the small circle of the General Staff and perhaps for those other officers in immediate contact with it. The real sentiments of the millions of conscripts and reservists who filled their divisions were practically unknown to them; they were certainly less known to the generals than to the people at home, to whom the soldiers bared their hearts when on one of their rare leaves. Least of all did the generals realize how unbearable to their men the pressure of the discipline and absolute subordination, so inextricably connected with the German military system, had become in the course of the four long years of war. Much has been said about social injustice in the army, and Professor Hobohm collected, in a book for the Committee on Investigation, over four hundred pages of considerable material to which even Major Volkmann's countertestimony is no satisfactory rebuttal.[69]

But the simple truth is that the German system was not fitted for an extended war. The system was designed for young men who could be brought by their officers into the desired physical and psychological condition. It failed completely when tried on older men, men who had already fashioned civilian lives for themselves and who, while bowing to the will of their military superiors, recalled with longing what they had left behind; men who were reminded with each letter from home how much their loved ones were suffering and how all that they held dear was being ruined. This was not class conflict but rather a sentiment common to most men of all classes and callings. It could weaken and even yield to a warlike spirit if a great goal beckoned, as at the beginning of the spring offensive, from which every officer and soldier expected a victorious end — but above all, an end — to the war. But it grew inexorably in strength when these same men saw that even this superhuman effort had proved fruitless, that nothing remained before them but, sooner or later, defeat. To the army the request for armistice (and everyone soon knew that the generals had demanded it) amounted to the hoisting of the white flag; no one wished to risk his life now that it was bound to be in vain. Even Ludendorff had to report, at the cabinet meeting of October 17, that "we learn from all sides

(Gallwitz' army for example) that the armistice negotiations are entailing very evil consequences. In Belgium our people ask themselves: 'Why should we go on fighting here if we only have to withdraw later?' And at Verdun they wonder: 'What purpose do our sacrifices serve if the French are going to get Alsace-Lorraine anyway?'" But could it have been otherwise? The only amazing thing is that Ludendorff was astonished at these results of his own deeds and that he could ask that somebody, anybody, somehow restore morale.

Interested parties have since tried to blame all this on "sedition." Now, there unquestionably was agitation on the part of the radical Left. But one reverses cause and effect if one thinks that this is what brought about the military collapse. The truth of the matter is just the opposite. Agitation was successful because the army had been decisively defeated. That spring, when everybody still believed the big offensive would work, there had been a by-election in a radical Berlin suburban precinct, Niederbarnim, in which the Independent Socialist Dr. Breitscheid, a brilliant orator and outstanding demagogue, had been defeated by the Majority Socialists. But in October, Scheidemann and Ebert were forced to watch their former supporters desert not only to the Independents, but even to the Spartacists, and to see Karl Liebknecht, who had just been released from prison, "hoisted upon shoulders of men who were wearing the Iron Cross." [70]

As soon as people in this mood became convinced that between them and their dearly desired peace stood just one man, the Emperor's doom was sealed. Prince Max could read the signs of the times as well as anyone. And he must have been particularly impressed when the Emperor's former aide-de-camp of long standing, General von Chelius, traveled from Brussels to Berlin solely to tell Prince Max that the Emperor would have to abdicate to save his country and his dynasty. [71] But what was Prince Max to do? All the Chancellor's attempts to persuade persons close to the Emperor to give him the advice to which there was no longer any alternative ended in failure. Then, on October 29, the prince decided to go to the Emperor himself. But before he could carry out this plan, he learned that William intended to go to the front that very day. Max did everything in his power to prevent this journey; he even put through a personal telephone call to the Emperor and stressed as urgently as he could how fateful this trip would be. But in vain. The Emperor left — and never saw Berlin again.

It was only natural that the news of the Emperor's departure from Berlin was interpreted everywhere to mean that he had taken refuge with the Supreme Command in order to be protected there from parliamentary influence. Hence with this one blow the sense and usefulness of the entire recent political reform was brought to nothing and the last vestige of William's reputation was destroyed. Even in those circles which had thus far opposed his abdication for general political reasons the impression was taking hold that William was now little more than ballast that might well have to be tossed overboard in this time of distress.

But he received the death blow from the admirals of his own fleet, that favorite weapon of his, for the sake of which he had sacrificed the possibility of a settlement with England in the critical prewar years. The idleness to which the fleet had been condemned ever since the Battle of the Skagerrak had been borne only with discomfort by its officers. And now, to satisfy Wilson, the unrestricted submarine war had been abandoned, thus rousing their ire all the more. Was the war to be brought to a close before the full weight of the battle fleet had been put in the balance? Its admirals decided to steam out and fight a decisive engagement with the English. Far from requesting the Chancellor's approval of this plan, they did not even tell him of its existence, although it was very clear that such a move in the course of the armistice negotiations constituted an act of extreme political importance.[72] Later they tried to defend themselves by saying that Admiral Scheer had given the Chancellor to understand in general terms that once the submarine campaign was over the battle fleet would again enjoy its former freedom of action. But this explanation was so obviously unconvincing that even the admirals must have known it was spurious.

They had been able to keep their secret from the Chancellor better than from their own crews. The sailors could tell from preparations what was planned; and so, on October 29, when the fleet was scheduled to leave, the stokers went out on strike. They struck so effectively that the orders had to be rescinded. Events now ran their necessary course: passive resistance turned into mutiny, and the officers showed themselves utterly unable to maintain discipline. On November 4 the red flag flew from every ship. Bands of revolutionary sailors wandered from the ports to other cities, kindling revolt as they went.

Mutiny is mutiny, and no one will try to excuse it. But if ever there was a pardonable mutiny, it was this one. Could the sailors regard the intended attack as anything but a deliberate attempt to sabotage the government's quest for peace, especially since many of their officers were openly opposed to this quest? Could they possibly believe that the attack would have a favorable effect on the

outcome of the war? Every German seaman knew the superiority
of the British fleet and could reckon on the fingers of his hands that
it would still be a grand fleet even if each German ship were to take
an English vessel with it as it sunk. Did it not seem more likely that
the officers were simply seeking that "death with honor" which their
naval code insisted upon? But did this code give the officers the
right to drag to their death thousands of good sailors, men who for
years had suffered the miserable life afloat and who now waited
only for the day that was to mean freedom and home? At that time,
the commander of the cruiser *Seydlitz* told Dr. Südekum, a Social
Democrat in the Reichstag, that his ship's company included "men
who would have completed voluntary four-year enlistments on October 1, 1914, but who now were in their eighth or ninth year on
board. This was frightful torture . . . And worst of all was the
feeling in the fleet that, throughout the war, the authorities, with
fatal shortsightedness, had failed to use the fleet when time was
ripe, yet Berlin now was toying with the idea of playing it as one
last, desperate trump. The commander had personally remained
completely loyal to his king, but could easily put himself in the
rebels' shoes." [73] The sailors' revolt can be explained without reference to any revolutionary agitation. The admirals had been playing
with fire, and now the fire consumed not only them but the German
Empire as well.

For the success of the sailors' mutiny was certain to fan other
sparks into flames if only because it had demonstrated that the
state had no means left with which to quell revolt. The soldiers who
were sent against the mutineers surrendered, declared themselves
"neutral," or else joined the revolt. The leaders of the Social Democrats lost more and more control over the party's rank and file;
finally they had no choice but to demand the Emperor's abdication. Prince Max tried in every way to make clear to William that
only in this way was the dynasty to be preserved. But the Emperor,
surrounded as he was by the generals and his military court, remained deaf to every plea. General Gröner, who had taken Ludendorff's place, was also an intransigent; yet even he, when he returned
to Berlin on November 5, was obliged to give the Chancellor a
completely hopeless report on the military situation. On Wednesday,
November 6, Gröner went so far as to say that the army would simply have to surrender if an armistice were not arranged before Saturday, November 9. That same Wednesday, Gröner met with leaders
of both the Social Democrats and the trade unions. These men had
collaborated loyally with the general when he was in charge of
the War Office. The Social Democrats certainly did not wish to turn

Germany into a republic at this time. They quite candidly told the general that they would be content with a parliamentary monarchy of Socialist bent, but that this would require the Emperor's immediate abdication and a regency in lieu of the crown prince. They urged Gröner to create these necessary conditions, but the general, considering himself bound by his military oath, rejected their request. Finally Ebert, finding the discussion at an impasse, broke it off, assuring Gröner that he and his colleagues would always have warm memories of their wartime collaboration. "At this point our ways part." Later, at the Munich Dolchstoss trial, when Gröner testified concerning this important conversation, he added: "I declare myself completely guilty for not having accepted Ebert's proposal then and there; perhaps we still could have saved the monarchy." [74]

Time was running out! On this same Wednesday Wilson's note arrived, stating the Allies' willingness to make peace upon the basis of the Fourteen Points and declaring Marshal Foch empowered to explain the conditions of armistice to representatives of the German government. Thus the German generals were spared the necessity of going to Foch with white flags. Gröner advised the Chancellor to appoint State Secretary Erzberger German representative on the armistice commission. Prince Max followed this advice, and Erzberger accepted the task — to his later sorrow. Perhaps it was also to Germany's loss; for Erzberger's industry and force were sorely missed during the next few days in Berlin, when everything fell into chaos. [75]

On the evening of November 6, Prince Max made the difficult decision to go in person to Spa in order to tell the Emperor face to face that he would have to abdicate to save the throne. The prince, to protect himself against a revolution while away, communicated his intention to Ebert the following morning, and Ebert promised him support. But Ebert could not keep this promise, for that very afternoon Ebert and Scheidemann delivered to the Chancellor an ultimatum which they had received from their party. This note threatened the withdrawal of the Social Democrats from the coalition government if certain demands were not met by noon of the next day, Friday, November 8. The most essential of these demands was the abdication of both the Emperor and the crown prince. The Social Democratic leaders were clearly not happy about this ultimatum, but twenty-six party meetings were scheduled for that evening in Berlin, at which the rank and file would certainly desert to the Independents if the leaders refused to endorse the ultimatum from the chair. These leaders were made even less happy when the Chancellor, who, as Schiedemann assured him, had their complete sympathy, answered their ultimatum with an offer to resign, and when the other ministers accused them vehemently of ruining everything at this critical moment.

While these men were still looking for some viable compromise, revolution spread throughout Germany. On November 8, a republic was proclaimed in Munich, and the Wittelsbachs were declared to be deposed; in Brunswick, the local duke, son-in-law of the Emperor, renounced his throne. But William, from the apparent safety of general headquarters, informed the Chancellor by wire that he could not accept the latter's recommendations and that he still regarded it as his duty to remain at his post.

William seems to have convinced himself that he, at the head of his armies, could still restore "order in the homeland." This was his final illusion. Gröner himself now realized that even the combat troops were in no mood to fight for the Emperor: "A division which had been considered particularly reliable had been selected to cover the rear of general headquarters against rebels advancing from Cologne and Aachen; the troops refused to obey their officers and, in spite of orders to the contrary, set off to march homeward." [76] With this the Supreme Command finally realized how matters stood. But the generals calmly waited until the following morning before advising the Emperor to do the unavoidable. They were even slower in informing the Chancellor of their moves, although they could hardly have been ignorant of the importance of every hour, perhaps of every minute, in Berlin. That very night the government felt itself obliged to wire Spa that the rebellion could no longer be checked if the abdication were not announced in the morning newspapers. But the All Highest had already retired and was not to be disturbed.

He arose the next morning still sovereign, but by the following evening, when he put himself to bed, he had ceased to be Emperor. He was now a refugee, forced to beg a roof on foreign soil, and the House of Hohenzollern had ceased to rule. It had required his own generals, Hindenburg and Gröner, to rip him from his dreams. But by the time they had done that, the morning of November 9 had already come, and everything that occurred in Spa occurred too late. The Social Democrats had already left the government, and mobs of workers were marching toward the center of Berlin and the government buildings. No one opposed them. This inactivity of the governmental forces is the truly characteristic element of this strange revolt. There were thousands of officers in Berlin who, under proper direction, would certainly have been strong enough to nip the Revolution in its bud. But no military command wished to lead them, and no one of them showed any desire to risk his life for his officer's oath. Neither hand grenades nor machine guns destroyed Imperial Germany, but rather a lack of faith in its right to exist.

The exact course of events is therefore of secondary interest. At about eleven that morning the Imperial Chancellor had learned from general headquarters of the Emperor's decision to abdicate. The precise wording of the Emperor's statement was to follow in thirty minutes. But the hour wore on and still no message came. Finally, in order to save the *institution* of the monarchy, Prince Max decided to announce at noon that the Emperor had abdicated and that the crown prince had declined to succeed him. But even this decision could not stop the tide of events. For at this same hour the Social Democrats came to tell Prince Max that they were taking over the government. The prince did the only thing left for him to do: he passed on to Ebert the office of Imperial Chancellor. When, a few hours later, he took his leave, he said: "Herr Ebert, Germany's fate depends upon your conscience now." And Ebert answered: "I have lost two sons for this country."

Only after he had resigned his office did Prince Max receive the official formula from headquarters: William had, to be sure, abdicated as German Emperor, but not as King of Prussia. If one had wished to take this message seriously, it would still have con- stituted a revolution. For the imperial constitution had bound the German and the Prussian crowns inseparably together. But by now this constitutional nonsense had become meaningless. For Scheide- mann had already proclaimed the German Republic from the steps of the Reichstag, and the shouted approval of thousands had greeted the news.

Things being as they were, the Republic became irrevocable with this shout, even though Scheidemann's announcement had been an improvisation for which he possessed neither direction nor au- thority. Ebert, who preferred quiet consideration while Scheide- mann gave himself up to the moment and to transitory party trends, was deeply disturbed by his colleague's proclamation. He was with- out doubt a republican, but he knew that the German Republic could not be born in less auspicious circumstances or at a less auspi- cious time. As late as November 9 the party organ *Vorwärts* had written: "The prospect of being obliged for perhaps thirty years to deal with royalist Don Quixotes within a young republic — and to see necessary inner developments thereby disturbed — is cer- tainly not very appealing." It was, presumably, Ebert who uttered these prophetic words from the very depths of his soul. Furthermore, he knew that a most demanding armistice awaited the German people, and that this was only a prelude to a no less rigorous peace.

On November 8, in the forest of Compiègne, Marshal Foch had handed the Allies' conditions of armistice to the German commission. They were the conditions of a conqueror who wishes to ensure in the fullest manner that his conquered foe will not be able to raise the sword again. Should Germany accept the armistice? The question was put to Hindenburg. In his reply he recommended that the German commission seek amelioration of some of the points. "But if these efforts fail," his telegram ended, "we shall have to accept it anyway." [77] And therewith he testified that there could be no thought of further resistance. There was certainly no prospect of continued resistance once the Revolution had begun. But even if Germany had been spared revolt, further bloodshed would have been both useless and mad.

And so, in the early morning of November 11, the German plenipotentiaries signed, and when the clocks struck eleven that day, weapons were dropped on all fronts. The hour had come for which all the world had yearned, an hour which bore within it an infinity of unseen complications.

II

FROM THE REVOLUTION
TO THE NATIONAL ASSEMBLY

THE Germans had suddenly found themselves not only with a Republic but with a Social Democratic national government as well. Those who remembered the position and opinions of the prewar Social Democratic movement were almost obliged to regard this new turn of events as a miracle. Yet, not only the affairs had changed, but the Social Democrats as well. In the Party Resolution of August 4, 1914 they had accepted Hugo Haase's proposition: "We will not desert the Fatherland in its hour of danger." This was an unalterable fact which was certain to entail critical consequences for the party's principles and passions whether or not later leaders continued to accept the resolution. For on this day Social Democracy had ceased to be what it had been up to then: the party of constant, dedicated opposition. At this decisive moment it had assumed its share of responsibility for the fate of the entire nation, a responsibility that it could not later dismiss.[1]

The resolution caused massive internal stresses and strains within the party when the quick victory everyone expected did not materialize and instead the war dragged on endlessly. This was a party which had not only opposed the imperial budget with regularity but which had also called any member to account who voted for the provincial budget in, say, the Hessian or the Baden Landtag. It was therefore only natural that, to countless Social Democrats, the party's approval of the military budget meant a complete break from the tradition in which they had grown up. Had they offered a toast every May Day to "Social Democracy, the liberator and uniter of nations," in order to approve now a war that was more terrible than man had ever imagined? A thousand times they had sworn that bourgeois society was their mortal enemy, but now the party leaders had become "bourgeois Socialists"; for the government they directed was most certainly bourgeois, not Socialist. And would not the owners and managers, rather than the "proletarian party" which had opposed them in all its past struggles, be the chief benefactors of a victorious war? Employers' groups had certainly done their share to encourage such doubts by becoming vociferous supporters of those leaders whose war aims included extensive annexation. *Every* Social Democrat, whether of conservative or radical persuasion, opposed such annexation. But when one wing of the party tried to use its influence in the Reichstag to hold the imperial government to the course of a strictly defensive war, the other wing was quick to seize this opportunity to throw their brothers into one pot with the annexationists and to declare a bitter war upon them there. Not all of these motives affected all the members of the opposition who left the party as "Independents." The very nature of the new group made that clear. Indeed, it had required a world catastrophe to bring into one camp men of such opposed opinions as Eduard Bernstein and Hugo Haase.

To the left of the Independents there stood the still more radical groups and subgroups who accused them, with passionate vehemence, of betraying the principles of international socialism. The Spartacists, then under the leadership of Karl Liebknecht and Rosa Luxemburg, were the loudest with this cry. In 1916 the Imperial Military Court had given Liebknecht an inhuman and senseless four-year sentence for taking part in a street demonstration; in October 1918 Prince Max's cabinet had set him free. Naturally enough, Liebknecht was now, if only because of this martyrdom, extremely popular among the Berlin radicals. The November flood tide of revolution turned this popularity into power. But neither his intellectual nor his political talents fitted him to be leader of a great movement. Intellectually superior to him was Rosa Luxemburg, whose many opponents never denied her intelligence nor her ability to employ the Marxist dialectic with extraordinary virtuosity. It was only natural that the Russian Revolution gave a strong impetus to the Spartacists. Even the weapons with which they fought came at least in part from the Russian armory. And their motto was derived from Russia too: "All power — legislative, executive, and judicial — to the workers' and soldiers' soviets!"

Once the Republic had been proclaimed, all these elements surged through the streets of Berlin, hailing either the German Republic or the Russian Revolution, using weapons they had legally or otherwise obtained, hurling themselves upon officers to rip off insignia of rank, and applauding Lübben's cavalry, which was summoned to keep order in Berlin, when it deserted to "the people." The various executive agencies of the authoritarian state which had stood so firmly a week before seemed to have disappeared. Peace and order seemed to rest solely upon the good or evil will, the wisdom or the folly, of the masses. No one knew how many people backed this group or that. Naturally, the radicals were loudest. To be sure, every reasonable man knew that this noise was no measure of their strength. But the reasonable man had also learned from Russia that even a small minority, well armed, can win its way.

Under these circumstances the leaders of the Majority Socialists could not possibly claim for their party the right to govern alone. They had to share the government at least with the Independents in order that it might rest upon a reasonably broad base. The Independents demanded, as a condition of their entrance into the regime, an acceptance of the principle of a "social republic," words which every man was free to interpret as he wished. Ebert and his colleagues experienced no difficulty in accepting this condition. The real issue lay between the proponents of a German democracy and those who demanded a dictatorship of the proletariat *à la russe*. The Majority Socialists wanted to place the power of final decision in the hands of a National Constituent Assembly to be chosen as soon as possible by the entire adult population in a democratic election. The Independents wanted to put all power in the hands of "elected representatives of the workers and soldiers." [2]

Although this difference was not settled, the Independents declared their readiness to join the cabinet (of course this bourgeois name was dropped in favor of the "Council of People's Representatives"). The "council" consisted of three Majority Socialists (Ebert, Scheidemann, and Landsberg) and three Independents (Haase, Dittmann, and Barth). Emil Barth was a metal worker who, on the strength of his talents as a demagogue, had clambered to the head of the workers' and soldiers' soviets in Berlin; the other five were members of the Reichstag, whose experience there had given them some training for their new tasks. Landsberg and Haase were also prominent lawyers and thus possessed the legal training and ability that would be necessary for the correct formulation of the council's decisions. Liebknecht had declined to take part in the regime, preferring to stick by his demand for a soviet government. This formula, however, was renounced by the great convention of the workers' and soldiers' soviets on November 10.

But the struggle did not end with this vote. On the contrary, it grew more bitter with every week. A nation which, after four years of war, was experiencing the collapse not only of all its hopes but also of its entire political structure, could hardly find a new equilibrium within a few days. This condition of uncertainty was increased by the addition of all the soldiers, returning in millions from the war. The armistice had required the German generals to withdraw their troops across the Rhine within set, short periods of time. This they did with their customary technical dispatch. But no sooner did the troops touch German soil than they melted away in their generals' hands. Whoever had a home or place of work went there forthwith; the rest wandered aimlessly in uniform through the streets of larger cities, taking part in the continual conventions or in meetings of soldiers' soviets.

This is not to say that demagogic words and idle talk prevailed throughout the land. Max Weber valued "the unassuming realism of the simple people, including many soldiers," of the Heidelberg workers' and soldiers' soviet, of which he became a member. But it lay in the nature of things that, especially in large cities like Berlin, the crowds of people who gathered were particularly easy prey for demagogues, whether idealists or tough-minded agitators; and the numerous weapons which found their way to the hands of the crowds gave these people the sensation of holding real power. In the streets of the government district in Berlin bullets whistled by at all hours of day and night. Newspaper offices were occupied by armed bands; a so-called People's Naval Division had taken up quarters in the palace; a representative of the extreme Left was directing the police; even the chancellery was threatened with violence.

Under these circumstances it was little wonder that the marriage of convenience between the Majority Socialists and the Independents did not last long. Ebert knew that the first duty of any government, even if it called itself the Council of People's Representatives, was the maintenance of "peace, security, and order" — to quote the time-honored definition of the policeman's mission as set forth in the Prussian Code. He also knew that this duty was not just a bourgeois class prejudice, but rather a real need sensed by every person, rich or poor, powerful or weak, who wished to enjoy the fruits of his labors in peace. And there was one further consideration, as simple as it was compelling: how were the large cities to be fed if the farmers refused to sell their crops and meat? The peasants and landowners were certainly most vigorously opposed to any Dictatorship of the Proletariat and were ready and able to act accordingly if the cities should declare a workers' state.

One dare not do a man like Haase the injustice of pretending that he was too dull to understand these facts. But his political position required him to cultivate the extreme Left, which alone could support him against the Majority Socialists (and, in a real emergency, against the bourgeois parties) and to which he felt himself bound by a common faith in the blessings of nationalization and a common enmity toward private enterprise. Most especially he shared the extreme Left's hatred of the old militarism, and every organized military force seemed to him to bring a rebirth of militarism a little closer. Thus, after Ebert had summoned troops to Berlin on December 24 for an unsuccessful attempt to clear the palace of the "people's sailors," the three Independents — on December 27 — announced their resignation from the Council of People's Representatives.

The Independents had already been forced to conclude that theirs was the weaker faction. The Congress of Workers' and Soldiers' Soviets, held at their behest in Berlin from December 16 to 19, was one great disillusionment for them. The elections to this congress had given the Majority Socialists an overwhelming majority. Liebknecht and Rosa Luxemburg had not even been able to win seats. Although the voters in these elections had been principally workers, they had shown very little sympathy for the methods and goals of the Russian Revolution. The debates of the congress were often confused and tumultuous; nevertheless it quickly became apparent that a great majority of the delegates wished to effect a return to ordered conditions in a democratic manner, that is, by means of a national assembly elected by the entire nation. On December 19 the motion of Cohen-Reuss, a rather conservative Socialist, that these elections be held on January 19, 1919, was accepted by a vote of four hundred to fifty. At this point the Independents withdrew, sulked petulantly, and refused to take any part in the selection of a Central Committee which was to serve as a sort of steering group for a new government. The committee was therefore made up exclusively of Majority Socialists. When, a week later, the Independents left the Council of People's Representatives as well, the Central Committee suddenly found that its only support lay in the streets.

The streets consequently became the battleground for the next struggle. In order to maintain its authority there, the government found itself obliged, for lack of any alternative, to depend upon remnants of the old army. One may well regret this decision — and the further history of the German Republic gives one every reason to regret it — but one cannot deny its sheer necessity. If the government had to reach agreements with its enemies on the Right, both present and potential, who was to blame for this but those on the

Left who gave it no peace? It is equally clear that at this juncture the generals, even though they had little use for the Social Democrats clustering around Noske and Scheidemann, came to realize that they would have to support these men in order to forestall utter anarchy. It was, as Friedrich Meinecke recounts,[3] General Gröner who convinced Hindenburg of this. As early as November 10 he sent "an oral message with Friedrich Naumann to Ebert, saying that the Supreme Military Command was ready to collaborate with him."

But six weeks later, when the situation in Berlin became unbearable and a resort to arms and bloodshed unavoidable, even the Supreme Command was unable to place an organized military force at the government's disposal. The honor of creating the necessary army belongs to Gustav Noske.[4] This former basket weaver, who had entered the Reichstag in 1905 after an austere life of trade union activities and newspaper editing, had accomplished as much in his role of imperial commissioner in Kiel at the time of the sailors' revolt as one could possibly have expected in the face of the extraordinarily difficult circumstances. He entered the Council of People's Representatives upon the resignation of the Independents. He now had the courage to accept appointment by Ebert as Supreme Commander and to undertake the mission of restoring peace to Berlin. He knew full well what lay before him. "Somebody has to be the bloodhound; I will not shirk the responsibility," he said when Ebert offered him the thankless task.[5] This was a deed for which he should never be forgotten, and it never will be forgotten by those who suffered through those awful weeks in Berlin. No less a man than Churchill honored him as "A son of the people, amid universal confusion acting without fear in a public cause." [6] Least grateful of all his judges were his party comrades, who attacked him in their press and at their meetings and who finally, when he was obliged to resign after the Kapp Putsch, dropped him from their parliamentary list as a "political liability."

Material for the new army was amply available. Thousands of young men who had served during the war were ready to offer their assistance until order could be restored and secured. But Noske had to turn to the career officers of the old army in order to find leaders for his volunteers. The troops themselves requested this move, for they credited only the professional officers with the experience necessary to assure success without unnecessary losses.[7] At the moment there was no political danger in this decision. Neither the diplomatic nor the domestic situation was such as to evoke general sympathy for a restoration of the monarchy. But success in quelling street disorders naturally enough brought renewed self-confidence to these officers, who were previously so depressed. And among the volunteers, most of whom came from middle class homes, there were many who saw in the street fights proof that neither a democratic society nor a republican form of government was suitable for Germany. And they came to regard each Social Democratic government as a curse. But the necessities of the immediate crisis forced them to suppress their antirepublican feeling for the moment and to fight in defense of democracy.

Noske's operation was quickly and completely successful. On January 19, the day of elections for the National Assembly, calm prevailed in Berlin and no one dared disturb the balloting. That this civil peace was not won without some excesses is regrettable, but hardly astonishing. The murders of Karl Liebknecht and Rosa Luxemburg on January 16 created great excitement, but news of the deaths was welcomed by the great majority of Berliners as relief from a great danger; few asked themselves if justice had been done. But the victims' friends cried loudly that the two had been murdered by reactionary freebooters. And today we can consider it established that at least Rosa Luxemburg was lynched by an excited mob.

One cannot excuse this murder by recalling the old saw that "those who live by the sword also die by it." And while it is true that we all have experienced too much violence at the hands of Liebknecht's and Luxemburg's friends to be able to feel a strong sense of revulsion at the manner of their death, nevertheless a curse clung to this wretched deed: by helping destroy distaste for violence and respect for human lives in Germany it helped teach the nation to accept brutal and bloody force as a legitimate tool of domestic politics.

In the course of these disturbed weeks, and even months, men were quietly working out the necessary preliminaries to the most important task the future National Assembly would face: the adoption of the Constitution of the German Republic. In November 1918, when the Council of People's Representatives was formed, the two groups of Social Democrats had decided that ultimate political authority should remain exclusively in their hands. But they quickly realized that they would have to look outside their parties for men to direct those offices which required professional competence. For the two Socialist parties simply did not contain sufficient numbers of such qualified men. They sought to solve this problem by excluding "bourgeois" ministers formally from the true cabinet, and making them instead responsible to the Council of People's Representatives.

Furthermore, these ministers were given Social Democratic under-secretaries or assistants. Thus, State Secretary Solf, who retained for a time the foreign ministry he had held under Prince Max, received Dr. David, a Social Democrat in the Reichstag, as his under-secretary and the Independent journalist Karl Kautsky as his assistant. Clumsy as this arrangement was, it at least expressed a certain understanding of the need for some form of continuity which might tie the new conditions to the past.

At the moment the most important question was that of naming a minister of the interior, for the task of drafting the new constitution was to be his; on November 15, the Council of People's Representatives appointed Dr. Preuss, the professor of constitutional law at the Commercial University of Berlin.[8]

Hugo Preuss, born in 1860, had joined the staff of the University of Berlin as a young man. But in spite of his success as a teacher and, both qualitatively and quantitatively, as a productive scholar, he had failed for a long time to win a professorial appointment, partly because he was Jewish and active politically on the extreme Left of the democratic liberals, and partly too because he did not always know how to keep under control his sarcasm and Berliner wit. It remained for the Commercial University, founded by leading Berlin merchants, to make him a professor just before the war. Intellectually a disciple of Otto Gierke, he gave the latter's theory of syndicalism a democratic twist that Gierke never sanctioned. In practical politics he remained close to his friend Theodor Barth, whose *Nation* he favored with many brilliant contributions. His hero in Germany history was Baron vom Stein; the captivating tale of vom Stein's reforms of the Prussian government after the defeat of Jena is the climax of Preuss's *Entwicklungsgeschichte der deutschen Städteverfassung* (History of the Development of German Municipal Law; 1906).

In the first year of the war Preuss published his basic political and historical conclusions under the title *Das deutsche Volk und die Politik* (The German Nation and Its Politics), which became famous through the antithesis presented in its text: "Democratic government versus authoritarian government." The treatise seeks to determine why Western Europeans find the German concept of the state so antipathetic; it finds the answer to the question in an analysis of modern German history, in the course of which the German nation was never able to select a political leader from its midst. Although in this book his conviction that the war would inevitably induce a change in this respect is implied rather than explicitly stated, Preuss became more and more convinced, as the war continued, that an immediate and fundamental change in the direction of democracy was essential if Germany were ever to regain contact with the rest of the world. The fruit of these thoughts was a memorandum composed in July 1917, while Bethmann was still in office. This document not only demonstrated the need for constitutional transformation with arguments no one can question today, but went on to describe in careful detail how reform could be accomplished within the framework of the German monarchy. The memorandum was never published, but those who had read it were convinced that Preuss was the one man able to deal with the constitutional task that lay ahead.

Preuss's fortunate combination of knowledge and courage was demonstrated in his article "Democratic Government or Distorted Authoritarianism?" in the *Berliner Tageblatt* of November 14, 1918, in which he warned Germany's new rulers against erecting, on the ruins of the Empire, an equally "authoritarian state, if upside down." He went on to tell his countrymen: "We have hope of escaping the dreadful shift from Red Terror to White only if a strong, energetic movement is formed within the German middle class, based candidly upon events that have occurred but not docile in the face of new authorities, and . . . only if these new authorities welcome the collaboration of this movement and tender it full equality of responsibility." Ebert understood this argument better than did the German bourgeoisie; for once their first fears passed, many middle class Germans bitterly reproached Preuss for precisely this sort of collaboration.

Every democratic constitution must solve the problem of arranging political forces in such a manner as to assure the eventual predominance of a sustained popular opinion, while at the same time protecting the ship of state from being rocked by every transitory fad and passion. But the German democratic constitution had to face still one further difficulty: that of balancing the powers of the central government with those of its constituent members. This was the persistent problem of German history. The generation of 1871 hoped that Bismarck had found a permanent solution, but this hope had collapsed with the monarchy. Bismarck had considered the German princes indispensable links between the German people and the German state. Now the princes had been swept away and a new type of political order had to be given to the people and to the state. Were the separate principalities, dynastic agglomerations for the most part, to remain untouched? Or had the time now come to grant more political power to the central government, to weaken the principalities correspondingly, and to revise their borders according to the demands of the present and the future instead of continuing to accept the legacy of the past? Preuss was outspoken in favor of a strong central government; he quoted vom Stein's words freely and emphatically: "I know only *one* fatherland, and that is Germany; therefore I can be devoted with all my soul only to all Germany, and not to just a part of it."

This was the tenor of the draft of the general part of the federal constitution which Preuss published on January 3, 1919, with a penetrating historical and juridical analysis appended. With candor and courage he stated that the new German state would have to be built deliberately upon a unitary base, the very base which Bismarck, in his work, had deliberately avoided. This was unwelcome news for those who, growing up in the Bismarck tradition, had come to identify their own good fortune with it. When Preuss now argued against "the continued existence of Prussia as a separate, centralized state within the future German Republic," he evoked particularly violent opposition. Preuss insisted that "the continual existence of a centralized republic of 40,000,000 people organizationally separated from a republic of 70,000,000" was simply "a juridical, political, and economic impossibility." His draft, therefore, would give the German people the right "to create new German states within the nation, without regard to the former boundaries of the principalities, but with appropriate attention to ethnic, economic, and historical association." The critics screamed that this would mean the dissolution of Prussia, the strongest unifying force in German history. The Rightists were not the only ones to express this concern; they were joined by many on the Left.

This criticism was strengthened by the concern evoked by separatist tendencies along the Rhine. In December active forces at work there set their goal as the establishment of "an independent Rhenish-Westphalian Republic." The orators of this movement had, it is true, always taken care to proclaim that this new republic was to remain *a part of Germany*. But at the same time they argued that they had to free themselves from Berlin's revolutionary confusion and decrees. The danger was clear that such a separate republic would sooner or later secede from the German union in order to win for its people, particularly at the peace negotiations, better living conditions. "The step from the Capitol of a separate German state to the Tarpeian Rock of secession from Germany" seemed "infinitesimal" to the *Kölnische Zeitung*; and the Social Democratic government of Prussia (Hirsch-Strobel-Braun) in a formal statement branded these tendencies as a public danger.[9]

But Prussia did not provide the only opposition to the pronounced tendencies of Preuss's draft to favor a unitary government. Many of the other individual states assumed a vigorous defense. True, their princes had been driven out and replaced by republican regimes under Social Democratic control. But these new regents guarded their "states' rights" with undiminished jealousy; indeed, in Bavaria a radical Socialist separatism took form which exceeded, by far, the blue-white * particularism of the Wittelsbachs.

This oldest German dynasty, the Wittelsbachs, had been the first to be swallowed by the revolutionary tide. The citizens of Munich, ordinarily the most stolid and phlegmatic townspeople of Germany, had hoisted the red flag even before the Berliners. It was, to be sure, not so much the old-time residents who raised the banner; it was rather the sensation-seeking bohemians of Schwabing, the "left bank" of Munich. Kurt Eisner, the former editor of *Vorwärts*, had pitched his tent among them after his comrades in Berlin had rather roughly turned him out. He was a brilliant journalist and an effective speaker, but without any practical experience; basically an idealist, he was deeply moved by the frightful war and felt himself called to make an end not only to the war, but also to those groups who, in his opinion, were responsible for it. The fact that this man — who had so little in common with the average man of Munich and who, as a Jew, was himself exposed to demagogic attacks — could unseat the Wittelsbachs shows how greatly the war had changed things in Bavaria. The nationalization of the agricultural market had aroused the farmers' wrath. And as the war grew ever longer and its outcome less auspicious, even those Bavarians who had nothing to do with agriculture considered themselves more and more the innocent victims of Prussian ambitions.[10] Their King Ludwig III was unpopular for several reasons; perhaps the most interesting of these was the blatant denial of the monarchical principle implicit in his not being content to be regent for the legitimate, mentally ill King Otto. By insisting on being crowned king in Otto's place, Ludwig sawed off the limb on which he sat. Not a hand was raised in his defense when Eisner proclaimed the Bavarian Republic at a mass meeting on the Teresienwiese on November 7, 1918.

The Independent Socialists — and Eisner, as a passionate opponent of the war, considered himself one — were too weak in Bavaria to let him form a government without the addition of Majority

*Blue and white are the traditional colors of Bavaria. During the postwar years the colors, particularly in conservative circles, evoked strong attachment for Bavaria's former rulers, the Wittelsbach dynasty. TRANSLATORS.

Socialists. So the leader of the Majority Socialists, Erhard Auer, became the minister of interior. But Eisner and his bohemian friends set the mood; and the mood was very anti-Prussian.

After the War of 1866, when Bismarck forced the South German principalities to enter into "treaties of mutual defense" with the North German Confederation, Dr. Jörg, the clerical leader of the "Bavarian Patriots," had damned the treaties as "the spring from whence the curse of militarism flooded the once so happy southern German lands." [11] This same feeling now seemed to motivate Eisner and the Independent Socialists — hence their cry *"Los von Berlin,"* the nest of the militarists and the home of the diplomats who had caused the war! For Eisner had convinced himself that the Emperor's diplomats had conjured up the war, and he reached greedily for every document in the files of the Bavarian Foreign Ministry that might help substantiate his conviction. On November 23, he even went so far as to publish from these files a report of July 1914 from the Bavarian chargé d'affaires which was supposed to prove his point. In doing this he so distorted the text as to shift at least the emphasis.[12] By omitting each of the author's references to the imperial government's hope of localizing the Austro-Serbian War, he created the impression that the government had marched to war with a grim, conscious determination which in fact it had completely lacked. He defended this exposé by explaining that "only through complete candor can that confidence among nations be established which is necessary for a peace of reconciliation." But he had violated his own integrity in publishing an incomplete copy of the report. Moreover, it was a typically amateurish illusion to think that one could come closer to this important goal by printing such a piece, and it was a monstrous example of overestimation to think that the victorious Allies would regard him as the representative of a new spirit in Germany. He never seemed to realize how welcome his indiscretion would be to the most violently anti-German members of the Allied camp. When the Foreign Office in Berlin protested against Eisner's playing with fire in this naïve way, Eisner, in a telegram of November 28, went so far as to break off further communication with the Foreign Office. But even earlier, at a conference of the separate states' regimes in Berlin, he had tried to unseat Secretaries Solf and Erzberger as "exposed, from now on useless" men.

To be sure, the newly founded "Bavarian People's Party," the continuation of the earlier dominant Centrists, did not join Eisner in all these adventures; but in its program of November 12, 1918, the party did announce: "Bavaria for the Bavarians! The present extreme economic and fiscal dependence of Bavaria upon the dominating North must be stopped at all costs. In all these areas we oppose unilateral, ruthless, Prussian rule because this led us to ruin in the past."

But now everything depended on the delegates whom the German voters would send to their National Constituent Assembly. No one was even certain that the majority would accept the idea of a republic. Here the attitude of the German middle class was obviously of paramount importance. One could easily assume that the workers would vote for the republic at least as strongly as they had voted for Social Democrats in the past. For by their Social Democratic vote they had advocated a republican form of government at a time when no one dreamed of its realization in Germany. But every reasonable Socialist knew that the German Republic could not be erected on so narrow a base. Among the moderate parties, the Centrists seemed most promising. Clericalism is not necessarily committed to any one form of government and can find a *modus vivendi* with each. In delivering the Centrists' statement at the National Assembly (February 13, 1919), Gröber declared: "In our opinion every government enjoys God's blessing, whether it be monarchic or republican." Furthermore, the great majority of German Catholics tended to identify themselves less with the Hohenzollern Empire than did their Protestant counterparts. On the other hand one could predict that the former Conservatives would remain loyal to the monarchy. Some of them realized that their time had passed, and retired, together with their former leader von Heydebrand, to private life. The conservative "old guard" formed the German National People's Party. That these conservatives had changed their attitude to parliamentary government, so recently anathema to them, is shown clearly in the new party's statement that parliamentary government was now "after recent events . . . the only possible" government for Germany. This party also attracted many former liberals who, in the course of the war, had cultivated too great an intimacy with the annexationists and the Patriots' Party to return to liberalism now. Dr. Traub, formerly a pastor and a Progressive in the Reichstag, was one of these. But the question remained whether, aside from such exceptions, the previously liberal middle class would accept and support the Republic.

This question received its most decisive assent from a group of men and women who published, on November 16, an open invitation to help found a Democratic Party.[13] The idea had originated among a small circle of intellectuals who, during the war, had reached the common conclusion that the traditional German political parties had become obsolete and ought to be replaced by parties more appropriate to the times. Members of this circle included, among others, Dr. Hjalmar Schacht, then director of a major Berlin bank; Professor Alfred Weber, in Heidelberg, Max Weber's brother; and Theodor Wolff, editor-in-chief of the *Berliner Tageblatt*, who had maintained the liberal, democratic position of his newspaper even in the most trying periods of the war. Although many of these men would have preferred a completely new party, devoid of all links with the past, their hopes yielded to the demands of practical politics. For they could help stem the proliferation of parties — which had been so harmful in the past and which was, in the final analysis, incompatible with a healthy parliamentary system — not by establishing new parties in competition with the old but by combining new ideas with old forms. Consequently the invitation was signed by many members of the Reichstag who had formerly belonged to the National Liberals or Progressive People's Party.

At first it seemed that they would be successful in merging the two former groups into the new Democratic Party. But Dr. Stresemann decided otherwise. He had originally been willing to go along, but he kept finding opposition to his views, particularly among the founders of the new party. One can hardly deny that his behavior during the war had done much to alienate these men. He had been among the loudest supporters of the fateful decisions in foreign policy and of the unrestricted submarine campaign. He had supported Ludendorff in his political ventures, and the latter's reputation was now at its nadir. One can therefore well understand that Schacht and Alfred Weber turned their backs on him now, and that even his former party colleagues who had become members of the Democratic Party begged him to remain quiet for a time. Yet this was a grave political mistake on their part. For whoever knew Stresemann must have realized that he was too active and self-confident a man to tolerate even a short exile in the wings and also that he was the only man with enough energy, intelligence, and powers of persuasion to enable the National Liberals to maintain a separate political existence. Indeed, on December 15, he succeeded in winning from a majority of the National Liberals' Central Committee a resolution to continue the party under the new name of German People's Party (*Deutsche Volkspartei*).

With this move, the hope of a single, unified Democratic Party, in which, regardless of shades of opinion, all liberals might have combined, was shattered forever. This was a misfortune for Stresemann too. For the remainder of the party which he now led was composed principally of men with Rightist tendencies, men with whom he had much less in common, with respect to the decisive questions which lay ahead, than with those who had joined the new Democrats. Later, when he became responsible for Germany's foreign policy, he repeatedly faced strong opposition within his own party and had to seek support from the Left.

The elections for the National Assembly took place on January 19, 1919, according to a decree of November 30, 1918, which the People's Representatives had issued over Secretary Preuss's signature. Political circumstances required the franchise to correspond to the Erfurt Declaration of the Social Democrats: no distinction was made between men and women, and the voting age was set at twenty, below the age of legal majority (a fact which had escaped the authors of the Erfurt Declaration). The moderate parties could only be thankful at this moment that the Social Democrats still adhered to their old demand for proportional representation; for this device increased the chances of survival for each of the newly formed parties and thus encouraged a sharp definition of their separate programs.

The major question whether the several Socialist parties would, together, comprise a majority at the National Assembly was answered with a negative. Of the 421 seats, the Socialists won only 185, and within this total the Independents with 22 found themselves far behind the Majority Socialists' 163. Only a diminishing fraction of the German people had accepted the concept of a Dictatorship of the Proletariat and a system of soviets. With just as clear a voice the nation had declined a return to monarchy. The German Nationalists, the only party to back the monarchy in unambiguous terms, won 42 seats, while the German People's Party, who were at least prepared to leave the question open, won only 21. The Center Party, successfully weathering this storm as it had so many others, received 88 seats. But this number included the Bavarians who were soon to leave and form the Bavarian People's Party (*Bayrische Volkspartei*). The fact that the German Democratic Party, with 75 seats, finished a close third to the Centrists represented a real victory on their part. But it would be wrong to assume that the 5,600,-000 people who had voted for them were all dedicated Democrats. A large number had voted Democratic for the simple reason that this party had seemed their last defense against the Socialist threat, and they turned to other idols as soon as they discovered that the danger was not as great as they had feared.

The Democratic delegation included many Progressives and National Liberals from the old Reichstag along with new men and women. But Max Weber was missing. He had sought to be included on the party's ticket in the Frankfurt Hesse-Nassau district. However, the party leaders had given preference to other men, with whom they were better acquainted after years of political collaboration. The withdrawal of this eminent mind from politics at this juncture was without doubt a severe loss to the political and parliamentary life of Germany. Less certain is an estimate of his ability, had he been elected, to accommodate himself fruitfully to parliamentary practice. Such a unique, forceful, and crisp personality would certainly have found it hard in party caucus to accept as binding a majority decision to which he was opposed; and he was already too old to learn this art. Unfortunately he had little time to live. In Munich, where he had succeeded Professor Lujo Brentano, he became ill and died suddenly in June 1920 at only 56 years of age.

Even Hugo Preuss had been unable to win himself a place in the National Assembly; he had to be content with a seat in the Prussian Landtag. The Berlin Democrats were, as Prussians, too loyal to risk sending a man to the Reichstag who was suspected of wanting to destroy Prussia.

On January 26, one week after the elections to the National Assembly, the balloting for the Prussian Assembly took place, and with similar results. The Bavarian elections had been held earlier, on January 12, and had shown that Eisner's supporters amounted only to a small fraction of the electorate. Less than 80,000 ballots had been cast in favor of the Independent Socialists, who therefore had to content themselves with three seats. On the other hand, the Centrists, now called the Bavarian People's Party, lost their former domination of Bavaria, although they did remain the strongest party in the state. At any rate it was evident that Eisner's regime would fall at the first meeting of the Bavarian Landtag.

Yet as late as January 25, Eisner was able to represent Bavaria at a conference of all the German governments, called at Berlin to discuss proposals for the future constitution. Eisner tried to persuade the conference to accept an emergency measure of his invention which would have strengthened the positions of the several states, giving them a decisive role in the legislative process of the central government. Although this move was voted down, Preuss was obliged to realize that his centralizing desires had struck immovable obstructions. The final result of the discussion was the draft, for the National Assembly's consideration, of a law concerning "temporary sovereignty." This draft readily accepted the exclusive jurisdiction of the National Assembly in drawing up the new constitution, but required any other legislative acts of the Assembly to be approved by a "States' Committee." The proposal also established, as constituent elements of the interim national government, a national cabinet and a national president, the latter to be chosen by the Assembly. Preuss, as representative of the national government, discussed the first public draft of the constitution with the States' Committee in rather exhaustive meetings which led to compromise on most points.

III

THE WEIMAR CONSTITUTION

THE National Assembly finally met. The central government had set February 6 for its meeting, which was to be held in Weimar rather than Berlin. Conditions in the capital were still too unpredictable to permit this type of meeting; there would have been constant danger of attempts to influence, if not to intimidate, the Assembly through putsches and demonstrations. Weimar was also chosen because of its great symbolic significance: the reconstruction of Germany was to be blessed by the spirit which, emanating from this small town, had once enlightened and inspired the world: the spirit of man's nobility, of his ethical freedom, and of a fruitful rivalry among the nations.

The Assembly immediately went to work with great energy. The emergency was so immediate and apparent that no one could ignore the necessity of establishing a provisional regime as quickly as possible to rule the nation until the adoption of the new constitution and also to enable Germany to take part in the critical negotiations with her former foes. Within the first few days the Assembly had organized itself and ratified the law establishing the provisional government. Then its members turned to the election of a provisional president; on February 11, they gave the former people's representative Friedrich Ebert 277 of 379 votes cast. This choice not only corresponded to the balance of political forces, it also expressed the personal confidence which Ebert had won for himself during years of war and days of revolution. Even his political opponents recognized that Ebert was a Social Democrat who considered not just his worker constituents, but rather the whole of the nation; that he was a patriot not of loud words but of sound deeds. Whoever had dealt with him praised him as a man whose word could be trusted. Even so conservative a journal as the *Kölnische Zeitung* recognized his decency and innate honor. Though the snobs affected distress at the sight of a former harness maker at the head of the Reich, less prejudiced minds were pleased to see that German trade unionism and politics had opened a path for the valuable talents of the German working class, a path up which a doughty and steadfast son of the people had been able to climb. On the day following his election, the *Berliner Tageblatt* wrote that "although German trade unionism has produced no stunning personalities, it has produced a sturdy, clear, and critical mind."

According to the law establishing the provisional government, the president's first duty was to create a cabinet. There were two ways to form a majority of the Assembly: either create a union of all the non-Socialist parties (the former bourgeois factions) from the Democrats all the way to the German Nationalists, or form a coalition of the Social Democrats with the Centrists and Democrats. Only the latter alternative was politically possible. The establishment of a regime with no Social Democrats would have involved dangers which no German government could meet. To include in the provisional cabinet German Nationalists, heirs of the old discredited regime, would have constituted a frivolous challenge to the Entente, and to Wilson in particular. Such a move would also have contradicted the popular will as reflected in the recent elections. One can therefore safely say that the German nation, even on the Right, was content to see its first constitutional cabinet made up of Social Democrats, Democrats, and Centrists. The Rightists in particular enjoyed the great — and, given the situation, unavoidable — political advantage of escaping the formal responsibility for the painful and stringent peace that was bound to come.

President Ebert selected his former colleague Philipp Scheidemann as Chancellor. From among the other former people's representatives, Noske assumed the leadership of the Reichswehr (as the army was now called) and Landsberg the Ministry of Justice. The Centrists were represented by Erzberger, Dr. Bell, and the trade-union leader Giesberts. Of the Democrats, Preuss received the Ministry of Interior, while Eugen Schiffer, formerly a National Liberal, accepted the thorny position of treasurer and Gothein the roving commission of minister without portfolio. Thus the Republic's first parliamentary cabinet was a coalition, as were all its successors. This first alliance of factions was known as the "Weimar Coalition" and represented three fourths of the Assembly.

In an introductory and explanatory address of February 24,

Preuss directed the National Assembly to commence its major task: the preparation of the constitution. It required three days' debate for all the parties to state their views on the issues of a centralized or federal, a republican or monarchic state. Then Preuss's draft was referred to a Constitutional Committee where, from March to July, every clause was considered twice.[1] Despite the sharpness of party differences, these meetings were carried out in a calm, businesslike manner. Particularly outstanding in this disciplined debate were such men as the Democrat Erich Koch, mayor of Kassel, and, on the Right, Professor Kahl of the People's Party and the German Nationalist Clemens Delbrück, formerly a state secretary.

Preuss, however, retained intellectual mastery of the Assembly. He not only controlled the discussion of specific points questioned by various party orators; he had also thought through broad questions involving the entire parliamentary system which the constitution would create. He was thus completely aware of the difficulties his colleagues would experience in freeing themselves from political conceptions that had become ingrained under a vastly different political system. It sounded like a cry of desperation and, at the same time, like a fateful prophecy when he complained, on April 8,[2] that in the course of the carping debates he had been forced to observe

how foreign a parliamentary system seems to even the most enlightened Germans. I have often listened to debates with real concern, glancing often rather timidly to the gentleman of the Right, fearful lest they say to me: "Do you hope to give a parliamentary system to a nation like this, one that resists it with every sinew of its body? Our people do not comprehend at all what such a system implies." One finds suspicion everywhere; Germans cannot shake off their old political timidity and their deference to the authoritarian state. They do not understand that the new government must be blood of their blood, flesh of their flesh, that their trusted representatives will have to be an integral part of it. Their constant worry is only: how can we best keep our constituted representatives so shackled that they will be unable to do anything?

Preuss's warning was all too well justified. The prohibition of formal orders and honors, adopted by the Constitutional Committee upon proposal by the Social Democrats, was a minor but significant example of the Germans' inability, mentioned by Preuss, to make the shift from an authoritarian state to popular sovereignty. It was certainly quite natural that, in the monarchic, authoritarian state, the Social Democrats, who were not only the constant opposition but also social untouchables, should regard with scorn and wrath the gentle rain of decorations which the German princes, both petty and great, let fall upon the heads of "loyal men." Many a man who was in no way a revolutionary harbored a deep distaste for this Vanity Fair. But was this really the right time to indulge in such aesthetic and ethical puritanism — now, when the former opposition was in power and depended upon the loyal cooperation of a civil service, only part of which had accepted the new regime, and then none too deeply?

In order to carry on the basic functions of government, it was obvious that the new republic required the support of professional civil servants who had grown to maturity in the service of the Crown. Since catastrophic economic conditions precluded high salaries and the political situation prevented any possibility of a restoration of the monarchy, there remained only one possible way of cultivating that support: the petty but time-honored means by which rulers had long assured themselves of loyal bureaucrats — the bestowing of titles. If the French Republic did not hesitate to continue the Legion of Honor, founded by an emperor, certainly the German Republic need not have feared granting republican honors to those who, as civil servants or otherwise, served the new republic well. But the Social Democratic proposal would also have done away with all honorific titles. When this suggestion was greeted with vehement protest by the experts, the proposal was considerably softened. In its final form it amounted to an abolition of the title of "Geheimrat." Certainly a great deal could be said in favor of this move. Nevertheless, the enemies of the former authoritarian state should have stopped to realize how greatly that state had profited from the fact that its officials expected, after years of careful duty, to acquire this title, which was so rich in social prestige and which more than made up for lack of wealth. And, perhaps even more important, a maiden who gave her hand to a civil servant of the monarchy could hope to die a "Frau Geheimrat." But such considerations seemed frivolous and petty to men who had just carried out a revolution.

On the whole, one must regard as remarkable the ability of the Constitutional Committee to complete its inspection of the 181 articles of the constitution in some forty sessions without making any sacrifice of quality to haste. Much of the credit was due to the wise and, when necessary, energetic direction of the chairman, the Democrat Conrad Haussmann, who, after thirty years of parliamentary service, had now his first opportunity to show his powers as a leader.[3] It was a real shortcoming of the former system that it had failed to make use of such resources precisely because they were in the parliament, and it was a misfortune for the new Republic that with every passing year this reserve of parliamentary political experience dwindled away further, with no prospect, in those inauspicious times, of new powers being developed to replace them.

The draft of the constitution, as reported back to the Assembly by the committee, was given second and third readings throughout July. It was then accepted by the 262 votes of the coalition parties: Majority Socialists, Centrists, and Democrats. Only 75 votes were cast by the opposition, in which the German Nationalists and the German People's Party joined the Independent Socialists. Whoever pondered these figures had every reason to believe that the work of Weimar rested on a sound foundation. The President accepted the Assembly's constitution on August 11, a day which was designated "Constitution Day" and proclaimed as an annual national holiday.

Naturally enough Preuss's draft had suffered many changes in the course of the committee's review. But his basic aim, the creation of a parliamentary, liberal-democratic government of law, remained untouched. The execution of this plan has, as we all know, occasioned a good deal of criticism from the very start; and today, when the entire structure lies in ruins, the critics are understandably all the more numerous and assertive.

The political situation, as well as Germany's historical development, made it obvious that the basis of the German Republic had to be democratic. Universal, equal vote for Reichstag delegates had existed, after all, for half a century, ever since Bismarck had played it as his trump against Austria in 1866. Although Bismarck himself had little cause to be content with the permanent results of his maneuver, the imperial franchise had nevertheless taken such firm root in the political consciousness of the German nation that not even the most dedicated die-hard could think seriously of abolishing it. But the times demanded, and not in Germany alone, more than Bismarck's franchise. A feminist movement, perhaps more apparent than real, insisted on the political rights of German womanhood, and the recent military service of the younger men seemed to argue for a lowering of the voting age from the former twenty-five years.

Both these demands, supported as they were by the platform of the Social Democrats, were satisfied by the coalition parties as far as seemed possible. Whoever was twenty-one years old could vote, whether man or woman. War is a powerful leveler, and with memories still warm of the four frightfully trying years of war, which had exacted equal suffering from all, no one dared raise his voice to ask whether political knowledge and interest among the Germans was in fact so widely spread and so mature as to make such a radical expansion of the franchise appropriate and, indeed, safe. Even Preuss had warned against putting the voting age into the constitution, arguing that it should be defined by law, which could more easily be altered in the light of experience. To the arguments of an Independent Socialist who had pressed for a constitutional voting age Preuss replied: "Dr. Cohn has employed the practical proverb, that one should strike while the iron is hot. But perhaps with time it will get hotter or perhaps it will cool off, one can never know." [4]

Indeed, it was not long until at least the wiser and more responsible Social Democrats realized that they had allowed themselves to be swept along too far by their theories. Toward the end of 1932 Wolfgang Heine was to write to Carl Severing, with respect to the Republic's early days: "We were not able to create a truly viable democracy, by which term I understand a society in which the nation feels itself a whole united by a tradition of spiritual and economic collaboration, feels itself a state. I know that the destruction by the old regime of all the necessary conditions for such a society had made this task particularly difficult. But I also believe that the proletariat was not yet ready for this democratic responsibility, and certainly we went about our business with the constitution in an all too *theoretical* and *lifeless way*." Severing not only agreed with this proposition, but also added: "The extension of the franchise to younger people and to women would, in a well-established democracy, mean the further enrichment of the democratic concept of the state. But in 1919 these changes wrought *confusion* rather than *education*." [5] The German women, at any rate, did not demonstrate that they considered their new political rights a valuable acquisition, one worth sturdy cultivation and defense. Nor did they repay this gift with support for the Republic. They went on to vote by enthusiastic millions for Hitler, who planned to shut them out of politics again.

And now the constitution saddled this inflated electorate with the task of voting not *persons* but rather *parties* into power. For this is the end result of the proportional ballot, particularly in the crass form of the "ticket vote" defined by the Franchise Law of April 27, 1920. The motivating factor here was the idea of justice: every vote was to have the same weight, no matter where it was cast and for whom. Such equivalence had become rarer as the Empire matured, for the voting districts of 1869 and 1871 had remained unaltered in spite of the massive population shifts since that time, and in spite of promises made by the Franchise Law of 1869. One can easily understand that the liberal political leaders, who had constantly observed and opposed this injustice, sought to preclude its return. And no system could better assuage their fears than one based upon the principle of one representative for every 60,000 votes. Working in this same direction was a partisan concern, namely the fear of the smaller parties lest they be smothered by the great blocs. The framers of the law were particularly conscious of the danger that all the metropolitan districts would inevitably be won by either the Social Democrats or the Centrists.

But none of these considerations could answer the cogent criticism directed at Preuss himself by Friedrich Naumann in the course of the committee's deliberations.[6] "A parliamentary system and proportional representation are mutually exclusive . . . Proportional representation is poorly suited to the determination of political leadership on any large scale." He foresaw all too well the spawning of splinter groups to which the proportional ballot would logically have to lead, and to which in Germany it actually did lead. He realized with equal clarity that in a parliamentary system the formation of governments requires large parties which can succeed each other in office. To be sure, the English and American two-party system is impossible in Germany for historical and confessional reasons. But precisely these reasons might have encouraged the development of a few great parties if only, under the pressure of experience, men had come to the realization that a political party does not imply or create unanimity among its members on all political, economic, cultural, and social issues; the party must rather serve as the means of constant compromise among those who are in basic agreement on the major issues of their time. Or, as Meinecke put it, the political party is "the first collecting and filtering basin of the confused national desires; the first synthesis of conflicting interests. It is formed on the basis of common political ideals."[7]

A second effect of the proportional ballot was just as harmful to the new parliamentary system: the disruption of the bond between the representative and his district. All Germany was divided into 35 districts. Any one district was, of course, far too large to allow any group feeling among the voters or between them and their representative. Indeed, fortunate was that voter who knew the face of the leader of the ticket to which he gave his vote. Of the other parties' representatives from his district he had, as a rule, not the slightest notion. He voted for a list of names. He had no voice in the composition of the list; that was the business of a small number of men who were dedicated to the party. And whoever excited the suspicions of these men had no prospect of election, no matter how popular he might be among the voters; he was simply deleted from the party ticket. Noske was enthusiastically applauded at gigantic Social Democratic rallies, but the party regulars denied him a place on their list because of reports of Noske's tendencies toward independence. Here Friedrich von Wieser's Law of Small Numbers begins to take effect.

All this could only lessen critically the voter's sense of sharing in the *responsibility* for his district's representation. And yet this sense of responsibility is the indispensable corollary of the right to vote, particularly when the right is as broadly enjoyed as under the new constitution. Moreover, the magnitude of the electoral districts increased the advantages of wealth. An election campaign required such financial reserves that ordinarily only those could afford to run who enjoyed the monetary support of an interest group, be it of workers or employers. An independent representative could never come to the Reichstag under this system, nor could a young, ambitious politician make his mark by wresting a district from his opponent's grip.

Parliamentary government would have experienced difficulty in taking root in Germany under any circumstances; and the unfavorable political and economic situation, both foreign and domestic, made any impressive successes almost impossible from the start. But the growth of German self-government was burdened still more severely by this voting system, a system which led necessarily to a continual change of governments, which did not lessen — but rather widened — the separation of the parliament from its constituents, and which seemed intentionally fashioned to favor the parties made up of those who can think only in unison.

The constitution went on to entrust to this broad mass of over-organized and underrepresented voters the election of a *Reichspräsident*. It had correctly accepted the necessity of having a national president who might represent Germany in foreign affairs, appoint the chancellor as head of the national government, and be commander-in-chief of the armed forces. The constitution also gave him the power of dissolving the Reichstag (and thus the means of appealing over its head to the national electorate) and the broad dictatorial powers of Article 48 for emergencies. The framers thought that they had satisfactorily grafted this sort of president onto a parliamentary system by requiring that all his emergency decrees must be countersigned either by the chancellor or by the appropriate minister.

The framers of the constitution saw two possibilities for the method of presidential election: parliamentary, as in France (by vote of the combined Senate and Chamber of Deputies), or popular, as in the United States. There was a strong movement against parliamentary election, led by no less a democrat than Max Weber.[8] He had argued to this effect even in the first review of Preuss's original draft. Members of this school were convinced that the Reichstag required an independent counterweight, lest parliamentary absolutism develop. The president could not be such a force if he were elected by the Reichstag; such a situation would, rather, lead to an "impure form of parliamentary government," as Redslob, a teacher of constitutional law, had recently written in an analysis of the French system. Redslob's chief argument was the fact that no French president since MacMahon had dared to employ his constitutional right of dissolving parliament. "Let us give the president a popular election, and thus his own two feet to stand on," argued Weber, who went on to call the right to participate directly in the election of one's leader "the Magna Carta of democracy."

This criticism of the French system was by no means completely unfounded. Whenever the parliament set about the task of electing a president, the prospects of its choosing a strong, distinguished leader were rather slight. The French parliament preferred, as a rule, men of average ability. Yet, even such mediocrities, who could at least claim some political and parliamentary experience, are less cause for concern than men who are utterly devoid of such experience and who have been able to attract the attention of the populace in some other way. The French had such an example before them constantly: the election of Louis Napoleon as president in December 1848. This was only the first "of those surprising results of universal suffrage, to which we have since become somewhat accustomed, but which still continue to remind us of the dark, irrational impulses of the so-called national soul. Such impulses tend to be dismissed as unseemly by those politicians who simply assume that voters are rational." Ludwig Bamberger, who had witnessed this election, was to write these words fifty years later.[9] But the Founding Fathers of 1919 were without the benefit of this experience. Instead, with few exceptions, they kept their eyes on the American example. In doing so, however, they failed to consider how much the American experience depended upon the existence of two mighty, national parties which, in one form or another, were as old as the American constitution itself.

Having misread the American example, they introduced something of the plebiscite idea at a critically important place in the German constitution. Nor were the democrats content with that. In accordance with the Social Democratic platform, they added the referendum, both of initiative and of decision, a device unknown to the constitutions of all other major nations. This plethora of popular power could only hinder the peaceful naturalization of parliamentary democracy in Germany.

Let us turn now to the basic German problem of the Reich and its constituent elements. The Republic was to be a federal state, as the Empire had been; but the centripetal forces were to be strengthened, even though these forces were not to be as strong as Preuss had hoped. The very fact that the members of the new government were no longer called "states" but had to be content with the colorless title "lands" is important, even if a majority of German jurists continued to pretend they still were states. The national government received in principle the power that Preuss had insisted on giving it to alter the boundaries of the lands (Article 18); but this power was so circumscribed by clauses and conditions that it cannot be said to have existed. As a matter of fact, apart from the merging of the petty Thuringian princedoms into a single Thuringia, things remained essentially as they had been. Most important, the land of Prussia retained the full extent, save for subsequent losses at Versailles, of the former Kingdom of Prussia. As a consequence the problem of Germany and Prussia stood untouched in all its massive complexity after the one moment when it might have been solved had passed.[10]

The national government was strengthened considerably in its legislative and executive powers. Perhaps the new financial relationship between the federal government and the lands had the most important consequences of all. The new arrangement was defined by the constitution, by the Federal Fiscal Law of September 1918, and by the Federal Tax Code of the following December. The axiom, so warmly defended by Bismarck, that the national government should be content with indirect taxes, leaving direct taxation to the states alone, had begun to yield to necessity in the last years of the Empire. Given the unfortunate outcome of the war, no one could deny the Republic's need of *all* kinds of taxes from which it might hope to derive sizable funds. Thus the transfer to the federal government of the most important direct taxes, in particular, the income tax, was in response not so much to platforms as to facts.

The fiscal legislation took another, more important, step in the direction of centralization by transferring the collection of these taxes from the lands to the national government. Consequently a small army of experienced bureaucrats moved into the federal civil service, strengthening the central power. In the same way the new definition of authority in questions of transportation involved further progress toward centralization. Necessity also forced upon the Germans the national railroad system for which Bismarck had pressed in vain. And, just as in Bismarck's time all the lesser states had fought to keep their railroads, now Bavaria assumed a vigorous defensive even in the Assembly's Constitutional Committee. But the conviction that the reconstruction of the devastated German economy would prove impossible without a centrally ruled and operated railroad system was so strong in the Reichstag that it outweighed the Bavarian opposition. The political importance of this step was implied in the observation made by the Prussian Minister Oeser during its consideration in committee that "this army of civil servants, clerks, and workmen," which was about to be transferred to federal employment, exceeded a total of one million and was in a state of political and economic unrest.[11]

The victory of centralization was not so complete in the realm of military affairs. To be sure, the constitution declared national defense to be a federal concern (Article 29) and gave the federal government exclusive jurisdiction over the organization of the armed forces (Article 6, Section 4). But when the Defense Law of March 23, 1921, was drafted the regimes of the smaller lands succeeded in establishing *Landeskommandanten* who were to "maintain, with their commands, a regard for the interests of their lands and, in particular, the special characteristics of their territorial units" (Paragraph 12). This directive, although harmless in itself, assumed a real political significance through the further provision that these *Landeskommandanten* were not to be appointed solely at the discretion of the *Reichspräsident*; the president simply approved the nominations made by the government of each land. Further political consequences of particular importance were apparent in the special concession made to Bavaria that the Bavarian *Landeskommandant* was also to be commander of the Bavarian Union. Thus the federal principle was retained in the German Army, and it was to make itself disturbingly evident.

The principal powers reserved to the lands included the administration of the courts, maintenance of law and order, direction of education, concern for religious affairs, and supervision of local government. These are all administrative tasks which in themselves presume little or no political, policy-making direction. Yet the political character of the land governments was not only foreordained by historical tradition, but it was also explicitly required by the new constitution in a way that exceeded by good measure any real need. For Article 17 stated not only that every land was to have a republican form of government, but also that the popular representatives in the lower chambers, as well as those of communities in the upper chambers, were to be selected in a fashion completely consonant with the election of the Reichstag. Thus the proportional ballot was prescribed, even though it was utterly unsuited to the smaller lands. Only with respect to the minimal voting age were the lands given freedom of decision. The national constitution's requirement that the land governments enjoy their lower chambers' confidence made sense only for those larger lands whose size could foster, and tolerate, meaningful political activity. In the smaller lands, which were better fitted to be administrative units, this pious provision could only lead to a most unhealthy situation; for it gave the local governments a political, indeed a partisan, flavor which contradicted their true mission.[12]

In a federal government the constituent elements have to participate, in some way, in making national policy. Preuss had wished to attain this end through a Committee of States whose members were to be elected by the parliaments of the several lands, a committee which was to have the character of an upper chamber, rather like the American Senate. The governments of the separate lands opposed this proposition with vigor and success. They wanted to participate directly in the national government, as they had previously done in the imperial Bundesrat. The National Assembly recognized this opposition and helped fashion a Reichsrat, in which the lands were to be represented by members of their governments (Articles 60 and 63).

But how were the seats in this new chamber to be divided among the lands? Again the Prussian problem raised its head. If representation of the lands were to be made directly proportional to their populations, then Prussia would rule both houses and the Reichsrat would be simply a rubber stamp. The constitution sought to deal with the problem in two ways: no land was to possess more than two-fifths of the Reichsrat's seats, and the Prussian seats were to be divided into two halves, one to be filled by members of the Prussian government and the other by delegates from the several Prussian provincial administrations. In this manner the danger of Prussian domination was, to be sure, avoided. But the political scales had perhaps been weighted too heavily against the upper house. The powers of the Reichsrat remained far less than those of the customary upper chamber. The most important power was that of vetoing the lower chamber's acts; but the veto could be overridden by a two-thirds vote of the Reichstag (Article 74).

So much, then, for the organizational aspects of the new constitution which are involved in any comprehension of the Republic's history. The second part of the document announced and defined the Fundamental Rights and Duties of a German. This part is largely the product of the Constitutional Committee, which here added freely to the draft with which it went to work. Preuss had been content with just a few articles which did little more than repeat the liberal axioms of the nineteenth century; after the bitter experiences of 1848 he was afraid that an expanded and detailed consideration of the axioms would only delay the pressing work at hand. Naumann, on the other hand, insisted with vigorous determination that the German nation had to make clear in its constitution its fundamental political assumptions, in order that they might guide its leaders in the future. A repetition of the time-honored liberal demands did not satisfy him at all; he conceived rather of a "sort of compromise peace between capitalism and socialism." His attempts to express these concepts with forceful informality could never win the committee's approval if only because, in eschewing juridical pedantry, he resorted to obscure and lapidary commonplaces which were almost impossible to debate.

The committee, on the other hand, went too far in the opposite direction. Every influential party and pressure group sought to have its particular point of view memorialized among basic German rights. These many cooks brought forth a broth which was neither consistent nor clear. In the course of the committee's deliberations Delegate Koch had said: "One never knows with fundamental rights whether they are positive law, or directions for future policy, or simply the precipitation of political and social opinions." [13] The final constitution contained examples of all three kinds. Then the German constitutional lawyers went to work and "positivized" (*positivierten*) these rights; that is, they tried to deduce from them positive rules of law and subjective rights which the future legislation of the Reich and of the lands was required to respect. Thus they erected, "out of these guarantees to private interests, a legalistic wall which hindered legislative freedom," often without paying sufficient attention to the state of emergency which the nation faced. [14]

These basic rights also led to a kind of economic parliament, the National Economic Council (Article 165, Paragraphs 3 and 4). It is an oddity in German constitutional history that here were joined old thoughts of Bismarck's and new Communist doctrines. Article 165 can well be considered a politically denatured version of the concept of soviets translated into democratic German. One of the practical consequences of this article was the creation of the National Economic Council, in which "all important trade and professional groups were to be represented according to their social and economic importance" (Article 3). Its duties were to consist in reviewing governmental drafts of social and economic legislation, as well as initiating such proposals. Only the reviewing power became real when, on May 4, 1920, a Temporary National Economic Council was called into being. The council went on to exercise this power to good effect. But the broader hopes with which various interests had regarded the birth of the council remained unfulfilled. It developed neither into a competing, economic parliament, nor into the center of a soviet system, nor even into a means of bridging the gaps between social classes.

One decision, the political consequences of which far exceeded its immediate importance, remains to be considered: the determination of the national flag and colors. The proposal that the old black, white, and red of the Empire be replaced by the black, red, and gold of 1848 came from many sources. Some wished to symbolize in this way the birth of a new Germany, one that no longer stood under black and white Prussian hegemony. Others regarded black, red, and gold as the colors of Greater Germany, colors under which Austria could join the Republic. Others saw in these colors merely the best means of avoiding the red flag demanded by the far Left. The opposition labeled the attempt to change the flag as sacrilege and ingratitude toward the colors under which imperial unity had been won and under which the German armies had fought in the recent war.[15]

This split ran through most parties. In the Democratic caucus the black, red, and gold won only by 23 against 19 votes. In the full meeting of the Reichstag the proposal of the Right that the black, white, and red be retained was defeated 190 to 110. By way of compromise these colors were reserved to the merchant marine, though with the proviso that the new national colors, black, red, and gold, be displayed in the upper inner corner. It was a compromise solution that contained seeds of further difficulties and that did not have the usual effect of compromise: the opposing parties were in no sense satisfied. On the contrary, the battle of the colors was carried on with ever growing bitterness. The opponents of the Republic were presented with an arena where they found it easy to arouse passions against the new state through oratory and agitation. They made ruthless and reckless use of their opportunity.

These aspects of the Weimar constitution need be mentioned here in order to make clear the role of the constitution in the history of the Republic. In evaluating the constitution one dare not forget that its consideration and adoption were carried out under the strong pressure of tumultuous domestic and, most particularly, foreign events, as well as the popular excitement kindled by these events. It is true that the Revolution formally ended with the revocation of the Law of Temporary National Authority (February 10), the election of Ebert as president, and the formation of the first

Scheidemann cabinet. But, in point of fact, the Revolution was still stirring; lawlessness and bloodshed continued sporadically throughout the country.

Events in Bavaria were particularly distressing.[16] On February 21 Premier Kurt Eisner was murdered in the open street, as he went to open the Landtag, by a twenty-two-year-old student, Count Arco-Valley. This was a completely absurd crime: the Eisner regime, having just suffered a heavy defeat in the provincial elections, was as good as over, and Eisner had been on his way, people learned after his death, to announce his resignation to the Landtag. One act of violence led to another. That same day in the Landtag a supporter of Eisner, a butcher named Lindner, shot at Erhard Auer, the leader of the Majority Socialists and a minister, wounding him severely. Lindner succeeded in killing instead an officer from the Bavarian Ministry of War, who had sought to shield Auer. One member of the Bavarian People's Party was also killed in the tumult.

A new, irrepressible wave of revolt now swept over Bavaria. A general strike was declared; newspaper offices were seized; a revolutionary Central Council was established. In mid-March the Landtag succeeded, to be sure, in erecting a constitutional government under the leadership of a Majority Socialist, a school teacher named Hoffmann. But the Landtag had become the chief target of revolutionary discontent even though its composition was based on extremely democratic principles. On April 4 the Central Council, in a dictatorial gesture, forbade the Landtag to meet again, and three days later the Republic of Soviets was proclaimed, which proceeded to name Socialist "people's representatives." This new republic referred openly and solemnly to its Russian model and refused "any collaboration with the despicable Ebert-Scheidemann-Noske-Erzberger regime." When Munich and most of the other Bavarian cities came under the power of the new republic, Hoffmann's government had no choice but to flee to rigorously Catholic Bamberg and from there to protest loudly against the injustice it had suffered. Not only the government of the Reich, but also those of Württemberg, Baden, and Hesse, immediately declared that they recognized only the Bamberg regime. These statements, naturally enough, accomplished nothing; only weapons could decide this debate.

The eventual success of the regular troops was at no time in doubt. It was the revolutionaries, with all their self-delusions, that had let matters come to open battle. Indeed, even some of them, especially Ernst Toller, the well-known dramatist, realized quickly not only that fighting was hopeless, but also that this so-called Republic of Soviets was completely incapable of governing and was instead, "a misfortune for the working populace." And so they resigned their offices. But this act only put the revolutionary power exclusively in the hands of a few extremists, some of whom were Russian Communists. The drearier their prospects became, the more ruthlessly they misused their brief powers. Just before their collapse on the last day of April, they had ten bourgeois "hostages," whom they had previously seized, executed without trial. The regular troops stormed Munich during the first two days of May, unfortunately with severe excesses. In a Catholic organization's meeting place twenty-one harmless people were shot down as reputed Spartacists. Further, Gustav Landauer, author of a brilliant book on Shakespeare and a Communist idealist who had originally taken part in the Republic of Soviets but who had had nothing to do with it during the last few weeks, was killed in prison by some soldiers. Once more men saw that civil war is most horrible of all.

Hoffmann's government was now able to return to Munich. Since the premier realized that his government could no longer exist as an exclusively Social Democratic regime, he formed a coalition cabinet with Democrats and members of the Catholic Bavarian People's Party. Even so, the new government's prospects for existence were extremely dim. The experience with the Republic of Soviets had swept away whatever brief revolutionary thrill Bavarians might have experienced during the first days of their revolution in November. Popular opinion about revolutions now swung completely about and sought to blame the Bavarian revolution on others, with the time-honored excuse that it had been instigated by foreign agents. And in this instance there was a kernel of truth in the charge. The Bavarians could no longer have their king, but they could seek consolation in the fact that even in a republic they could remain particularists. They could curse the national government as the seat of all evil and damn as "Marxist" whatever did not suit their fancy.

But external difficulties, born of the peace negotiations, pressed upon the National Assembly even more than these and similar domestic confusions.

IV

THE TREATY OF VERSAILLES[1]

In the year 321 B.C. the Samnites trapped a Roman army in the Caudine Forks, forcing their surrender. Thereupon, the Samnite leader asked his father, Herennius, what he should do with his conquered foe. "Let them all go," replied the wise Herennius. When the son said he could not possibly follow such advice, the father counseled him to have every Roman killed. But this seemed too cruel to the son, who asked his father for some middle course. "No," replied Herennius firmly, "a middle course would neither make the Romans your friends nor relieve you of your enemies."

Herennius' counsel was wise, and the Samnites soon had every reason to regret that they ignored it. But wise as his advice was, it was extraordinarily difficult to follow. And this has been the experience not only of the Samnites but also of those countless conquerors who have been thwarted in their attempts to secure the fruits of victory. Extermination of the foe, from which the ancient Italic chief recoiled, has become an even less real alternative among nations committed to humane Christianity; only a barbarism like Hitler's National Socialism could try to ignore the elementary demands of humanity. But the other choice, to forget all enmity and hate in the moment of victory and to extend the hand of brotherhood to the conquered foe, is unfortunately just as unreal. It is particularly unreal now, when wars can be waged only with the exertion of the last bit of the entire nation's strength and when the people, naturally enough, insist on playing a role in the final settlement. No war, especially a long war, can be waged in cold blood. The sacrifices which it requires of every person are too contradictory to every natural human impulse. People would reject these sacrifices in disgust or dismay if they could have the dispassionate outlook of some future historian pondering the pros and cons of war in the tranquility of his study. Hence hatred of the foe has become a normal and, indeed, indispensable tool of warfare. This hatred grows and captures men's hearts all the more as the war wears on. A nation of millions, once brought to such a peak of excitement, requires years before it can again find psychic equilibrium. In the moment of victory nothing seems more reasonable to people than the notion that the defeated enemy should be made to pay for everything that they have lost or suffered: for their casualties in both men and money as well as for the torments of worry and woe which they had to endure day after day and night after night. A truly great statesman, one who leads by dint of his superior personality and wisdom, may perhaps overcome this tendency. But how many peace treaties in the history of man have been the product of such exemplary statesmanship? People like to recall, reasonably enough, Bismarck at Nikolsburg in 1866. But they should not forget that his war had lasted only seven weeks and that the Prussian eagle's appetite, which Bismarck had restrained in the face of Austrian delicacies, had been satisfied in full measure with Hanover, Hesse, Nassau, Frankfurt, and Schleswig-Holstein.

In the year before the Austrian-Prussian conflict, another civil war had been concluded in the United States of America. There a great statesman had come to the fore, armed with an awareness of the necessary bases for any lasting peace. Abraham Lincoln announced those principles solemnly in the Inaugural Address of March 4, 1865, with which he commenced his second presidential term: "With malice toward none, with charity for all, with firmness in the right as God gives us to see the right, let us strive on to finish the work we are in, to bind up the nation's wounds, to care for him who shall have borne the battle and for his widow and his orphan, to do all which may achieve and cherish a just and lasting peace among ourselves and with all nations." But a few weeks after Lincoln had spoken these imperishable words he himself fell victim to the mad passions which the long war had unleashed. A fanatic, who mistook himself for Brutus, shot Lincoln and thus destroyed for many years all hope for a peace of reconciliation.

Now, in 1919, Woodrow Wilson occupied the presidential chair that Abraham Lincoln had graced.* He, too, hoped to lead mankind away from the rule of passions and avarice, of force and revenge, into the kingdom of reason and of peace. He is one of the most tragic and complex personalities of modern history.[2] Seldom has a man

* This sentence and the preceding paragraph, which differ from the text of the German original, have been inserted into the English translation at the request of Dr. Eyck. TRANSLATORS.

enjoyed higher esteem not only among his own people but among all nations. Seldom has any man suffered such complete failure and, at least for a time, such misunderstanding and calumny. And not without cause. Wilson was a high-minded idealist who had the ability to state his ideals with a force which gripped the hearts of men around the world. In his best moments he rose to the heights of an Old Testament prophet. It is no wonder, therefore, that he finally became consumed by the conviction that Providence had elected him to fulfill a mission for all mankind.

This sort of conviction entails the gravest dangers, as history up to this very day has demonstrated all too often. Everything depends upon the personality involved. Gladstone, for whom Wilson had deep respect, also had such a faith in his mission. But his deep humility preserved him from those perils of overestimation to which Wilson succumbed. Then too, in the constant give-and-take of decades of parliamentary struggle with outstanding opponents, Gladstone had had a better opportunity to acquire a sense of political tolerance than had the President, who, coming from the professor's chair, found himself elevated by his office and his country's constitution high above his political contemporaries. At Versailles, true enough, where the two other great powers of the Entente were represented by two extraordinarily gifted statesmen, he could not help but realize that negotiation involved mutual concessions. One would do him a real injustice if one did not recognize the disciplined devotion with which Wilson set about familarizing himself with European problems. But he had first to overcome his prejudice that only reactionary forms of thought and traditional avarice had kept Europeans from considering these problems with the cool dispassion which came so easily to the objective American who viewed Europe from three thousand miles across the sea. The more he steeped himself in Europe, the more he lost rapport not only with public opinion in America but also with his own colleagues and advisers. In the end, those who had put most faith in him were disillusioned most. It was not indeed they who defeated him; it was rather the shortsighted "political realists" among his fellow Americans. But it was the disillusioned who for years shaped our memory of the man.

Wilson is like the man depicted in Goethe's "*Grenzen der Menschheit*" who tries to raise his head to the heavens only to become prey to clouds and winds; his two most important partners in the negotiations, Clemenceau [3] and Lloyd George,[4] resemble more the man who stands "fast with sturdy bones on the firm, enduring earth" and who, instead of towering too high, is content instead "to measure himself by oak trees and the vine." Both Clemenceau and Lloyd

George had spent many years in national parliamentary struggles, learning the bitterness of defeat and the pleasure of triumph. Both were accustomed to keeping a careful finger on the national pulse. And though it is true that they, more than any other men, were able to direct this pulse according to their wish, they knew, nevertheless, the limits of their charisma and their skill.

Lloyd George had learned these limits particularly well when he tumbled his country into the confusion of a general election immediately after the armistice. For the election campaign had, naturally enough, aroused the people's passions even more and had therefore rewarded with election those who screamed for a complete exploitation of the victory. Lloyd George had later reason to regret the extent to which he personally had yielded to this mood, particularly in respect to reparations. He had felt obliged to promise that the Germans would pay to the last penny for the damage they had wrought. He had been careful enough to add "in so far as they are able," but this qualifying clause, quite understandably, was not remembered as well as was his promise to exact ruthlessly a payment which his people considered just. Also of importance to the peace negotiations was the fact that, in this campaign, Lloyd George destroyed the Liberal Party from whence he had sprung. In so doing he destroyed a support which would have proved welcome on a later path of moderation, and he made enemies of those to whom, in his best moments, he felt himself most close. It is doubtful that he had ever seriously intended to take Asquith, the leader of the Liberals, along to Versailles. At any rate, the party passions kindled by the campaign made such a move impossible. Had he taken Asquith with him, not only would the clarity and calm of the former Prime Minister been most useful in the negotiations, but also the pendulum of British popular opinion would probably not have swung so far to the other side as it did within a few years.

Clemenceau's position, on the other hand, was determined by the same fact that had marked his whole career: in 1870 he had experienced, as an active politician and passionate patriot, France's collapse and Germany's triumph, the seige of Paris and the loss of Alsace-Lorraine. Fate had favored him with a long life of seventy-eight years in order that he might lead his nation to its triumph and revenge. He knew well that through all the long years since their defeat the lust for *revanche* had lain heavy in the hearts of his people. He had shared this passion to its fullest extent and he did not for one moment doubt that someday revenge would also stir the hearts of the Germans after their defeat; not the first day and perhaps not the second, but sooner or later, when the sorrows and the losses of this terrible war would have been surmounted and forgotten. But what then? How would France, with its stagnating population of forty million, particularly in the absence of her former ally, Russia, defend herself against the Germans, who already numbered sixty million and who, in another generation, would certainly grow to seventy million or more? The losses which this victorious war had cost France were there to be counted in all their horror: almost 1,400,000 dead and 3,750,000 wounded; almost half the soldiers under thirty years of age lost; more than 4,000 villages ruined; 20,000 factories and shops destroyed. *Sécurité*! The insurance of France in the face of this future, but inevitable, danger of a resurgent Germany was therefore the foremost demand which Clemenceau brought to the negotiations.

Wilson's answer to this life-and-death matter was this: in the future the League of Nations will make any attack by one country upon another impossible; for the League will so bind them together that they will all immediately come to the aid of the attacked member, and no country will dare provoke such superior force. Wilson had come to Paris principally to bring the League of Nations into existence. The League was to give a blessing to the treaty of peace; it was to distinguish this peace radically from all that had gone before, making permanent end to the age of murderous wars. For this reason Wilson placed all his authority and political power behind his insistence that the League be made an integral part of the peace treaty, that, in fact, its covenant became the treaty's first section. The members of this League were supposed to guarantee each other's independence and territorial integrity (Article 10) and adopt common financial and economic sanctions against any aggressor (Article 16). Having suffered so severely from the allied blockade, Germany would certainly not run the risk of such treatment from the entire world.

But could one expect a bitter, hardened, and skeptical realist like Clemenceau to regard this proposal of Wilson's as a satisfactory answer to the fateful question of France's security? Clemenceau knew from his own experience the efficacy of international alliances, and he knew how difficult it is, when one party to the pact is in a crisis, to persuade the other nation that its fortune is also at stake. The history of the Franco-Russian alliance offered more than enough examples of such difficulties. Could one expect with any sort of certainty that the nations of the world, and their governments, would be any quicker to risk their peace and private interests and perhaps run the danger of war for the sake of another country just because they all had solemnly subscribed to the League of Nations?

Would not each nation seek excuses, squeezing the League's charter dry of convenient interpretations, before sacrificing itself for a matter that was another land's concern? The "twenty million too many Germans" were a fact; the aid of the members of the League was only a hope, whether true or false only time would tell. Therefore the French demanded, as a minimum guarantee, that the League be provided with an international army for the immediate punishment of aggressors.

The French representative on the committee considering the League, Leon Bourgeois, long a proponent of the idea of the League, fought unceasingly and in every way for such an international force. But Wilson's firm, categoric refusal balked his every attempt.[5] The President had no choice. He knew that the American constitution places the power to declare war and to conclude peace in the hands of the Congress, and that the Senate, which would have to ratify the treaty now at hand, would under no circumstances accept this limitation of its powers. Wilson therefore stressed all the more emphatically the moral effect which the duties of membership would have upon all the member nations of the League. But Clemenceau could find no reason to believe that the American Senate would be any more disposed to think and act in an international manner in a specific case of aggression than in the general instance of establishing the League. He firmly insisted, therefore, upon concrete and convincing protection for France.

Public opinion in France was convinced that the only sure security lay in a Rhine border, that is, in separating from Germany the provinces on the left bank of the Rhine. Marshal Foch, whose military successes had won him not only overwhelming popularity at home but also a high repute among his allies, proposed and defended this argument with special emphasis. He did not, to be sure, insist that France annex these German provinces; he was content to see them become a neutral, demilitarized buffer state. For further security he proposed a thirty-year occupation of the bridge-heads on the right bank of the Rhine. Together, these two provisions would make it impossible for German divisions to invade France again.

But Foch's arguments left his Anglo-Saxon allies unmoved. Lloyd George firmly declined to take part in the creation of new "Alsace-Lorraines" which would disturb Europe for fifty years as had the original. Wilson was naturally unconvinced. But Clemenceau did not give up his efforts. He made it perfectly clear that France would sign no peace treaty which did not satisfy, at least in some measure, her need for protection. And so the Allies finally arrived at a compromise: Germany was to keep its left bank, but the Allies decided to occupy it and the most important bridgeheads, such as Mainz and Cologne, for fifteen years, and to require of Germany the permanent demilitarization of the entire left bank and a fifty-kilometer strip along the right bank. In this region no fortresses might be established and no soldiers recruited or stationed. Every five years the area of occupation was to be reduced as long as Germany continued to carry out fully the conditions of peace. And along with the required reduction of the German peacetime army to 100,000 men, Clemenceau could find further promise of future safety for France in an additional concession which he had obtained. Both Wilson and Lloyd George agreed to sign treaties with France, guaranteeing American and British armed assistance if Germany mounted an unprovoked attack against France. These two treaties were separate, but each was to be conditional upon the existence of the other. While there could be no doubt concerning the prompt execution of the British treaty, that is, its ratification by Parliament, the prospects of the American pact were not so clear. Every international agreement made by the President of the United States requires, for its ratification, the approval of a two-thirds majority of the American Senate. But could one count on this? Wilson's Democratic Party had suffered a defeat in the election of November 1918, losing control of the Senate to the Republicans. The Republicans, his opposition, could hardly be expected to approve a step so contradictory to the whole tradition of American foreign policy. Had not George Washington himself solemnly warned his nation against entangling alliances? As a matter of fact, the treaty was never even presented to the Senate; it became a worthless piece of paper and the English pact thus lost its validity.

The problem of the Saar, like that of the Rhineland, was settled by compromise among the victors. The French had claimed the region, with its rich coal fields, for historical as well as economic and strategic reasons. A century earlier part of the Saar had been French. Now the region's coal deposits were to serve as repayment for the French mines which had been deliberately destroyed by the retreating Germans. To these arguments the English and Americans replied that the people of the Saar were clearly German and wished to remain so. The Allies finally agreed that the French might have the mines for fifteen years, during which time the region would be administered by a commission to be appointed by the League of Nations. At the end of this period a plebiscite would determine the allegiance of the Saar.

The fate of Alsace-Lorraine had been sealed with Germany's

defeat. Its return to France had been that nation's goal throughout the war, and, in his Eighth Point, Wilson had promised that the peace settlement would right the wrong which Prussia had done to France in 1871. The Allies were in complete agreement on this point. They even went so far as to assume that the region had been ceded back to France by the terms of the armistice which had required the Germans to quit both provinces (Article II of the armistice, Article 51 of the peace treaty).

The peace treaty cut much deeper into Germany's eastern borders than in the west. For here it was a matter of undoing one of the most critical events of the eighteenth century: the partition of Poland (1772–1795). The Central Powers had begun the work themselves by proclaiming the Polish Kingdom in 1916. They had, of course, meant to limit this kingdom to Russian Poland, but this restriction had collapsed with their defeat. The Poles had always found in the West strong sympathy with their struggle for independence. And Wilson had gone so far as to demand expressly, in the thirteenth of his Fourteen Points, an independent Polish state including all areas of clearly Polish population. This clause alone meant that Germany would lose considerable amounts of land formerly belonging to Prussia; the second provision of the Point, namely, that Poland have free access to the sea, involved even more. For between the Baltic and the indisputable land of the Poles lay East Prussia and Danzig, the population of which was obviously German, not Polish. And in all this part of Europe, where the course of history had tossed whole nations one among the other, it was exceedingly difficult to draw a border which would correspond to the theory of Wilson's Third Principle as set forth in his speech of February 11, 1918: that all national boundaries be fixed to serve the interests and the welfare of the peoples concerned. The Allies decided to leave East Prussia to Germany but to make Danzig a free city under the control of the League of Nations, with certain economic privileges granted to the Poles. Between East Prussia and the body of the Reich a "corridor" leading from Polish lands to the sea was created and given to Poland. But all the fears that Wilson's program had already aroused in Germany were surpassed when the Allies announced that the whole of Upper Silesia was to be given to Poland.

Turning to the question of Germany's northern border, the Allies demanded a plebiscite in North Schleswig to see if the people wished to be German or Danish. This decision fulfilled a promise which Prussia had made in the Peace of Prague, 1866, but had never carried out. For in 1878 Bismarck had traded his support of Austrian demands at the Congress of Berlin for Austria's willingness not to insist on a plebiscite.

Fully as important as the matter of boundaries, and far more difficult to solve, was the question of reparations, the payment for all the damages which conquered Germany had wrought upon its victorious foes. Since this topic will be discussed in more detail below, it may suffice here to note that the draft treaty declared an unconditional German liability (Article 231) but failed to set any definite reparation figures. Article 253 left this task to a future reparations commission.

It is little wonder that the negotiations over these and countless other extremely complicated problems required several months. The time required can scarcely astonish a generation which, after the end of World War II, has watched years go by without seeing a formal peace. But Germany, which had just experienced revolution and was still threatened with Bolshevism from the East, had a particular need for a speedy peace, since the Allied blockade was still in force.[6] Here too both sides had contributed to confusion. The armistice agreement of November 11, 1918, explicitly declared that the blockade was to be continued in full force; but the Allies had also assumed responsibility for feeding Germany in case of emergency. Nothing was done during the initial thirty-six day period of the armistice. One of the reasons adduced for this delay was that, after the ravages of the submarine campaign and in the face of their many postwar responsibilities, the Allies could not spare the shipping to bring food to Germany. In granting the second extension of the armistice on January 16, 1919, they therefore required that the German merchant marine be put under their control "to ensure the relief of Germany and the rest of Europe." The ultimate disposal of the fleet was not to be prejudiced by this move. The German government accepted this condition (Paragraph 8). Thereupon the Allies promised the immediate delivery of 200,000 tons of grain and 70,000 tons of preserved meat. But the German government gave no indication of making the ships available. At the conference of delegates at Spa on March 5, the Germans declared that they would deliver the ships only if the Allies assumed formal responsibility for feeding Germany until the next harvest, that is, until September. At this, the Allied delegates broke off the conversations and returned forthwith to Paris. Keynes, financial adviser to the British delegation, has reported that the Allied delegates decided upon this crisp, sharp break in negotiations in order to bring the ever worsening situation to the attention of their superiors.

They succeeded in so doing. On March 8, the Allied Supreme

Council devoted an entire session to the problem of feeding Germany. Lloyd George, Clemenceau, and Foch took part in this most dramatic meeting. Clemenceau was, to be sure, essentially in favor of the project, but he, and still more Klotz, his minister of finance, protested against having the Germans pay for these shipments in gold, since, in the eyes of the French, the Reichsbank's reserves served as ultimate assurance that reparations would be paid. And Foch did not wish to lay aside the weapon of blockade, for only by its means could the Germans be forced to accept the peace conditions without further military measures. Lloyd George, on the other hand, argued strongly, almost passionately, for the feeding of the German people. He quoted the statement of General Plumer, commander of the British Army of Occupation, that he could not be responsible for his troops if they continued to see starving children on the streets. In order to lend his arguments greatest effect, Lloyd George had Plumer send him a telegram. It arrived during the course of the meeting and was read aloud with tremendous success. Thanks to this man's skillful energy the Supreme Council decided to assure the Germans of a steady supply of provisions provided that *before* negotiations the Germans accepted and fulfilled their obligation to deliver the ships.

The German delegation accepted this condition at the conference at Brussels on March 13, whereupon Admiral Wemyss, leader of the Allied delegation there, promised them 300,000 tons of grain and 70,000 tons of meat each month until September. This promise was to become null and void should Germany break the conditions of armistice or prove dilatory in delivering the ships. This happy solution was, Keynes tells us, due to his personal intervention. For, just before the decisive meeting at Brussels, he succeeded in having an intimate conversation with the deputy chairman of the German delegation, Dr. Carl Melchior, a partner of the Max Warburg Bank in Hamburg. Keynes had observed that Melchior seemed to excel his German colleagues in wisdom and in speed of comprehension; he explained to him how important it was that the Germans accept the Allies' provisions quickly and without counterconditions. Melchior understood immediately and took care that Under-Secretary von Braun, chairman of the delegation, made an appropriate statement. With this statement, the feeding of Germany could be resumed, and only a few days passed before the first provisions arrived in Hamburg's harbor. The blockade remained in formal force, although relaxed in many respects, until the conclusion of peace. But to say that the Allies continued to starve the Germans is clearly to distort the facts.

By April 14 the Allies had progressed so far in their work that they could invite the Germans to send a delegation to Versailles for the purpose of *receiving* the peace terms — just to receive the terms, not to negotiate them. It had been Wilson's original plan that the Allied governments would arrive at a tentative draft which could then serve as the basis of discussions with the Germans. But the task of setting the victors' conflicting interests into one mold had proved so tedious that even the President decided not to risk the hard-won unanimity of the Allies before the Germans. For Wilson's differences with the Italians had already led the latter to leave the conference. So the Big Three agreed to regard their common conditions of peace as final, and simply to hand them to the Germans for signing. Naturally this attitude evoked considerable consternation in Germany, and the government there, under the influence of the new foreign minister, Count Brockdorff-Rantzau, replied on April 20 that some official of the Foreign Office would be sent to receive the document. Clemenceau, as chairman of the peace conference, immediately retorted that he was not content with a mere messenger, but insisted rather upon plenipotentiaries empowered to sign the treaty. The German government was obliged, of course, to yield; on April 21 they gave the Allies the names of the empowered delegates.

At their head stood, logically, the German foreign minister, Count Ulrich von Brockdorff-Rantzau,[7] who was born in Schleswig fifty years before, and who had been an imperial ambassador, most recently in Copenhagen. In December 1918, when the post of foreign minister was about to be relinquished by Solf, Scheidemann turned to Brockdorff in the name of both Social Democratic parties. He agreed to assume the office, but only with certain clearly stated stipulations. Among them was the power to decline the Allies' conditions of peace should these deny the Germans an opportunity to lead halfway decent lives.[8] At the same time, he made it perfectly clear that he accepted the new form of the German state and was a member of the Democratic Party. It was on this basis that, at the beginning of 1919, he undertook the leadership of Germany's foreign policy. To his new office he brought not only his professional knowledge of international relations, but also a keen mind and sense of style, thanks to which his communications were penetrating and emphatic. On the other hand he lacked, as do so many diplomats, the gift of extemporaneous speaking. Faced with any large audience, such as in parliament, he could only cling nervously to his prepared manuscript and plunge ahead. One certainly has no reason now to doubt the man's democratic convictions and his liberal point of view. Nevertheless he not only gave the impression of being an extremely self-conscious aristocrat, but *was* one at the bottom of his heart. He considered himself superior by far to the politicians with whom fate had teamed him as well as to the populace. And in intimate conversations, especially after a good bit of his well-loved brandy, he loved to exercise his biting wit at their expense.[9] To give the man his due, one must add that he spoke no better of the generals. He probably had real respect only for Ebert; Erzberger, with his brash manner and constant bustling, must have got on his nerves. Since Brockdorff took everything personally, he always interpreted opposition as downright enmity. Indeed, the two ministers soon found themselves on different sides of the critical issue of peace. For Erzberger, who was of course more familiar than the count with the domestic and the parliamentary scene, became more and more certain that Germany would have to accept whatever sort of peace was offered her.

The other delegates were Dr. Landsberg, minister of justice; Giesberts, postmaster general and leader of the Christian Workers' Movement; and Leinert, the Social Democratic president of the Prussian Landtag. Professor Walter Schücking, a Democratic member of the Reichstag, was the delegation's specialist on international law. For years he had fought, in striking contrast to the majority of his German colleagues, for the principle of justice and peaceful arbitration in international affairs. He could, therefore, be regarded as the ideal man to reply in the full spirit of Wilson's ideals to the demands of the Entente. But he was basically not a practical politician and did not possess that sensitive sixth sense which is necessary for diplomatic success. The delegation's economic expert was Dr. Carl Melchior, another man of strong ethical convictions, whose clear and steady mind was armed with a broad professional competence. Just as important as these delegates was the general commissioner, Dr. Walter Simons, the ministerial director of the Foreign Office, who served as their adviser in legal and factual matters. Dr. Simons, a distinguished jurist, was named president of the German Supreme Court only a few years later. He had found his way to newer forms of thought through ethics and religion. A sturdy Protestant, he was soon to become president of the Evangelical Social Congress. He had a particularly warm regard for Hugo Preuss and defended his contribution to Germany's new development against Preuss's vilifiers. At Versailles he had the formal task of maintaining unity in the work of the various German committees. Yet his advice could not but influence the delegation, and the letters he sent home provide valuable insights into the activity of the Germans at the conference.

At the end of April, when the German delegates left for Versailles, they had no official knowlege of the treaty which was about to confront them. For the leaders of the Allies had not only negotiated behind closed doors; they had also kept their decisions confidential, fearful lest untimely publicity impede their freedom of movement. But what can remain secret when the most cunning journalists of the world lurk, thirsting for news, in every corridor and at every door? Indeed, the press, especially in France and America, had exposed so many diplomatic secrets and political differences, that the Germans already knew quite well what awaited them at Versailles. A commission under the direction of the former ambassador, Count Bernstorff, had been collecting such data for months, distributing them to specialists for annotation and reply. A small army of experts in every field — law, economics, politics, and history — along with a limited number of German reporters, accompanied the German delegation.

The delegation's route lay through the ruins of northern France. "Our journey was an overwhelming experience," Simons wrote. "The train deliberately went slowly through the desolate fields, once rich with fruit, now torn apart by bombs, past the ruins of former villages and towns, where no one was to be seen save those removing the rubble. We paused at stations amid hollow dwellings, gutted warehouses, and exploded trains until we had seen all that we could stand." [10] When the delegates arrived at Versailles they first suffered the unpleasant surprise of discovering that they would be cut off from the outside world by a high board fence. The official explanation spoke of protecting them thus from hostile demonstrations on the part of the local population. The real reason, obviously enough, was the desire of the Allies to preserve the weaknesses in their unified front from discovery and exploitation in private conversations between Germans and individual parties of the West. The ghost of "Talleyrand at the Congress of Vienna" was wandering here. For the Allied historians had sedulously studied the great negotiations of a century before and had even equipped the delegates with an account of their course. Had the Allies read Treitschke's colorful description of the Congress and the triumphs associated with Talleyrand's "iron countenance," their worries would certainly not have been diminished.[11]

The handing of the peace treaty to the Germans had been set for May 7, 1919. This important event was to take place in the Trianon, not far from the Palace of Versailles, where, on January 18, 1871, Bismarck had proclaimed the German Empire. Bismarck's choice of Versailles, which symbolized to the French so much that was glorious in their history, had struck them as a mean and deliberate provocation under which they had suffered for more than four decades. Now the day of retribution had come. And the French statesman who presided over the ceremony embodied the nation's memory of those days of defeat, days through which he too had lived and suffered. It is therefore no wonder that Clemenceau, in his address to the Germans which opened the solemn session, alluded pointedly to this "Second Treaty of Versailles" which he now placed before the Germans. And the bitterness of this reference lost none of its edge from the tone in which he spoke. Clemenceau then went on to say that the battle had proved so costly to the victors that they would spare no measure to ensure a lasting peace.

While Clemenceau's short speech was being translated into English and German, the secretary of the conference handed Count Brockdorff-Rantzau the thick volume which contained the treaty draft. Without opening it, Brockdorff laid it to one side. The moment had now come when Germany's representative could address all the assembled leaders of the West, perhaps the only time that he would have this chance. Would he make full use of his opportunity?

His opening created a sensation: Clemenceau had risen to address the Germans; Count Brockdorff elected to sit. Was this a deliberate affront as everyone present had to — and did — assume? Lloyd George tells how, years later, another member of the German delegation explained to him the true reason for Brockdorff's behavior: "The poor man was so nervous that he was physically incapable of standing up. He made an effort to do so. But he trembled at the knees and could not rise." Brockdorff always refused to accept this kindly interpretation. In fact, Simons wrote in a letter of May 10 [12] that the count had told him in advance that he planned to sit. His reasoning was as follows: in a cartoon depicting the Germans at the conference, a French journal had labeled them "the defendants," and Brockdorff feared that if he stood he would resemble a culprit to whom the judge is saying: "Defendant, arise!" But can one believe that this really constituted Brockdorff's motivation? Can one imagine that an experienced diplomat and responsible statesman, mindful that the fortunes of his fatherland depended on him at this fateful moment, could let an arrogant newspaper influence his actions rather than govern himself so as to make the best possible impression upon the men who held his country's fate in their hands? One probably would do well to combine the two versions of the scene. Brockdorff was conscious of his weakness: he knew in advance that he would suffer a violent attack of stage fright if obliged to address this large assembly of men whom he knew to be politically as powerful as they were unfriendly. He knew that his strength would fail him if he were to attempt to speak on his feet; unwilling to provide the world with such a scene, he made up his mind beforehand to remain seated, offering an excuse which concealed his real reason.

This behavior brought him great acclaim in Germany. He became something of a national hero for simply having sat. But what was most important was the impression the affair made upon the Allied statesmen, and that was as bad as possible. Wilson felt himself deeply affronted and muttered to Lloyd George: "Isn't it just like them?" Nor can one say that the count's speech struck the right note. From the several drafts which lay before him, he had clearly chosen the sharpest for reply. And he read it in such a manner as to emphasize its bitterness. Simons wrote: "It is to Clemenceau's credit that he controlled his temper to such an extent as not to interrupt Brockdorff's speech; but his face was red with rage." Lloyd George relieved his emotions by breaking a letter opener before him on the table. And after the session Wilson said: "The Germans are really a stupid people. They always do the wrong thing . . . This is the most tactless speech I have ever heard. It will set the whole world against them." [13]

If one reads Brockdorff's speech today, in cooler blood, one can find little to justify such indignation but less that might have been designed to elicit a cooperative attitude from his audience. Brockdorff's position was difficult, to be sure, in that he enjoyed no official knowledge of the contents of the treaty just handed him while at the same time he had already unofficially learned much that he would find in reading it; hence his gruff polemic against the idea of attributing to Germany sole guilt for the war. But was it clever of him to accuse the Allies of having made the Germans wait six weeks for an armistice? Every man there knew that the Germans had caused this delay themselves by addressing their requests for peace to Wilson alone rather than to the whole Entente. Moreover a few sentences later, Brockdorff himself said that the victors had, "in the period between October 5 and November 5, declined to press for unconditional surrender." And was it not careless, to say the least, to make the accusation, neither demonstrable nor true, that "the hundreds of thousands of noncombatants starved by the blockade since November 11 were deliberately killed after our foes won and secured their victory"? This indictment later became one of the trump cards of Hitler's propaganda. Only after Brockdorff had clubbed the Allied leaders in this way did he turn to those problems to which he could properly direct their attention.

It is perhaps indicative of Lloyd George's nature that Brockdorff's remarks concerning famine in Germany after the armistice impressed him particularly. But when he voiced these thoughts at the meeting of the Council of Four the next day, Clemenceau not only reminded him that Brockdorff's reports had yet to be proved, he also offered to introduce to President Wilson a group of women, ranging from 14 to 60 years of age, who had been raped by Germans. Whereupon Lloyd George admitted that Sir Ernest Pollock, one of England's outstanding judges, had told him that many of the affidavits submitted to the Committee for the Investigation of German Atrocities had been too revolting to be read aloud to the commission.[14]

The Allies allotted the Germans fifteen days in which to prepare in writing, in French and English, whatever objections, questions, or proposals they might have. This period was later extended by one week. Oral communication was still prohibited. The fact that a few individuals succeeded in establishing private contacts with members of the Allied delegations had little effect on the final result. The Germans went busily about their work, and whoever reads their countless memoranda on each clause and their final, enormously comprehensive note of May 29 cannot but be amazed at their tireless energy and the magnitude of their achievement. Yet perhaps even here, less would have meant more. Perhaps they would have made a greater impression if, rather than answering each point in detail, they had instead restricted their attention to a few critical areas where the Allies had differences of interest and opinion and where there was, therefore, at least some hope for compromise.

The German delegation went to work on the so-called war-guilt question with a special zeal.[15] Article 231, the first in the section on reparations, contains the declaration on the part of the Allied governments and its acceptance by Germany of "the *responsibility* of Germany and her allies for *causing all the loss and damage* to which the Allied and Associated Governments and their nationals have been subjected as a consequence of the war *imposed* upon them *by the aggression of Germany* and her Allies." Originally this statement, as its position at the beginning of the section shows, had had a restricted connotation. It is an ancient axiom of human history that the loser pays for the war. Every conqueror has reaped the benefits of this truth without anyone's worrying whether the victor had been the attacked or the attacker. When Bismarck, in 1871, saddled the French with an indemnity of five billion francs, neither he nor his victims took the trouble to determine whether in this case, too, "World History had been the World Court." But in 1919 the victors believed that this sort of raw *Realpolitik* no longer sufficed; it had to be replaced by more refined legal arguments. Just as in civil law damages are paid by those who cause them, whether out of fore-thought or neglect, so the requirement of reparations from Germany and her allies was to be based upon the demonstration that they, as aggressors, were responsible for the war. The Allies felt themselves especially called upon to assume this attitude since Lansing, the American secretary of state, in his note of November 5, 1918, had required with emphasis that Germany accept the obligation that "compensation will be made by Germany for all damage done to the civilian population of the Allies and their property *by the aggression of Germany,* by land, by sea and from the air." And Germany had accepted this commitment in the armistice (Article 19).

The German delegation, however, regarded Article 231 as a forced confession by Germany that it alone was guilty for the war, and they decided to oppose the accusation firmly. They summoned four experts of top quality, Hans Delbrück, Max Weber, Albrecht Mendelssohn-Bartholdy, and General Max Montgelas, to their aid and finally presented the Allies with a memorandum by these men on the question of war guilt. Now these were certainly gentlemen whose quality of character and independence of mind even their former foes had to accept. They certainly were right when they in-sisted that the question of war guilt could not be determined uni-laterally by one party and that the archives of all nations concerned would have to be available to anyone seeking an objective conclu-sion. It is not their fault if today their memorandum strikes us as scanty, a bit forced, and casuistic. It was written too soon. The Allies, on the other hand, would have had a simple task had they been content to restrict the implications of Article 231 sharply, leaving the grand issue to future historians. Instead they let them-selves be seduced into legalistic debate and answered the Germans, on June 16, with a smoking note full of pontifical pronouncement on German diplomatic and military policy. The author of this note was Lloyd George's private secretary, Philip Kerr, later the Marquis of Lothian, a strong proponent of English rapprochement with Ger-many. The note was a piece of brilliant journalism but poor states-manship. For it gave the debated article an objectionable connota-tion which it did not originally have and thus paved the way for that passionate, often demagogic, discussion of the "war-guilt lie" which helped kindle German nationalism once again.

Naturally the Allies had every reason to regard Germany as the cause of the war and to pronounce this judgment to the world. But they had no right to require the Germans to accept this statement regardless of whether they thought it true or false. What the West could properly require of the Germans was something entirely different, namely their acceptance of liability for reparations. In a civil suit of similar nature any half-skilled attorney would have been able to hit with ease upon a formula which, while guarding the creditor's interests, would have spared the debtor's feelings.

But more important at the time was the question of whether and to what extent the intended mutilation of Germany would hinder or indeed preclude economic reconstruction there. The German delegation presented a memorandum on this subject, written by Melchior, which, as was to be expected of this man, kept coolly and closely to the point. When, therefore, this memorandum came to the conclusion that the proposed treaty was tantamount to a death sentence for millions of German men, women, and children, it could not help but make a deep impression. Nor can there be any doubt that every German who knew or thought he knew anything at all about economics considered Melchior's memorandum extremely apt and the Allies' answer, which called the German fears exaggerated, frivolous and superficial. But the optimism of the West proved to be correct. Germany's postwar problems were overcome in an astonishingly short time due to the resiliency of modern industry, the diligence and energy of the Germany people, and the willingness of the world, which recognized these virtues, to grant more than sufficient credits to the German economy after the inflation had passed.

On May 29 the German delegation was able to submit its final "Observation" on the peace treaty. It was a thick volume, convincing evidence of the thoroughness and speed of German work. A "Letter of Enclosure" preceded it, presenting the principal points in clear, emphatic, and less formal language. Brockdorff had assigned the composition of this letter not to a diplomat but to a journalist, Bernhard Guttmann, a correspondent of the *Frankfurter Zeitung*. He sensed correctly that Guttmann would find words which would evoke an echo in the world. A consultation between the delegation and members of the German cabinet, on May 23 in Spa, preceded the delivery of the note.[16] This meeting had become necessary since differences of opinion between the two bodies had become evident. The delegates were united in their view that Germany could not sign the peace treaty unless the Allies granted several essential concessions. The German government had originally taken this same position. On May 12, a few days after the delivery of the draft treaty at Versailles, the National Assembly met in the great hall of the University of Berlin. Prime Minister Scheidemann made a firm, sharp speech there in which, amid wild applause, he pronounced the treaty unacceptable to the German government, lapsing even into the pathetic words: "What hand would not wither which placed this chain upon itself and upon us?" With only one exception the speakers of all the parties adopted this same standpoint. This one exception was Haase, the Independent Social Democrat, who, while protesting the terms of the treaty, still insisted that "our nation has no choice but to make peace." He consoled himself over its terms with the hope that the world revolution was on the march and that it would quickly annul the work of Versailles.

Haase's argument for signing the treaty made little impression on the Assembly, but his words sounded ominous to a war-weary people. For he forced them to realize that rejection of the treaty was feasible only if the entire German nation were prepared to resume the war. The patent impossibility of this alternative was one of the reasons why Erzberger, in particular, was convinced that a break with the Entente had to be avoided at all costs. And he evidently suspected that such a break would not disappoint Brockdorff at all.

The statesmen of the Entente were rather distressed at the thought that the Germans might decline to sign their peace. They certainly had the military and economic means available to resume hostilities. They agreed to re-establish the blockade in full force if Germany said no; and within a few days Marshal Foch drew up and issued plans for the invasion of unoccupied Germany. But everyone knew full well that such a resumption of hostilities would be extremely unpopular. The soldiers wanted to go home and the parents of those not yet discharged were calling for their sons. In nations like England and America, unaccustomed to conscription, such a cry has much more force than it would have had in Germany — and most of the German soldiers had already gone home.

Lloyd George was most disturbed of all. His critics accused him of making concessions to Germany because he fell into panic at the prospect of having to face Parliament without a concluded peace. It is true that the British Prime Minister had to be mindful of the mood of Parliament and his people. Indeed Wilson, who had lost as much in his last election as Lloyd George had gained in his, could have profited if he had paid more attention to American opinion. But the English statesman's motives lay deeper than party politics. As early as the end of March, in the course of negotiations among the Allies, he had spent a weekend at Fontainbleau composing a calm and penetrating memorandum on what the aims of the victorious nations should be.[17] They should, he argued, proceed in as detached a manner as possible, like dispassionate judges who had left the fevers of war behind. The peace should be one that a responsible German government could sign with good conscience and with the intention of fulfilling the obligations thus undertaken. And this peace should not contain the seed of new wars, but must rather, through its universal acceptance as a fair and rational solution to Europe's problems, serve as a counterweight to the blandishments of Bolshevism.

Although it is possible that, for a time, the English Prime Minister cherished the belief that the Allies' final draft corresponded to his wise axioms, it is clear that this faith dissolved rapidly in the face of his most trusted colleagues' criticism. Bitterest of all in his criticism of the treaty was General Smuts, the great South African who less than twenty years before had been fighting against the British Empire and was now one of its most respected and popular leaders.[18] He criticized especially the Rhenish occupation and the Polish boundaries. When Lloyd George sought to persuade his Allied partners to consider changes in the treaty, it was to be expected that he would not find Clemenceau accommodating. But Wilson too argued that it was unwise to alter the treaty at this late date simply in order to win German signatures. The President concluded that the British "ought to have been rational to begin with and then they would not have needed to have funked at the end." [19] Though he met opposition from his allies, Lloyd George did succeed in persuading his own cabinet, summoned to Paris for this purpose, to arm him with authority to say that Great Britain would furnish neither occupation troops nor blockade ships unless granted certain concessions.[20] The pressure of this statement brought about a compromise which met the German pleas in several ways.

The major concession concerned Upper Silesia. The draft treaty would have given it to Poland without further ado. Now the final decision was made dependent upon a plebiscite. The stipulations concerning the eventual plebiscite in the Saar and the future German payments for the coal mines there were adjusted so as to facilitate the return of the region to Germany after fifteen years. Indeed, this transfer was accomplished smoothly after the plebiscite of 1935 had displayed an overwhelming majority in its favor. In Schleswig German wishes were accommodated only insofar as the area of the plebiscite was somewhat decreased. The Germans' desire to be admitted immediately to the League of Nations was not satisfied; they were told instead to wait until they had demonstrated through deeds that they had met the conditions of the peace and had forsworn the ways of war. Nor was the German hope for a definite reparations bill realized, even though numerous experts in the Allied delegations had urged such a move. The determination of this sum was delegated to the reparations commission created by the treaty. The Allies granted the possibility of another manner of determination only if Germany made acceptable proposals within four months' time. Neither the period nor the area of the Rhenish occupation was altered in the least. But Lloyd George and Wilson finally got Clemenceau to agree to limit the number of occupation troops and to ensure the continuity of German civil administration in the region.

Most important, however, was the note's last paragraph in which the Allies made clear that this was their final, immutable position, and asked to learn within five days' time, later lengthened to a week, whether the Germans intended to sign. If no assent were heard within this time, the armistice would lapse — in other words, the Allied invasion of Germany would commence.

This required the German government to make a decision of the most critical importance in little more than minutes. Brockdorff-Rantzau's opinion was already formed: he urged refusal, and the other delegates agreed with him. A majority of the German delegates left Versailles at the end of the day in which they received the Allies' ultimatum. The citizenry of Versailles, taking this move as evidence that the Germans did not plan to sign, began a violent demonstration which even led to stoning the German delegation. The demonstration distressed the Allied governments, as an extremely correct, apologetic note from Clemenceau made clear.

But on the morning of June 18, when Brockdorff arrived in Weimar, the seat of the German government, he found little sign of the near unanimity that had filled the Berlin hall on May 12. Not only the cabinet but every party was sharply split. In the government, acceptance of the treaty was opposed by Scheidemann and the Democrats, including Gothein and Preuss, whom no one would call chauvinistic.[21] Other ministers pointed out that they, too, were dismayed by the treaty, but even more by the prospect of Germany's refusal to sign it. For the Allies would then certainly advance while their blockade threatened the German nation with starvation. This entailed the danger not only of widespread unrest and Bolshevism but even perhaps of the disintegration of Germany. And they argued that particularism, which already pressed for cession of the left bank of the Rhine, would raise its head throughout the Reich, especially in the south. Finally, after another period of desperate tumult, Germany would have to sign anyway. For nothing warranted Brockdorff's hope that "the further peaceful progress of mankind will soon admit us to that objective court where we shall seek our equity and rights." Erzberger opposed the argument that Germany should reject the treaty with all his energy of mind and force of tongue;[22]

Noske and David, of the Social Democrats, supported him. Noske was clearly quite worried about the danger of Bolshevism. "The German people has so lost its sense of morality and of national identity that we have to sign," he declared.[23] Neither side could persuade the other.

The same heated and fruitless debates took place in the caucuses of the coalition parties. Neither the Democrats, nor the Social Democrats, nor the Centrists were able to maintain a solid party front. In the course of these discussions the debate gradually centered upon two points, both of no material relevance. One was the acceptance of war guilt; the other, the delivery to the West of Germans indicted for war crimes. A strong and passionate public opinion in the Allied nations pressed for the punishment, in a court to be established by the Allies for this purpose, of those guilty either of the war or of crimes committed in its name. Leading the list of these war criminals was the German Emperor, whom everyone in the West considered most responsible for the war. "Hang the Kaiser!" had been the most popular slogan in the British electoral campaign. It was, of course, true that William sat safely in Holland; the Allies could not hope nor the Germans fear that he would be extradited to a victors' court. More serious was the plight of those whom the Allies intended to indict "for acts against the laws and customs of war" (Article 228). One could foresee that many of the German commanders would be included. Here, at least physically, the possibility of extradition did exist; for they all were in Germany, including Ludendorff, who had fled incognito to Sweden at the cessation of hostilities. A sense of national pride violently opposed this extradition without regard to the truth or error of the indictment. Not only the opposition parties of the Right and the officers' associations, but also the coalition parties, thought that German honor was at stake.

Now Erzberger, on the strength of reports from the enemy camp, had reason to believe that the Entente was prepared to accommodate the Germans on these two points if the rest of the treaty was signed. Under his influence the Centrists decided in caucus to cast their party's votes in favor of signing, with the provision that neither the acceptance of war guilt (Article 231) nor the obligation to extradite the so-called war criminals be binding. The Social Democrats took essentially the same position.[24] Whereupon, on June 20, Scheidemann and his cabinet resigned.

But first Noske, as the minister of defense, had inquired of the Supreme Command, then in Kolberg, what the prospects were of armed resistance in the event of further hostilities. Hindenburg had replied that they could resist in the east but not the west. With this he officially confirmed something every layman already knew. When he went on to declare that, as a soldier, he would prefer honorable annihilation to a disgraceful peace, he said something which one might well respect as a personal point of view but which one could hardly make the base for policy. A government which decided to lead the people in its charge to certain ruin would be acting in a clearly criminal manner. And in any event this foolish resistance would have had only the practical effect of postponing, not obviating, the "disgraceful peace." The Bolshevists had discovered this at the Treaty of Brest-Litovsk. The responsible ministers and the *Reichspräsident,* who was personally against signing the treaty, could only conclude from Hindenburg's reply that no hope was to be laid in military resistance.

The resignation of Scheidemann's cabinet confronted Ebert with the task, as pressing as it was difficult, of finding a new government, one prepared to sign the treaty with the two-point proviso. He would have much preferred to resign, but his friends managed to convince him that resignation was out of the question. Since the Democrats had decided in caucus to take no part in the next government, the cabinet had to be drawn from Social Democrats and Centrists, but without the services of Otto Landsberg, who continued to refuse to have a hand in signing the treaty. The Social Democrat Bauer, formerly a trade unionist and most recently minister of labor, headed the new cabinet. Brockdorff's successor was also a Social Democrat, Hermann Müller, one of the more powerful members of the party's central committee. It was not insignificant that Erzberger became minister of finance, since this was bound to become an increasingly critical post in the months ahead.

It was at the meeting of the National Assembly on June 22 that the universal sense of shock at the Entente's treaty found its strongest expression. But every responsible member knew that his words would do nothing to alter his nation's fate and that the only question was whether the government was empowered to sign the treaty with the two proposed provisos. The Rightists remained obdurately opposed. A moderate German Nationalist, Count Posadowsky, formerly an imperial minister, spoke for his party. He described as transitory the consequences of refusing to sign, while arguing that the treaty, if accepted, "would deliver countless generations of our people to misery." For the other side, Haase insisted that refusal to sign would invite certain ruin. The resolution which stated the National Assembly's declaration in favor of accepting the treaty was passed, 237 to 138. The majority included, besides most of the

Social Democrats and Centrists, six Democrats. Among these was Friedrich Payer, former vice-chancellor and, until his vote, chairman of his party's delegation.[25] Of the Social Democrats, Scheidemann, Landsberg, and Wolfgang Heine, among others, chose to be absent.

But anyone who thought that with this act the tragedy had run its course was quickly torn from his dreams. The German militarists, as could be expected, were quick to do their share to stifle a tendency on the part of any Allied statesmen to view the German plight with sympathy. On the same day that the Allies received from the German ambassador, von Haniel, his government's statement that it was ready to sign the treaty with two provisos, they learned that at Scapa Flow the German crews had scuttled the fleet due, by treaty terms, to be delivered to the West, and that in the Berlin armory the similarly destined French flags had been lost in fire. Naturally the Big Three were enraged. Wilson said he finally realized that when dealing with Germans one was not dealing with honorable men. He, as well as Lloyd George, refused any further extension of the armistice for this very reason.[26] In full concord with them, Clemenceau replied immediately with the statement, amounting to an ultimatum, that the time for German requests was past, that the Allies would accept neither changes nor provisos but demanded of Germany a clear declaration of its acceptance or rejection of the treaty in its present form. His allusion to the fact that the Germans had less than twenty-four hours of their week left could not be misunderstood.

The excitement in Weimar upon receipt of this ultimatum was tremendous, and it was increased by the threatening attitude of the officers' corps. For weeks the officers had been protesting the "shameful paragraphs" of extradition and now they threatened open resistance or, at the least, their resignations if the government were to yield upon this point. This movement received support through a telegram from Hindenburg, alluding to a conference held on June 16 at which, in the presence of the Supreme Command, spokesmen for a large number of officers threatened with their resignations any government that might accept the "shameful paragraphs." "On this issue there has been no change in the position of the Supreme Command." [27] General von Märker who, with his National Defense Forces, had the task of protecting the National Assembly and the government, told the Centrist leaders that his men would not defend a government which signed the treaty and he thus could no longer guarantee law and order.

The pressures became so acute that Noske felt obliged to tender his resignation — which Ebert refused. Ebert then took personal part in the affairs: he called the Supreme Command in Kolberg by tele-phone in order to ascertain clearly the generals' attitude toward the signing of the treaty and the threatening officers' revolt. Gröner spoke for the generals; Hindenburg chose to leave the room.[28] Gröner declared once more that military resistance was useless. He then went on to urge that Noske should not only stay in office, but under-take the leadership of his people and assume responsibility for signing the treaty. Noske should explain in a manifesto the necessity of such a step and demand of every officer that he remain at his post and do his duty in order that the fatherland be saved. Only thus, Gröner argued, could the government remain sure of its officers and prevent military uprisings at home and adventures in the east. In other words, he advised Ebert in unequivocal terms to sign the treaty even with its "shameful paragraphs." There is no doubt that Hinden-burg knew of this advice. But he did nothing to counteract its effect even though his previous — and, of course, well-publicized — telegrams had given the nation to believe that he entertained quite different opinions on the matter. Thus he made it possible for the German Nationalists to quote him in support of their irresponsible political game. And those better acquainted with the facts declined to make it clear that it was Hindenburg who had advised the Em-peror to flee to Holland. The Hindenburg Legend had to be main-tained at any cost. This is certainly what Gröner meant when he later said that, in the years after 1918, he had deliberately sacri-ficed his reputation to his country, in order that Hindenburg's might be preserved.[29] But if Gröner thought that he had thus earned a claim to Hindenburg's gratitude, he erred just as surely as did those who later placed their faith in Hindenburg's much-vaunted loyalty.

The national government could no longer ignore the fact that, things being as they were, there was no choice but to sign the treaty as it stood. It would really have been a case of swallowing camels but straining at gnats to have let the peace founder on these "points of honor" after accepting all the infinitely more important and more burdensome demands of territorial losses and reparations.[30] But the government needed the assent of the National Assembly, convoked on June 23, for such a step. One can hardly doubt that by far the majority of the delegates shared the government's opinion that the treaty had to be signed. General Seeckt, certainly no man disposed to accept surrenders lightly, wrote at that time to a friend: "Be-lieve me, very many who voted against signing did so because they knew that if they spoke in favor of signing the treaty would be held against them personally."[31] But the coalition parties feared, and with good reason, lest their assent serve as grist for the chauvinistic mill of the demagogic Right.[32] Ebert therefore asked the opposition to form a government, naturally with negative results. At this point Heinze, a delegate of the People's Party, found a way out both for the government and for the opposition, a way which would avoid another ballot. He proposed that the preceding vote be interpreted to mean that though the Rightist opposition did not favor signing, the government was empowered to sign the treaty with no provisos, and further that the opposition would not use this arrangement for their own partisan political advantage. Leaders of the Right eagerly snatched at this solution. Payer, who took part in this critical conversation later observed, "Under the pressure of events, the desire of the antisigners to avoid an imminent catastrophe became so strong that they accepted this solution even at the cost of sacrificing their official policy." [33]

The coalition parties consequently required the opposition to state explicitly and publicly that, in their opinion, those who favored acceptance of the treaty were impelled by patriotism alone. Democrats and members of the *Volkspartei* made this declaration in the open Assembly without condition. The statement by the German Nationalists was more guarded, but there was no doubt that they too wished to help avoid disaster. The armistice had only four more hours to run! The Assembly moved that the government be empowered, without regard to provisos, to sign the treaty. And eighty minutes before the time was out a telegram was handed to Clemenceau informing him of Germany's unconditional acquiescence. Five days later, on June 28, 1919, the actual signing took place, again in the Hall of Mirrors at Versailles, thus bringing the war, after almost five years, to formal close. Hermann Müller and Bell, his Centrist minister of transport, had volunteered for the thankless task of signing.

More than thirty years have passed since that June day. The world has seen parts of the treaty never put in force and others — some sooner, some later — rescinded. The world has watched Germany, once seemingly doomed to permanent weakness, recover, indeed, become monstrously strong, and use its new powers to challenge its old foes to war again, again to lose. Thirty years' time means that the generation which lived those days in fevered excitement has grown old or died. Can one assume, to use a phrase of Hegel's, that a form of life has now grown old and that the dusk has fallen in which wisdom, Minerva's owl, can take her flight? It ought to be possible now to discuss the treaty of 1919 dispassionately and without total acceptance of any one party's point of view. Both sides must have learned by now that a world-wide war of such duration involves unspeakable evils for *all* contestants, no matter who may be said to have won; that its consequences press inescapably upon victors and victims alike; and that only demagogues with neither conscience nor restraint can say the treaty alone shaped the aftermath.

To say this is certainly not to say that the treaties which brought World War I to an end were examples of masterful statesmanship. Everyone today recognizes their basic error: the dismemberment of the Austro-Hungarian state. Bismarck had always insisted that the health of Europe depended upon the integrity and strength of Austria-Hungary, and history has proved him right. Even many a Czech in Prague must find himself longing for the good old Hapsburg days when the greatest curse he had to bear was the flag-waving Sunday promenades of the German students.

But the peacemakers of Versailles were not the only ones who must bear responsibility for this fateful development. Franz Josef's amateurish, incapable advisers who led the Empire to catastrophe were also heavily responsible. And so were those nationalistic hotspurs in *all* the states of the Hapsburg monarchy who sought to further their own so-called "national rights" rather than to promote the welfare of their common state. Actually the dismemberment of the Hapsburg Empire was less a work of the peace conference of 1919 than it was of 1918. The last year of the war had given to the restless national groups an opportunity to fashion faits accomplis which the victorious great powers themselves could not have altered even if they had not already been bound to their doctrine of "self-determination of all nations."

It was tragic but, on the basis of Wilson's program, which Germany had accepted with its armistice, predictable that this doctrine would also cut deeply into Germany. For in his Thirteenth Point, Wilson had insisted not only upon the establishment of an independent Polish state, but also on its "free and secure access to the sea." To be sure, the determination of territories with "undisputably Polish populations" was not as simple as Wilson obviously had first believed, and one may well assume that the border which the treaty finally drew gave many a predominantly German district to Poland. But this could not be avoided in the face of the region's ethnic confusion, a product both of history and of Germany's deliberate colonization policy. The principal source of German complaint was the Polish Corridor between East Prussia and Danzig on the one side and Germany proper on the other. This was a most strange creation indeed, for which scarcely an example was to be found in all history. But the Entente could quote Wilson's Points as authority for even this. The German delegation had made the counterproposition that "the Poles be assured free and secure access to the sea through an international guarantee which would establish free harbors in Danzig, Königsberg, and Memel; grant shipping rights upon the Vistula; and conclude special railway agreements." But the Allies preferred the reciprocal solution of giving Germany special traffic rights through the Corridor (Article 89). Lloyd George pointed out that, if the Germans had considered a privileged route through foreign lands good enough for Poles, they could hardly argue in the same breath that such a route between East and West Prussia would not satisfy the provinces' needs, particularly since most of this traffic customarily went by sea. Anyway, the population of the Corridor was principally Polish.[34] The great powers were probably influenced in their decision by the consideration that they would always find it easier to hold Poland to these international guarantees than Germany, which was bound to remain a great power and which would in all certainty tower over Poland once again.

One must also admit that the Allies tried hard to respect the right to self-determination of the German population in this area. Evidence of these efforts includes not only the plebiscites required in Allenstein, Marienwerder, and especially in Upper Silesia, but also the establishment of the Free City of Danzig. Yet even here the seeds of tragedy were already sown. In every geographic sense Danzig was Poland's natural seaport; ethnically, however, it was a completely German city. How were these two conflicting vital truths to be reconciled? The Big Three thought they had found the solution in the free city, under the supervision of the League of Nations but with explicit economic privileges reserved for Poland. This was probably the best answer; at any rate, no one suggested a better. But at the same time it was an extremely artificial solution, and, like all artificial solutions, it not only provoked unceasing quarrels, but also invited, through its provisional appearance, any and every one to find another answer.[35] Thus Danzig became a constant source of international unrest. This all might have been avoided if the Allies, with brutal favoritism, had joined Danzig to Poland, and restricted their own subsequent role to an effective, international protection of minority rights there. Had this been done, Danzig would perhaps have been spared the present fate of becoming a purely Polish city from which the Germans have been driven out empty-handed.

Equally unfortunate was the decision to separate, in furthest East Prussia, the city of Memel — where once Frederick William III and Queen Louise had sought refuge from Napoleon — from the rest of Germany. Memel was another German city in the corner of a foreign, here Lithuanian, land. But the Lithuanians in this area had always considered themselves Prussians and certainly did not wish to be separated from the Reich. The real reason for their separation from Germany was the Allies' wish to give the new Republic of Lithuania access to the sea. The three Baltic States, Estonia, Latvia, and Lithuania, which, like Finland, had torn themselves free of Bolshevik Russia, were now of as much interest to the Entente as they had been to Germany before her defeat. But the effective influence which the West could exercise here was by no means as great.

Originally the Memel region was to be governed by the League of Nations. But after the Poles had robbed the Lithuanians of Vilna while the League only looked on helplessly, the Lithuanians felt free to make good their loss by annexing Memel. Again the League had no choice but to legalize the crime after the fact (January 1923), contenting itself with the imposition of a Memel Convention on Lithuania, which assured the region some autonomy and its German minority some degree of protection (May 6, 1924). It goes without saying that Lithuania was much too weak to hope to defend her booty against an arisen Germany.

There is little to be said about the boundary changes in North Schleswig. Not only did they correspond to local wishes, as the plebiscite revealed; they also enjoyed historical precedents. In the west, the temporary internationalization of the Saar was opposed with the argument, in particular, that this was the first step toward annexation of the region by France. But this indictment has already been answered by historical fact.

Much more important and, in a certain manner, especially painful to German sentiment was the loss of Alsace-Lorraine. But the nation should have expected this once it accepted Wilson's Fourteen Points — although Hindenburg, as we saw above, evidently never comprehended what was at stake. As a matter of fact, the German delegation asked only for a plebiscite on this issue. But Wilson, in his Eighth Point, had made no mention of votes. He had simply insisted that "the wrong done to France by Prussia in 1871 in the matter of Alsace-Lorraine . . . should be righted." And even the Germans, who in no way regarded their acquisition of the provinces as unjust, always knew that these provinces would be lost again whenever France should win a German war. The denial of a plebiscite made perfect sense to the French since Bismarck had refused one in 1871. At that time the population had clearly manifested deep opposition to German annexation, and their subsequent representatives in the German parliament continued to protest in unison. There was not the slightest sign of such distress at the prospect of reunion with France.

To these territorial losses in Europe must be added that part of Upper Silesia which was awarded to Poland on the strength of the plebiscite of March 1921. But we will deal with this at greater length below.

Total German losses in Europe approximated six million souls and 70,000 square kilometers, or 13 percent of the prewar Reich. These losses would, of course, have been more than counterbalanced if the Allies had granted the German request for union with Austria. If you rob us of old lands in the name of Wilson's "right of self-determination," the Germans argued, then you should be willing to let the German Austrians join themselves to us, as their constitution clearly shows they desire. Logically the argument was completely sound; but politically it was, just as completely, unsound. Could anyone seriously expect that the Allies, after summoning up their last ounce of strength to defeat Germany, would allow their enemy to use the peace in such a way as to grow even stronger than before? Would not the French, already alarmed by the numerical superiority of the Germans, be certain to fear a war of revenge launched by a Greater Germany united, for the first time, into one national state? Could any politically sophisticated man, even in Germany, expect the French to say "yes" and "amen" and thus declare all their recent, massive sacrifices to have been wasted and in vain?

In any event the conquerors sought to avert the danger of a war of revenge by drastically limiting Germany's ability to arm (Articles 159–213). They abolished German universal military service (Article 173) and restricted the Army to 100,000 men. The great General Staff, in which the Allies saw concentrated the embodiment of German militarism, was dissolved and permanently banned (Article 160). Similarly the Navy was reduced to six battleships and a few smaller craft; the rest was to be turned over to the victors (Article 185). Submarines were simply forbidden (Articles 188–191). Aircraft were permitted only for civilian purposes (Article 198). Inter-Allied inspection committees, armed with broad powers, were to supervise the execution of these provisions (Article 203 ff.).

All these articles cut deeply into the flesh of German sovereignty, reminding the historian of the hard terms of the Peace of Tilsit in 1807. But some sort of precautionary measures of this kind were indispensable from the Allied point of view. For four years they had witnessed the unexampled military capabilities of the German state, against which an entire world in arms had been able to prevail only at the cost of extreme exertion; and they found the root of this dangerous power in universal military service, which always struck at least the Anglo-Saxons as an inhuman and barbaric institution. They had disdain and fear for the German military spirit, the twin supports of which they thought to be the great army of German career officers and their kindred reservists.

It was true that they now faced a German government which certainly was not militaristic; indeed many of its members had fought German militarism throughout their lives. But who could guarantee the Allies that this or similarly minded governments would always be in power? All the reports that Lloyd George and Wilson received from their agents in Germany agreed that the present government was weak and anything but beloved by its people. And who would follow this one? The Independents, who, according to the reports of some observers, were constantly gaining ground? Or Rightists, whose cries against the peace treaty kept twanging on the German people's nerves? Did not the popular approval of the scuttling of the battle fleet at Scapa Flow and of the burning, in the Berlin Armory, of the flags owed to France show how far these sentiments were spread throughout the land? During the critical debates on signing the treaty had not the officers of Noske's new army demonstrated that they still claimed a voice in their government's most important and most sensitive political decisions? And had not even a Social Democratic government experienced great difficulties in surviving this challenge? And had not these officers and the parties of the Right succeeded in winning the nation's support in the question of the so-called war crimes? It is certainly quite comprehensible and in fact justifiable that the Germans were opposed to the extradition of their soldiers and officers to foreign courts. But how many of these vehement protesters had a sufficient sense of justice to demand, or even wish, trial in German courts of those who had broken the laws of warfare or who had brutally misused their power? The honor of the German people, so frequently and so passionately invoked, would hardly have been stained by the just punishment of such criminals. The fuzzy thinking which manifested itself in these ways showed all too well that, after the brief, sobering experience of November, large elements of the German nation had returned to the worship of their military gods.

But this fact hardly justified all provisions of the treaty, particularly the sharp decrease in the Army to 100,000 men. In view of the disturbances which flamed throughout Germany, sometimes here, sometimes there, this number was insufficient to maintain

order. At the same time, the necessity of quickly reducing the officers'
corps proportionately, and thus of discharging countless officers, including those who had done their duty through these last months
of constant crisis, presented the republican regime with an almost
insoluble problem. The discharged officer and all his close friends
naturally regarded his misfortune as yet another foul trick played on
him by the Republic that he already despised. To be sure, many
industrial firms hastened to offer the former officers positions of
varying degrees of attractiveness. But this only gave them another
opportunity to recount their woes and disappointments to a wider
circle. Thus in a certain respect the requirement that Germany disarm fostered the rebirth of that militaristic spirit which the conquerors had tried so hard to exorcize.

Now, whether or not one considers these provisions for disarmament too severe, one must agree that they could accomplish their
desired end only if executed in rigorous detail. The Allied control
commissions were to see to this. But the commissions, as we shall
see, were completely inadequate for their task. Furthermore, the
Allies themselves had tied the disarmament of Germany to a plan
for general international disarmament. Part Five of the treaty, which
deals with military provisions, begins with the explanatory pre-
amble: "In order to render possible the initiation of a general limitation of the armaments of all nations . . ." The treaty thus embodied
the program which Wilson's Fourth Point had proposed. This program reflected the hopes of great numbers of English and Americans. People of both these countries regarded massive armament as
an irritating obstruction to more fruitful uses of the state and thought
conscription an obsolescent burden. These people tended to believe
that arms breed wars and that, therefore, international disarmament
provides the best way to lasting peace. This theory enjoyed very
little support among the Germans, who therefore placed little faith
in promises of general disarmament. It was precisely to dissolve
these suspicions that the Allies took care to explain, in their final note
of June 16, 1919, that their requirements in regard to German armaments were not *exclusively* directed against Germany with the purpose of making it impossible for Germany to resume her policy of
military aggression. "They are also the first steps toward that
general reduction and limitation of armaments which they seek to
bring about as one of the most fruitful preventatives of war and
which it will be one of the first duties of the League of Nations to
promote." Thus international disarmament, was, according to the
expressed program of the Allies, not to be a *condition* (*Bedingung*)
peculiar to Germany but rather a general *consequence* (*Folgerung*)

of German disarmament. Unfortunately, however, it was much easier to erect a theoretical program in this area than to execute it in reality, for its execution presumed among the great powers a unison of wills which was quickly lost. And so this problem provided the stuff for years of political debate until every possibility of its realization was lost.

The Germans sought to connect their disarmament with their admission to the League of Nations in the company of their conquerors. And the rulers of Germany at that time pressed for admission in all good faith. It is not clear, however, to what extent German popular opinion supported their attempt, to what extent, in other words, the Germans had freed themselves from their former distaste for international organizations designed to keep the peace. One has every reason to assume, however, that a deep and strong current of public opinion would have moved in this direction had the Allies quickly granted this request. But here again one sees how difficult it is for men to turn from the bitter moods of war to the calm and thoughtful ways required by peace. For it was little more than such residual bitterness which kept the Allies from making room for the Germans at the table of nations, around which men were to seek and debate their way to lasting peace. Lloyd George had originally desired Germany's immediate admission to the League.[36] But in the course of the cabinet meeting of June 1 he confessed to a change of opinion: the Allies had first to settle the differences among themselves before inviting Germany to join. Consequently the Allies rejected the German request, explaining that the present temper of national feelings gave them no other alternative and advising the German people to wait until they could "prove by their acts that they intend to fulfill the conditions of the peace" and "have now become a people with whom it is possible to live in neighborly good fellowship."

This attitude only sharpened the bad impression which the Allies had made in taking the German colonies. Every German must have expected the loss of some colonies in the event of defeat. No one could imagine, for instance, that the Japanese would tolerate the ninety-nine year lease of Kiaochow which Germany had extorted in 1898 from a helpless China. But no one was prepared for the total loss of the German colonial domain. Nevertheless one cannot be surprised to learn that the British Dominions in Africa and Australasia opposed the continued existence of German "protectorates" which would constitute direct threats in the event of future war. The Australian Prime Minister Hughes, a Socialist, went so far as to tell Wilson to his face that Australia would not be kept from annexing nearby German colonies even by the protest of the entire civilized world. The old Boer Generals Botha and Smuts were a bit gentler in voicing the demand of the Union of South Africa for the annexation of German Southwest Africa, as was Massey of New Zealand in pressing for Samoa.[37] All these Dominions had made heavy sacrifices of men and treasure and did not wish to give away what had cost so dear.

But in his addresses Wilson had expressly declared himself opposed to annexations, and in his rather obscure Fifth Point he had proposed the general rule for colonial problems: equal consideration of the interests of the population and of the just claims of the mother country. If the Germans thought that these words assured them of keeping at least some of their colonies, they were completely ignorant of Wilson's attitude. At the beginning of the Allies' discussion of the issue Wilson, as Lloyd George recounts, had declared categorically: "We were agreed to oppose the restoration of the German Colonies." [38] This extreme position could be made to conform to the President's published program only if one assumed that a continuation of German colonial rule anywhere in the world would necessarily and without exception be opposed to the best interests of the people concerned. As a matter of fact the Allies had made precisely that assumption. In their letter of enclosure of June 16 they declared roundly: "the native inhabitants of [all] German colonies are strongly opposed to being returned to German control. The record of German rule . . . makes it impossible . . . to give the colonies back to Germany or to entrust Germany with the responsibility of training and educating the natives."

Now this was quite a sweeping statement. It is true enough that the Colonial Office had not been a showpiece of German policy. Before the war the office had often been the object of sharp criticism in Germany itself, and the Allies took pleasure in quoting Reichstag speeches which two present ministers, Erzberger and Noske, had made when in the opposition. But no neutral party could have denied not only that Germany's colonial administration had had its good side and fruitful results, but also that it had been of a distinctly better quality than those of Belgium and Portugal, both members of the Entente. This one-sided moral indignation, directed at the German colonial rule alone, was therefore *bound* to create the impression of hypocrisy and to evoke passionate indignation in Germany.

It was something quite different when the Allies went on to declare that the German government had made use of its colonies in order to threaten world trade. A later sentence explained what all this meant: "[The Allies] felt themselves compelled to safeguard their own security and the peace of the world against a military imperialism which sought to establish bases whence it could pursue a policy of interference and intimidation against the other powers." The German colonies in Africa and Australasia were indeed so situated that they could harbor threats to those avenues of world trade upon which the British Empire was peculiarly dependent. During the war these threats had, to a certain extent, become real, and it was clear that in a future war, especially with the demonstrated efficacy of her submarines, Germany would make even greater use of these bases. At a peace conference of former times this argument would doubtless have sufficed to justify a claim to the German colonies; the Allied statesmen would have been honoring a venerable European tradition if they had rested their decision on these grounds alone. But Wilson's Points and the general American distaste for colonialism forced them to change the old tradition. And thus they coated their realistic designs with a moralistic plaster which hardly matched.

At any rate, the Versailles treaty did make one important and real departure from former practice: there was no mention of open annexation. The lost colonies were turned, instead, into "mandates" of the League under whose supervision and as whose agents the respective great powers were to carry out their trusts. Article 22 of the League's Covenant announced that the purpose of the mandates was to provide for "the well-being and development" of the indigenous populations. The mandates were, in other words, not to be made to serve the interests of their guardians. Consequently the erection of fortifications and of military and naval bases was prohibited, as was the military training of the natives. But the one consolation that this turn of events might have afforded the Germans was destroyed when Germany was refused admission to the League and thus was passed over when the mandates were assigned.

The "theft of the colonies" became a sore spot among the Germans, one out of all proportion to the economic losses it involved. For the colonies had always played an extremely minor role both in the German economy and in emigration from the overcrowded Reich.

But it was not so much their territorial losses, nor the so-called points of honor, but rather the reparations which gave the Germans cause for deepest concern.[39] And in time reparations were to give even the statesmen of the West more headaches than all the other clauses of the treaty. They represented one of the most complex and bitter problems which peacemakers could be asked to face. For this war, the books of which were now being closed, exceeded by far, in its extent and effects, all the wars of history. Where before had such armies of millions ever been set in march? When before had battles of such monstrous size and of such duration raged, destroying every flower that bloomed? When before had men reckoned by the million the tons of shipping lost? When before had massive armies of the ultimate loser occupied their foe's land for years, deliberately destroying thousands of factories and mines? Napoleon's campaign against Prussia in 1806–1807 had lasted nine months; the Franco-Prussian War of 1870–1871, only six. But in this war men had fought for fifty-one months. If ever Hegel was correct in saying that beyond a certain point differences of degree became differences of kind, that point was reached here. Repayment for all the misery that this war had brought mankind, if only in the sense that the loser pay his victors' damages, was clearly impossible.

But the problem was made even more complicated by the fact that Wilson, in his program, had taken an explicit stand against what had previously been called "indemnities" to meet the costs of war. Earlier conquerors had simply rounded off, upwards, their military expenses and presented the victim with the bill. This is what Napoleon did after Jena, and Bismarck after Sedan. The victor tended to rationalize this course of action by arguing that his vanquished foe would have more difficulty in waging a war of revenge if he were well drained of his financial blood. Everyone is familiar with Bismarck's disappointment that France, thanks to Thiers' fiscal mastery, was able to repay the sum, astronomical in those days, of five billion francs in only two and one-half years.

President Wilson completely rejected this practice. In an address to the American Congress as early as December 1917 he had argued against avenging one evil with another, and on February 11, 1918, he had declared with his customary crispness: "There shall be no annexations, no contributions, no punitive damages." These words stood in the sharpest opposition imaginable to the official plans of Germany — as long as it could hope to win the war. Indeed, the imperial minister of finance, Helfferich, had justified his irresponsible financing of the war through bonds and bills with the argument that the defeated foe could be made to pay it all. We cling fast, he stated, to the hope of being able to present the bill for this war we did not seek to our enemies when they come begging peace. If, to the war debts, one adds the treasury bills issued during the war, one arrives at a figure in excess of 150 billion gold marks. This was, in other words, the minimal burden which Helfferich would have had a victorious Germany impose upon her foes. Had the Allies followed the same formula, they could have presented the Central Powers with an indemnity of almost 500 billion marks.[40]

But did Wilson's rejection — which the Allies had perforce to accept — of war damages in the traditional sense mean that the reparations question had ceased to exist? By no means. For there were still the damages which the German forces had inflicted upon the Allies' civilian populations, particularly in the occupation of Belgium and northern France and in the submarine campaign. Here Wilson had quite different views. In his Fourteen Points he had demanded the restoration of Belgium and northern France (Points 7 and 8). His demand was clarified by Lansing's note of November 5, 1918, immediately before the armistice: "Compensation will be made by Germany for all damage done to the civilian population of the Allies and their property by the aggression of Germany by land, by sea, and from the air." This was, as explained above, accepted by Germany as a condition and constituent element of its armistice. Hindenburg and Ludendorff, at any rate, in their message of September 15, 1917, to Chancellor Michaelis, had nonchalantly declared: "The mutual understanding that our neighbors will bear the costs of the severe damages we have caused will hardly strike anyone as a gain of consequence for us." Yet Germany's obligation, pressed upon her in defeat, to make good these "severe damages" proved to be the greatest, the most burdensome, and the most exasperating problem of the postwar years. And among those who complained the loudest about this "tribute" was, of course, General Ludendorff himself. In considering this aspect of the peace, one dare not forget that the allies, especially the French, accused the German Army of having deliberately destroyed factories and mines in northern France, not out of military necessity, but rather to weaken for a long time France's ability to compete with German industry. As proof of this charge they cited an extensive memorandum of February 1916 from the quartermaster-general of the German Army which had been circulated among German chambers of commerce and trade associations.[41]

The assembled statesmen of the West faced as their first task, therefore, the determination of just which kinds of damages were to be regarded as covered by the critical clause and what these damages amounted to; then, since it soon became apparent that astronomical sums were at stake, they had to calculate what fraction of all this Germany could possibly be made to pay. The simple truth that one cannot squeeze blood from a turnip was hardly unknown to a man like Lloyd George; he had even voiced it, if only softly, in the heat of the British election campaign.

It proved almost impossible to determine these sums. The damages were naturally thought higher by those who had suffered than by those who were going to have to pay, or by those neutral parties who wanted a quick settlement of this part of the problem. This has always been the case in civil suits. No one can therefore be surprised that the French demanded sums for the restoration of their ruined north which seemed fantastic not only to the Americans but to the British as well. Scholars still debate the restoration's total cost, which France finally had to bear essentially alone, reckoned in the gold francs which no longer existed.[42] But at least in these questions of actual damages one had a concrete base from which one could proceed, whereas the estimation of Germany's ability to pay required the manipulation of unknowns and guesses about the future. For it was obvious that at best the payments would have to be extended over several decades. But who could pretend to know with any sort of accuracy what the state of the German economy would be in twenty or twenty-five years and what manner of reparation it would then be able to pay? No wonder then that the so-called experts' estimates differed widely. The British Treasury set 40 billion gold marks as the upper limit of what Germany could be expected to pay within one generation. Yet a commission of economic experts hit upon a figure twenty times higher, and among these experts were such men as the governor of the Bank of England, Lord Cunliffe.

All these estimates regularly ignored one special factor of uncertainty: the subjective attitude of those who were to pay. Reparations have to be drawn from the members of the debtor state through assessments and taxes. But one is foolish to believe that these payments can be made to come in automatically, as though from robots. Their yield will always depend to a certain extent upon the cooperation of those being taxed. Now this spirit of cooperation will strike its lowest ebb if the tax returns serve a purpose which the taxpayers oppose, especially if the taxpayers oppose the government as well. This attitude was all too common among many Germans of means. These people, who in the final analysis would pay a good share of the reparations, did not recognize the German Republic as their legitimate government and either contested or ignored its claim to rule.

In any event these variables were so numerous, and the aims and interests of the relevant countries so disparate, that no definite sum could be arrived at in the months of the peace conference. The financial experts, particularly those of the United States and England, emphatically recommended that a definite sum be set in the peace treaty, for only in this way could the uncertainties be obviated, uncertainties which would obstruct every step in German reconstruction and every move in international finance. But they did not succeed. What the Americans proposed seemed utterly insufficient to the French; and what the French demanded, the Americans thought impracticable. In the face of these differences the Allies found themselves forced to settle for a provisional compromise. The task of determining a final reparation figure was delegated to an Allied Reparations Commission which was given until May 1, 1921, to establish a system of payments designed to begin at that date and to erase the reparation debt in thirty years (Article 233).

To this the German delegation responded with a request for an immediate definition of the debt, and itself proposed the sum of 100 billion gold marks, to be paid in annual installments with no interest. Dr. Helfferich's description of this offer as "mad," "irresponsible," and "bankrupt bungling" serves to illustrate the moods prevalent in many German circles.[43] The Allies for their part calculated that a non–interest-bearing debt of 100 billion marks amortized over fifty or sixty years represented a present value of only about 30 billion marks.[44] Even so, they would have done well to accept the Germans' offer. The future was to show that they would thus have received more money than the Germans actually paid and they might have snuffed out a smouldering fire which kept Europe uneasy for years. But they insisted, instead, on carrying out their treaty compromise and gave the German government only the right to make proposals, within the following four months, concerning the determination of the reparations.

Still another issue remains to be mentioned, one which played a large role in journalistic and political discussions of the next few years. Among the damages for which Germany was held responsible, according to Annex I to Article 232, were "all pensions and compensation in the nature of pensions to naval and military victims of war (including members of the air force) . . . and to the dependents of such victims." The Germans were not alone in their vehement objection that such pensions could not possibly fall under the category of "damages done to the civilian populations of the Allies" as set forth in the American note of November 5, 1918. Originally President Wilson shared their view.[45] He abandoned this position because of General Smuts' memorandum of March 31. More forceful perhaps than its argument was the personality of its author, whose sense of justice was undoubted and of whom even the Americans reported that throughout the conference his head stayed cool.[46] Such a man could not fail to make an impression when he said that it was only common sense and a clear interpretation of the note of November 5, if one took it to include all damages suffered by any Allied national, whether or not in uniform. But an objective jurist must insist that common opinion distinguishes between civilians and military personnel, that when a document states that only civilian damages are to be paid, it means thereby to bar all military persons and their dependents from making such a claim.

The full significance of this controversy can be regarded from many points of view. In the first place, the capitalized value of all these pensions was extremely large, larger in fact than the sum of all other civilian damages. In the second place, the Allied leaders were resolved that, while Germany was to be made to pay all that a generation possibly could, even under the best of circumstances this sum would fall far short of Western claims. From this point of view the addition of pensions was seen to effect no real increase in the German debt.[47] But this addition was of utmost importance in determining the allocation of Germany's payments among her creditors, the Allies. For while France, for example, had borne a greater share of the material damage than had England, these nations' roles were reversed with respect to pensions. This fact affected the attitudes of such men as Lloyd George. But if one asks how much of these pension claims Germany ever paid, the answer can only be: none.

Along with the entire burden of reparations, the treaty adjustment of private prewar debts among nationals of the two sides was settled to Germany's disadvantage. The treaty stated that this adjustment should be made exclusively between the states of the parties concerned. These states then had the further responsibility of satisfying the private creditors and of collecting from the debtors. The treaty went on to stipulate that the prewar debts were to be settled at prewar rates of exchanges, that is, German debts to England were to be paid at twenty marks to the pound sterling. The German government had to accept this rate in adjusting its foreign accounts. But the private German creditor paid his debt to his government at the going rate of exchange, which, by the time the treaty was signed, had fallen by a third and was soon to fall much further still. The consequence was that the Reich had to assume a loss that amounted to millions of pounds.[48]

It is not our intent here to examine all the countless provisions of this thick treaty. Our remarks are designed solely to provide some general basis for a critical evaluation of it. Undoubtedly this was a very severe, very burdensome peace for Germany. The question whether it was also a "just" peace is hard to answer because there was no one norm that was commonly recognized by the parties involved and because so many different points of view were represented. Even those who would deny the Allies' thesis that the Central Powers started the war cannot deny the simple fact that the victors believed it true and thus thought themselves justified in placing heavy punishments upon their vanquished foes. And similar differences existed among the parties' forecasts of the future. The German representatives at Versailles could state in good faith that with this shattering defeat their nation had lost all taste for militarism and would never entertain the notion of revenge. But these earnest protestations did not alter the fact that the French did believe firmly in this danger and were deeply intent upon using the treaty to forestall it. And who today can still maintain that these fears were groundless? One might perhaps argue that the war of revenge would never have come if the Allies had made a gentler peace. The merits of this argument will become apparent in the account of later experiences in general and of Allied concessions in particular.

Germany's territorial losses were very considerable when taken as a whole and thus could not but occasion sorrow in the nation. But Germany's *unity* had been preserved, and this was more valuable than any territories lost. Even after her losses Germany remained a country of over 460,000 square kilometers, with a population of more than 60 million, which made it, except for Russia, by far the largest European nation. In the face of the bonds imposed by the treaty these facts afforded little consolation in a military sense but were all the more encouraging from an economic standpoint, especially to a nation so industrious and technically apt. It was only human that the Germans overlooked this in their excited debate about the treaty, and one should not let oneself be too surprised at the words the otherwise calm and reasonable labor leader Leipart used in February 1920: "The slavery which was abolished in Africa is about to be introduced in Europe." But as soon as the inflation was over, every fair-minded person had to agree that the Germans had by no means become, nor did they feel like, slaves.

The final point made in the German counterproposals sounds odd to us today: that this treaty marks "the last frightful triumph . . . of a dying *capitalist* civilization." We now know that "imperialist" tendencies can be combined with a most vigorous anticapitalism and that a Communist state can exact reparations from a defeated foe more ruthlessly and forcefully that can a "capitalist" state, which is ever mindful that someday the facts of international economic life will have to be faced and that yesterday's enemy is not only the competitor, but also the customer, of tomorrow. It was exactly this truth which large circles of German thought refused to face. Those who before the war had pressed for a German battle fleet lest England be free to destroy the German commercial competitor felt encouraged by the rotten fruits of their advice to argue after the war that England was now using the peace treaty to rid itself of its most dangerous economic rival. But whoever is familiar with the English literature on the treaty knows that the responsible leaders of Great Britain never lost sight of their national interest in as prompt a resumption as possible of full world trade and were fully aware of the important share that Germany would necessarily have in this market. In any event they stuck to their policy of free trade, and thus afforded Germany its best opportunity to find its place once more in international commerce.

Considerably better grounded, as we have seen, was the German complaint that the treaty diverged sharply from Wilson's stated program. At any rate the treaty contains several points which require a great deal of clever casuistry if they are to be brought into harmony with the Fourteen Points. The Germans, to be sure, in their heated polemics tended often to ignore those of Wilson's Points which were not in their favor, or else altered the meaning of these at will. It was simply grotesque that Bernhard W. von Bülow, later state secretary for foreign affairs, opened his book about the "Versailles League of Nations" with a bald reference to the "Versailles betrayal." [49] And Bülow was clearly no nationalistic war hawk; he had, as a matter of fact, joined the Democratic Party. Any man of his experience should have realized from the beginning that a dozen or so principles sent from across the Atlantic would hardly solve the enormous problem of fitting together all the pieces of a Europe that had been blown apart; and he should have known that Wilson, like every idealist, would have to water his wine when faced by hard fact. But the worst part of this sweeping condemnation, which was repeated by millions of the uninformed, was the false notion it created that Wilson's promises had seduced Germany into accepting an armistice it would otherwise have disdained. People were only too willing to ignore two facts which contradict this legend: Germany laid down her weapons only when military leaders could find no alternative; and only then did she accept the Points she had previously rejected with scorn.

If one wishes to arrive at some reasonably balanced judgment on the issue of the Points, one might say that, in many ways, the Allies did in fact fail to fulfill Wilson's program. But the Germans were also at fault, for they too wanted to bend the Points to suit their own needs and they too overly exaggerated the significance of later modifications of the treaty. These faults bore tragic fruit for the next generation of Germans. Franklin D. Roosevelt, then assistant secretary of the navy, had an intimate view of Woodrow Wilson's tragedy, the lesson of which was not lost on him. As a constant reminder of this grand failure Roosevelt kept a picture of the earlier president constantly in his office. He had pondered the unfortunate effects that the publication of the peace aims had worked upon Wilson's reputation, both at the time and in history, and was resolved to avoid these dangers for himself. This was certainly one of the motives which impelled him to the other extreme when, in January 1943, he suddenly announced the dictum that only Germany's *unconditional surrender* would bring the Second World War to an end.

In 1918 this was all part of the uncertain future. At that time the falsification of the facts, abetted by popular indignation at the treaty, had important domestic consequences. For it played into the hands of the defeated generals and their militaristic admirers. From this point it was only a short step to the further legend that the German Army really had never been defeated at all.

This militaristic turn taken by the popular indignation at an "imposed" peace was the most dangerous consequence in the long run. For it was to threaten not only the peace of the world, but also the very existence of the German Republic. It soon became apparent that the German statesmen had taken a step that was loaded with fateful implications when they, rather than the generals, trod the thorny, thankless road to Marshal Foch and signed the armistice. Hindenburg, who had prudently stayed far from Compiègne, quickly rewon his place in his nation's heart, while Erzberger, whose name was signed to the document of surrender, saw all responsibility heaped upon himself. It is true that the German government's official white book, where the armistice details are set forth at documentary length, made clear that the field marshal had also recommended acceptance of the armistice even if the softening amendments he had asked for were not granted. But who bothered to read collections of official documents in those times? And for those who did, the answer was quickly found that Hindenburg had made his decision not under the pressure of defeat but rather under that of revolution. The legend of the "stab in the back" was already smouldering; it needed only the proper provocation to be whipped into flames. It was so much more comfortable to one's sense of national pride if one blamed Germany's misfortune on the unruly men of the streets, who had won a hollow victory at their Emperor's expense, rather than on the generals, who had been revered for years not only as men of battle, but also as statesmen. In Germany it had been customary to label the French as a vain people and to attribute their cry for revenge after 1871 to injured vanity. But even Bismarck had written: "We are a vain folk, irritated even by not being able to display our vanity." [50]

It was only natural that this mood worked to the advantage of the parties of the Right, who mocked the illusions of the fuzzy-minded republicans, and reminded all who would listen that they had always recognized the "enemy's intent to destroy us." The pledges they had given to the coalition parties in the anxious hours of June 23 were of course quickly forgotten. They now employed every demagogue's trick to brand the coalition as cowards guilty of a "shameful peace." Nor were the Democrats saved by the fact that most of them had voted not to sign. For it was remembered that only a few days earlier they had sat in the cabinet of Centrists and Social Democrats and had collaborated with them in fashioning a constitution for a republic. And many Germans were only too glad to blame this Republic for all their misfortunes. The republicans were in too vulnerable a position to fend off this attack. If only because the treaty was so unpopular, they could not afford, for political reasons, to give the opposition a monopoly in damning Versailles. Furthermore it was hardly possible to point out the share of the public tragedy borne by the annexationists, let alone to remind the German electorate that the major portion of the treaty should surprise no one who had read the Fourteen Points. At the Social Democratic convention in June, when old Eduard Bernstein tried to distinguish justice from injustice in the treaty, he experienced utter defeat, and was even damned by Scheidemann for refusing to transcend his principles for his party's sake.[51]

Keynes's book *The Economic Consequences of the Peace* [52] appeared at this time with important results. It was a brilliant polemic, comparable to Burke's criticism of the French Revolution in its cogent effect. John Maynard Keynes possessed all the talents necessary for such a tour de force. The clarity and keenness of his mind were equalled by few of his contemporaries. He had thought carefully and long about many problems of many kinds and was a source not only of reasoned conclusions but also of flashing insights. He was one of the first men to specialize in the study of national economics, a subject which he taught at Cambridge, and of fiscal policy, which he had directed for the British Treasury throughout the war. Moreover, he possessed an able style, one which not only permitted him to present the most complex and difficult problems with apparent ease, but also enabled him to sketch unforgettable portraits of the men he criticized. All these talents stood at the disposal of Keynes's wrath at the injustice which he believed the Germans had suffered at Versailles. Just before the transmission of the final Allied note, Keynes resigned his post in the English delegation to the conference principally because of the decision of the Big Three to include in the bill for reparations pensions owed to widows and the wounded. Keynes regarded this move as a violation of the Fourteen Points, upon the strength of which the armistice had been signed; in his book he spoke of the "masterful sophistry" to which Wilson had submitted. But Keynes did not disclose to his readers that the memorandum thus described stemmed from that same General Smuts whom he considered his partner in the fight for a just peace and who had encouraged him to write this very book. He was especially obligated to mention this man's name since he went on to place this interpretation of the concept "reparations" on the same level as Germany's violation of Belgian neutrality.[53]

Indignation can lend wings to prose, particularly if the prose is as clever and precise as that of Keynes. But at times, especially when his arguments are pouring forth with ease and he is finding truest pleasure in his wit, indignation can bear the author farther than he can later justify in cooler blood. This danger becomes all the greater when he fails to restrict his writing to the fields of his competence. Winston Churchill has said of Keynes: "His qualifications to speak on the economic aspects [of the treaty] were indisputable; but on the other and vastly more important side of the problem he could judge no better than many others." [54] Today one can even add that with his doctrinaire prejudices Keynes was even less qualified than many others. In 1919, when he wrote that "future dangers do not lie in boundary and territorial questions, but rather in questions of food, coal, and commerce," he was sure of approval, for he was echoing certain general attitudes which passed at that time for a particularly modern philosophy of history. To all this the reader of today, who has lived the real history of the last thirty years, can only shake his head. We all have learned through experience that the attempt to institute "a new Napoleonic hegemony" did not, as Keynes had sought to persuade his contemporaries, exist solely "in the imaginations of the timid."

Most important of all was Keynes's failure to realize that in Germany, where his book naturally was read with great interest and approval, he was dealing with a reading public radically different from the Englishmen he knew. In England political self-criticism, that is, the critical examination of the policies of one's own country, not only is traditional, it also fails to reflect upon the critic's patriotism in any way. In Germany this sort of national self-criticism is considered objectionable and unseemly. Keynes's ecstatic German readers never asked themselves what would have befallen a countryman of theirs who had dared to criticize Bismarck's Peace of Frankfurt even half as sharply. General Vogel von Falkenstein had had Johann Jakoby arrested and brought to prison for opposing the annexation of Alsace-Lorraine as a violation of "a people's right to selfdetermination" — this at a time when the annexation was not yet even official governmental policy. This outspoken behavior made Jakoby so unpopular among his fellow Democrats that he finally left them for the Social Democrats, a step politically and socially tantamount to self-exile in the desert. Keynes's book made him, to be sure, quite unloved by the English government of that time, but neither academically, politically, socially, nor in any manner did that government impede or harm the brilliant career which he concluded as one of his nation's most respected men, as its official representative, and as a member of its House of Lords.

Thus it was that his manifesto had a quite different effect in Germany from what Keynes himself had wished. For it served as a complete confirmation to all those who had been shrieking about the "shameful peace" and the "*Diktat* of Versailles"; those who insisted that the primary, indeed the single, purpose of German policy should be to circumvent the treaty; those who branded as treason any policy of "fulfillment" or rapprochement; and those who sensed a pleasant relief from any feeling of guilt over their violation of Belgian neutrality once Keynes had accused the Allies of an equivalent violation of international morality. It was in the nature of things that the brilliant and often, necessarily, quite abstract passages in which Keynes argued for a reduction of the reparations to an economically feasible sum were comprehended by only a small minority of his German readers, while his sharp condemnation of the way the reparations were dealt with in the treaty burned itself indelibly into every German mind, where it generally was simplified into the conclusion that one was justified in opposing any and every reparations bill. No German with any serious hope of a political career dared even imply the thought that Germany was legally obligated to pay for even part of the damage she had inflicted on the neighbors she attacked. And if the Germans finally went so far as to attribute all their economic ills not to their having lost a war but simply to the reparations that they paid, Keynes cannot be relieved of his share of the blame; for he had failed to distinguish with sufficient care between these two different chains of cause and effect.

It was of special importance in Germany that Keynes had not

let his title limit his discussion to the economic consequences of the peace. The portraits which he sketched of Wilson, Clemenceau, and Lloyd George were literary masterpieces, all the more likely to impress their German readers since they intentionally emphasized the less attractive traits of each man. Even his biographer, R. F. Harrod, admits that Keynes was not fair to his subjects.[55] Harrod defends him, however, by saying that Keynes was trying through his book to direct popular opinion toward a softening of the peace. As far as his English readers are concerned this may constitute a reasonable excuse for his method; but its effect was bound to be quite different in Germany. For what could be more welcome to a German nationalist than a description of President Wilson as a "blind and deaf Don Quixote" who let an avenging Clemenceau lead him around by the nose? It is quite true that the worst Keynes could say of Clemenceau was that he shared Bismarck's political philosophy. But this did not keep the average German reader from joining Keynes in damning Clemenceau on the one hand while continuing, upon the other, to regard Bismarck as the greatest statesman of all time. Why should the German reader ponder France's need for security if Keynes could so glibly ignore it?

It is therefore little wonder that ninety-nine of every hundred Germans were convinced they had been duped by the armistice, and little wonder too that they felt themselves excused from any careful examination of Wilson's Fourteen Points to see whether and to what extent the Points had been violated by the peace. This mental attitude began to nourish the "stab in the back" legend. Thus to the two villains who had betrayed Germany, the armistice and the revolution, was added yet a third: "that old Presbyterian Wilson" who, as Keynes had so brilliantly proposed, was plagued by a Freudian complex which kept him from accepting rational compromise, lest he thereby admit his former course had been wrong and harmful to the mission given him by God. What could be more soothing to the German conscience than to see an Englishman blame the President of the United States for everything that had gone wrong?

It was precisely in this respect that Keynes's polemic had a further consequence which occasioned considerable pleasure in Germany at that time, but which later worked to the great disadvantage not only of the world peace, but of Germany itself.[56] The American Senate's rejection of the Treaty of Versailles cannot, of course, be blamed on Keynes alone. The principal responsibility for Wilson's severe defeat rests partly upon Wilson's stubbornness, which his illness had now made pathological, and partly upon his short-sighted, narrow-minded opponents, led by Senator Lodge, who were united by partisan politics and personal hatred for the President. But Keynes's book played its part, too. The Senate's initial rejection of the treaty on November 19, 1919, cannot very well have been influenced by the book. But Wilson's opponents felt so uncomfortable with this success that they returned the matter to the Senate floor. At this juncture Keynes's polemic appeared. Not only did it very rapidly become a best seller, but a liberal magazine also hastened to reprint entire sections.

The purposes of these liberal friends of Keynes could not have been more unlike those of Wilson's opponents in the Senate. The liberals wished to soften a peace which Lodge and his supporters already found too mild. Wilson's opposition objected principally to the League of Nations, exactly the *one* part of the treaty on which the liberals set their hopes. But when Keynes's sharp pen lacerated the President's prestige, the Senators could only profit from their opponent's loss. For now they were safe from a popular reaction against their isolationism, especially in the forthcoming presidential election. And so they calmly weighted the treaty down with the "reservations" which finally sank it on March 19, 1920. On this day the constitutional two-thirds majority was missed by seven votes. In the presidential campaign the following November, Warren Harding, the man of "normalcy," was elected. No one could accuse Harding of harboring one bit of the idealism which had inspired Woodrow Wilson. One would do Keynes an injustice if one proposed that he had sought these ends. Indeed an American historian who took part in the peace conference has rightly said: "It would be hard to find in the literature of controversy a work in which the author has so completely ruined his own case as in this instance." [57]

The gaps created by the American failure to ratify the Treaty of Versailles were closed by a separate treaty between Germany and the United States on August 25, 1921. The state of war which had formally existed between the two nations had been unilaterally ended on July 2, 1921, by resolution of the American Congress. In this resolution the United States claimed for itself and its citizens all rights and privileges included in the Versailles treaty. The separate treaty of August 25 embodied this demand. It specified further that America had not joined the League of Nations and did not regard itself obliged to take part in the Reparations Commission. But in their joy at having split the Entente, many Germans failed to see that this isolation of America meant a heavy loss to them. For nothing would have better suited German interests than the active participation of Americans in the execution of the treaty, especially in the adjustment of reparations. Since they had no direct interest in the payments, their presence would have provided a beneficial balance against French demands. One can even assume that the English had been counting on having American colleagues in this work; and Lloyd George openly complained that America's retreat had completely changed the nature of the Reparations Commission.[58]

Similarly, only myopic Germans could find joy in the fact that the American Senate had not only rejected the treaty but had also refused to guarantee the integrity of France. Therewith the English guarantee lost its strength, and France found that she would have to find security by relying solely on her own resources. Consequently, and inevitably, France felt all the more obliged to use to the fullest her present advantage over defeated Germany. She felt equally constrained to ignore completely the moderating counsel of those former Allies who had now, she felt, left her in the lurch.

V

FROM THE TREATY
TO THE KAPP PUTSCH

Now that peace had finally been concluded, the Germans were obliged to start putting their own house in order. The first task was the promulgation, on August 11, 1919, of their new constitution, which legally brought an end to the Revolution and laid the foundation upon which a new political structure might be built. The individual states of Germany also completed their constitutions, although the most important one, Prussia's, was not ready until November 1920.

The Prussian constitutional convention had faced, of course, the same problem that Preuss had tried in his own way to solve: the question of the future relationship between the governments of Prussia and of Germany. A majority of the Prussian convention proposed a far more radical solution than had Preuss; namely, the transformation of Germany into a centralized state. In December 1919 the parties of the Prussian government, Democrats, Social Democrats, and Centrists, introduced a joint resolution instructing their government to request the national government to enter into discussions with the governments of the several lands for the purpose of establishing a truly unitary system for Germany. In spite of vehement protests from the Right this resolution was adopted by an overwhelming majority (210 to 32). It led, however, to no practical results; the obstacles were too great. Yet the understanding these men showed of the problem at hand as well as their desire to assist, where possible, in the nurture of the central government found expression in their decision that Prussia should have no super-parliamentary chief of state. For it would have been an intolerable situation if in Berlin two presidents had been at work, either with or against each other. This meant, of course, that there was no other way to select the Prussian premier than by election in the Prussian Landtag; it also meant that the premier would have to be personally responsible for forming the Prussian cabinet. In practice any parliamentary coalition intent on forming a regime had to arrive at a common understanding concerning their basic policies, their premier, and the number of seats in his cabinet which each party to the coalition might receive. The premier thus chosen by the Landtag would normally proceed to install as "his" ministers the men who had been nominated by each party delegation. Yet later Otto Braun, for one, was to make free use of his constitutional powers, at the particular expense of his own party's wishes.

To the Landtag, which had thus become Prussia's constitutional center of gravity, there was added the Staatsrat, a second house comprised of representatives from the Prussian provinces. This was not an upper chamber in the sense that its approval was necessary before any new law was passed. It is true that it did have a kind of veto power, but the Landtag could, and during the first decade very often did, override the veto with a two-thirds vote. In general the authority of this second house lay in the interpretation and execution of new laws. Its president enjoyed a special function, since he was ex officio a member of the three-man board which had the power to dissolve the Landtag. (The other members were the president of the Landtag and the Prussian premier.) That the constitution also contained numerous provisions for referenda was, in the climate of opinion at that time, quite unavoidable.

Only in one part of Germany did the unification of petty principalities into a larger, viable political body take place. In January 1920, seven small Thuringian states united to form the single land of Thuringia. Their action was ratified, according to Article 18 of the new German constitution, by a federal law of April 30, 1920. In 1924, on the other hand, a Guelphic attempt to undo the work of 1866 and to make Hanover once more free of Prussian rule failed to receive in the referendum even one third of the votes required by the constitution (Article 18, Paragraph 4, Section 2).

But constitutions can only provide the legal framework for the real work of reconstruction, and, after four years of war and months of revolutionary change, this work was more than timely. The poverty of the public purse was especially acute. The war, and particularly the way it was financed, had ruined the finances of the state and the value of the mark. For the Empire had sought to pay for the war not through taxes but through loans; in other words, it had asked future generations, rather than the living, to pay the costs. Now it is true that the expenses of a long modern war are so great that even the wealthiest country cannot meet them without mortgaging its future to some extent. But none of the belligerent states went as far as Germany in sparing the present generation the costs of war. This policy makes sense only when one remembers Helfferich's plan, noted above, of having a prostrate foe pay for the war, and when one recalls the blind assurance of victory which filled the hearts and minds of influential Germans at that time. There were, to be sure, exceptions, like Chancellor Bethmann-Hollweg; but it was his being just such an exception that made him so unpopular among those men of power who, like their Emperor, "had no use for pessimists."

The result of this financial policy was that Germany ended the war with a national debt of 144 billion marks, of which 89 billion were in long-term bonds and 55 billion in paper.[1] One might compare these figures with Helfferich's estimates of 1913: that Germany's national income was 40 billion marks and her total national wealth between 290 and 320 billion.[2]

To be sure, the mark of 1919 was a far cry from what it had been in 1913. Its value had fallen by more than one third, and, with it, the war debt's weight. But here an even more fateful aspect of Helfferich's policy became apparent: it obviously did not cause the inflation, but it certainly sharpened and accelerated the inflationary trend. A certain amount of inflation is the necessary consequence of any protracted war; for the longer the war continues, the greater the volume of currency becomes, while the supply of goods, especially in an isolated economy like that of blockaded Germany, decreases. Equally inevitable was the abolition of the gold standard by the law of August 4, 1914, which freed the Reichsbank from the obligation of redeeming its currency with gold at demand. But other belligerents had absorbed this excess buying power with higher taxes and thus had kept inflation within reasonable bounds. In Germany, with the exception of the ineffective war-profits tax, this was not done. The war loans served their purposes of sopping up newly created purchasing power only in the first years of hostilities. In the spring of 1916 the acceptance of war bonds began to lag behind the issuance of new currency, and the lag began to feed upon itself. The Empire was forced to take constant recourse to its money presses. On September 30, 1918, 34 billion paper marks were in circulation, or approximately 500 marks for every German.

Thus inflation was already present at the end of the war. But the public was not yet conscious of it. People still spoke of the high prices caused by shortages of goods, by the blockade, and the like. Cut off from the outside world, they knew nothing of the fallen value of the mark. But after the armistice, first the merchants and then ever widening circles of the nation discovered that the mark had lost about 40 percent of its former worth in dollars.[3]

The Revolution and the tumultuous months which preceded the formal conclusion of peace, along with the extraordinarily high costs of demobilization, made the bad situation even worse. The presses had to print their money faster. The financial status of the Reich and lands threatened to collapse into chaos.

Under these circumstances it required high courage for Erzberger to accept the national Ministry of Finance in June 1919. One can certainly believe him when he told the Reichstag on July 8 that he was frightened when the President offered him that thorny post. But a healthy self-confidence was one of Erzberger's most characteristic traits, frequently to the detriment, but often to the advantage, of his cause. Immediately he placed before the Reichstag ten drafts of new tax laws which the Ministry had prepared under his predecessors' directions. He defended these measures on July 8 in an address which did not try to hide the almost overwhelming difficulties at hand. The greatest achievement which he could announce was the new federal sovereignty in the realm of tax collecting according to the provisions of the still embryonic federal constitution. It was due principally to his initiative that the federal government assumed authority over the administration not only of customs and consumers' taxes, but also of direct taxes. (See the Federal Financial Administration Law of September 10, 1919, later included in the Federal Assessment Ordinance of December 13, 1919.) This represented an irrevocable step toward centralization.[4]

Under the prevailing conditions it was inevitable that the new tax laws sought to seize upon all possible sources of revenue. No less necessary was an increase in the traditional taxes on property and income. But none of these steps was such as to engender love for the new Republic — nor for its eager, brisk minister of finance — among those Germans most directly affected. And it proved easy to sharpen these negative attitudes with the reminder that all these taxes were destined to enrich the former foe as reparations. One of the most debated points of Erzberger's program was the so-called national emergency contribution (Reichsnotopfer), and, as later developments showed, the debate was not without good reason. One could not, of course, oppose the principle that every man of means was obligated to sacrifice a certain portion of his fortune to help overcome the common emergency. But no one could pretend that this sort of contribution could be exacted in one stroke. The government therefore proposed that this assessment be paid in thirty annual installments. These installments were to be set immediately, a provision which assumed, in defiance of all experience, that the fortunes to be taxed would remain constant for a generation's time. This law, which was passed by a strong majority of the National Assembly, was enveloped and dissolved by the rising tide of catastrophic inflation.

Between the introduction and the implementation of Erzberger's financial program lay the formation of a new national government. In early October the Democrats decided to accept Chancellor Bauer's invitation to rejoin the coalition and thus afford the government a broader base. Schiffer, who had been minister of finance until April, now became minister of justice and vice-chancellor. Erich Koch, the mayor of Kassel, became minister of interior. Hugo Preuss, who had held this post up to the resignation of Scheidemann's cabinet, at which time he became federal commissioner for the preparation of the constitution, was never again proposed by his party for a cabinet seat. Somewhat later a third Democrat, Dr. Otto Gessler, mayor of Nuremberg, was named minister of reconstruction. As far as party politics was concerned, there was little profit for the Democrats in entering the cabinet at this time of domestic and of foreign difficulties, especially since they would have to share the responsibility for the execution of those measures which the government had initiated when it had consisted of Centrists and Social Democrats alone.

A particular source of their embarrassment was the Factory Council Law (*Betriebrätegesetz*), the first draft of which had been read in August, receiving at that time rather sharp criticism from the Democratic bloc. The origins of this law were related to the council or soviet idea which had played such a large role in the days of the Revolution and which large numbers of workers considered one of their greatest gains. This idea had even found expression in Article 165 of the new national constitution, although bereft of its original revolutionary character. Among other things, the constitution had now given workers and salaried employees hope of having official factory councils for the defense and promotion of their social and economic interests. The Factory Council Law was designed to realize this hope. But some of its provisions went rather far, as, for example, in the requirement that management open its books annually to the councils and that these councils be represented on the boards of corporations. These provisions were opposed not only by the affected entrepreneurs, but also by more detached groups who regarded them as an invasion of that range of activities and decisions which must necessarily be reserved to the management responsible for the firm. A majority of the Democratic bloc found ways, nevertheless, to overcome these doubts, and on January 18, 1920, the law was passed by the great majority of 213 to 56.

The confused political picture is illustrated by the fact that the opposition to this law consisted of the Right and the extreme Left, the Independents. For these latter had become convinced that this law which purported to further social peace was, in fact, designed to "ease the workers back into their capitalistic yoke" by "turning workers' councils into company unions." [5] The Communists naturally took vigorous part in this agitation. On the day of the second reading of the bill the Independents and Communists organized a mass meeting in front of the Reichstag. It ended in a bloody battle with police which cost forty-two men their lives. The government found itself obliged to declare a state of emergency in most of Germany and to give Noske, as minister of defense, full power to restore the public peace.

This revolutionary flickering on the Left was especially dangerous for the young Republic since, in the meantime, the flame of militaristic nationalism had again risen high, impelled by the activities of the investigating committee of the National Assembly.

The establishment of this committee was the fruit of an acute and inspired thought. After the catastrophic military defeat the same questions were on every lip: Did it have to happen? Could not this war have been avoided? Could it not have been ended sooner? Who are the men who led us into such misfortune? Who is responsible and for what? As the representative of the whole nation, the National Assembly had the clear responsibility of asking these questions in order to find clarity and perhaps answers. This was the purpose of the establishment on August 19, 1919, of the Committee on Investigation. It is to be attributed to the gross political inexperience of the Germans that many of them regarded this as an illegitimate move on the Assembly's part, and declared the committee an affront to national honor; some people even believed these countercharges. Those who directed this agitation knew, of course, exactly what they were about: no spot was to sully the memory of the old regime and its army. In truth the effect of the committee was, on the whole, quite beneficial — and of particular use to historical research. [6] It gathered valuable and fruitful opinions from experts of many points of view. The political education of the Germans would have been promoted if the committee's publications had reached a wider audience. The gentlemen of the

Right, who objected so loudly at first, were to take active part in the committee's labors later, when a different political balance of power gave them a stronger voice in the Reichstag.

This is not to say that no major difficulties lay in the matter at hand, nor that the members of the committee knew how to solve these problems from the start. The composition of the committee lay in the hands of the several party blocs, each with a number of committee places at its disposal according to the party's strength. The parties, especially the smaller parties of the two extremes, quite naturally took care to fill their places with men whom they could trust to represent the party's point of view with emphasis and skill. This is always the practice with parliamentary investigating committees, nor is it an injurious one so long as men remember that it is only through the resolution of differing, even opposing, points of view that enlightenment occurs. But since the committee's meetings were often held in public, prejudiced reporters were able to make irresponsible use of the statements and inquiries of individual members. The secretary of the second subcommittee, which investigated peace overtures made during the war, was the Social Democrat Hugo Sinzheimer, a distinguished jurist, later professor at the University of Frankfurt, whose articles on labor law enjoyed a wide repute. Sinzheimer had totally immersed himself in the documents, displaying what Haussmann called "a phenomenal memory." But there was something petty and arrogant about his manner of interrogation that irritated his political opponents. His critics, however, were content to attack him chiefly for being a Jew. The same was true of the Independents' representative, Oscar Cohn, another attorney. Cohn also suffered from the public statement made by Joffe, the former Bolshevik Russian ambassador to Germany, that he had given Cohn the funds with which to organize the November Revolution in Berlin.

The first sensation occurred on November 15, 1919, during the testimony of the former minister Dr. Helfferich. Karl Helfferich is one of the most famous of the many liberals who turned to the Right as a consequence of the war and defeat. As a youth he had been intimate with liberals of the Bamberg-Barth school; now he was one of the sharpest tongued German Nationalists. His powerful intellect and massive knowledge, particularly in economic matters, could not be denied. But his ministerial fiasco had made him a bitter, spiteful man, glad to let his extraordinary talents for debate serve the ends of a personal vendetta. The subject of his testimony, the unrestricted submarine campaign, was especially suited to irritate him, for Helfferich had originally opposed the notion strongly and

then, after the Supreme Command had had its way, defended the
decision with equal vehemence. If, therefore, this topic was not
one calculated to bring him new laurels, he was all the more determined to use his testimony to strike a blow against his opponents
on the Left.

His opportunity came with a question from the Independent
Cohn. Helfferich refused to answer as a matter of principle, citing
the rules for criminal trials, which, he argued, had been given
"appropriate application" to the committee's operations by Article
34 of the new national constitution. In a statement that had clearly
been well prepared in advance, Helfferich claimed the defendant's
right to decline a judge if he fears a possible conflict of the jurist's
interests. Legally this argument was without merit: Helfferich was
no defendant, but a witness; Cohn was not his judge; and in criminal
procedure the right to request another judge must be exercised
before the trial begins. But legal logic was not Helfferich's goal.
What he sought and achieved was the public opportunity to accuse
Cohn of having used Russian money to buy the revolution that
stabbed the German Army in the back. And with this charge, especially since Cohn's answer was not convincing, he scored such a
smashing success in many minds that he could suffer with equanimity
the subsequent rejection of his legal point. A majority of the committee refused him the right of silence and punished him, according to criminal procedure, with a fine of 300 marks, a sum which,
if ever paid, had first shrunk to meaninglessness as the mark lost its
value. The chairman of this subcommittee, a German Nationalist
judge who had declined to overrule as invalid Helfferich's refusal to
testify, took further pains to link his own name to that of his recalcitrant witness by resigning his chair. His former deputy, the Democrat delegate Gothein, replaced him and soon found himself on
the brink of an even more dangerous cliff.

For in its desire to find out how the Supreme Command had
been able to effect the decision on unrestricted undersea warfare
in January 1917 against the wishes of the Chancellor Bethmann-
Hollweg, the subcommittee decided to invite the testimony of General Ludendorff. The general eagerly accepted this chance to display himself once more upon the public stage. Immediately after
the outbreak of the Revolution he had fled to Sweden in disguise.
But after he had observed that the German revolutionaries had no
intention of following the French example of guillotining their
unsuccessful marshals, he had returned, making his excuses in his
memoirs of the war. But this had not sufficed. Filled, in spite of his
defeat, with an inexhaustible ego, he now cherished the ambition

of playing in German politics that leading role which would hence-forth be denied him in military affairs. Could there be a better scene for his return to public life than before this subcommittee, where he could make clear his standpoint to these miserable politicians and, at the same time, declare to the German nation that he had always been right and that only those who had refused to follow him were responsible for the fatherland's misfortunes? A certain amount of precaution was, of course, required. He was not ignorant of the tarnish on his own reputation. But the reputation of Field Marshal von Hindenburg was still without a blemish. Republican statesmen and journals had taken pains to avoid attacks on Hinden-burg, in part because they assumed that he had merely given his name to Ludendorff's decisions and in part because, through lending his name to the young Republic in its darkest hour, he had helped it keep the peace. It was, therefore, a carefully considered maneuver on Ludendorff's part when he told the subcommittee that he wished to testify only in Hindenburg's presence. The subcommittee would have been perfectly justified in declining to meet this condition. It is the duty of the citizen to give testimony when called upon to do so, and no one has the right to make the fulfillment of that duty dependent on private provisos. Nor could the committee expect to gain further factual enlightenment by hearing additional testi-mony from the old field marshal, since Hindenburg certainly could not tell them things that Ludendorff did not know. Nevertheless the subcommittee acceded to Ludendorff's demands. One can only wonder why.

The subcommittee soon had reason to regret this move. On No-vember 18, while its members were still standing at Hindenburg's entrance as a sign of respect, the field marshal made clear in every tone and gesture his disdain for both the members and the institu-tion of parliamentary investigation committees. When the chairman presented Hindenburg with the first of the subcommittee's questions, the field marshal, instead of answering, delivered a prepared state-ment which had nothing to do with the subject at hand. We do not know the author of this statement; that Hindenburg did not write it can definitely be taken as true. It is clearly not the work of any general, but rather of a clever political mind; Helfferich's name suggests itself. Word by word Hindenburg recited what someone else had written for him, remaining unruffled by interruptions or suggestions from the chair. What concern was it to him whether his conduct as a witness was correct? The newspapers of the world were taking down his words and would soon set before their readers his statement — or better, his plea.

For that is what it was: a plea for the Army and its leaders, who everywhere and always had done the best they could, and a denunciation of the German nation and its political parties, which had deserted the Army and even attacked it from the rear. It is fruitless to try to criticize this fictionalization of fact. Hindenburg's chief point was his statement that some English general had said the German Army was knifed from behind. Just who this English general was, Hindenburg did not say, nor, unfortunately, did the subcommittee think to ask. But even if, as is probably true, no English general ever spoke these words, they were now on the lips of millions of Germans: Our Army was stabbed in the back.

And thus was born the legend of the stab in the back. It is truly one of those legends which Adolf Harnack has characterized so well:

> The historical lie is the most wretched form of legend for, instead of creating truth, it deliberately distorts it. And we ourselves are guilty of fashioning such wretched legends when, influenced by various moods, we treat facts too lightly. Above all we must guard against the convenient lie . . . That we have already gone rather far in this direction (if only as dilettantes) is shown by the Party Legend, which uses history to serve its ends and is careful to ignore whatever does not suit its purposes.

Ignore whatever does not suit your purposes! The authors of the legend of the stab in the back knew how to do that well enough! The dictatorial and dilettantish political adventures of the generals, their military defeats, their obstruction of any useful steps toward a negotiated peace, their sudden insistence that the Army drop its arms — all these facts were swept under the rug with a majestic gesture. The German nation had of course experienced these events; but now millions of Germans found pleasure in forgetting them, even as the Parisians who, on September 4, 1870, after the defeat at Sedan, unseated Napoleon III for having brought about the war, took pleasure in forgetting how they had thronged through the streets on July 15, 1870, shouting "On to Berlin!"

The same psychological cause lay behind the two phenomena: the utter disappointment of all hopes. How many Germans who turned, on November 9, 1918, from the old gods to the new, did so because they thought democracy and a republic the best way to the mildest possible peace? This expectation had not been fulfilled, and in circumstances like this the psychological effect remains the same regardless of whether one was truly duped or simply duped oneself. The more readily people had been to seek comfort in illusions as the war came to its close, the quicker they were now to console themselves with the legend that the German Army had never been defeated. The younger folk in particular sought this false solace. "Invictis victi victuri" * were the words of the memorial erected by the Berlin students to their fallen fellows. To be sure, this motto would have the nation take the blame for the defeat. But this was unimportant, for every one that talked this way excepted himself from the indictment and blamed instead "the others," particularly those responsible for the November Revolution. And people found it all too easy to group with those responsible for the Revolution those men who, accepting responsibilities in that dark hour, had set to work at the hard and thankless task of reconstruction.

It was, of course, Hindenburg's name that reinforced this legend. Who dared contradict the hero of Tannenberg? Few of his admirers noticed that he was content to play a very minor role in giving the testimony that formed the real purpose of the hearing. The field marshal left the answering to Ludendorff, who sought to replace factual argument with bold personal attacks and angry explosions. Ludendorff behaved with special belligerence toward the former ambassador to Washington, Count Bernstorff, also present as a witness. The latter answered Ludendorff in a calm and therefore less effective manner. Then, before it was possible for others to tear apart the general's fables, Ludendorff declared he was too exhausted by the hearing to continue. The subcommittee, considerate as always, adjourned; and since the Assembly also adjourned shortly thereafter, months passed before the hearings could be resumed. By that time the political scene had greatly changed and the nationalists had had full time to make their demagogic use of the field marshal's historical lie. They operated with the motto, as effective as it was false, of "Hindenburg versus Cohn" even though Cohn had scarcely taken part in the interrogation of the two generals. Among the leaders of the German National Party the idea was already taking shape of running Hindenburg as their candidate for president of the Republic.[7]

German armed adventures in the new Baltic States offered to the Rightist parties and their journals still another opportunity for nationalistic, militaristic propaganda. These three new nations, Estonia, Latvia, and Lithuania, which were trying to separate themselves from Russia were the product of German advances since 1917 on the one hand and of the Russian Revolution on the other. German policy in this region had sought to achieve a loose attachment of these states to Germany through the cultivation of the economi-

* "Those who have been conquered, but will yet conquer, salute the unconquered."

cally and culturally important German-speaking elements of their populations. These hopes, of course, collapsed in defeat. But German troops were still stationed in these countries, particularly in Latvia. The political situation was extremely confused since the various national groups, although united in defense against the Reds, were otherwise at violent odds with each other. The German forces, welcome as protection against the Bolshevists, were at the same time hated as supporters of the German-Baltic landowners, the so-called Baltic Barons. This situation became especially critical when, in April 1919, German forces took part in the coup that toppled Ulmanis' regime in Latvia, replacing it temporarily with a more friendly government. The policy of the Entente was equally uncertain. At first the Allies had insisted that Germany leave her soldiers there to protect these lands against the Bolshevists. But after the treaty had been signed at Versailles they reversed their position and demanded the immediate, total evacuation of these forces.[8]

Now this was much easier to demand than to accomplish. For the German officers and men in this area had, for the most part, an independent will and policy. They could be regarded as components of the German Army only in so far as they received German pay and had a Prussian general, von der Goltz, at their head. But most of the soldiers were pursuing private ends, principally free land for settlement. They cited a promise Ulmanis had made, according to which they were to be repaid with homesteads for their aid against the Reds. For months this false hope enticed young men first to recruiting offices in Germany and thence to Latvia. Injunctions issued by the German government were ignored. One cannot be astonished that, after four years of war, many soldiers now turned eastward for adventure or even for plunder. The troops were largely gathered into Free Corps, among which Major Bischoff's Iron Division was the most prominent.[9] The leaders of these groups and their officers pursued private political goals, among which the preservation of the local German culture was only the most immediate and innocuous.

The Order of the Day for June 16, 1919, from the commander of the Baltic troops found its way to the hands of the British commissioner. This document babbled of a coming alliance between Germany and Russia and of the future falling-out between England on the one side and the United States and France on the other. This order can best be taken simply as another example of the ineptitude with which the military mind meddled in politics. Nevertheless, the idea of Russian alliance did have deep roots in traditions of the

German Army. Naturally these officers were thinking of a Russia freed from Communism and even restored to the tsars. They operated in concert with White Russian, monarchist troops. Among all these an adventurer by the name of Bermondt — who called himself General Prince Bermondt-Awaloff — played an increasingly important role. But the German officers clearly were not thinking of the Romanoffs alone. More important to them was a restoration of the German monarchy. The officers, especially those of the Iron Division, spoke with utter candor of these hopes. Rumor had it that their leaders were in touch with Ludendorff, that the general had even visited them in Mitau. Although one must be skeptical about these reports, one cannot doubt the willingness of these men to assist in a monarchist coup.[10] At any rate, when the government ordered them home, they had not the slightest inclination to obey the Republic they despised. Certainly it was with their officers' concurrence that representatives of the Baltic troops met in Mitau on August 24, 1919, and proclaimed their refusal to obey the order as well as their intent, instead, to "preserve under all circumstances our claims, won with blood and confirmed by contract, to citizens' rights and homesteads in Latvia."

The Baltic troops received passionate support for their rebellious attitude from the nationalist press at home. The papers even castigated the Republic for not having defended the just rights of their fellow Germans with sufficient force. But the government had not done so for very good reason. It knew that the supposed treaty, on which the soldiers based their case, had in all likelihood never been signed; nor could the government ignore its agreement in the Treaty of Versailles (Article 293) to the annulment of all special rights of Germans in the Baltic States. Still less did it dare ignore the fact that the Entente had all the power it needed to enforce its will. The nationalistic journalists knew this too, of course. But, after all, it sounded much more patriotic to accuse the government of failing to uphold the national honor and to glorify the troops in Courland as defenders of the fame of German arms — in spite of the plundering and other excesses which they committed from time to time at the expense of the defenseless Latvian pople.

And so the inevitable finally occurred. In early October, Bermondt-Awaloff, in whose corps most of the German soldiers had found a place, made an attack upon Riga, seat of the Latvian government. The attack was partially successful.[11] Thereupon the Entente prohibited German marine traffic in the Baltic and threatened, further, to cut off shipments of food and supplies. Fortunately, the Allies also accepted the German government's proposal that they send an Allied commission, including one German representative, to the area of disturbance. The commission, which arrived in Berlin on November 7, was given every assurance that the German government, and especially Minister of Defense Noske, sincerely wanted to carry out its obligations. The German delegate to the commission, Admiral Hopmann, also proved to be completely reliable. But the impression the commission received in Königsberg, both from the Commanding General von Esdorff and from the Social Democratic president of East Prussia, August Winnig, was disturbingly different. In view of later events it is worth noting that General Turner, the English member of the commission, wrote from Tilsit in his concluding report of December 9, 1919:

> East Prussia does not realize that Germany has lost the War. The Military Party is all-powerful and Militarism in all its forms is rampant. Personally I have little doubt of the plot to overthrow the Government at the opportune moment, or of the power of the Military Party to do so. They are simply waiting for the time when the Peace shall have been ratified and the whole onus of it can be thrown on the present Government. Propaganda encouraging Militarism is being disseminated everywhere, especially by the Ober President of East Prussia, Herr Winning [Winnig].[12]

Today those words sound like a prologue to the Kapp Putsch.

The Allies were primarily concerned with the withdrawal of the German troops from the Baltic States. This achieved, they released the German shipping in the Baltic, and any lasting damage was avoided. But in December 1919, Minister Koch could rightly tell the Democratic convention: "All the woes that pelted us this fall would never have occurred if the German Nationalists had not convinced the troops that they were strong enough to hold the Baltic States against a victorious world." The Bolshevists' attack on East Prussia, which had been predicted to follow in the wake of the German retreat, never took place. But the attitude of the officers and men, as they petulantly obeyed their order to withdraw, was so insolent that the interested observer could hardly expect them to feel at home as citizens of the new Germany.

The alacrity with which the lessons of catastrophe were forgotten is illustrated by the rapid reappearance of even the Pan-German League. The Pan-Germans bore a full measure of guilt for their nation's present woe. Before the war their immoderate agitation had provoked a good deal of hostility, and during the war it had whipped into passionate frenzy those annexationist tendencies which seduced the German nation from the path of a purely defensive war. But so great was their confidence in the shortness of the public's memory that they felt free to assemble in September 1919. The convention chairman, Judge Class, demanded the restoration of the monarchy and accused those "presently in power" of having no thought for the nation. Their own "subjugation" and their "refusal to collaborate with the present regime" became the league's platform. And it soon became apparent that these gentlemen would use any means to gain their goal.

The further the year 1919 wore on, the clearer it became that the parties to the Weimar Coalition were losing their popular support, and indeed in two directions at once. The middle classes streamed back to the parties of the Right, while on the Left the Independent Socialists made large inroads among the workers. And each movement toward a political extreme tended to increase the other. The efforts of the Independents and Communists to drive the wave of revolution further gave the country no peace and poured turbulent water on reactionary mills. At the same time the growing strength of the monarchists excited among the workers not only a fear of losing their revolutionary gains but the concomitant resolve to meet this threatening force with forces of their own. Both tendencies concurred in the common effort to terminate the National Assembly as soon as possible and to hold new elections, which each side expected to win. On March 9, 1920, the Assembly considered a petition from the German Nationalists and the People's Party that it declare its intention to dissolve on May 1 and undertake immediate steps for the election of a Reichstag and a president. The petitioners argued that with the acceptance of the constitution the Assembly's mission was complete. The government pointed, in reply, to the necessity of the legislative program still to be passed and to the plebiscites about to be held along the occupied borders of the Reich. The government preferred to hold elections after the harvest in the fall. A majority of the body agreed, rejecting the petition by a vote of 176 to 60, the Independents voting with the Rightist minority.

But even while the members of the cabinet were fighting their way to this parliamentary victory, they knew that they were about to lose their most active and politically important colleague, the minister of finance. For Erzberger had to battle for his political life in a libel suit against Helfferich. Bitter enmity had existed between the two men at least since the Reichstag Peace Resolution of July 1917. The animosity was naturally increased when Erzberger, in front of the National Assembly, called Helfferich "the least responsible of all ministers of finance." Helfferich replied in an extremely sharp article in the conservative *Kreuzzeitung* which he later condensed in a pamphlet entitled "Away with Erzberger." [13] Here he was not content simply to oppose Erzberger's policies, but made violent personal attacks against his probity and veracity. It was apparent that he was seeking to force Erzberger to bring the matter to court. And this he succeeded in doing. Erzberger sued for libel and demanded damages. The state's attorney, as was his duty, found the public interest to be involved and issued an indictment. And so it was that on January 19, 1920, the financial ministers of the Empire and of the Republic faced each other in a chamber of the First District Court of Berlin, one as defendant and the other as coplaintiff and witness. The trial lasted until March 12, 1920, and ended with a complete victory for Helfferich.[14] He was, to be sure, sentenced to a fine of all of 300 marks and was required to pay the costs, which were quite considerable. But the court had accepted as proved almost all the accusations he had brought against Erzberger, and this was all that had really been at stake.

As legal counsel Helfferich had secured the most prominent and ablest defense attorney in Berlin, Dr. Max Alsberg, who directed Helfferich's case with consummate skill and winning rhetoric. But Helfferich could claim credit for a large part of this forensic success. His mastery of the almost infinite material, furnished him in part by an army of volunteer assistants; his unremitting energy; his nimble mind and his cutting logic: all these qualities had to impress even his political opponent. But equally apparent were his almost demonic hate and his unbridled temper, which drove him from one impulsive outburst to another. The president of the court was repeatedly obliged to threaten him with penalties. These threats, of course, were no more carried out than were those which had warned the audience that disorderly conduct could mean dismissal from the chamber. For the audience was part of the act and seized every opportunity to give loud expression to its distaste for Erzberger and his policies. The audience's own political attitudes were disclosed at such times as when the Reichstag's Peace Resolution of July 1917 was under discussion. When, for instance, Erzberger said he was proud to have effected the passage of the resolution, the audience broke out in a demonstration of disapproval so loud as to require a formal call for order from the bench. To these onlookers Erzberger was the man who, with this Peace Resolution, had knifed their victorious army from behind; who, by signing the armistice, had brought about the shameful capitulation; and who, by offering to sign the Treaty of Versailles, had shown his satisfaction with its terms.[15] And because it was he who kept his party in coalition with the Democrats and Social Democrats, the audience saw in him the chief support of the republic they despised. Many others hated him also as the minister who was trying, with his severe tax measures, to reach deep into the pockets of the propertied classes.

The excitement aroused by this trial found tragic expression in the attempted assassination of Erzberger by a twenty-year-old student, the former Officer Cadet von Hirschfeld, on January 26, 1920, that is, when the trial had only begun. His revolver shot wounded Erzberger in the shoulder. Yet the latter managed to return to court a few days later, thus avoiding what had seemed the inevitable adjournment of the case. It is significant that the jury which heard Hirschfeld's case on February 22 acquitted him of charges of manslaughter and attempted murder in spite of all the evidence. They found him guilty only of "inflicting serious bodily harm" — and this under mitigating circumstances. He was sentenced to prison for eighteen months.

Erzberger's position in the trial was difficult from the start since he was obliged, as a witness, to recount on oath events which had in part occurred several years before and which had been elements of a critical development at a highly critical time. He was expected to give an account of his attitude toward Bethmann-Hollweg in almost every day and hour of the latter's fight against the submarine campaign, out of which fight the Peace Resolution had sprung. The ease with which the most conscientious man can be tricked by his own memory is shown by a statement of Bethmann's, whose truthfulness no one can doubt. He said that he could not have made a statement attributed to him by Erzberger because, at the time of the conversation in question, he had been already bound by a resolution of the Federal Council. Accepting Bethmann's word as definitive, the court found Erzberger guilty of perjury on this point. Yet a later inspection of the Federal Council's minutes showed that the resolution had not been passed until several weeks later. It was also most unfortunate for Erzberger that the state's attorney, as a rule on the side of the plaintiff, turned about and opposed him. While one cannot take juridic exception to this, such a maneuver against a minister would have been inconceivable under the old regime. And in the course of the trial Erzberger was obliged to request a leave of absence from his Ministry after the *Hamburger Nachrichten*, a Rightist paper, had published his stolen personal tax records, accusing him of irregularities. He immediately called for an investigation of his case, which, after many months, gave public assurance of his innocence. But by then the ambiguous outcome of the trial had long since forced him to resign his post.

In the long course of the trial much had come to light which reflected no credit on Erzberger's sense of tact or official ethics. Yet the judgment did not fit the facts at all. It can rather be regarded as an example of the difficulty legal officials experience when required to judge events of the political world, so foreign to their own. They were unduly severe in accusing Erzberger of using public office to serve his private ends. For this problem is much more complex than may appear to a secure and tidy civil servant's mind. A landowner who, as a member of the Reichstag, votes to raise the import duties on grain or to lower the tax on liquor seeks in this way advantages not only for agriculture in general; he regards the promotion of such legislation as his proper political goal, and as advantageous to his private purse as well. And the same applies to an iron magnate who demands high tariffs on imported ore; in fact an alliance between these very groups determined decades of German economic policy. Naturally, the "contacts" which any active, influential parliamentarian makes can be used only with the greatest caution and only after close examination. But their use is, in itself, just as unavoidable as the use of contacts in society or even in the court. Is it worse for a member of the Reichstag who is also member of a corporation's board to represent his firm with candor before a governmental official who then can examine, and deny, its case from the viewpoint of the state, or for a trusted minister to use his influence upon a senile king to obtain special, royal exception from a general law, as did Bismarck and Minister of Agriculture von Lucius when faced with a tax on entailments? It was only natural that many members of Reichstag were also members of the board of one or several corporations, and Helfferich expressly agreed that no objection could be made to such a practice.

But these, he said, were men of commercial reputations, and with Erzberger this was not the case. Now it is true that Erzberger had originally been no more than a schoolteacher with the simple background of a Swabian country town. But everyone who had really come to know him recognized that, in the course of his seventeen years of parliamentary service, Erzberger's untiring industry had won him a highly respectable knowledge of economics and finance. Indeed it was this very knowledge that had gained him so much influence even among members of the Emperor's government. Why should not such a man strike the director of a corporation as being fully as desirable an addition to his board as, say, some Reichstag lawyer? Was it necessarily corruption for Erzberger to do what others freely did? To be sure, an experienced judge would not have done many things that Erzberger did, not because he had superior human qualities, but rather because he had had a different education. In any event that strict measure of bureaucratic propriety which a judge is obliged to observe privately is not quite appropriate to the worlds of business and politics.

All those instances where the court had been of the opinion that Erzberger had wandered from the truth were given close, judicial examination in the perjury trial which followed immediately upon his testimony in the Helfferich case. This second trial was quickly halted when it became apparent that no evidence of either willful or negligent perjury could be found. At this point the attorney general announced that in most of those instances where the libel court had assumed false witness, the suspicion had to be regarded as disproved. Such a statement certainly does not cast a favorable light on the libel court's use of evidence.

So much, then, for the Erzberger-Helfferich trial. In retrospect the suit seems like a curse which attached itself to all participants: in 1921 Erzberger was murdered; in 1924 Helfferich lost his life in a hideous train accident; in 1933 Alsberg, driven from his homeland by the persecuting mania of the National Socialists, took his own life; and the presiding justice of the court was obliged, having first become presiding justice of his district, to quit the bench a few years later because of compromising personal affairs.

The political effects of the trial were enormous. Helfferich's victory appeared as a triumph of the old regime, as a vindication of nationalism and militarism; Erzberger's defeat, as a blow to the Republic. The new state's reputation seemed so shaken by these events that its opponents believed a single thrust would bring it down. On March 12 the court's verdict regarding Erzberger was announced, and at six o'clock on the morning of March 13 the rebellious troops of the Ehrhardt Brigade marched through the Brandenburg Gate. And only one hour later Dr. Wolfgang Kapp, provincial director-general of East Prussia, appeared at the national chancellery on the Wilhelmstrasse to seize the authority and title of chancellor.

For months now there had been ferment among the officers and troops. Their restlessness was understandable insofar as it pertained to the diminution of the Army as required by the Entente. For many officers this meant a forced separation from their chosen profession, and no one knew just whom the axe would hit. By April 1920, 15,000 officers had been dismissed, but 5000 more would have to go since, by September of that year, the Army was to be cut still further from 200,000 to 150,000 men. Understandable as their resentment was, it was foolish of them to demand that the government refuse to carry out the treaty. And it was irresponsible of discharged officers, like Captain Pabst, to take revenge upon their government by arousing and organizing nationalistic agitation. The problem was made even more complex by the existence of the *Freikorps*. These private armies had been active during the weeks of revolution and in battles against the Poles. Their members believed they had found a military career and, following the lead of the Baltic Volunteers, they refused to obey the Allied order to disband.

Another stipulation of the treaty which kept the Army in a state of unrest was the required extradition of war criminals (Articles 228–230). The German government correctly pointed out that it simply was in no position to execute this provision. It offered, instead, to prosecute in the German Supreme Court whichever Germans the Allies wished to indict for crimes against the laws of civilized warfare. A law passed by the National Assembly in December 1919 afforded a legal base for such proceedings. Fortunately the Entente had sense enough to agree, if only tentatively, in their note of February 17, 1920, and so, as Ludendorff has put it, "the whole question of extradition dissolved into air." [16] In other words, he and his political partners found themselves robbed of a weapon. For, as the general later testified in court, he had already discussed this very subject with Kapp and General Lüttwitz.

Kapp had been one of the loudest nationalists throughout the war and had distinguished himself particularly by his venomous attacks on Bethmann-Hollweg. He had founded the Fatherland Party; after its collapse he had become the East Prussian representative on the central committee of the German Nationalists, whose meetings he never attended. The story of Kapp's life is the story of the political tragedy of the German middle class. He was the scion of a thoroughly enlightened family. His father, a revolutionary of 1848, who was forced to spend many years in American exile and later became a liberal member of the Reichstag, was Friedrich Kapp, chronicler of the German princes' trade in mercenaries in the eighteenth century. Wolfgang Kapp became a conservative Agrarian and nationalistic war hawk, possessed of a boundless ambition inversely proportional to his political talents. In the summer of 1919, just after Germany accepted the Treaty of Versailles, he wished to start a new war against Poland from East Prussia in order to recover the lost province of Posen. When even the army had to make it clear to him that his project was nonsense and that even in East Prussia the people were tired of war, Kapp began to busy himself with creating domestic strife. But he did not find much encouragement here, even among leaders of the Right. He naturally claimed as his own idea the

German Nationalists' demand that the National Assembly be dissolved and a new president be elected. For all this he found a willing ear in Baron von Lüttwitz, the rather aged commander of the First Army District in Berlin. General von Lüttwitz had his own reasons for being bitter.

Originally Lüttwitz had been among those officers who set their trust in Noske as minister of defense.[17] But Noske had no choice but to become suspicious as the utterly naïve general fell under the influence of former Captain Pabst and former Colonel Bauer, Ludendorff's agent in intrigue. Two excellently equipped marine brigades, Ehrhardt's in Döberitz and Löwenfeld's in Silesia, stood under Lüttwitz' command. Upon the Allies' demand, Noske had to order that both brigades be dissolved. Lüttwitz vehemently protested this move in a conversation with Noske on February 29, 1920. And when Noske continued to insist that the operation be carried out by March 10, the general became enraged. Shortly afterwards, at an inspection of Ehrhardt's Brigade, he announced that he would never execute their dissolution.

At this point Lüttwitz became vulnerable to the revolutionary influences of Kapp, Pabst, and Bauer. On the evening of March 9, after the National Assembly had rejected the petition to dissolve, the general visited Hergt, the chairman of the German Nationalists and former Prussian minister of finance. Lüttwitz proceeded to unfold before him all sorts of schemes for violence, quite without acquiring his host's assent. On the following day he was received, at his request, by President Ebert with Noske also present.[18] The general then delivered a set of demands: an immediate Reichstag election, the popular election of a national president, the appointment of so-called specialist-ministers, and several military measures. Among these was to be the removal of General Reinhardt, army chief of staff and too faithful to the new constitution to be of use to these adventurers. While Ebert calmly tried to talk the general out of these ideas, Noske, who had been warned of projected disturbances, became impatient, reminded the general of his proper place, and made quite clear to him that his civilian superiors would take no pleasure in an officers' manifesto.

In the course of the next few days Noske received alarming, but insufficiently concrete, reports. On March 11 he ordered the arrests of Kapp and Pabst; but the police dallied, and the two had time to find safe hiding. Lüttwitz was relieved of his command. In the evening of March 12, the day on which the verdict of the Erzberger-Helfferich trial was announced, a cabinet meeting was held at which Noske offered a general description of the situation but was unable to give a precise report on any planned revolt. He sent an Admiral von Trotha to Döberitz for purposes of reconnaissance. Trotha found everything in fine order, naturally enough, for he had previously announced by telephone his plans to visit there. But about midnight the news arrived that Ehrhardt's Brigade had commenced its march upon Berlin. Two generals set off to intercept Ehrhardt with the hope of bringing him back to reason. But all they brought back was a political ultimatum from the captain, convinced now of his mission to save the state. Noske declined to parley with a rebel and instead urged the generals gathered in his office to undertake the proper military measures for defense. But now the catastrophe occurred. General von Seeckt, chief of the *Truppenamt* and, in effect, chief of staff of the army, declared: "Reichswehr does not fire on Reichswehr," [19] by which he clearly meant that the loyal troops would not shoot at the rebels, not vice versa. All the other generals, except Reinhardt, also saw no hope in military resistance, and thus, in a decisive moment, the government found itself deserted by the Reichswehr of Berlin.

What was it to do now, in this desperate situation? Remaining in Berlin meant being taken hostage by the rebels. And so the cabinet decided that night to leave Berlin for Dresden. Only the vice-chancellor, Minister of Justice Schiffer, stayed in Berlin.

Thus Ehrhardt was able to make his triumphant entry through the Brandenburg Gate early the next morning. A small group of the faithful were gathered there, including no less a personage than General Ludendorff. When a later court inquired what had brought him thither, the general replied: "The principal question to me was, will the soldiers shoot at one another or will they not? I should have been deeply saddened if they had." [20] Everyone is free to draw his own conclusions. Was he one of the conspirators? It seems clear that they were counting on him. But perhaps he had not yet decided whether it was advisable to join this movement. And before he could make up his mind, the whole dream was over.

From its very beginnings the Kapp Putsch was nothing but the work of overgrown juvenile delinquents. That the *Herren Offiziere* among them had no idea what their undertaking meant could really astonish no one. Noske characterized them as people who showed that their political sophistication had not progressed beyond that of an eighteen-year-old cadet.[21] Even the new "chancellor," Dr. Kapp, who had thought himself possessed of all political wisdom, and who had looked down with disdain upon the parliamentary ministers because they were not "specialists," could find no more to do with the power that was suddenly his than make a few arrests,

issue a few absurd proclamations, and, for the rest, have his soldiers
parade the Berlin streets with hand grenades and helmets, shooting
a bit when they pleased. The general level of this nation-saver's
mental processes is perhaps best illustrated by his proclamation
which forbade further examinations at the Berlin University, or
the one which triumphantly announced that the matzo flour for the
forthcoming Passover had been confiscated. One of Kapp's confidants
was a former lawyer who had been disbarred for gross malpractice.
But even more odd was his choice for a press secretary. For this
post he found an international adventurer, Trebitsch-Lincoln, by
birth a Hungarian Jew, who had dabbled in British politics until
finally jailed for embezzlement. Perhaps it was he who planted the
mad "confidential reports" which the rebels peddled, according to
which the English government looked with favor on the putsch.

Witnesses friendly to the coup afforded, in their later testimony
in court, our clearest descriptions of the utter confusion that reigned
in Kapp's Chancellery.[22] No one led and no one followed, for no one
had a plan. Only the countless office seekers who suddenly appeared
in the Wilhelmstrasse seemed to have any definite goals. One of the
rebels later characterized the Chancellery of these days, in the
private argot of the coup, as a "pack of Jews." One morning they
arrested all the Prussian ministers; the same noon they set them
free because the rail workers had threatened to strike if their Minister Oeser were not let out, and Oeser had declined the honor unless
his cabinet colleagues were also released.

If the gentlemen had imagined that the people of Berlin were
going to greet them with jubilation, they were severely disillusioned.
Naturally they had a few disciples, but the vast majority of even the
middle class Berliners would have nothing to do with them. A
blond-bearded demagogue climbed upon the Postdamer Bridge and
proceeded to malign "King Ebert" for being afraid to face a vote;
icy silence was all he evoked from the crowd. The parties of the Right
were trying to eat their cake and have it too. On the one hand they
spoke of the "new government," thus recognizing the traitors' regime, while on the other they pressed for a speedy restoration of
constitutional conditions, thus praising what they had none too
faintly damned.

The putsch was defeated by two principal forms of resistance:
the general strike of the workers and the refusal of the higher civil
servants to collaborate with their rebel masters.[23] A government
needs money not only to make war, but also to carry out rebellion;
and so Kapp asked the Reichsbank for 10,000,000 marks. But the
officers of the bank would honor only the order of an authorized

official and no such signature was to be had. For all the under-secretaries in the ministries refused to sign, and it did not seem to the cashier of the Reichsbank that the signature of "National Chancellor Kapp" offered quite the financial security required. The Kapp government was, of course, hit by a much stronger force: the general strike. On the first day of the coup, the Social Democratic Party had called for the strike in a proclamation which appeared over the signatures of Ebert and other Social Democratic ministers, but without their official approval. The call was accepted and completely carried out by all unions, regardless of their political affiliations. All public service ceased throughout Berlin; no streetcar ran, no light went on, no news was printed. The Berliners had a few unpleasant days, but most of them bore the strike without grumbling.

After four days Kapp realized that he had shot his bolt. In an effort to retreat with some semblance of dignity, he tried to enter into negotiations with the government. But when both Minister Schiffer in Berlin and the rest of the cabinet, now in Stuttgart, refused his entreaties, he found himself with nothing else to do but to declare, on the morning of March 17, his formal "resignation." That evening Ehrhardt's Brigade marched away, but not without adding one last deed to their bloody record. When the crowd at the Brandenburg Gate began to give vocal expression to their joy at his retreat, Ehrhardt's officers had machine guns turned on the crowd. This was the "liberators'" final deed.[24]

The putsch lasted only four days, but the miseries it caused lingered longer. Not only had it cost hundreds of people their lives, but it had also sowed the seed of hate and distrust and had disrupted the slow course of Germany's political recuperation.

What had failed in Berlin succeeded for a time in Munich. Under pressure from the military, especially from the Volunteers, who were aided by Pöhner and Frick of the Munich police, Hoffmann's cabinet was forced to resign.[25] A new coalition government was formed, this time without the Social Democrats. Now the psychological and political effects of the former Republic of Soviets came to full light. For the Bavarian Social Democrats this was a final farewell from the cabinet; they never were members again. The party that really ruled was and remained the Bavarian People's Party, which had seceded from the Centrists to cultivate its particularism, that is, its exclusively Bavarian patriotism, with greater freedom. The attitude expressed later by its party bulletin was already manifest at this time: "The Bavarian People's Party must at all times keep this single point of view, namely the promotion of Bavarian interests. Party policy must never seek anything other than to serve the Bavarian ideal." As a part of this program the party chose as premier von Kahr, a man who readily admitted that he "had heretofore had nothing to do with politics" and who was, at the bottom of his heart, a Bavarian monarchist who yearned for the restoration of the Wittelsbachs. This political change conformed to dominant opinion in Bavaria. It was a defeat, however, for both the Weimar Republic and German unity. From now on each central government was forced to see every national program nullified in Munich. The sturdy Bavarians despised Berlin and Berliners almost as much as they did their former foes. Whoever voiced an attack on the Berliners, as did, for example, a certain Adolf Hitler, could be sure of loving protection in Munich. It almost seemed as though the Bavarians wished to punish Berlin for having first driven out their king and then having submitted to the Reds.

It was inevitable that the military mutiny during the Kapp Putsch made republican Germans, which is to say Socialist Germans, highly suspicious of the entire Army. And, unfortunately, the whole domestic history of Prussia and of Germany since the constitutional crisis of the 1860's had created an atmosphere in which neither the Left nor the Right could regard the military or military affairs with anything approaching nonpartisan objectivity. Antimilitaristic prejudice on the part of the Social Democratic workers discouraged them from enlisting in the Republic's army. This antipathy could have been overcome only if Germany had been granted years of peaceful development and only if the workers had been given enough evidence to convince them that the officers' corps had changed fundamentally and was no longer dominated by the monarchist-conservative traditions of the old Prussian military Junkers. But now a mutinous brigade had marched through the Brandenburg Gate under the old black, white, and red banner, driving the constitutional government from the national capital. This event destroyed any possibility of constructive development in the foreseeable future. It is true that only a few units stationed east of the Elbe in Prussia had taken active part in the putsch. Troops in the west and south either remained loyal or tried to maintain their "neutrality." Even in Berlin General Lüttwitz could at best count on only part of his forces. In his memoirs he tells with moral indignation, and as though he were the last of the Gracchi lamenting the fickleness of his helpmates in revolt, how the Guards Engineer Battalion "mutinied" on the night of March 16–17.[26] An attempt by General Märker in Dresden to mediate between the rebels and the government failed in the face of Noske's and Ebert's resistance and led to the general's dismissal. And though it may be true that the Army's treason was not so great as outraged republicans thought, it remains clear that the Army had failed in its role as that shield of the constitution and the state upon which the nation and its government could rely. Seeckt's categoric statement, "Reichswehr does not fire on Reichswehr," had perhaps avoided a sanguinary meeting at the Brandenburg Gate, but it had also brutally exposed the helplessness of the nation's government and president and had served to destroy the people's faith in their Army.

Several segments of the Prussian police and provincial administration had made themselves equally subject to suspicion. Most remarkable is the fact that there were two Social Democrats among the provincial presidents who failed to do their duty; Philipp in Breslau and Winnig in Königsberg; and to these one should add Eugen Ernst, commissioner of police in Berlin.[27] In Winnig's case, which was the most severe, an inner distaste for the Social Democrats' party strategy had found expression.[28] This gifted but unsteady man slipped more and more into the wake of the nationalists.

On the other hand the general strike had been an event to give even convinced supporters of the new regime every reason to reconsider. The strike, to be sure, brought the coup of Kapp and company to an end after only four days. Since the regular tools of the state had been found wanting, only immediate intervention by the populace could have saved it so soon. The central committee of the Democratic Party recognized this fact, publishing a manifesto in favor of the strike in its early days. Yet a general strike remains, by its very nature, a revolutionary measure by means of which one segment of the nation tries to force its will upon the rest, and many men feared that this one segment would feel all the freer to use this weapon in the future if it were found justified and legal in this case. Indeed, otherwise calm and responsible labor leaders were momentarily dazed by their sudden success. In their negotiations with representatives of the coalition parties, the leaders sought to make their halting of the strike conditional upon the parties' acceptance of their political demands. Although they finally had to be content with half a victory, leaving the decision to the Reichstag as the proper constitutional authority, many workers and their leaders nevertheless nourished long memories of how effective their weapon had been. They forgot that their endeavor had found success only because clerks and officials had joined the workers in their fight, and because they enjoyed the sympathy of more than half of Berlin. Thus their later disillusionment brought all the more pain.

Still worse was the Communists' attempt to use for their own ends the enormous excitement which the Kapp Putsch had aroused among the workers. They made their move in the Ruhr, the industrial heart of Germany. Here, too, the movement had at first assumed the form of defensive action against a coup. The workers thought such a step particularly necessary since the local army commander, General Watter, could not be brought, in those first days, to take a clear, unambiguous position of loyalty, and several *Freikorps Führer* had made themselves distinctly suspicious. But fortunately in this region the government had a representative who combined wisdom with energy: Commissioner Carl Severing, a Social Democratic delegate to the Assembly and a man well versed in union affairs. It was due principally to his efforts that those workers who really wished to save the state calmed down within a few days. But others had quite different goals and had weapons in their hands. Severing writes in his memoirs:

In the early instance of a march upon Dortmund, which a military detachment had tried in vain to block, it became apparent that the Communists were aiming at the annihilation of all governmental instruments of power. They made no distinction between soldiers, police, and volunteer security guards. Whoever, in the execution of his duty, sought to oppose the onrushing masses was rendered harmless, was chased away, or was killed. Individual members of the Security Police in Essen, who had tenaciously defended especially threatened points within the city, were murdered in a particularly brutal fashion. This was . . . no longer the prevention of revolt; it was the bestial slaughter of loyal civil servants.

The population was obliged to suffer frightful weeks of fear, plundering, and mistreatment. Finally a strong military force had to be sent in to restore order. And now the same dreadful discovery was made as at the time of the subjugation of the soviets in Munich. Severing laments: "The terroristic measures taken by the troops against the peaceful population — the arbitrary executions without trial or sentence, the mass arrests on the strength of unilateral denunciations, the mistreatment of prisoners — were fully up to the Red atrocities." [29]

The entrance of German troops into this disturbed area led in turn to international complications, since part of the area lay in the demilitarized zone where, according to the Versailles treaty, no German soldier dared stand. On March 19, after the Kapp Putsch collapsed, Allied representatives in Berlin had tendered their congratulations on the quick smashing of the plot. The French chargé des affaires had even hastened to be the first with his good wishes. And the Supreme Council of the Allies went so far as to decide to stop the delivery of foodstuffs and raw materials if a monarchic or Communist regime should come to power in Germany. In sharp contrast to this Allied attitude, the French, now led by the Socialist Millerand, replied to the German troop movements with the occupation of the German cities of Frankfurt, Darmstadt, Homburg, and Hanau. With this step France separated herself from her most important allies.[30] The English government in particular took clear and public pains to dissociate itself from this French move, not only by declaring openly that no English soldier would assist this act of force, but also by telling the French government in a crisp note that Paris would tear apart the Entente's united front if it persisted in taking military measures against the Germans without prior consultation with its allies. More than merely national differences of temper were involved. It may well be true that the Englishman is inclined to forgive and forget once the battle is done, while the Frenchman takes years to rid himself of wartime hate. But what the British government realized, and what the French failed to comprehend, was that every act of force would only strengthen German nationalistic desires for revenge and thus strike at its most tender spot every hope for Europe's gradual pacification. Indeed this became apparent all too soon.

After the revolt was over, the Republic's list of casualties carried the name of Gustav Noske. During Kapp's days in March the national government had settled in Stuttgart, where it also convened the National Assembly. In the session of March 18, Scheidemann directed an extraordinarily critical address at the Reichswehr, an address which everyone took as aimed at Noske, although his name was never mentioned. Noske immediately tendered his resignation. Ebert certainly understood the situation and the personalities involved far better than did most members of his party; and it was Ebert who always, even in the most tumultuous times, preserved "the holy, ever bounteous gift of calm" that Scheidemann was always so quick to lose. Ebert insisted that Noske stay and was supported in this policy by a large part of the Social Democratic delegation. But Scheidemann did not give up. He reminded Ebert that the directors of the general strike and especially Legien, the president of the Social Democratic unions, demanded that Noske resign for having shown more energy against striking Communists than against mutinous generals. With a heavy heart Ebert had to yield. But in the letter to Noske, in which he accepted the latter's resignation, he made quite clear how little he thought of all these doings. In this letter he not only alluded to Noske's "purposeful, hard work," but he also praised Noske's achievement of bringing Germany back to the ways of peace and fruitful labor as a "deed which will never be forgotten in the annals of our fatherland." These words, however, did not keep the Social Democratic press from celebrating Noske's fall. Yet, thoughtful members of the party began to doubt the wisdom of their heroic deed when it became apparent that they had absolutely no one to propose as Noske's successor and therefore had to see this critical post in the new state pass into bourgeois hands.

But "each man learns no more than what he can." The party organization was not content with excluding Noske from the cabinet; they also dropped him from the party ticket and thus banned him from the Reichstag from then on. He had become "a liability." Put in other words, this means that the Social Democrats did not wish to propose as a candidate a man against whom the Independents and Communists daily fired their heaviest cannonades of calumny. Perhaps the party heads hoped with this sacrifice to win back the labor vote which had been seduced by Leftist agitation. If so, the next elections showed how false their hopes had been. The Social Democratic Party had robbed itself of one of the few men who had the ability to lead and govern. Every time Noske spoke at a party rally he showed he could still make a deep and moving impression on his listeners. Under the prewar system of single-candidate districts, a system in which the delegate's personality played a role, more than one district would have fought for the honor of electing him, and he would have returned to the Reichstag in triumph. But with the proportional ballot, which counts votes for each party only, a politician could get along quite well without personality; and the nobodies, sure of their seats in this way, had every interest in playing the game as safely as they could. It was due to the Prussian government, and in particular to its new minister of interior, Severing, that Noske was not completely lost from public life. Severing gave him the presidency of the Province of Hanover, the former incumbent of which, von Richter of the People's Party, had not behaved correctly during the Kapp Putsch. Here Noske enjoyed a fruitful career until the National Socialists came into power; then his new masters chased him from office without even waiting the few months that separated him from retirement.

In the Reichswehr Noske had especially enjoyed the intimate respect of those generals who had come to personal terms with the Republic. General Walter Reinhardt, the chief of the high command (*Chef der Heeresleitung*) who had distinguished himself in the creation of the new army and who, in the night of March 12 and 13, had been the only general to argue for military resistance to Kapp, declared his confidence in Noske by resigning. In his place Minister Schiffer, who represented the entire cabinet in Berlin, appointed General von Seeckt who, on that fateful night had uttered the axiom: "Reichswehr does not fire on Reichswehr." Noske, who had lost his taste for Seeckt because of these words, would never have made this choice.[31]

Seeckt was, without question, a strong personality of outstanding military capabilities and he dedicated his tireless and intelligent labors to creating and equipping the new army. Even so, was he really the proper man to lead a republican army? It was only natural that his sympathies would remain attached to the former regime, under which he had grown up and made his career. Yet he realized, at least in his calmer moments, that no person and no force could bring back those days and that it was his patriotic duty to serve the new political order even though it was not to his taste. "My world is very different from the world of today," he wrote to his wife in February 1919. "But I will do my part to make it possible for both of us and a few more Germans to live in the world of the future . . . I find no conflict between this opinion and my fundamental political convictions and am certain that I am doing what is right."

Seeckt was enough of a realist to see through the Junkers' nationalistic froth to the hollowness behind and even to recognize the false game of the German Nationalists, loud in their demands that the treaty be rejected but happy that a German majority had voted to sign. Another advantage was his skeptical attitude toward Ludendorff. Furthermore, his self-confidence and the jealousy with which he hoarded his authority gave one every reason to expect that he would suffer no subordinate to step out of line and would maintain, in general, the strictest discipline. On the other hand, Seeckt was not the sort of man to be content with an exclusively military, nonpolitical role. Particularly in foreign policy he had his own ideas, nor was he in any sense without political ambitions. Might not the national need some day be so great that the nation would summon him to lead, either as chancellor or even as its president? Thoughts like these could hardly have escaped Seeckt and his intimates, especially his extremely ambitious wife, and one would do him no injustice to assume that in his opinion a call to power under such circumstances would have meant personal dictatorship by Seeckt.[32]

It was the arduous task of the new minister of defense simultaneously to assist this man in his military activities and to keep watch on his political moves. At Ebert's suggestion this post was given to the former minister of reconstruction, Dr. Otto Gessler, whom Ebert had come to know well and to value while in Stuttgart. His relationship with Seeckt was not Gessler's sole difficulty.

Gessler belonged to the Democratic Party, yet he found himself the object of continual criticism from the Left, not only from the Independent and Social Democratic papers, but also from parts of the Democratic press. Yet he held his post for eight long years, until January 1928, through a ceaseless succession of governments and changing coalitions. This tenure testifies not only to his unusual ability, which no one would deny, but also to his political acumen. He was indeed a man of many gifts. In the Reichstag men admired the dialectical skill with which he defended his often difficult position, and even larger assemblies could escape neither the force of his personality nor the excellence of his arguments. He possessed to an extraordinary degree the ability to win over hostile audiences. The certainty of his political judgment was recognized by such utterly different men as the two presidents Ebert and Hindenburg, both of whom valued his counsel highly. While there can be valid differences of opinion concerning many of his actions, one dare not forget that his was perhaps the thorniest office of the German Republic.

The Defense Ministry was not the only one that needed to be refilled. Upon its return from Stuttgart the entire government had to undergo reconstruction. Chancellor Bauer resigned. Former Foreign Minister Hermann Müller took his place. The unions had protested against Schiffer, vice-chancellor and minister of justice, because he stooped to treat with the Kappists. Although the Democratic Party properly rejected this protest as unwarranted, Schiffer voluntarily resigned.

Members of the Prussian government were also victims of the putsch. Wolfgang Heine, minister of interior, went first. The premier, Paul Hirsch, formerly chairman of the Social Democratic bloc in the Landtag, had also failed to meet his party's expectations and thus was replaced by his minister of agriculture, Otto Braun, a stronger and more energetic man. To Heine's place Braun named Carl Severing, whose talents he had come to know well during the fighting in the Ruhr. The government remained a coalition of Social Democrats with Centrists and Democrats.

The legal liquidation of the putsch took a rather long time. The normal course of justice was interrupted by the Amnesty Law of August 4, 1920, the first of the many measures of that name which, in the final analysis, contributed not a little to the dulling of the Germans' legal sense. This law was principally a result of the disturbance in the Ruhr and the so-called Bielefeld Agreement of March 1920, with which it had been settled.[33] Since this agreement had promised impunity to those who had broken laws in quelling the revolt, the parties of the Right, much stronger since the June elections, demanded a similar treatment of the participants in the abortive coup. This the law granted "insofar as they were neither instigators nor leaders of this treasonable enterprise." Indicative of opinion in the South was the fact that Bavaria succeeded in keeping this general amnesty from being extended so as to include "treasonable enterprises" in Bavaria, that is, the Red republic there. Most of the leaders of the Kapp Putsch fled from justice. Wolfgang Kapp escaped to Sweden and most of his lieutenants simply disappeared. They had good friends who hid them on country estates or in other fitting spots until they found an opportunity to cross the border, leaving their nation behind.

When the dust had settled, only three rebel leaders stood before the Supreme Court, indicted for high treason: the former police commissioner of Berlin, Traugott von Jagow, who had played at being Kapp's minister of interior; Baron Konrad von Wangenheim, long the leader of the Agrarian League (*Bund der Landwirte*); and Georg Wilhelm Schiele, M.D. Ludendorff was not required to sit upon the defendants' bench. The attorney general assumed, to be sure, that the general had been aware of the rebels' attitudes and purpose and had followed their undertaking with evident interest. But he said he could not find sufficient grounds for prosecution, and the Social Democratic minister of justice, Professor Radbruch, agreed.[34] The Supreme Court delivered its sentence on December 21, 1921. Jagow alone received five years' "fortress confinement" for having been accessory to high treason. The cases against Wangenheim and Schiele were dropped since these men could not be regarded as "leaders" of the putsch.

Jagow was obliged to serve only a portion of his sentence. Pardoned in December 1924, he immediately sued the land of Prussia for back payments of his pension. He won his case before the Supreme Court, thanks to a literal interpretation of law which flew in the face of seventy years' practice.

Kapp waited until the spring of 1922 for his return to Germany and his judges. At this time he was mortally ill, and on June 12, 1922, death took him to a higher court. Thus his heavy debt remained unpaid. But in Hitler's time a fanatic racist [35] dedicated to this would-be traitor a panegyric which he called "A Word of Atonement" (*Ein Wort der Sühne*). The author insisted that Kapp owed no act of atonement to the German people. Rather it was the nation which owed a great debt to the allegedly misunderstood statesman. Here was an inversion of moral concepts to bring joy to the hearts of the witches in *Macbeth*!

VI

WEAKNESS AT HOME
AND THREATS FROM ABROAD

K<small>APP</small>'s rebels produced one beneficial result. Because of their putsch, it was necessary to advance the date of the Reichstag elections. On March 29, at the first meeting of the National Assembly under the new government, Chancellor Müller, speaking for his cabinet, declared that the nation "demanded prompt elections now, after the Kapp adventure." Perhaps the coalition parties assumed that the putsch had a sobering effect on the electorate, bringing the nation to the realization that the time had come to strengthen and concentrate those forces that were prepared to cooperate in the peaceful organization of the new state. But the elections of June 6, 1920, completely dashed any such hope. To the opposition, both of the Right and of the Left, they brought massive success; to the governmental coalition, severe defeat. Votes for the coalition dropped from a former 19 million to 11; those on the Right increased from 5.6 to 9.1; those on the Left, from 2.1 to 5.3 million. Neither in the electorate nor in the Reichstag did the coalition command its former majority.

The heaviest losses were suffered by the German Democratic Party. In the elections for the National Assembly the Democrats had received 5.6 million votes; they now won only 2.3 million. The number of the party's seats consequently dropped from 75 to 45. On the other hand Stresemann's German People's Party, which had campaigned under the slogan "Von roten Ketten macht Euch frei/ Allein die Deutsche Volkspartei," * had gained over 2.5 million

---

* "Only the German Populists can save you from the Communists."

votes and now had 62 instead of 22 delegates. The voters who in 1919 had regarded the Democratic Party as the last dike against the Socialist tide had deserted this defense when the Democrats joined the Social Democrats and Centrists to pass laws as unpopular among bourgeois circles as were the Emergency Contribution (*Notopfer*) and the Factory Council Law. The defection was probably increased by the party's attitude toward the general strike; Erzberger's general unpopularity may also have been influential. Furthermore, many people had voted for the Democrats in 1919 because they had hoped that a democratic Germany would receive a milder peace. Once this hope was shattered, the electorate had little use for either democracy or Democrats. The party had also lost several of its more popular leaders: Friedrich Naumann died prematurely in August 1919 and Friedrich Payer returned to private life because of advanced years. But the decisive factor — and it had lasting importance — was the electoral defeat. The party not only failed to recover from this blow; it continued to languish. This erosion of the Democratic Party proved fatal to the life of the Weimar Republic because this party was the single reliable support of German republicanism for those who were neither Socialist nor Catholic.

The weakness of republican sentiment was manifested in another way when the openly antirepublican German National Party gained more than one million new votes and the German People's Party more than two and one half million. While the *Volkspartei* cannot be labeled explicitly monarchist, it most certainly was not republican. At best it barely tolerated the new German state. No system of government, however, can long remain healthy unless it is genuinely and positively supported by at least a significant part of the country's intellectual, economic, and social leaders. In Germany the preponderance of such leaders castigated the Weimer Republic as the "state of surrender" and indicted it for its inability to arouse the nation against the victorious enemy. The nationalist militarist spirit had taken root again.

The Socialist workers, like the Democrats, had also hoped to play a constructive role in the new Republic. Their plans suffered just as great a defeat. It is, of course, true that the Social Democrats, with their 113 seats, were still the strongest party in the Reichstag. But they had lost over 50 delegates, while the Independents, who had formerly to content themselves with 22, now controlled 81 seats of their own, having gained the allegiance of 2.7 million new voters. And beyond them to the Left were almost 600,000 Communist votes. For the first time in German history, two Communists, Dr. Paul Levi and Clara Zetkin, sat in the Reichstag. This drift of the workers to the Left was, of course, strengthened by Kapp's foolish revolt and its aftermath. But it can also be considered a natural consequence of labor's shattered hopes of socializing Germany and of the dreary economic situation, inflation and rising prices, the fruits of a lost war. These factors gave the workers grounds for discontent and provided the raw material for agitators' mills. While the Independents' success quickly proved ephemeral, it made a great impression for the moment, particularly upon the Majority Socialists, at whose expense the Independents had made their gains.

For the Social Democrats drew from this experience the conclusion that their voters had deserted them precisely because they held the party responsible for shortcomings of the government. Thus the Social Democrats wished to take part in the formation of a new government required by the change in party strengths only if the Independents also joined the cabinet. But the latter much preferred the easy role of opposition or, as their doctrinaire jargon put it, "the continuation of the ruthless proletarian class struggle with the aim of abolishing the capitalistic-militaristic bourgeois rule." They said they would take part only in a "purely socialistic government" although they knew well enough that the composition of the Reichstag made such a regime impossible. None of these protestations, however, kept several of the Independents' leaders from accepting posts in later bourgeois cabinets.

And so the Social Democrats left the government, while the German People's Party, after protracted parleys, stepped in. The latter, together with the Centrists and Democrats, comprised the new coalition government. The Democrats had blocked a further drift toward the Right with their refusal to take part in a government which included German Nationalists. The last president of the old Reichstag, Dr. Fehrenbach, a Centrist from Baden, became chancellor. Dr. Walter Simons, former commissioner-general of the German delegation to Versailles, became foreign minister. Dr. Heinze of the People's Party became vice-premier and minister of justice. The Ministry of Finance remained, as in the former cabinet, under Dr. Wirth, a Centrist. The Ministry of Transportation was given to General Gröner, who, like Dr. Simons, belonged to no party. In a Reichstag of 466 members the coalition parties controlled together only 176 votes. The regime was thus a minority government, not even able to ask its parliament for the customary vote of confidence. It could exist only so long as the Social Democrats gave it their benevolent toleration. This neutrality was granted for the time being because of imminent negotiations with the Allies.

An international conference was about to be held at Spa, a meeting where, for the first time, the Germans had been invited to join, rather than face, the Allies. A plethora of interallied conferences had already taken place, yielding only the evidence that the Allies were finding it constantly more difficult to maintain a common German policy. In Great Britain Lloyd George, still in command, was returning more and more to the frame of mind that he had expressed during the negotiations at Versailles, in his memorandum of late March 1919. That is to say, he wanted to proceed from a formal peace to a real one, and German reconstruction was a necessary condition of such a settlement. In France Clemenceau had departed from the scene. A majority of the senators and deputies, fearful of his liberal use of power, had preferred Deschanel to the "Tiger" as president. But France's German policy was set less by her leaders than by public opinion, and this was, in the main, a combination of hatred and fear. The French wished to let the Germans suffer as they had made the French suffer and also to make as sure as possible that no German soldier would ever again enter France. This explains their insistence on a strict execution of the Versailles treaty down to the last subclause. The new Premier, Millerand, endorsed this position.

Clearly the task of German diplomacy was to take advantage of this difference of opinion among the Allies and, quietly and unobtrusively, to steer a course in the direction of Germany's national advantage. Whether such a course would have attained its goal, no one can tell. But one certainly can say that the German representatives in Spa made no use of this opportunity. It would be unjust to heap the responsibility for this strategy on them alone. They stood under the pressure of public opinion which had become painfully clear after the Reichstag elections. "Don't yield one inch!" was the message from the polls. "The softness of the Weimar Coalition saddled us with this shameful peace. We have chased the rascals out and now we shall see that a firm stand will lead to success."

The first item of the agenda at Spa (July 5–16, 1920) could serve as an example of the mood of the German delegation. This item concerned the execution of the military provisions of the treaty for the disarmament of Germany. Today hardly anyone would wish to contradict the argument of the responsible leaders of the German Army that a force of 100,000 was utterly insufficient. For these leaders had twenty months of bitter experience behind them. Nor will anyone today find wisdom in the provision that this 100,000-man army should consist of career soldiers on twelve-year enlistments. It was a matter of concern not only for German domestic policy but also for the Allies that, things in Germany being as they were, pro-

fessional soldiers came almost exclusively from Rightist circles; the
Leftist urban workers avoided military service almost to a man.

But the Allies thought that the Germans had been busy from the
start with the creation, parallel to the official Army, of other armed
ogranizations which could quickly double or triple German military
power at the desired moment. It was with suspicious eyes that they
regarded the security police (*Sicherheitspolizei*), armed and organized in a military fashion, and more particularly the armed Home
Guards (*Einwohnerwehren*) which had been formed in many regions, especially in the south. To the Allies all these things smacked
of German militarism, the unreconstructed vigor of which had been
fully proved to them by the Kapp Putsch.

But in point of fact the Home Guards could not be dispensed
with so simply. The men of Moscow were preaching world revolution while armed bands threatened the peaceful citizen with arson
and looting. In April 1920 Max Hölz, the leader of a Communist
band, had terrorized the Saxon Vogtland for several weeks. In a
time like this it was inevitable that the threatened citizenry should
reach for weapons and band together with their neighbors to protect their life and property. That the Home Guards, especially in
rural areas, were useful in this way is attested by such an informed
and unprejudiced witness as Severing. But many Home Guards
sought political ends as well. In Bavaria, where they were headed by
the forester Escherich, they had helped to create Kahr's Rightist
government in March. Throughout Germany the parties of the Right
understandably considered these groups to be their political brethren. This fact became apparent when, on April 8, Koch, the national
minister of interior, obeying an Allied directive, ordered the governments of the lands to dissolve the Home Guards. When the government of Prussia yielded to this command, it was most violently attacked from the Right in the Landtag and in the press,[1] while these
same forces praised the Bavarian regime for having refused to obey
the order. Under such circumstances it is quite understandable
that many German republicans regarded the Home Guards as an
instrument of the counterrevolution and that the Allies saw in them
a ready reserve for the Army.

Gessler and Seeckt presented the German military point of view
at Spa.[2] Their demand that German armed strength be fixed at
200,000 men, double the treaty provision, was all the more doomed
to failure at this time since they had to admit, while asking this
favor, that the provisions for demilitarization and deliveries of arms
had not been carried out. Lloyd George retorted that the existence
of millions of uncontrolled arms constituted a constant threat not

only to the German government but also to neighboring states. When Seeckt then proposed that the time allotted for the cut in the Army to 100,000 men be extended to fifteen months, he also met with absolute refusal. The Allies were convinced that there was no use in further negotiation, so they reverted to dictation. They gave the Germans a protocol to sign in which they granted the Germans the maximal time permitted by the treaty to reduce their forces, that is until January 1, 1921, but threatened to occupy additional parts of Germany, perhaps the Ruhr, if the new deadlines were not met. It seemed to the Germans that this threat exceeded the rights granted the Allies in the treaty, and they therefore declined to accept it with their signatures. They had, however, no choice but to sign the protocol requiring them to disarm the Home Guards and to complete the delivery of weapons. Materially these protocols did not involve any alteration of the treaty to the Germans' disadvantage; but their form implied another German defeat, and the threat of further occupation could only arouse concern for what might lie ahead.

There were also negotiations concerning German deliveries of coal under the provisions of the treaty. This was a technically difficult problem and one in which (and this fact should have warned the Germans) France, among all the allies, was involved to the greatest and most immediate degree. It is undeniable that France had need of German coal because her own mines had been destroyed or made useless by German soldiers. It is equally undeniable that the required deliveries placed an extraordinary weight upon a German economy plagued, particularly in the industrial Ruhr, with disturbances which made these shipments dear. Moreover, in consequence of shortages of Upper Silesian coal, the Germans had made the error of lessening unilaterally the amount of coal delivered every month. Thus it well behooved the German delegation to treat this matter with the greatest care. Their formal advocates, Minister Simons and the German representative on the Reparations Commission, the realistic Secretary Bergmann, were guided in their conduct by this thought. But then the expert Stinnes rose to speak.

Hugo Stinnes, "merchant in Mühlheim" as he liked to call himself with pretentious simplicity, was the most successful German industrialist of his time. In good times he had made good money, and he made it no less in the bad. He kept extending the range of his interests ever further: into coal and mining, shipping, hotels, and even newspapers. And in every undertaking to which he lent his name he remained the leading, decision-making man. He knew how to get things done and was a tireless worker. A unique personality, he distinguished himself from his fellow magnates not only in his face and beard, which gave him almost the appearance of an ancient Assyrian king, but also through his poorly fitting suits and his disdain for all those pleasures in which the wealthy customarily indulge. Unfortunately he had somehow become convinced that, since he had reaped the greatest economic successes, he was in a position to win political laurels as well — not in the Reichstag, where he was a *Volkspartei* delegate, but rather at the conference table, where the real decisions were made. One has no right to doubt his desire to further German interests as he saw them. But with the naïveté of many a self-made man, he identified the welfare of Germany with that of his private enterprises. This habit of his was of special portent at this time since his affairs were prospering from the inflation that was ruining the Reich. Clever as he was in his own way, in politics he remained a dilettante. Probably more than he realized, he became increasingly subservient to the nationalistic sentiments which were so popular in his social set. Since he knew more about mining and handling coal than did the politicians at the table, he thought he could treat them like recalcitrant stockholders who could be quickly brought to reason by a few sharp words delivered at the annual meeting.

Even the first sentence of his remarks, prepared in advance and read from manuscript, was a clear challenge: "I rise in order to be able to look the hostile delegates straight in the eyes." He went on in this style, referring to such things as "our insane conquerors" and underscoring his unyielding words with a coarse manner and uncompromising tone.[3] Lord d'Abernon, who had gone as British ambassador to Berlin with every desire of reaching mutual understanding, writes: "The Allied delegates were pale with anger and surprise . . . M. Hymans, the Belgian foreign minister, remarked: 'What would have happened with such a man, if he had been in the position of the conqueror?' "[4] Stinnes' behavior led to utter catastrophe at Spa, but in Germany this speech had made him a national hero. "He really gave it to them!" men chortled in the local taverns and in the editorial offices of the "nationalistic" newspapers.

"Whoever contradicts his conqueror is a fool," were the words of Platen's Harmosan. Bismarck had warned the Germans in vain that every nation must sooner or later pay for the windows broken by its pugnacious press. But it is not only the press that practices this expensive sport; those much-revered captains of industry often join the game.

Simons and the more responsible members of the German delegation had all they could do to repair the damage wrought by

Stinnes. Stinnes had threatened that all coal deliveries would be cut off if the Allies occupied the Ruhr. But the Allies did not appear to take fright at this dark warning. Not only did they give formal notice of their intent to extend their occupation if deliveries continued to be delayed, but they also summoned Marshal Foch and the English Commanding General Wilson to Spa to begin preparations for the Allied march. With the help of Professor Bonn,[5] who was with the German delegation as the Chancellor's adviser on reparations, Simons succeeded in re-establishing rapport with Lloyd George before any military steps were taken. After further, heated negotiations Fehrenbach and Simons signed a protocol, prepared by the Allies, which determined the coal deliveries for the next six months. With respect to quantity the Allies had, on the whole, worked their will. But they had made a most important concession to the Germans: a cash credit of five gold marks was set on each delivered ton of coal, and the funds were to be used expressly to purchase food for German miners. Stinnes objected to this agreement to the end but, having failed to convince his colleagues, was forced to yield.

Naturally these results were received very badly by German nationalists. One can go so far as to say that many segments of the population were as astonished as they were indignant. What Simons said in the Reichstag was true: "Up to the last few months many of our nation nourished the false notion that the peace treaty was not to be taken seriously and would not be taken seriously by the other side. Only now are the people gradually beginning to comprehend the full weight of the nation's burden." In the Reichstag a speaker for the German Nationalists accused the delegation of having failed to preserve the national honor, and this time the reproach was made by an otherwise rational man, the historian Otto Hoetzsch. Even Stresemann, who, as leader of a coalition party, had the duty of defending the agreement, managed to thank Stinnes for his contribution. An occurrence at the French embassy in Berlin illustrates the nonsensical consequences of this nationalistic furor. There the French flag, flying in celebration of July 14, was ripped down by a young man. Of course the German government had to present formal apologies and a company of German soldiers had to salute the flag of France as it was raised again. But the manner in which these acts of international courtesy were carried out served only to evoke further protests from Paris. And when Simons, in the Reichstag, permitted himself a mild reproach, his remark excited such spirited objections that he half retracted his words. A Berlin court fined the author of this stupid prank only 500 paper marks, which corresponded at that time to approximately 50 gold marks.[6]

In an atmosphere like this it took real courage for Conrad Haussmann to label, in Reichstag debate, the scuttling of the fleet at Scapa Flow as an act of consummate injustice, wrought upon Germany by her admirals. With the aid of the Social Democrats, a considerable majority of the Reichstag accepted a resolution approving the government's course. And the Disarmament Law, which the Spa Protocol required of the German government, was passed by a large majority; even most of the German Nationalists voted for the bill.

The German problem was not the only cause of Allied headaches at Spa. In the spring of 1920 Russo-Polish tensions had exploded into a real war which, in July, took a decided turn in Russia's favor. When Warsaw was seriously threatened, Grabski, the Polish Premier, hastened to Spa to call for Allied aid. The Entente dispatched an Anglo-French mission to Warsaw, the most important member of which was General Weygand, Marshal Foch's chief of staff. Weygand succeeded in bringing order to the military and moral chaos of the Polish Army and was even able to organize a counterattack that met with complete success. Now it was the Red Army's turn to collapse with astonishing speed; and in October Soviet Russia had to accept an armistice which subsequently led to a peace very favorable to the Poles. Poland received an eastern border that met its wishes in every way.

People in Germany were following these dramatic events with lively interest. They sensed that a definitive defeat of France's protegé, Poland, would considerably weaken the continental position of the Entente. On July 20 the German government made a formal declaration of German neutrality in the Russo-Polish conflict. This move had the practical effect of barring Allied shipments of troops or weapons to Poland through German territory. It came as no surprise that the sympathies of the Independents and the Communists lay with Russia and that the spokesman for the Independents in the Reichstag, Dr. Breitscheid, sent the Russians "the greetings of their German brothers in the holy battle for the fruits of revolution." Considerably less expected was the calm and calculating manner with which, at the same session of the Reichstag (July 26), the foreign minister, Dr. Simons, discussed the Russian government, taking care to praise it warmly for its achievements and explicitly denying the notion that "the Soviet Republic might turn against Germany with fire and the sword." In fact there was at that time a strong tendency on the Wilhelmstrasse to favor a rapprochement with Russia which would improve Germany's position vis à vis the Entente. The most prominent and energetic proponent of this view was Ago, Baron von Maltzan.

But even Seeckt, who was naturally opposed in every way to Bolshevism, was rather inclined to find ways to let Russian military successes serve German ends. On the one hand he hoped to persuade the Entente to treat Germany as a "wall against Bolshevism," giving him the stronger army that he wished. On the other hand he rejected "any support of Poland, even in the event that Poland is devoured . . . Although we are unable to help Russia regain her former borders, we can at least refrain from hindering her attempt." In early August, when he was still counting on a complete Russian conquest of Poland, he recommended that the Germans "try to obtain guarantees of the 1914 borders and, further, to overcome the nation's domestic differences in the quest for a common foreign policy." [7] The Russian defeat soon made such considerations quite pointless.

Reparations had not been on the agenda at Spa. From the German point of view this fact was perhaps not to be regretted. For what could they have offered to the West? The Allied members of the Reparations Commission, who earnestly wished to reach some feasible arrangement, agreed with Secretary Bergmann and Dr. Melchior during a confidential conversation, that, at the moment, the German delegation faced an insoluble dilemma: [8] if the Germans were to declare that their political and economic distress made them unable to offer reparations at this time, they would evoke a storm of indignation in France and England; yet if the Germans offered an amount which actually corresponded with their depressed circumstances, this figure would fall so far short of their creditors' expectations and demands that it would be rejected out of hand. This route, too, would thus lead to crisis. Yet some hope was seen in the idea of a so-called *Besserungsschein*,* that is, in the combination of the minimum practicable offer with the agreement that that amount would be increased proportionately as the German economy improved.

But sometime the moment had to come when the Germans would clearly and unambiguously say how much of the reparations bill

* *Besserungsschein* is the technical term in German law for the written statement of a bankrupt debtor, given in a general settlement, in which the debtor promises to make additional payments to his creditors as and when his economic position improves. TRANSLATORS.

they would assume and how they planned to amortize their debt. The Versailles treaty required that by May 1, 1921, the Germans pay their initial installment of twenty billion gold marks and also, according to Article 233, that the Reparations Commission fix the total sum of the German debt. In the meantime, however, even the Allies had discovered that the problem was much more complex than it had appeared to the men at Versailles one year before. Was not the stipulated date much too early to set a final, total sum? Would it not be to the advantage of both sides to establish first a provisional plan for payments through the next five years and then, in the breathing space thus won, to work out the definitive schedule? Could one not hope that during this period public opinion, both in Germany and the West, would have calmed down and popular illusions dissipated; could not one also expect that objective economic data would have become consolidated and the whole economic situation become clearer? This was the standpoint of one of the keenest and most influential of the French experts, Seydoux, chief of the commerce division of the French Foreign Office. In January 1921, at one of the numerous international conferences which took place in the months after Spa, Seydoux made the concrete proposal that Germany pay three billion gold marks annually for the next five years.

Bergmann took this proposal, which, though not official, might have become so under proper treatment, to Berlin. And so the German government found themselves confronted by the choice of accepting this provisional answer or proposing a better one themselves. This was a most difficult problem. In the short run it was of course simpler to purchase five years' respite from the awful question. But could one ever count on economic calm and consolidation as long as this great riddle of Germany's future remained unsolved? The industrial leaders with whom the cabinet consulted declared, under Stinnes' decisive influence, that they needed an *immediate* solution of the *definitive* problem in order that they might arrange their business affairs accordingly. It is probably true, however, that there was a more compelling reason why the industrialists urged immediate action on reparations. They were afraid that postponement would increase the amount of reparations demanded if, after a few years, the German economy should rise from the ruins of defeat and revolution to ever higher levels of production. Certainly one could expect a demand for increased reparations if, during provisional period, the German currency were stabilized and the inflation ended.

It is one of the more insidious characteristics of inflation that it displays its pernicious side only gradually. At the beginning of an inflation, disadvantages are obscured by immediate benefits more striking to the eye. These visible benefits are well described in Goethe's *Faust* by the Emperor's marshal who has been lulled by Mephisto's deviltry:

> The money-counters now are opened wide . . .
> Then off to butchers, bars, and bakery shops.
> Full half the world thinks only of their chops;
> And while the rest in newest raiment struts,
> The merchant measures out, the tailor cuts.

Such bliss was only for those at the top of the business, economic, or political ladder. The investor, who from his fixed savings drew a fixed and definite income, was naturally quick to notice that the value of his capital and income shrank with every week. But no one worried about him. On the contrary, he was quite unpopular, and, to the extent that his investments lay in real estate, legislators took care, through sundry sorts of rent controls, lest he try to raise his rents as their real value fell. At first the industrialist and the merchant, and to a certain extent even the workers and clerks, did not suffer from inflation in the least. Merchandise floated away in the flood of new money, and the devaluation of the mark made German exports cheaper. It was only natural that stock prices rose as the mark fell; the market became fantastically active, and whoever was not too stupid about it found himself able to supplement his shrinking income amply with speculation's profits. The export trade was in the best position of all of course, for exporters received payments in the form that all desired, foreign currencies, while paying salaries, interest, and taxes in paper marks. Salaries in this field were admittedly rather high. But the export companies could reckon that taxes would shrink between imposition and collection, along with their debts at the bank. Industry thus did not share the nation's general desire to check inflation, but rather, and this is the relevant fact here, regarded inflation and the expansion of currency as a veil which might hide from foreign experts the real state of German affairs.

Restrained by this negative attitude of the industrialists, the government hesitated to accept Seydoux' proposal. But after the English and French chargés d'affaires called upon Simons to present their governments' recommendations that he accept this temporizing solution, he finally realized that an utter rejection of this plan by the Germans would be particularly dangerous since no German was able to make a counterproposal for a final solution which could be presented to the Entente with any hope of success. He therefore

assigned to Bergmann the task of negotiating further on the basis
of the Seydoux plan. It was only proper that in these negotiations
Bergmann sought to lower the annual payments and, further, to set
some limit to the ever mounting costs of occupation. More questionable, however, was his insistence that these German proposals be
linked to assurances that Upper Silesia would remain German. For
the plebiscite promised at Versailles still lay in the future (March
1921). Furthermore, this plebiscite had been a last-minute concession to the Germans, a concession which Lloyd George won from
Clemenceau only after a struggle. It was therefore obvious that the
French, who were just about to conclude an alliance with Poland
(February 1, 1921), would under no circumstances yield on this
point and that Lloyd George, if only to preserve his political reputation, was in no position at all to ask such a concession of France.

Whether in spite of these difficulties the negotiations might have
led to some provisional solution must remain a moot question, for,
at their conference in Paris on January 24, the Allies suddenly
changed their course and dropped the whole idea of the Seydoux
plan. Briand had just assumed the reins of government in France,
although he allowed his minister of finance, Doumer, to carry the
French burden at the conference. Doumer's extreme demands were
opposed sharply by Lloyd George. But even he finally agreed to
join in requiring Germany to pay an annual bill, for forty-two years,
rising gradually from two to six billion gold marks; and to deliver,
throughout this time, twelve percent of German exports to the
Entente.

These decisions (which, to be sure, were simply labeled "proposals") were received in Germany with a storm of indignant protest, the echoes of which could be clearly heard in the Reichstag
session of February 2. But all this did not relieve the government
of the necessity of presenting counterproposals in return. For the
Germans had been invited to confer with the Allies at London on
March 1, and Simons knew quite well that he would not be able
to satisfy his hosts with a simple pauper's oath. He was also sufficiently far in advance of public opinion in Germany to realize that
a completely negative attitude would put him morally in the wrong.
On February 13, in a speech at Stuttgart, he said the German government was convinced that the nation which had decided to sign
the Treaty of Versailles was also prepared to labor to the limit of
its ability to make good the damages of war. In contrast to many
others, Simons really meant these words. He full realized that German popular opinion much preferred illusions and loud words to
his sober rejoinders. He also knew that this public opinion was his

source of strength, and so he sought, in a speaking tour through southern Germany, to win it to his side. He should have presented a simple, direct exposition of his case. Instead he tried to win the approbation of the crowd by criticizing sharply the proposals from Paris and by raising once again the question of war guilt. Naturally the Germans applauded merrily when he denied that the guilt was theirs. But his speeches were also read in Paris and London, where the belief in German's guilt still stood firm and where people could only interpret such untimely utterances as deliberate provocations. Hence the Allies assembled at the London Conference regarded Simons in a much less favorable light than his ethics and his politics deserved.

Probably even the most brilliant diplomat could not have presented a plan to the conference which, on one hand, restricted itself to the maximum amount the Germans thought they were able to pay and on the other hand corresponded even slightly to the amount the Allies thought they needed desperately if they were to repair only their severest damages. But an offer of 30 billion marks in easy payments and with no provision for a *Besserungsschein* when the bill of damages had heretofore hovered above 200 billion marks could clearly only irritate and embitter the Allies to such an extent that they would overlook the wise and well-considered portions of the German plan.

The cornerstone of this plan certainly deserved serious consideration. The Germans' reasoning had as its base the *present value* of what they were to be required to pay. This value would be considerably less than the sum of its installments to be paid for more than forty years, for each installment included a large payment of interest. At interest of 8 percent the 226 billion gold marks which the Paris proposals would have set as Germany's bill had a present value of only 53 billion. In this way one arrived at handier figures, easier to discuss. The Germans took the figure of 53 billion and rounded it off — downwards — to 50 billion. But how had they reduced this result further to the 30 billion marks which Simons offered? The answer was simplicity itself, or seemed to be.

According to Article 235 of the Versailles treaty, Germany was required to deliver 20 billion marks' worth of reparation before May 1, 1921, that is, before the final determination of the total reparation bill, in what was expected at Versailles to take the form of goods, not credits. The German government claimed now that the German anticipatory shipments had already reached this figure if indeed, they had not exceeded it; their itemized bill showed a total of 21 billion marks. But of all this the Reparations Commission recognized only 8 billion at most. Now it is quite true that men can differ honestly in their appraisal of the value of payments in kind. But various items of the Germans' calculations were such as to excite real doubts concerning their authors' good faith, either because the item clearly did not belong in the bill or because the item's estimated value stood in screaming contradiction to its actual worth. The mines of the Saar, for instance, had been assessed by Helfferich in 1913 at 300 million marks; now, having been turned over to the French, they were valued at 1000 million. In 1935 Germany paid only 140 million gold marks for their return. In 1913 Helfferich had estimated the total value of German shipping, both domestic and international, at more than one billion marks. Germany had been obliged to give over half of its maritime fleet to the Allies. As recompense the affected owners received a total of 550 million marks through the government's Bank for Maritime Reconstruction, payments which made possible an astonishingly quick revival of the German merchant marine. But in calculating reparations paid in kind the Germans now entered these delivered ships as an item of 3426 million gold marks. Even worse was their attempt to include among these reparations the value of materials lost in war, including that of the battle fleet scuttled at Scapa Flow.[9] In brief, the errors and exaggerations in the Germans' reckoning were so apparent that one cannot hold against the Allies their conclusion that this was one more sign of the bad faith of the Germans, who, however much they might protest to the contrary, simply did not wish to carry out the peace.

Unfortunately this was not the only basis for the Allies' conclusion. Another cause of Allied complaint was the continued delay in the trial of German war criminals. No action had been initiated before the Supreme Court; indeed none was undertaken before May 23, 1921. Far more significant was the Allied complaint that Germany had failed to carry out its disarmament according to the protocol of Spa.

This accusation contained a kernel of truth, but in this instance the guilty party was not the government of Germany. As we saw above, the government had succeeded in steering the Disarmament Law through the Reichstag, but the administration of this law was sabotaged and even blocked by Bavaria. For here the belief in the indispensability of the Home Guards had become an article of faith which no one could question without being taken for a supporter of the Reds, and in the defense of which Kahr saw the *raison d'être* of his regime. Whether Bavarian defiance of the disarmament order attacked the national government from behind at a time when it was trying desperately to spare Germany new misfortunes and whether this defiance gravely endangered the unity of the Reich, a unity they liked to laud in rolling tones, was all a matter of complete indifference to the men of Munich. On the very day that Simons was forced to sign the disarmament protocol at Spa, Kahr announced the "permanent opinion" of his government "that under no circumstances can Bavaria dispense with her Home Guards." The Bavarian Government adopted this same position on August 11, 1920, when the Disarmament Law went into force. Not only did the Munich regime refuse to carry out the law in Bavaria, it even went so far as to let the Bavarian Home Guards publicly organize a "Bavarian Shooting Match" and triumphantly announce it as an annual event. In conversations with the national government, for which Kahr had traveled to Berlin, he did not dispute the necessity of the national law but did claim for his regime the right to decide for itself *when* the law should be executed in Bavaria, where a state of siege and extralegal "People's Courts" (*Volksgerichte*) still existed.

This was the first time in the history of a united Germany that a member state had dared to disobey. But so great was the confusion of ideas when a question of militarism was involved that in the Reichstag debate of January 19, 1921, the spokesman for the German Nationalists managed to defend this disobedience with the argument that Bavaria was required to recognize nation-wide provisions only when they did not affect matters of vital interest to the Bavarian state. This spokesman, a professor of Protestant theology at the Bavarian University at Erlangen, then had to listen while the national minister of interior, Erich Koch, explained that his arguments amounted to a clear invitation to constitutional chaos. But neither the worthy Kahr nor the Bavarian People's Party were afraid of that. Even after January 1921, when the conclusions of the Allied conference in Paris had made the severity of Germany's plight apparent to even the most myopic nationalists, and while the national government was preparing for the London Conference, the Bavarian government was so stupidly tactless as to announce formally that its position would not be changed by new events.

The battle over the *Orgesch (Organisation Escherich)* was just one detail of this domestic war. The forester Escherich, leader of the Bavarian Home Guards, founded what he hoped would become a national union of all the German "Self-Defense Units" (*Selbstschutzverbände*). The platform of this national union was impeccable, as was its official goal of uniting all those German elements "who take the battle against Communism seriously." But the actual behavior of this organization and its members was by no means so inoffensive. They had military weapons at their disposal and almost every week their caches of arms, according to Severing, were uncovered.[10] The Prussian minister of the interior was therefore only doing his duty when he banned the *Orgesch* from his land. This move naturally excited a loud cry not only in Bavaria, but also in the entire German Nationalist press, which did not shrink from calling him "the slave of his party, the destroyer of Prussia, and the saboteur of German unity." The national government hesitated at first but later found itself with no alternative but to outlaw the organization throughout the Reich.

Naturally the Allies followed carefully the conflict between the governments of Germany and Bavaria. Since July 1920 the French had even had a special emissary in Munich, although the rights of the German states to send and receive ambassadors, left to them by Bismarck, had been revoked in the Weimar constitution. But France had used a contrived, pseudolegalistic argument to circumvent this clause. The French clearly hoped that Bavarian particularism might someday grow into secession. None of the other Allies followed French example here, but they were extremely irritated by the inability of the national government to force its will against the recalcitrant Bavarians. Was German *unable* or merely *unwilling* to act? As Lloyd George put it at the London Conference, the Allies had become convinced that either "the German Government does not intend to carry out its treaty obligations, or that it has not the strength to insist, in the face of selfish and shortsighted opposition, upon the necessary sacrifices being made." [11]

These words were part of the reply that the British Prime Minister, speaking for all the Allies, made to the German foreign minister on March 3. Lloyd George had come to the conference with every desire to effect a rapprochement. He was, as Lord d'Abernon's notes of the time make clear, in a critical mood toward the French, whom he accused of being unable to decide whether they preferred payment or the pleasure of trampling on Germany.[12] But Simons' address had gravely disillusioned him. And even Bergmann [13] noted that Simons' "manner of delivery, which hammered, so to speak, the despised 30 billion marks into the minds of the assembly, while the debt seemed to shrink at every blow," made an unfavorable impression on the Allies. Now the British Prime Minister, who up to that time had unconditionally rejected any "military adventure," could no longer withstand the French pressures for armed sanctions. And so in his address he announced the Allies' decision: (1) to occupy the cities of Düsseldorf, Duisburg, and Ruhrort; (2) to retain a portion of the purchase prices of German goods exported to the West; and (3) to seize the German customs' receipts in the occupied areas, establishing another customs barrier between these areas and the rest of Germany.

These sanctions were to take effect on March 7 unless, by that date, the Germans had either accepted the Paris proposals of January or made appropriate counterproposals in their stead. The British Prime Minister clearly hoped that the German delegation, pressed by this announcement, would make some sort of proposal which would permit him to avoid the threatened steps. Aided by Lord d'Abernon and Philip Kerr he entered busily into private negotiations with Simons on the one hand and the French plenipotentiary on the other in search of some solution. For a moment it seemed that agreement could be found on a provisional plan. But this hope quickly vanished. The negotiations led to no result, and so the three Rhine ports were occupied on March 8, 1921. The German delegation protested this Allied move and left the conference.

Lord d'Abernon, whose honest desire for agreement no one can doubt, and who had come, in the course of intimate conversations, to respect Simons highly, saw at least three reasons for the failure of the London Conference. First, German public opinion did not support Simons in his quest for compromise; second, the French delegates were too tightly bound by a firm and narrow mandate. Finally, all efforts were doomed to failure so long as the Germans refused to make any payments unless Upper Silesia remained theirs.[14]

The correctness of d'Abernon's estimate of popular opinion in Germany was demonstrated when the German delegation returned to Berlin. At the rail station Simons, and also Seeckt, who had accompanied him, were hailed as victors by the cheering crowd. Why victors? Because they had said no. No one seems to have asked himself whether this no would spare Germany further injury or what its influence on later events was going to be. The crowd applauded the defiant gesture; Simons can hardly have been pleased by their joy.

The great question was whether this no could be maintained. An overwhelming majority of the Reichstag approved it on March 12, but only after a debate which disclosed a wide variety of views concerning the methods employed at London and the course to be taken in the future. Actually one cannot speak of a unified German attitude toward this tense international situation. The Communists not only staged a childish attack upon the Victory Column in Berlin, they also plotted a rather dangerous armed revolt in central Germany, making explicit reference to "the critical position of the national government, caught between sanctions in the West and the plebiscite in Upper Silesia." [15] Legally, this move amounted to treason; politically, it was an attempt to transplant the World Revolution from Russia to Germany via Bitterfeld and Merseburg. The links tying these rebels to Moscow were particularly clear since in October 1920 Russian emissaries like Zinoviev had succeeded in persuading many of the Independents to join the Communists, thus giving the latter party a new importance. On March 24 the German President found himself obliged to declare a state of nonmilitary emergency in the Prussian province of Saxony. With rapid deployment of Prussian police, supported by Reichswehr units, Severing quickly succeeded in suppressing the revolt. It was typical of German politics at that time that Severing was subsequently attacked sharply for this intervention not only by the Communists but also by German Nationalists in the Prussian Landtag.

And still worse, even now, when the flames consuming Germany had almost reached the roof, the Bavarians persisted in stubbornly refusing to yield up their weapons to the Reich. When the national government sent Dr. Heinze, minister of justice and vice-chancellor, to Munich in the hope that he might effect a last-minute surrender on this issue through personal negotiations, the men of Munich, after consultation in their cabinet, saw fit to reject his overtures. At the same time they had to admit to their Landtag that the Bavarian Home Guards consisted of 320,000 men equipped with 240,000 rifles, 2780 machine guns, 44 light cannons and 34 mortars.

In the meantime Simons was trying in every conceivable way to reweave the threads that had been torn apart at London. He even hit upon the curious notion of inviting the new President of the United States (Harding had succeeded Wilson on March 4) to serve as referee over reparations, giving advance assurance that Harding's decision would be accepted unconditionally by Germany. He should not have been surprised that Harding demurred, offering only to transmit to the Allies whatever appropriate proposals the Germans might make. Simons had new proposals prepared, but they were nothing more than revisions of the old. He had no choice, since a majority of the Reichstag had already found the first offers too generous. This path, of course, was fruitless. On May 3 the United States declared the latest German proposals unacceptable and declined to transmit them, having earlier announced officially that, with respect to reparations, America still shared the Allied point of view.

Meanwhile the deadline of May 1, 1921, had arrived. The Versailles treaty had given this date a double importance. Article 235 required the Germans to deliver by this day the first 20 billion marks of their debt. By the reckoning of the Reparations Commission Germany had, at most, furnished only 8 billion of this sum and thus was at least 12 billion in arrears. The Germans insisted, of course, that their shipments had a higher value; yet Simons, in his Reichstag speech of April 26, was careful to avoid his earlier statement that the full required sum of 20 billion had been paid. Germany had therefore unquestionably defaulted to a greater or lesser degree. But even more important was Article 233, Paragraph 3, according to which the Reparations Commission should have set the precise total German debt by this day. On April 27 this figure was set at *132 billion gold marks.* Remarkably enough, the commission, whose members came from six nations, was unanimous in arriving at this figure. The sum, high as it was, fell short of the previous Allied estimates by a considerable amount and was approximately the same as Keynes's calculation of 137 billion.

With this decision made, the Allies felt they had grounds for renewed action against Germany. Their Supreme Council met in Paris, whither the Reparations Commission was directed to return. The result of these meetings was a new ultimatum, which Lloyd George handed to Sthamer, the German ambassador in London, on May 5. But when it arrived at Berlin, there was no government there to receive it. After being turned away by Harding, Simons realized that he had exhausted his hand. The German People's Party did not wish to bear the responsibility for what was certain to come — at least not as a member of such a weak, minority government. The aged Fehrenbach was thankful for any excuse to cast aside a burden that had grown far too heavy for him. And so, on May 4 the cabinet resigned.

Before pursuing the chain of events touched off by the Allies' ultimatum and the cabinet's resignation, it is necessary first to turn back to the recent happenings in Upper Silesia. The requirement, in the final form of the Treaty of Versailles, of a plebiscite in this region had gravely disappointed the Poles. They had been counting on getting all of Upper Silesia, as the initial draft had provided; now they tried to win with brutal force what they feared to lose at law. In August 1919 a carefully prepared Polish revolt erupted, gained great initial success, and then was quickly suppressed by German troops. But on January 10, 1920, the day the Versailles treaty took effect, these forces had to relinquish the plebiscite zone to Allied occupation troops. Most of these troops were French, openly sympathetic with the Poles. The plebiscite was held in a peaceful atmosphere on March 21, 1921. The result constituted one more disappointment for the Poles: only 479,000 had voted to join Poland,

while 707,000 preferred to stay German. The "patriotic Silesians"
(*heimattreuen Öberschlesier*), that is, the men and women who had
been born in Silesia and had subsequently emigrated to other parts
of Germany, had responded by the thousands to the call of their
threatened homeland. They deserve no small credit for the favorable result of the plebiscite. In the light of later events it needs to
be noted here that a large number of critical votes were cast by
Jews.

The German government now took the position that on the
strength of this majority decision the entire province should be
given back. This contention was clearly contrary to the treaty, which
provided rather that a border be set on the basis of the votes in
each commune. (See Annex to Article 88, Paragraphs 5 and 6.) But,
as the English historian of the League of Nations has remarked,
"Soon, in their characteristic way, the whole German nation had
convinced themselves that every legal, moral, and economic principle was favourable to their claim and that the cession of any part
of the area would be a tyrannical violation of the laws of both God
and man." [16] The Allies had, indeed, imagined that it would be
easier to set the boundary than it proved to be. For in Upper Silesia
the German urban votes had often won majorities while the coun-
tryside voted Polish. What the Germans hoped to gain through diplomatic notes, the Poles tried to win with force. On May 1 the Allied
Plebiscite Commission declared it was about to draw the boundary.
Two days later, under the leadership of Korfanty, a former member
of the German Reichstag, Polish volunteers broke into the disputed
region.[17] This was one more of those carefully prepared attacks
which the Polish government helped in every way, and again it
met with great success at first. Among the Allies only the Italians
assumed an active defense; the French assisted the insurrection by
remaining passive.

At this point the plight of the German government was most
acute. It dared not send its regular army, for the French threatened
to occupy the Ruhr in such event. And so it had to be content to let
German volunteers (*Freikorps*) take up the fight against the Poles.
Seeckt helped them unofficially as much as he could; officially he
was powerless, for any open act would have conflicted with the disarmament to which, under the renewed pressure of the Allied ultimatum, the national government had been forced to subscribe.[18]
The Upper Silesians had Herr Kahr to thank for this situation. For
in the Allies' ultimatum of May 5 Kahr's failure to disarm stood
first again on the list of German failures to carry out the treaty. The
second point was the 12 billion marks still due as of May 1; the

third, the delay in the war-crimes trials. The Reparations Commission's schedule for the payment of 132 billion marks was presented simultaneously with the ultimatum. Its essential requirements consisted of annual payments of two billion marks, together with one fourth of German exports. The ultimatum required an unambiguous declaration on the part of the German government that it would unconditionally accept and execute four demands. Among these were the fulfillment of the payment plan, disarmament, and the trial of war criminals. The time allowed for answer: six days, that is, until May 12. The penalty in the absence of an appropriate response: occupation of the Ruhr.

This blow was fully as staggering when it struck as it had been clearly visible in coming. What help was it now to the Germans if they passionately argued that the terms could not be met or that the threatened occupation would be an international crime? On the other hand, some intentionally exaggerated the impact these steps would have on Germany, while the leading national expert on the subject, Secretary Bergmann, in his final analysis found the terms for payment no worse than those Germany had offered in its last note to America.[19] The situation repeated that of June 1919. An infinitely difficult decision had to be made, but no government in sight was willing to assume the responsibility. Needless to say, countless voices urged that the conditions be refused, voices not only from the aroused masses but also from the parties in the Reichstag. No sober thinker could delude himself about the catastrophic effects of an occupation of the Ruhr; but the opposition argued that, since the Allies were bound to occupy the Ruhr sooner or later, any new negotiations were a waste of time. Most responsible statesmen, however, found this the counsel of despair and insisted that any government with the welfare of Germany at heart simply had to try with all its power to avert this catastrophe, even if it should succeed only in postponing it. Bismarck's argument against preventive war: namely, that no one knows what the future will bring, was relevant here.

Among those who had arrived at this conviction through the bitter experiences of the preceding years was one of those party leaders who initially had demanded a flat and uncompromising rejection of the Allied terms — Gustav Stresemann. On May 9, 1921, when Lord d'Abernon returned to Berlin from London, he was met by his deputy, Lord Kilmarnock, with the news that Stresemann had just sought him out in order to direct, through him, four questions to the English government. Stresemann's third question concerned the occupation, on March 8, of the three Rhenish ports: he wished to know whether the ports would be released if Germany accepted the ultimatum. The fourth and most important question touched on Upper Silesia. Stresemann sadly realized that at least a part of the province would be lost. But he gave the British to understand that, if most of the industrial regions were to remain German, he would be ready to assume the responsibility of forming a government that would attempt to fulfill the Allies' terms. The ambassador was unable to communicate his government's reply to Stresemann until May 12. The answers to the first three questions were unconditionally favorable. With regard to Upper Silesia Lloyd George was able to say only that the German government could rest assured that "in our discussion with our Allies [the] German Government may rely upon our desire to pay due regard to the important German interests involved and to press for equitable settlement on [the] basis of strict and impartial execution of [the] Treaty of Versailles." When the ambassador communicated this telegram, whose style as well as message boded well, he gained the impression that one thought was running through Stresemann's mind: had this answer arrived forty-eight hours earlier, I should now be German chancellor.[20]

For in the meantime, on May 10, the former minister of finance, Dr. Wirth, had formed a cabinet. This was to be a government dedicated to a policy of fulfillment (*Erfüllungspolitik*). Negotiations among the parties of the Reichstag had shown that a majority supported an acceptance of the ultimatum, with the division running through the parties of the middle. A majority of the People's Party opposed the ultimatum and hence participation in the regime. Stresemann expressed his party's decision in a formal speech, and one could tell how much it disappointed him. From among the Democrats the new cabinet drew, in addition to Gessler, Eugen Schiffer as minister of justice. Otherwise the government consisted chiefly of Social Democrats and Centrists. The Independents had joined these parties in voting solidly, 220 to 172, to accept the ultimatum. On May 11, one day before the time expired, the Allies could be told that their terms had been met.

Joseph Wirth stood at that time in the prime of life. He was born in 1879 in that same Freiburg of the Breisgau where his predecessor, Fehrenbach, had enjoyed a long political and professional career. Both men exemplified the South German sort of democratic Roman Catholic politician, their only difference being that the democratic component was even more apparent in Wirth. Like Erzberger, he originally had been a teacher, but a highly trained one, teaching mathematics in a gymnasium. His courage and his delight in making decisions were his greatest political assets. He had shown them earlier in taking over the Ministry of Finance after Erzberger's fall. And now he showed these qualities again in forming a new government in the clear knowledge that it would have to pursue a policy which would require of the German people the greatest spirit of sacrifice and cool reason, and that it would be exposed to the full weight of nationalist demagoguery. He also possessed extraordinary forensic talents which often lent his words a force which bore them throughout the land. There was something candid and refreshing in his appearance. Lord d'Abernon, who thought most highly of him, gained the impression of a man who spent much time outdoors and who had nothing of the bookworm or the bureaucrat about him.[21] Wirth realized that the ceaseless German protests served only to worsen foreign opinion of Germany and that it behooved Germany to make an earnest effort to comply with the Allies' terms to the fullest of its ability. Only in this way could it show the Allies where the limits of its ability really lay. One cannot assume that Wirth had mastered all the problems implied by such a move. For this reason he leaned upon the counsel of men who were superior to himself in expertise and new ideas, but united with him in their common goals. Prominent among these was Walther Rathenau, whose inauguration on May 28, 1921, as Wirth's minister of reconstruction caused a great sensation.

Walter Rathenau [22] was known to the broad German public both as an industrial magnate and as an author. In the first capacity he was heir to his father, Emil Rathenau, the enterprising, farsighted founder of Germany's world-famous General Electric Company (*Allgemeine Elektrizitäts-Gesellschaft* or A.E.G.). But he was more than just an heir. In the first year of the war he had shown that he could carry his own weight in commerce when he recognized the critical importance, overlooked in official quarters, of ensuring Germany's supply of raw materials and met this problem successfully by organizing and directing the Division of Military Raw Materials (*Kriegsrohstoffabteilung*). In his literary capacity Rathenau tried to put on paper the many thoughts on economics, sociology, politics, and religion which constantly concerned his fertile and eclectic mind and which, in the course of time, altered more than once. His efforts in this direction did not always take a clear and simple form. His oral mastery of the German language, which worked magic in conversation, often lapsed in writing into verbose and artificial prose. But he always had something to say that stimulated thought, and often opposition. It is tragic that men with minds too narrow or too untrained to comprehend his works felt free to extract and denounce single statements from his books — statements they could never understand — and that on the strength of these isolated words they were able to persuade a maddened crowd that Rathenau neither loved his country nor had hoped that it would win. This false image was not dispelled even by the passionate, if misdirected, words with which he had called for a *levée en masse* in the *Vossische Zeitung* on October 7, 1918.

Actually Rathenau not only loved the German nation with the affection that every man of normal feeling has for his fatherland, but he had even constructed for himself an idealized concept of the nation and waxed ecstatic over his thoughts of blond and blue-eyed Teutons. For Rathenau was a Jew who suffered severely under his heritage. Too proud to take the step to Christianity that was so common among upper-class Jews, he could never forget the many personal slights which he might have been spared had he taken that step and which were doubly painful to him because he was so aware of his superiority over those who had profited from his disadvantage. At the same time he was a ruthless and often unjust critic of his fellow Jews. A man like this is clearly not likely to be universally loved. His plethora of inspired phrases, so exciting to some, put others off. And yet the magic of Rathenau's personality is certainly shown by the fact that among his friends and admirers was Ernst Troeltsch, whose studies of religion, philosophy, and history place him among the greatest of German scholars. But in spite of all his friends and his connections, Rathenau remained essentially a lonely man.

After the Revolution his extraordinary gifts and insights gave him every right to yearn for a position of political leadership. But a man like Rathenau, who has never had anything to do with the less dramatic chores of actual politics, cannot easily win a place for himself in a party, especially when he is famous for his independent mind. The Democratic Party, which he joined, never offered him a place upon its ballot, and it is fruitless to ask whether the fault lay more with the party or with the man. It must have seemed an act of Providence when Wirth offered Rathenau a position in his cabinet. And he felt deeply compelled to accept the invitation in spite of all the warnings of his intimates, among them his mother, and all the doubts of his own more rational self. Not that he might have found it hard to leave suddenly his widespread commercial activities and responsibilities. But he was all too well aware of the difficulty and challenge of the proffered post and the necessity for its occupant to swim vigorously against the stream of popular opinion. What he wrote to a friend at that time rings true: "This was the hardest decision of my life . . . Man after man will have to throw himself into this trench before it can be crossed. Yet it never will be crossed unless some one goes first." [23] He could not foresee the terrible truth of this prophecy. But this spirit of personal sacrifice was with him from the first day on.

Rathenau clearly saw all the difficulties and obstructions that would confront a policy of fulfillment. Nevertheless upon entering the government he was convinced that an honest attempt at compliance had to be made. In a trope quite typical of him but not common in the Reichstag, he illustrated his position with reference to the "difficult decision" of the last movement of Beethoven's Quartet in F Major, Opus 135: "It begins with faint tones and finishes with a decisive and powerful 'It must be.' Whoever faces his task without this 'It must be' will only produce a half-toned resolution." He shared this point of view with the Chancellor. Gustav Radbruch, who sat in the cabinet with both men, characterized the mutual relationship of Wirth and Rathenau in his memoirs:

From the tenderness with which Rathenau dealt with the Chancellor, one gained the impression that he was fully aware of the worth and sensitivity of the man, who, though he looked like a healthy farm hand, was infinitely more complex than he appeared, and that he admired in Wirth what he found lacking in himself. Rathenau was a man of calculation. Whenever Wirth tried calculation he made mistakes, for he was completely a man of instincts, of strong political instincts rare among Germans. And so each of this pair saw in the other what he lacked and what he needed to complement himself.[24]

The first practical step that Rathenau took toward a solution of the reparations problem was the agreement, reached in conversations with the French Minister Loucheur, that Germany would make payments in kind especially for French reconstruction. Their basic idea was to replace political, bureaucratic negotiations and agreements between their two governments and the Reparations Commission with simpler commercial agreements between French and German parties. It was in this sense that the Wiesbaden Agreement, concluded by Rathenau and Loucheur on October 6–7, proposed the establishment of a German private corporation that would assume responsibility for deliveries to those individual Frenchmen who had suffered war damages, thereby satisfying them directly, without recourse to either national government. Where satisfaction could not be reached through this sort of direct negotiation, a balanced court of arbitration would decide. Detailed rules were set forth explaining how these shipments were to be credited to the reparations bill.

This agreement was the object of much criticism and tedious

debate, and it bore only modest fruits. But its fundamental idea was nonetheless sound, for it sought at least three necessary ends: to remove the question of reparations as far as possible from the over-heated political atmosphere; to give a practical demonstration, especially to her most bitter creditors, of Germany's honest desire to pay her debt; and, through a resuscitation of commercial relations, to lead the way toward mutual understanding and thus to a lessening of hatred, distrust, and enmity.[25] From the point of view of national economics one can well debate the relative advantages of payments in money or kind; but in any event the payments in kind which really stemmed from these talks were much more valuable than the money payments, which proved unworkable.

In this respect Wirth tried out his policy of fulfillment on the first billion marks, which the London plan of payments required every three months. This schedule was indeed observed through August 1921, but only at the price of a further devaluation of the mark. The foreign currencies which the German government needed grew rarer and more dear with every week. By the time the entire operation came to a halt in September, the dollar, rather stable in July at sixty marks, had risen to more than one hundred, with the end not yet in sight.

That part of the London ultimatum which referred to war-crimes trials was satisfied by the opening of such proceedings before the Supreme Court (*Reichsgericht*) on May 23. Leading these cases were four indictments concerning mistreatment of British prisoners of war and the sinking of a British hospital ship. A judgment of guilty was found in three cases; in the fourth the defendant was found legally innocent, although the facts of his indictment were unquestioned. Neither the official observers from the English government nor the special correspondent of the *Times* made any objections to the conduct of the trials. But they did criticize the sentences as much too mild. And today, with our knowledge of German sins of this sort in the Second World War, one has to agree that the critics were right. Certainly the few months' arrest which the court required could have no lasting effect as a warning, particularly after the expert witness for the defense, General von Fransecky, had been able to find a military justification for almost every misdeed. Later several more cases were tried on indictments for actions against the French. Most of these defendants were set free. Meaningful punishment was exacted of only two men, submarine officers who, having torpedoed an English hospital ship, raked and sank the lifeboats full of nurses and wounded. These two were sentenced to four years' arrest — but a few weeks later they managed to escape and were never found. Unfortunately such "war heroes" could always count on help.

Twelve cases came to judgment and that was all. The Allies saw no use in transmitting further indictments to the German court, nor did they choose to employ their formal right to hale Germans accused of war crimes into Western courts.[26] They concluded that the time for this had passed. It is reasonable to assume that it was this experience which led the victors in the Second World War to prosecute war criminals themselves before negotiating for a peace.

On the question of disarmament Bavaria finally gave way. In early June the Bavarian *Einwohnerwehren* (Home Guards) were officially ordered to turn in their weapons. With this act the conflict between the Reich and its second largest member seemed to have been settled. But a tragic event was about to renew it.

After his severe defeat in the Helfferich case Matthias Erzberger had gone into complete political retirement. It is true that his loyal Württembergers had returned him to the Reichstag in June 1920, but he had remained silent there throughout his perjury trial. In the spring of 1921 this latter action was halted with an official declaration which relieved him of the first court's accusation of false witness. And the investigation of his personal tax returns was progressing so favorably that Erzberger could expect that it too would be dropped in the near future. Under these circumstances he felt justified in stating, at a caucus of the Center Party on June 29, that he was ready to resume a more active governmental role if the overall political situation seemed propitious. But there were people prepared to obstruct at any cost Erzberger's return to political activity. And so on August 26 he was murdered by Schultz and Tillessen, onetime officers in Ehrhardt's Brigade. They had lain in wait for their victim along a path near the Black Forest resort where he had gone for a rest. As the former minister approached, they fired their pistols at point blank range. False passports took the murderers safely to Hungary, which declined to yield them up to German justice. A former lieutenant commander — and participant in the Kapp Putsch — who was suspected of having been accomplice to this murder was found innocent by an Offenburg jury.

Almost more terrifying than the murder itself was the shameless glee of many Germans at the news. The evidence of this delight is so manifold that one may no longer doubt that it was there. A Lutheran theologian, Professor Martin Rade, wrote with proper indignation in the *Christliche Welt*: "It is monstrous with what joy uncounted Lutherans greeted this report. They baldly give expression to this feeling in the streets, on the trains, and among their families." [27] In many instances this hate may have been an honest wrath at errors imputed to Erzberger. But in many more it was solely a political reaction directed against the man whose energies and competence might have served as strong supports for the Republic. Such a man as Lord d'Abernon thought he had even seen signs of true political genius in Erzberger. What Erzberger's enemies could never forgive was his going to Compiègne to sue for peace. This is why they cheered at the news of his murder. And Field Marshal von Hindenburg, who had been spared utter humiliation by Erzberger's willingness to sign in 1918, was later to be chosen by these applauders as their national president.

Of course those who were so happy at this crime comprised only a minority of the Germans. Their opponents, the supporters of the Republic, were deeply moved; they took this assassination as a blow against their new state and demanded that this open, massive subversion be opposed. For Erzberger's had not been the first murder of this kind. In June the leader of the Bavarian Independents, Gareis, a member of the Landtag, had been shot on a Munich street. The antirepublican press, as was seen at Erzberger's death, greeted these anarchic acts of violence with unbridled enthusiasm. And there was much talk of secret Rightist organizations that would not shrink from terroristic acts, groups like Organization Consul, for example, to which both of Erzberger's murderers belonged.

The national government was convinced that a sharper attack upon the Republic's enemies had become necessary. The Chancellor, Dr. Wirth, was strongly of this mind. His life in those days was extraordinarily full and his speeches, packed with honest pathos, made a deep impression on the nation. "The present plight of our country makes it doubly necessary to take severe steps against these actions of unscrupulous or misguided Germans," were his words accompanying a presidential proclamation of August 29, 1921, ordering the restoration of public peace and order. The order, based on Article 48 of the constitution, empowered civil authorities to ban temporarily any newspaper which incited people to alter the constitution by violent means or which otherwise encouraged sedition. The order also restricted the freedoms of speech and assembly under similar circumstances.

That the parties of the Right protested, thinking themselves and their press threatened by this move, was only to be expected, however odd this indignation at "emergency legislation" sounded in nationalist mouths. More important was the refusal of the Bavarian government to execute the decree, ostensibly because it impinged without constitutional authority upon "private concerns of the individual land." No fundamental distaste for emergency legislation was a factor here, for the Munich regime still maintained the state of emergency it had decreed after the suppression of the Red Republic in May 1919. But this "emergency" was directed exclusively against the Left, and Bavaria was always very shocked indeed when Berlin suggested that that emergency had passed. The German Nationalists opened their party conference in Munich on the day the presidential proclamation of August 29, 1921, was issued. The Nationalists worked hard at pouring oil upon the fire. A few days later in a pre-arranged commemoration of the anniversary of the victory at Sedan (September 2), an orator — and a nobleman and former general at that — called his national government "the executors who are dispensing the profits they inherited from the World War, the bailiffs of King Mammon," and he reviled the flag of the Republic by employing the aristocratic accusation that it contained "the yellow stripe of Jewry." [28]

Fortunately there were some among the leaders of the Bavarian People's Party who did not wish to push these matters to their limit and sought compromise instead. When Kahr, stupid to the last, obstructed them, the executive committee of the Bavarian Landtag refused to support him, and he was obliged to resign. In his place the Landtag selected Count Hugo von Lerchenfeld, a man who was convinced of the necessity of cooperation with the Reich and who, as a former diplomat, had greater tact at his disposal. Through personal negotiations with Wirth he succeeded in arriving at a mutually tolerable compromise. The presidential order was toned down in several ways, while Lerchenfeld promised shortly to declare the Bavarian emergency to be over. This agreement was faithfully carried out by both parties. Thus another threat to Germany unity had passed, at least for the moment. But the leader of the German Nationalists in the Reichstag, the former Prussian Minister Hergt, insisted on stirring up trouble again on September 30 by ridiculing the Chancellor for his alleged retreat. The Chancellor did not leave him waiting for an answer.

The extent to which the Bavarian situation had deteriorated under Kahr is shown by a report of the Prussian commissioner of state for public order, a Dr. Weismann, which accused the Bavarian authorities of harboring men wanted for rebellion under Kapp. Captain Ehrhardt, he wrote, hunted by police throughout the Reich, was the intimate companion of Pöhner, head of the Munich police. To be sure, the Bavarian government denied these statements energetically; but at least in Pöhner's case one cannot accept their denial. For in 1923 Pöhner was one of the leaders of Hitler's putsch, and among the aides who helped Hitler plan the march on Berlin was Ehrhardt.

Meanwhile the shadow of Upper Silesia's uncertain fate still hung over Germany. In those May days which saw Germany confronted with the Allied ultimatum, armed Germans and Poles stood face to face in Silesia. Korfanty was unable to hold the gains of his illegal offensive when the German militia, led by General Hoefer, finally grew strong enough to attack. The Germans demonstrated their military superiority in the successful battles around the Annaberg (May 21–June 6). It was natural that people throughout Germany should rejoice at this news and at the liberation of several portions of this suffering region from the Polish bands. But unfortunately it was equally clear that these ephemeral military successes could not possibly influence the final settlement of the border. Now soldiers in battle, especially those in private armies, are not likely to sympathize with such an attitude. The Upper Silesian volunteers were therefore furious when the national government, yielding to increasing Allied pressures, tried to hold them back. Hence still another source of domestic conflict was prepared.

This entire military interlude could have been avoided if, from the very beginning, the occupation authorities had done their duty. This was clearly the view of Lloyd George, who, in the House of Commons on May 13, pleaded for "fair play," finding it "unfair" of the Allies to forbid the Germans to use their Army to restore order. There was much excitement, of course, in Paris at *this* thought, and Briand prophesied the direst consequences if the Germans were permitted to invade Upper Silesia. And so another divergence of French and English policy occurred. It is true that at the end of June an Interallied Commission succeeded in establishing, through negotiations with the Upper Silesians and General Hoefer, a peaceful modus vivendi in the region, ensured by a neutral zone between the two armed sides. But attempts to reach a British-French agreement on the ultimate division of the province met with no such luck. The Supreme Council of the Allies, which met in mid-August at Paris, could arrive at no decision and finally could think of no solution other than to turn the entire matter over to the League of Nations.[29] The council based this decision upon Article 11, Paragraph 2 of the League's Charter, according to which the Council of the League was to concern itself with any question "which threatens to disturb international peace or the good understanding between nations." The League Council set up a Committee of Four from nations not involved in the dispute — Belgium, Brazil, China, and Spain — and asked them to work out a plan. Their proposal was accepted, first by the Council of the League, and immediately thereafter, on October 20, by the Supreme Council of the Allies.

The committee's border line proved much less favorable than people in Germany had expected, or even feared. Whether it was less favorable than was warranted by the plebiscite and the geographic and economic factors which, according to the treaty, had to be weighed, and whether it might have been possible to draw a fairer line are questions which are much harder to answer and with regard to which disinterested parties cannot agree today. Without doubt, with this new boundary Germany lost most of the economically important industrial part of the province, together with cities like Kattowicz and Königshütte which were overwhelmingly German. The Committee of Four were the first to admit that the new boundary cut regions apart which required the closest economic ties. They therefore proposed that the execution of their plan be preceded by the formulation of a German-Polish convention assuring commercial intercourse and the protection of ethnic minorities during a transitional period. This convention was to be worked out by a German-Polish commission headed by a neutral chairman. To this chair the Council of the League later named a onetime Swiss president, Dr. Calonder. At first the French objected to this convention, but Briand was finally convinced that actually and politically it was a necessary complement to the division of the province.

Although the Germans' shock at this loss of parts of Upper Silesia was understandable, their reply, another governmental crisis, made little sense. Eugen Schiffer is proud of the promise he exacted from Wirth to resign with his entire cabinet if any meaningful parts of the province were lost.[30] It is hard to imagine what effect this intelligent gentleman sought to achieve through such a demonstration of what Lord d'Abernon called, in his diary, "suicidal mania." [31] And indeed Wirth was too much the realist to commit political suicide for the sake of theatrical effect: four days after resigning he had formed a new cabinet. He as well as Ebert had first sought a broader base for the government, one extending from the Social Democrats to the People's Party. This failed. Not only the People's Party but also the Democrats declined to join the new cabinet. Gessler was free to remain, but no longer as a representative of his party. He stayed on as a "nonpartisan specialist" (*Fachminister*). Along with Schiffer, Rathenau too was obliged to relinquish his portfolio. But not for long. For Wirth had used this reorganization as an opportunity to drop his former foreign minister, Dr. Rosen. At first the Chancellor served as his own foreign minister, although he probably regarded this arrangement as provisional from the start. His candidate for the post was Rathenau, whose brilliant, creative mind he could not spare. But it took him a few months to carry out his scheme.

The *Volkspartei* carried its policy of petulance one step further by formally protesting the dispatch of a German commissioner to the negotiations for the provisional treaty in Upper Silesia that the Committee of Four had proposed. His appearance, they argued, could be regarded as German recognition of the new border. "Our refusal to recognize this border," orated their Reichstag leader, Professor Kahl, "must be clearly and unambiguously set forth once and for all before the court of human history by open and dramatic action!" The Democrats at any rate refused to join in the proposed demonstration, a demonstration that was as harmful as it was pointless. Hence Schiffer, with his party's approval, took a place as representative of Germany on the three-man commission that had the important and difficult task of working out the convention. An excellent jurist and skillful negotiator, Schiffer performed his mission well, sharing with his chairman, Calonder, credit for creating a treaty which represented real progress in international law. On May 15, 1922, the German-Polish agreement was signed in Geneva. Its more than six hundred articles comprise an attempt to define and execute the idea that for the next fifteen years all elements of the affected population should enjoy full civil rights without respect to their place of birth, their language, their religion, or their race. Although this intent may not have proved perfectly successful, one fact that far outweighs the rest remains true: when, under Hitler, Germany sank far below the level of European culture, Upper Silesia was the only place where, until the fifteen years elapsed, the principle of equal justice for all stayed in full force.

Two international bodies were created to deal with the many conflicts which were bound to attend the execution of this rather complicated treaty: the Mixed Commission, chaired again by Calonder, and the Tribunal of Arbitration. As president of the Tribunal the League appointed the Dutch jurist G. Kaeckenbeck, who later described "the International Experiment of Upper Silesia" in a searching and judicious book.[32] His study exposes the complexity of the problems created by the partition of the province, a good many of which remained unsoluble in spite of the best intentions. But after weighing all the pros and cons he comes to the conclusion that on the whole the experiment was a success. Above all this international treaty preserved the rule of law in an area that was an arena for embattled and rabid nationalism. Neither those who wrote this treaty nor those who administered it bear responsibility for the way its fruitful, pacifying provisions were brutally ignored after it lapsed in 1937.

Stresemann's behavior during the cabinet crisis of October had impressed Lord d'Abernon highly; in his diary he noted with approval that Stresemann had not used the government's embarrassment to serve his own ends. And in fact Stresemann had gradually convinced himself that the government had to be strengthened and widened in order that it might better withstand the stormy times. But the idea of a grand coalition, a union of Social Democrats, Democrats, Centrists, and the *Volkspartei* in one majority government, could not yet be realized in Germany. The aftermath of the Upper Silesian treaty was not propitious. It was nevertheless a great step forward when the Social Democratic convention at Görlitz (September 17–24) passed a resolution smoothing the way toward collaboration with the *Volkspartei*. Of course, even this was not accomplished without a fight. The "old-line" Socialists did not wish to give up the class struggle they had preached and glorified so long. Severing answered them with words of moving clarity: "I often feel that those who talk so bravely on the streets and at our rallies are exactly the ones who would find themselves a bit short of what we call civil courage at conference tables, in parliaments, or governments . . . What sort of democracy and republic do we have that has to entrust its care either to monarchists and militarists or else to men who support the Republic only halfheartedly?" [33]

The situation in Prussia made this observation particularly relevant. The Landtag elections there in February 1921, like those for the Reichstag in the summer of 1920, had destroyed the power of the Weimar Coalition, and Braun's government, based upon these parties, resigned. Since all other combinations failed, the Centrist Stegerwald tried to form a cabinet of Centrists and Democrats — much too narrow a political base. This makeshift solution lasted only through October. The Democrats in particular demanded a broadening of the government so that it might better cope with all the problems of the time; thus the "grand coalition" was realized after all. Members of the *Volkspartei* joined the cabinet, receiving the two important ministries of Finance (von Richter) and Education (Boelitz). The Social Democrat Otto Braun became premier, while Severing went back to his Ministry of the Interior. The Centrists received two portfolios; the Democrats, one.

A government in which men of such differing opinions as Severing and von Richter had to work together was no simple operation. But things worked out better than had been expected. Traditional taboos and partisan prejudice dissolved in the face of the sheer necessity of achieving practical results. Severing himself said of Finance Minister von Richter that "in the course of their three years' service together . . . a spirit of cooperative collaboration had developed" between them which even his "boldest hopes had not foreseen." [34]

VII

THE MURDER OF RATHENAU
AND THE FALL OF WIRTH

THE devaluation of the mark remained the most difficult problem. Throughout the late summer of 1921 it fell steadily until, by November 8, the dollar was worth over 200 marks. The Germans believed that the most important reason for this ruin of their currency lay in the payment of reparations which obliged the government to procure, with ever mounting difficulties, the necessary foreign exchange. Consequently the problem of devaluation was being exacerbated by speculation. For, so long as men were sure that in a few weeks their hard-pressed government would have to buy at higher prices whatever foreign credits they themselves could buy immediately, they sought these foreign funds in every possible way, legal and illegal. Plans to fight devaluation through a loan from German industry or American banks fell through.

Naturally the Germans pointed to their financial plight at international conferences in the hope thereby of gaining a postponement or a reduction of their debt. But it was just as natural for their creditors, especially the French, to reply that they too had burdens to bear and that Germany's economy was active and its unemployment negligible. The creditors also insisted that the German taxpayers were not being pressed hard enough. Now it is true that in November and December the German government succeeded, after a considerable parliamentary struggle, in pushing through a comprehensive and much more stringent tax reform. But no tax reform could really help while the currency kept losing its value and while prices, necessarily, continued to rise. The state had to pay more for everything it needed. Wages and salaries climbed faster than did tax receipts. When one minister spoke of setting taxes in terms of real value, Helfferich indignantly replied that a compliance with the London ultimatum "would mortgage Germany's capital to the Entente for years to come."

In November the entire Reparations Commission came to Berlin to inspect the evidence on the spot.[1] Although their negotiations there with the German government yielded no positive results, their visit was itself a sign that, even among the victorious Allies, men had begun to realize that the present path led nowhere and that Germany was not the only country which would be hurt if it were followed much further. Perhaps it was due to this visit that the mark recovered slightly at the end of November and hovered near 200 to the dollar for the next few weeks.

No one was more eager in his search for a solution than the British Prime Minister, Lloyd George. Of the men who had written the Versailles treaty, he alone was still in power. And, in spite of many minor wanderings from his course, he continued to strive for the same goal: a genuine and enduring European peace. If he sought to attain this goal primarily by the use of international conferences, he did so in part because he was aware of his quite remarkable talents for such negotiations, namely, his incomparable ability to sense the feelings of others and his elasticity of mind. These talents often enabled him to find a way out of seemingly hopeless blind alleys. One has no reason to doubt the sincerity of his efforts to help relieve the sufferings of mankind even though it is also true that he earnestly sought a diplomatic success to solidify his political position at home. For Lloyd George found it no simple task to remain in power. He was the Liberal leader of a coalition whose parliamentary center of gravity had clearly shifted to the Conservatives; furthermore, many of his former Liberal friends now resented and bitterly opposed him for good reason. But Lloyd George's tenuous political position was not unique in the postwar period. No leading statesman in any country was sure of his footing. None could carry out a policy of reconciliation without looking anxiously over his shoulder to see whether he had been deserted by his party, rejected by his parliament, or accused by his people of being a soft-hearted traitor to national interests. The atmosphere of war does not clear in just a few years. And it remains as clouded among those who think themselves cheated of the just fruits of victory as among those who cannot forget the sorrow of surrender and who find the burden of their plight intolerable. Anyone, on either side of the Rhine, who failed to share such emotions and sought instead to pursue a purely pragmatic policy was suspected of insufficient patriotism.

Such uncertainties were particularly the lot of the French Premier Briand who, though unfamiliar with the economic and financial problems involved, was nonetheless sincerely convinced that what Europe needed most was real peace and that even France could thrive only upon such a ground. But when he faced his parliament, he was constantly conscious that its greatest fear was that of losing the advantages gained by France in the Treaty of Versailles, and that it was most certainly in no mood to abandon these advantages for the sake of some idealistic dreamworld of the future, however enchanting the prospect might appear. To be sure, Briand's brilliant oratory always gained him victory over his critics, but each debate served to remind him all the more of how careful he had to be. He shared Lloyd George's hope of finding, at new conferences, some solution to these ever growing difficulties. Consequently, when Germany declared itself unable to make the payments that were due on January 15 and February 15, 1922, the two premiers agreed at a December meeting in London to convoke the Supreme Council on January 6, 1922, and to recommend there that a general European economic conference be held, to which Germany and Russia would also be invited.

A German delegation took part in the meeting at Cannes. Its chairman and spokesman was Walther Rathenau, who had previously represented the German Chancellor in discussions of the reparations problem at London. There he had made a special attempt to convince Lloyd George personally of the necessity of postponing and reducing Germany's payments; and the British Prime Minister had for the first time gained the impression that he was dealing with a German negotiator who did not simply mouth the same old phrases of complaint, but who instead had his own ideas and knew how to couch them in brilliant form. Lloyd George was not alone in this belief; the opinion was quite general outside of Germany that in Rathenau the Reich had found a spokesman whose words were worthy of attention. It is true that his critics accused him of being all too conscious of his verbal successes and of cultivating international conferences so that he might sparkle there. But if in doing so he served his people well, they surely had no reason to complain. It is unfortunate, but in no way a fault of his tactics, that the effect of his grand address before the Supreme Council at Cannes on January 11 was completely obliterated by the news, which arrived while he was speaking, that Briand had fallen from power.[2]

The apparent cause for Briand's defeat was the negotiations that he had been carrying on with Lloyd George in Cannes concerning the Franco-English treaty of alliance. But the real reason was that his country feared lest he be persuaded by his English counterpart to make concessions at the cost of French reparation claims. Nothing illustrates better the tense anxieties of the French concerning this point than the fact that the vote of no confidence was touched off by an utterly innocuous event. Briand had taken advantage of a recess in the meetings to be introduced by Lloyd George to the mysteries of golf. The pictures which the French press immediately published of the two, the one directing the efforts of the other, served to convince their readers that Briand was no fit defender of French rights but would instead fall willing prey to the crafty Welshman. And so France turned to a man who was certain not to yield or grow weak. Raymond Poincaré, a man of rigorous mind and rigid heart, was a perfect expression of the mood of France. During the Great War he had been President of the Republic, and it was known that he had regarded the peace treaty from the start as an inadequate guarantee of his nation's interests. Later he had become president of the Reparations Commission, and there was no doubt that he had mastered the attendant problems in every detail. His countrymen were sure that he would neither ignore nor yield a single one of the rights assigned them at Versailles. His strong will could be trusted to keep his parliament in line, while his dialectic skills would carry every international debate.

Lloyd George's epigram, "Poincaré knows everything and understands nothing; Briand understands everything and knows nothing," characterized the difference which the British Prime Minister sensed between himself and his new counterpart in France. To Lloyd George, who always sought to avoid extremes and to obscure distinctions, no partner in negotiations could be less congenial than this man who, with the sharpest logic, deduced the ultimate consequences from each treaty paragraph and defended them with an untiring will, and who unconditionally sought only the interest, as he saw it, of France, refusing absolutely to subordinate it to any so-called general interest or future hopes. This difference between the two men was a surface manifestation of their deeper divergence on the cardinal question: How should one treat the Germans in order to ensure the longest peace? One can well describe their quandary with Vergil's famous words: *parcere subjectis et debellare superbos* — "Spare the humble and humble the proud." While the one argued that the Germans had been conquered and subdued and thus deserved fair treatment, the other replied that the Germans were as arrogant and demanding as ever, even though they tried to hide the fact by loudly lamenting their fate. Poincaré argued: It may be true that your Wirths and Rathenaus are honest when they talk today about trying to comply with Versailles; but they do not speak for the real Germany which only lets them talk that way because, given the political situation, it is expedient to do so. No, the true voice of Germany sounds from the mouths of the Stinnes and the Helfferichs who call this policy of compliance (*Erfüllungspolitik*) "suicidal mania." Mark my words: once Germany has recovered from the catastrophe of 1918, these men will lead her again, and once more Germany will threaten the peace of Europe. For this reason the Germans must be kept down as long as their victors have the strength. (Poincaré was convinced that the period of France's superiority would be short and, thus, that these few allotted years would have to be put to good use if the victory were to bring any lasting advantage at all.)

At first Poincaré had to take the situation as he found it when he stepped into power on January 15, 1922. He was obliged to accept the postponement that the Reparations Commission had granted on January 13 for the German payments due January 15 and February 15. Nor could he block the European Economic Conference at Genoa, on which Briand and the other Allied chiefs had agreed and which Germany and Russia were expected to attend. But he immediately made clear his firm intent to oppose with all his energy any attempt on the conference's part to tamper in any way with the reparations question or, indeed, the Treaty of Versailles. Lloyd George made another attempt to reach an understanding with Poincaré about the conference when the two met in Boulogne on February 25. But this meeting only showed how far apart the two men really were.

Shortly after his return from Cannes Rathenau was named minister of foreign affairs. Wirth, who had been occupying this post provisionally since October, welcomed Rathenau's appointment, especially since Poincaré's rise to power had made Germany's position so much more dangerous and difficult. Rathenau himself was by no means certain that he had done the right thing in accepting the position. In a confidential letter he confessed that he confronted "this task . . . with deep and earnest doubts . . . For what can one man do when faced by a cold world, with foes behind his back?"[3] These "foes behind his back" did not let him forget for one moment that he would have to fight on two fronts. The Rightist press greeted his appointment with expressions of utter indignation. To compose their diatribes against him, they ransacked all of Rathenau's works for sentences that lent themselves to misinterpretation. And many of his friends, knowing how virulent and unscrupulous German anti-Semitism could be, were seriously concerned. Rathenau's mother, who never let herself be fooled by external signs of success, was particularly disturbed. Rathenau might quite rightly tell her that "they cannot find anyone else," but what concern was that to those who branded the policy of compliance as treason and who were driven into a frenzy to see it directed by a Jew?

No one knew better than Rathenau how extremely difficult it was going to be to make the policy of fulfillment work; and if by any chance he had been temporarily inclined to underestimate the complexities at hand, a communication from the Reparations Commission as early as March 1922 relieved him of every illusion. In granting postponement at Cannes, the commission had not only required lesser payments of 31 million gold marks every ten days but had also insisted that the German government present a plan for budgetary reform, for currency control, and for reparations payments to be made in the course of that year, 1922. The German government had accepted this stipulation, describing in its reply the broad set of new taxes which it was then pushing, and which it succeeded in pushing, through the Reichstag. But the commission was not satisfied with this. To be sure, it lowered the cash payments due in 1922 to 720 million gold marks and the payments in kind to 1450 million. The Germans, as Wirth explained in his Reichstag address, had been counting on this not inconsiderable compromise. But this arrangement was only provisional. Its realization depended upon Germany's reforming its system of taxation as the commission proposed. For in the commission's opinion the taxes planned and passed up to that time would not suffice to meet the demands of the treaty. Another billion gold marks, that is, 60 billion paper marks, were needed. The Reich was given until May 31, 1922, to write and pass new tax laws which would procure this sum. The Guarantee Committee of the Reparations Commission was to be granted an effective control of Germany's finances. All this was stated in an exceptionally sharp-toned note, the result, clearly, of pressures that Poincaré exerted upon the French members of the commission.

It is completely understandable that the Germans received this note with great hostility, and that they overlooked its concessions in their shock at its demands. But it was of critical importance that both Wirth and Rathenau, in addressing the Reichstag on March 29, assumed this same attitude, displaying an air of indignation which was as sure to find approval in the Reichstag and the nation as it was to provoke renewed resistance from the commission. "The two supporters of the policy of compliance had now declared open feud with the commission," wrote Bergmann, the best and most realistic German expert on the subject of reparations. Rathenau sharpened the debate still further by blaming Poincaré for the new note, and committed the tactical error of suggesting that Lloyd George had yielded to the French Premier.[4] It was especially dangerous to alienate the British Prime Minister with words like these just before the scheduled conference at Genoa, where Rathenau would certainly try to further German interests through personal conversations with Lloyd George. In this address Rathenau went on to adduce another factor which had clearly influenced his attitude and mood: the many allegations and inquiries concerning imaginary or real violations of the disarmament provisions of the treaty with which the Allied Military Commission had been overwhelming him. As early as mid-March he had complained to Lord d'Abernon that the constant stream of complaints which plagued his office day and night would drive him wild.[5] Naturally, he regarded these as another part of Poincaré's game. And he was probably right — although this is not to say that all these complaints were unjustified.

The attempts at conciliation which Bergmann undertook in the matter of reparations proved fruitless. In its formal reply the German government declined both to impose the demanded taxes and to grant the demanded fiscal control. On April 10, the day on which this reply was given to the Allies at Paris, the European Economic Conference at Genoa got under way.

This was the first conference at which the victors and the vanquished of the world war met as fully equal partners in their search for ways to solve their economic problems. It seemed particularly significant that Soviet Russia had been invited to participate and that it had accepted. Lloyd George, who had to suffer attacks from the *Times* and other domestic opponents for this invitation, was eager to effect a rapprochement with Russia because he was convinced that the economic reconstruction of Europe was impossible without Russia and that this basic fact outweighed one's disgust for the Bolshevists' atrocities. He did not envisage a merely unilateral reconciliation; he expected the Russians to reciprocate by recognizing at least part of the foreign debts incurred, especially in France, by Russia under the tsars. He also assumed that at least a limited compensation would be paid to foreigners who had suffered damages as a result of Bolshevik destruction and confiscation. This position was considered a part of the agenda agreed upon at Cannes. The Germans hoped that, in spite of the limited official program, the gathering of leaders from all nations at Genoa would afford an opportunity to settle ticklish questions, excluded from the formal discussion, in personal, private conversations and perhaps with more success than is usually found in the politically charged atmosphere of multinational negotiations.

Germany demonstrated the importance it attached to this conference by sending no less than four national ministers. Chancellor Wirth personally led the delegation, to which, of course, Foreign Minister Rathenau also belonged. Accompanying them were, among others, Baron Ago von Maltzan, chief of the Eastern Division of the Foreign Office, and Professor Julius M. Bonn, the Chancellor's consultant on reparations. The Russian delegation was headed by the clever and cunning Chicherin, foreign commissar. Lloyd George was naturally there, as were the leading statesmen of most other countries. Poincaré was conspicuous by his absence. However much other nations wished to emphasize the significance of the conference through the size and composition of their delegations, Poincaré did not wish to help in any way. Then too, he had the same reasons as Bismarck for eschewing personal participation in such international conferences at especially critical times: a chief executive retains a greater degree of flexibility if he lets himself be represented by an instructed deputy or colleague. For the man who was not there is never wrong. Louis Barthou, the deputy minister, was placed in charge of the French delegation.

The conference split into four groups, in each of which a German had a seat. But parallel to the official negotiations there were confidential conversations between the Allies and Russia on the one hand or among the economic experts of all countries concerned with reparations. Then suddenly it was learned that on Easter Sunday, April 16, Germany and Soviet Russia had concluded a private treaty in the seaside resort town of Rapallo, just east of Genoa.

Contrary to contemporary opinion, the Treaty of Rapallo was not the result of extemporizing inspiration but rather the fruit of a long, if indirect, development. It was fairly obvious that the two losers of the World War would join together in order to offer a counterweight to the overwhelming force of the victors. The Peace of Brest-Litovsk, which might have obstructed such rapprochement, had been abrogated by Allied decree (Article 116, Paragraph 2 of the Treaty of Versailles). It was even more comprehensible that German commercial interests sought revival of trade with Russia, for this country had been one of Germany's best foreign customers before the war. The reconciliation had not been blocked so much by Russian Communism in itself as by their promotion of world revolution. Germany had learned directly what that meant; in its worst years it had suffered numerous Communist disturbances which everyone assumed had been instigated, organized, financed, and armed by Moscow. In the face of this threat from the East, the Germans could hardly take Bismarck as their model; for his concept of Russo-German amity involved, as every reader of Chapter 29 of his *Reflections and Reminiscences* knows, the hope of confronting "socialistic republicanism" with "an orderly system based on monarchy." But if there was a major difference between the policies of the two centuries, there was also a similarity: Bismarck's anti-Polish policy was revived. Most candid among the proponents of this policy was the leader of the Army, General von Seeckt. In a somewhat later memorandum, written in the autumn of 1922, he concluded crisply: "Poland is the nub of our Eastern problem. Poland's existence is intolerable; it is incompatible with the conditions of Germany's existence . . . *Poland must disappear* and it will disappear thanks to its own internal weakness and *to Russia — with our help*. For Poland is even more intolerable to Russia than to us; no Russian regime can abide a Polish state. Nor can Germany ever hope to derive any advantage from Poland, neither economic, for it is incapable of development, nor political, for it is a vassal of France." [6]

In the presence of such conflicting hopes and interests it is not astonishing that the policies of Russia and Germany with respect to each other were groping and unsure. It is perhaps illustrative of this uncertainty that the first Russian to try to restore ties with Germany was the Jewish revolutionary Radek, who had been arrested by the Prussian police in 1919 because of suspicious activities. Among the visitors to his cell in the Moabit Prison at that time were certain generals — and Walter Rathenau. Even more significant was Lenin's change of policy after Russia's defeat in its Polish War. At the Soviet Congress of December 1920, Lenin announced the proposition that, under the pressures of the Versailles treaty, Germany "would naturally be forced to ally herself with Russia." [7] Simons, then the German foreign minister, answered him on January 21, 1921, in his grand Reichstag address on Russo-German relations: "Communism in itself is no block to collaboration between a capitalistic regime and the Soviet Government." Simons went on to express his "honest desire" to enter into such collaboration with Russia as soon as possible. At the same time, however, he was obliged to make clear how many difficulties lay in the way of any practical realization of this hope. And indeed official rapprochement proceeded very slowly. On May 6, 1921, a commercial treaty was signed, but it, too, had the air more of a first step than of arrival. Real political significance, however, was attached to the German recognition of the Soviet government as *the only legitimate* representative of Russia; for this meant, in other words, a final German rejection of all Russian counterrevolutionary groups. This was a success with which the Soviets could be well satisfied no matter how trade relations might develop.

Far more important, however, than these official negotiations on commercial affairs were the highly secret military talks. Here the Germans hoped to circumvent the disarmament required by the Treaty of Versailles by establishing in Russia those forms of military arming and training which the treaty expressly denied them, such as, most particularly, an air force (Article 198). In all this the leader was, of course, General Seeckt, even though he tried to remain as obscure as possible in the course of negotiations. The talks took place at Major Schleicher's home.[8] The fact that the generals did not hesitate to violate in this way the treaty which their government had signed will astonish no one familiar with their ideas. It is, however, rather surprising that the Chancellor, Dr. Wirth, also had his hand in this game. The generals had originally been carrying on these conversations behind the cabinet's back. But when it became apparent that their plot required considerable funds, Seeckt had no choice but to inform the Chancellor. He discovered that Wirth was in complete agreement with this move. "Whenever our policy in the West has run aground," he explained, "it has always been wise to try something in the East." [9]

This same policy was being pursued in the Foreign Office by the director of the relevant division, Baron von Maltzan. Here was a man of exceptional intelligence; Lord d'Abernon, who liked but did not trust him, thought him the cleverest man to serve on the Wilhelmstrasse since the war. Although a wealthy, pleasure-loving aristocrat by nature, Maltzan cultivated political friendships with Leftist leaders. And when, in foreign affairs, he promoted reconciliation with Russia, he was not motivated by rational arguments alone; this adventure satisfied his inclination toward cynical intrigue. He found delight in showing these Russian conspirators, whom he trusted no more than did anyone else, that he could beat them at their own game. He was richly entertained when the Russian Kopp showed him, by bending a steel ruler, that it was simpler to join the ends than two adjacent points, and thus that the Bolsheviks could more easily collaborate with conservative professional diplomats than with their own Social Democratic neighbors.[10] If Maltzan had had his own way, Germany would have concluded a pact with Moscow even before the Genoa Conference. Russian agents in Berlin were busily working to this end, and agreement had been reached on almost all points. On their way to Genoa the Soviet delegation, headed by Chicherin, paused in Berlin to complete the treaty. Rathenau, however, was not prepared to commit himself to such a separation from the West lest he put Germany at a disadvantage before the conference had begun.

But the conference turned out quite otherwise than Rathenau had expected. He had thought that the leaders of the Entente, especially Lloyd George, would quickly give him opportunities for confidential talks. Nothing of the sort occurred. Quite the contrary, he had the impression that they were studiously avoiding him. It was said that they were negotiating with Chicherin in the privacy of Lloyd George's villa. Rathenau became increasingly fearful that Russia and the Entente were reaching a common agreement and that it was directed against Germany. Now, imperturbability was not one of Walther Rathenau's strong points. More and more he became obsessed by the conviction that he was being threatened with a blow which would annihilate not only his diplomatic strategy but his entire political career. The night before Easter he was pacing his hotel room, unable to sleep, when suddenly, between one and two o'clock, Maltzan appeared at his door. "Are you bringing my death sentence?" the excited minister asked. But Maltzan brought quite different news: Chicherin had just telephoned him to say that the Russians would soon conclude an agreement with the West unless the Germans accepted the Russians' offer immediately. Chicherin had gone on to invite the German delegation to meet secretly on Sunday with the Russians in Rapallo. At this meeting the agreement, already drafted in Berlin, could be completed and signed. Wirth was quickly called, and the three men in pajamas pondered whether they should take the fateful step of accepting the Russians' Easter invitation.

Rathenau's first instinct was to inform Lloyd George immediately that they were about to treat with Russia. Maltzan opposed this move with all·his energy and skill. That would, he insisted, be a betrayal of Chicherin's confidence. Maltzan's chief argument referred to the third paragraph of Article 116 of the Versailles treaty, where the Allies had expressly reserved "the rights of Russia to obtain from Germany restitution and reparation based on the principles of the present Treaty." According to Chicherin the Allied statesmen were ready to grant Russia these reserved rights now, and thus to heap new burdens on Germany's already broken back. Only the immediate acceptance of the Russian proposal could avert this enormous danger.

It is hard to believe that this argument could have impressed as intelligent a man as Rathenau. For not only is its fallacy obvious today, but it was there for Rathenau to discover on second thought. The Reparations Commission had already set the maximum that Germany could pay at 132 billion gold marks, a sum which did not even cover all the Allies' claims. In the meantime it had become apparent that Germany would probably not be able to pay even this much. One did not have to be an optimistic opportunist at that time to assume with certainty that a good part of this reparations debt would be forgiven. It was extremely unlikely that the Allies would pile a second load of billions on this first mortgage of 132 billion; it would have been an empty gesture from the start. States are no different in this respect from citizens in heavy debt. Were Russia accepted in fact as one of Germany's official creditors, its gain would be only at the other creditors' cost. As in a bankruptcy, each creditor would then receive a smaller share of what he claimed; the Russians would have taken payments not from Germany but from France. Could any rational man believe the Allies would agree to this? But Rathenau gave way. A critical factor in his decision was certainly the fact that Wirth gave Maltzan his complete support. And the wily Maltzan knew quite well how little choice this left to Rathenau. When he later spoke to friends about this nocturnal struggle, he expressed pride in having "raped Rathenau that night." [11]

And so the German delegation went to Rapallo on Easter Sunday, and on Monday afternoon the delegates in Genoa learned that there a Russo-German pact had been agreed upon and signed. Their excitement was immense. At first it seemed as if the whole conference would dissolve.

To be sure, the contents of the agreement scarcely warranted this excitement. Both parties mutually renounced claims to reparations and indemnities. Germany also renounced damages for losses suffered by its nationals through Russian nationalization and expropriations, provided that Russia did not make any such payments to other nationals. Both parties gave the other the rights of the most favored nation in commercial relations. Of greater political significance was their immediate resumption of diplomatic and consular relations. For with this move the diplomatic boycott of Russia was pierced. And the Russians had gained this goal without having to give satisfaction to Germany for the murder of its ambassador to Moscow, Count Mirbach.

But if the literal contents of the Treaty of Rapallo were justifiable, the manner in which it was signed gave cause for uneasiness. "The first and foremost attributes of every human deed are its time and place," says Seni in Schiller's *Wilhelm Tell*. In this case the choice of time and place could not have been less diplomatic. It had meant a great step forward to general European postwar settlement when the victorious Allies had, for the first time, invited Germany and Russia to participate in a general European congress; they could hardly think it tactful of these two parties to confer behind the others' backs. This was the reaction in Genoa not only of the Western delegates, but also of many members of the German group who had been equally surprised by the dramatic Easter message. They had just been negotiating with representatives of the Entente in an atmosphere of rational amity and now suddenly found themselves suspected of having played a false and double game.[12] The thin strands with which they had carefully begun to bridge the reparations gap were, as Bergmann testifies, immediately cut. The respected Swedish banker and friend of Germany, Marcus Wallenberg, who had taken part in these confidential talks, lamented their disruption by the treaty, and called Rapallo the most stupid step the German government had taken since the war.[13]

Lloyd George was bound to feel this Russo-German reconciliation as an especially heavy blow. Up to this time he had been trying to gather the non-Socialist countries into a united diplomatic front that could force Russia to recognize the tsarist debts and the damages inflicted by the Reds on the property of foreign nationals. For these matters were of common concern to all Europe. But the moment he had the Germans' receipt in his pocket, Chicherin naturally gave up every thought of satisfying the others. Instead, with a brashness that was beautiful to see, he gave the conference to understand that Russia's participation in the reconstruction of the European economy would consist of the new loans which the "capitalistic" West would have to grant to Russia.

The other aim of Lloyd George's strategy had been to isolate Poincaré as much as possible and thus to render his intransigence less harmful. This hope was empty now. For now Poincaré, passionately supported by his countrymen, could lead an oratorical crusade against the perfidious Germans who would throw their treaty obligations to the wind unless they were held in a firm grip while there was still time. In lurid colors, he could now paint a vast and horrible mural of a Russo-German alliance. On April 24, while the Genoa Conference was still in session, he delivered a policy speech in Bar-le-Duc, the city of his birth. Here he not only reiterated his ruthless insistence on the complete fulfillment of the Versailles treaty, but also voiced the threatening proposition that, if the Allies could not agree on how to secure their treaty rights, then each of them would have to resort to unilateral steps against the Germans.

Nor was it in France alone that opinion turned sharply against Germany. The belief was commonly held and expressed that the Treaty of Rapallo contained secret military provisions. Both Chicherin and Wirth categorically denied this allegation in emphatic notes. And their protestations were formally quite true. The Rapallo treaty had indeed no secret clauses but, rather, had been immediately published in full. Yet the secret negotiations, still under way between Seeckt's agents and the Russians, had been strengthened and encouraged by the pact. Shortly before, in February 1922, Seeckt had even had a secret conversation with Radek. That July he received Rosenblatt, a Soviet agent, and on July 29 a secret treaty was signed. It was called a "Provisional Trade Agreement" but related, in all probability, to military matters.[14]

Even German opinion on Rapallo was sharply divided. The President was outraged at the way Wirth and Rathenau had concluded a treaty of such significance without his consent — indeed, without his knowledge.[15] His reaction was based not only on the most solid constitutional grounds but also, and most importantly, on urgent political considerations. Ebert was a proponent of a general German inclination towards the West, as Rathenau had been until that nocturnal council in the Genoa hotel. But Ebert was less willing to put about just because their former course had, for the moment, become difficult. He knew the deep gap which separated Communist Russia from even the German Republic. He knew the menace which the constant Communist agitation, backed by Russian aid, constituted to the pacification and reconstruction of Germany. And he most certainly doubted that the Soviets were going to desist from their agitation for the sake of a treaty like Rapallo, whatever their momentary protestations might be. It seemed to him that however skeptical one might be about the Allies, it was most dangerous to offend the West at the very time Germany had such need of its good will. This same coolness over Rapallo marked the reactions not only of many conservatives, who rejected any traffic with the Reds, but also of many liberals, who regarded this turn toward the East as an abandonment of Germany's traditional place in the Western European cultural community.

It is indicative of the confusions of the time that Wirth sought Seeckt's support in the hope that the general would exercise a helpful influence upon the parties of the Right. Naturally, the general regarded the treaty in quite a different light. In mid-May he wrote to General Haase, who had been at Genoa that Easter: [16] "I am not so interested in the treaty's contents as in its moral effect. This move constitutes the first, and a very important, improvement of Germany's international posture. For others suspect that the treaty contains more than is, in fact, the case. Actually there are no political-military agreements whatsoever. But people *suspect* that some exist . . . Is it to our interest to destroy this flattering mirage?" Given Seeckt's cunning, it is not surprising that we find him criticizing his naïve friend for an "almost pathological desire to play the role of peacemaker at all costs." And one should be even less surprised that Seeckt's biographer took especial pleasure in quoting this letter to a Nazi reading public in the year 1940, that is, in the period between the conclusion of the Russo-German Pact of August 1939 and its violation by Hitler's invasion of Russia in June 1941.

It is principally to the credit of Lloyd George that the Genoa Conference did not adjourn at the news of Rapallo. After he had first expressed his indignation sharply and had even demanded the annulment of the pact, he turned back to the work at hand, declaring the incident closed. He sincerely hoped the conference would prove successful, not only for the sake of Europe, but also because he needed this success to strengthen his political position at home. He was denied this success. To be sure, the delegation took pains to obscure their failure, but everybody knew that the conference had not reached its goal. In the final plenary session Rathenau succeeded once again in making a strong impression. In his address he tried, through a brilliant summary of all the problems at hand, to put the results of the conference in as favorable a light as possible and thus to smooth as best he could the way to further attempts at reconciliation. And when in closing he quoted Petrarch's words, "Io vò gridando Pace, Pace, Pace!" ("I keep on shouting, Peace, Peace, Peace!"), the assembly replied to this reminder of suffering mankind's deepest hope with loud and sustained applause. Thus the conference concluded with a personal triumph for Germany's foreign minister, though certainly with no triumph for Germany's foreign policy.

But the peace Walther Rathenau had wanted for all mankind was not granted to him. Perhaps he had no reason to complain when the policy of Rapallo, a policy he had accepted rather than initiated, found a mixed reception in Germany. For men could arrive at quite different conclusions about the treaty — as they still do today. And he knew from the start that he would have to reckon with the opposition of men otherwise quite close to him. When he returned from

Genoa he told his friend Max Warburg he presumed that Warburg now considered him "an ass." [17] Such an unprejudiced man as Bergmann put the matter neatly in his *Der Weg der Reparationen* (1926): "We are still waiting today for the fruits of the Treaty of Rapallo." [18] But what really aroused passions against Rathenau was not the ambiguous value of the treaty but rather the fact that Rathenau had become the spokesman, and, to some extent, the successful spokesman, of Germany to the world. This was intolerable to racial fanatics, for Rathenau was a Jew. The doctrine of the racial fanatics insisted that a Jew was infinitely different from a German, that a Jew lied when he said that he loved his country, and that even the deepest deterioration of Germanic feeling and Germanic thought could not obscure the basic difference between German and Jew. This racist cant had been spreading widely throughout defeated Germany and had become a sort of substitute religion for the half-educated or the uneducated, as well as for the more sophisticated who used it for their own political purposes. Misfortune is easier to bear if someone else can be made responsible for it, and one's debasement is less sorely felt if one can debase and look down upon someone else. This psychological projection is shown in the words of a song which the nationalist fanatics sang behind their beer steins. The aesthetic quality of the verse is on the same level as the ethical sensitivity it reveals.

> Schlagt tot den Walther Rathenau,
> Die gottverfluchte Judensau! *

This Jew was also a proponent of the fulfillment policy and thus the perfect target for those politicians who sought to persuade the German people that they could relieve themselves of the oppressing consequences of a lost war by constantly and loudly saying no. And so this minister, labeled a "fulfiller," found no favor in their eyes even when he sought to align himself with their own attitudes. On June 21, 1922, Rathenau was obliged to reply in the Reichstag to several interpellations which dealt with French separatist schemes in the Rhineland and violations on the part of the Governing Commission in the Saar. In his speech, as reported by Schulthess' *Geschichtskalender*, Rathenau "sharply criticized the policy of the Entente as a typical example of foreign rule." Indeed when one reads this address today,[19] one is forced to conclude that throughout the entire speech Rathenau resolutely defended the German position. Toward the end, for example, he referred "with pride to the fact that in these severely trying years of foreign rule . . . the people of the

---

* Knock off Walther Rathenau/The dirty god-damned Jewish sow.

Saar have drawn all the closer together in order to defend what they consider to be their most precious possession: their *Deutschtum*."

This patently patriotic speech, however, did not satisfy Karl Helfferich who, two days later, replied for the German Nationalists with a fire-eating oration. Since Rathenau's realistic appraisal gave Helfferich no grounds for rebuttal, he complained all the more passionately about the "tone" of the speech. Here, of course, Helfferich was on safer ground. Naturally Rathenau had not spoken like a beer-hall demagogue, but rather like a minister of foreign affairs who was mindful of his responsibilities. Even so, the way he spoke certainly did not give the former minister of William II any cause for lamenting that "By God, that lemonade is weak," or to damn angrily "the weak words in which shock and indignation are scarcely heard," or to insinuate that Rathenau's words smacked more of a fear "of French displeasure than of concern for the sufferings of the Saar." [20] In fact, even more significant and an utter distortion of the truth was Helfferich's insistence that the fulfillment policy had caused "the frightful devaluation of German money" and "the pulverization of our middle class." This was a demagogic appeal to the passions of those hit hardest by inflation, an appeal made all the more demagogic by dint of Helfferich's expertise: he knew far better than that. The Reichstag realized what he was doing; even the Leftists flooded him with interrupting cheers.

Karl Helfferich was certainly no anti-Semite. He was too intelligent, too educated for that, too firmly rooted in the liberal milieu in which he had grown up and where he had won his first successes. But with his youth he had lost, too, his ability to check his passions, and he had become so much a party-minded man that the annihilation of his opponent, naturally not in the sense of brute force, appeared the principal goal to him, one that justified even the most cruel and unjust words. Rathenau was deeply disturbed by this attack. We learn this from Mr. Houghton, the American ambassador, at whose residence Rathenau appeared for a state dinner immediately after the Reichstag session closed.[21] Here a discussion developed about German coal deliveries. At Rathenau's special request Stinnes had been invited to the embassy, and later he appeared. It was clear that Rathenau sought an interview with this man, who long had been his keen opponent, in order to convince him of the wisdom and necessity of his policies. The two men became so involved in their conversation that Rathenau accompanied the magnate back to his hotel and continued the discussion, evidently not without success, until well after three o'clock that morning. Only then did he return to his Grunewald villa.

Later that morning, about eleven, when he rode to the Foreign Office in his open auto, he was followed by a large touring car in which two men sat. In the Königsallee, at a spot where the minister's vehicle had to slow down, the large car passed his, and when the cars were closest one passenger shot him several times with a submachine gun while the other hurled a hand grenade that almost tore him to shreds. The assassination was a complete success. There was nothing but a shattered, bleeding corpse for the chauffeur to bring back home.

Rathenau had been prepared for violent death. He knew how men were being taught to hate him. He had declined with firmness and, unfortunately, success the detectives whom the police had offered as a guard. With a fatalism strange in such a complicated man, he had waited for what Providence would bring and what no mortal hand could stay. And so the assassins had had a clear field.

Rathenau's murderers were two twenty-five-year-old examples of the blond and blue-eyed type he loved so well: the former naval officer Kern, and Fischer, an engineer. The Berlin Criminal Police, under the energetic leadership of Dr. Weiss, quickly succeeded in tracing the two. But the police were not able to make an arrest. For on July 17, after they had cornered the pair at the home of a certain Stein in the castle Saaleck near Kösen, a good bit of shooting ensued, in the course of which Kern lost his life. At this Fischer shot himself. Nazi Germany later erected a monument to them upon the spot. The assassins' car had been driven by twenty-one-year-old Ernst Techow, who, along with his seventeen-year-old brother, Hans Gerd, was arrested and brought to trial. The name Techow inspires melancholy reflections on the political deterioration of the German middle class. An artillery lieutenant by the name of Techow, of this same family, had helped storm the Berlin Armory in 1848 and then had been exiled to Australia; forty years later, when he begged to see his now glorious fatherland once more, a word from Bismarck kept Emperor Frederick III from granting the septuagenarian's request. The deceased father of these juvenile killers had been a respected member of the Berlin Council and an active figure in the Progressive Party.

Other accomplices, in addition to the two Techow brothers, were brought before the Court for the Protection of the Republic in Leipzig.[22] Their trial took place in October 1922, under the able prosecution of Dr. Ebermayer, the solicitor general. To be sure, it proved impossible to prove the existence of an organization expressly dedicated to the slaughter of political opponents. But the trial did make frighteningly clear that an atmosphere of murder, conducive to such deeds of violence, hung over Germany. Scheide-

mann and Maximilian Harden, the political journalist, were objects
of similar attacks within the year, but they survived. It became apparent that many Germans were prepared, with no qualms of conscience whatever, to assist in crimes like these or to help the assassins in their flight. The killers always had money, and it certainly
was not their own.

Fully as shocking as the ethics of these people were their politics.
The delirious rantings which the defendants and their witnesses
offered by way of defense were as much to be pitied as scorned.
These youngsters, who had taken it upon themselves to interrupt
political developments with bloody hands, had no idea of the real
facts and recited, in their place, fantastic fairy tales. Techow testified that Kern had told him Rathenau was a supporter of "creeping
Communism" and had married off his sister to the Bolshevist Radek.
When they blamed the fulfillment policy for Germany's ills, they
were, of course, only repeating the words of politicians like Helfferich. The objections they raised to the Treaty of Rapallo must have
warmed the heart of General von Seeckt; for Techow stated as a
"demonstrated fact that behind this treaty the Entente constantly
suspects a secret Russo-German military pact and treats Germany
severely for this reason." One need only compare this exegesis to
Seeckt's triumphant explanation of the treaty's consequences. And
the anti-Semitism of the older generation found grotesque expression in the mouths of these young men and boys. They cited the
"Protocols of the Elders of Zion," an anti-Semitic forgery which was
distributed through Germany in hundreds of thousands of copies at
that time. Techow quoted Kern as saying that Rathenau had revealed
himself as one of the three hundred "Elders of Zion," seeking to
achieve in Germany what "that Jew Lenin" had accomplished in
Russia. Techow proceeded on his own to maintain that the Jewish
press, the *Frankfurter Zeitung* in particular, had said that this exposé of the "Elders of Zion" had unfortunately come too late: "the
plot had progressed so far that it could no longer be restrained."

Such was the caliber of the youngsters who murdered one of
Germany's most intelligent, most educated, and most far-seeing
men. A submachine gun in the hands of a fool outweighs a wise
man's arguments. Walther Rathenau had been Germany's foreign
minister for scarcely six months. This was certainly too short a time
for him to show what he might have achieved, and one can hardly
say that what he in fact accomplished assures him of high rank
among the statesmen of history. But there can be no doubt that he
was a man of extraordinary talents, talents which he freely and
willingly put to work for his fatherland in its hour of gravest need.

His reward was bullets, a hand grenade, and malicious slander which did not stop even after his murder. General von Rabenau wrote in his biography of Seeckt that "the nomination of this ethnic alien" had constituted "a sharp challenge to those Germans mindful of their race." And Rabenau was not one of the worst, otherwise he would not have been murdered by Hitler's henchmen.

Let us turn from this political field of carnage to the letters which Rathenau's mother wrote to Frau Techow, the mother of his murderers. Seldom has humanity's voice sounded as clearly as in these few lines, which only a barbarian can read without being moved deeply: "In unspeakable sorrow I extend my hand to you, most suffering of women. Say to your son that in the name and in the spirit of his victim I shall forgive him — as I pray God will forgive him — if he makes a full confession to earthly justice and a repentant one to God. Had he known my son, the noblest man the earth has ever borne, he would rather have killed himself than shot the other. I hope these words will bring your soul some peace."

Rathenau's murder caused greater and more general excitement than had Erzberger's. This time no normal man could say that the victim had deserved his dreadful end. Republican elements of the nation were the most disturbed, for they regarded the assassination as a crime against the state. Rathenau had been murdered because he had served the Republic; indeed, because his remarkable talents had lent the new state a certain prestige. The anxious supporters of the Republic therefore focused their apprehension on those who were working night and day to disturb the public peace, who inundated the Republic with mocking accusations, and who regarded its representatives with enmity or scorn. The Republicans were justified in their concern, although it was never proved that certain Rightist, so-called "National," organizations, had been directly responsible for the murder. Nevertheless, this ceaseless agitation had prepared the atmosphere, had set the scene, for the assassination. In the Reichstag democratic wrath was unleashed in stormy attacks on Helfferich, who was finally forced to leave the chamber. Helfferich was blamed for having incited passions against Rathenau in his violent and unjust speech the day before the murder. Technically this accusation was false, for, as the trial revealed, the plan for the assassination had been completed before Helfferich made his address. But a man who proceeded against a political opponent in this thoughtless way has no grounds for complaint when reminded sharply that he reaps the whirlwind who sows the wind.

Gigantic mass demonstrations filled the streets. Labor protested with a twenty-four hour strike. A few unfortunate incidents occurred, as was to be expected at a time of such tension. But in general a sober discipline was maintained. And everywhere it became apparent that some thorough, radical step had to be taken for the protection of the Republic and of republicans.

This was the undivided opinion of the government. Wirth immediately summoned his cabinet and proposed a presidential decree to be issued for the protection of the Republic under Article 48 of the constitution. The decree included penalties for whoever might glorify, encourage, or approve acts of open violence against the republican form of government or the members of a republican regime, whoever might mock the national banner, and the like. The decree empowered the governments of the lands to forbid public meetings if fear of their revolutionary nature seemed justified. This, of course, was an infringement upon the freedom of assembly. For the trial of antirepublican crimes it established a special Court for the Protection of the Republic in Leipzig, at the seat of the Supreme Court.

This special court was to consist of three justices of the Supreme Court and three lay members, to be appointed by the President of the Reich. The solicitor general, Dr. Ebermayer, whom the minister of justice had summoned quickly to Berlin to study the draft decree, objected to this provision. He was fearful of commingling "the Supreme Court and partisan politics." The minister of justice was Professor Gustav Radbruch, a student and admirer of Franz von Liszt, the gifted and controversial founder of the modern school of criminal law. Radbruch was an idealist who had joined the Social Democrats in the hope of being most able to realize his hopes within their program. In the days of the Kapp Putsch he had fought with all his energy for the Republic; and his party, which did not boast of many famous jurists, rewarded him in 1920 with a Reichstag seat and, in 1921, with a place in Wirth's second cabinet. He was in no sense a radical, but he did regard the situation as serious and was convinced that the Republic had to defend itself vigorously with all the means at hand and that, in light of recent experiences, this vigor could not be expected of the regular courts which were still occupied, on the whole, by judges from the days of the monarchy. And so he held fast to his ideas of the special court, convinced that its very link to the Supreme Court would preserve it from the danger of becoming a "revolutionary tribunal."

The presidential decree was issued on June 26, 1922. Its publication had been preceded by a Reichstag debate which revealed clearly that the decree was directed against the Right. The high point of the debate was the Chancellor's great, impassioned, and moving oration on Walther Rathenau and his frightful death. Because Wirth had been deeply moved by these events, his words touched all whose hearts were not already completely closed. He certainly was completely justified when he made the appeal "to cleanse Germany, finally, of this atmosphere of murder, rage, and poison." But it was his final, dramatic sentence which contained the political point of his speech: "There stands the enemy, where Mephisto drips his poison into a nation's wounds; there stands the enemy and there can be no doubt about it: the enemy stands on the Right."

These words not only expressed the general feelings of millions of Germans; they were also an accurate analysis of the specific political situation. Indeed the future would show that the speech was even more accurate than anyone realized at the time. The minister of justice, Professor Radbruch, followed Wirth's speech with the explanation that the presidential decree had been made necessary by the "excesses and pronouncements of Rightist radical groups," adding: "Labor's worry lest this decree, directed immediately at the radical Right, be later turned against the Left is quite unfounded." This was clear, he argued, in the requirement that the forbidden acts had to be "against the republican form of government."

Naturally Radbruch's statement was most vigorously attacked, and not by the Rightists alone. Moreover, the interpretation had not been easy to construct.[23] In the cabinet not only the Centrist minister of finance, Hermes, but also the nonpartisan state secretary for the Ministry of Justice, Dr. Joël, had opposed it strongly. Only the Chancellor's personal authority had won acceptance for the planned defense. Radbruch, a man quite ready to admit past errors, insisted in his memoirs of a much later date that he still thought his explanation sound. He based this argument upon subsequent experience with the Law for the Protection of the Republic, in which the decree's formula was amended to read "acts against the republican form of government as defined in the German constitution." He went on to insist that he could not have foreseen that this law would later be directed "primarily against the radical Left."

Even if one admits that Radbruch could not predict the future application of the law, one must still have reservations about such an argument. For a judge must adhere to the literal wording of the law; it is the task of the original drafters of that law to word it in such a way that the judge cannot misinterpret its meaning. Furthermore, if the lawmaker is convinced that a thing of common right (*Rechtsgut*) requires protection against attacks from two different sides, he is hardly justified in directing his attention to one attacker while closing his eyes to the other. Radbruch's argument exposed a tragic weakness of the Republic: it could not trust its courts. For how many of its judges were really republicans at heart? This is not to say that a majority of them were sworn enemies of their new state nor that they let themselves be influenced in the performance of their judicial duties by their coolness toward the Republic. But their new master had not won their hearts, and when the chips were down they found it easier to defend the Republic against its enemies on the Left than against those on the Right, to whom they felt connected by bonds of their "national sense."

Another weakness of the Republic likewise came to light. A few days after the publication of the decree the Bavarian government issued a sharp declaration protesting that the presidential order was tantamount to "class legislation by virtue of its political background." What the Bavarians meant by this became clear in a speech delivered by the former Premier von Kahr who was now, as president of an administrative district of Bavaria, an important governmental official. In this official speech Kahr expressed his hope that some day he would be able to salute the former Crown Prince Rupprecht as his king. The Bavarian attitude was further illustrated when Kahr's superior, the minister of interior, defended him in the Landtag against protests from the Left. Even more ominous was the way the Bavarian government made clear in advance its opposition to the national law that was planned to replace the Decree for the Protection of the Republic. The law was nevertheless passed. Not the least credit for this should go to Stresemann, who had been truly shocked by Rathenau's murder and who recognized that racist agitation was a threat to the future of the Republic and the unity of the nation. This realization also led several of the best German Nationalists, men like Düringer and Siegfried von Kardorff, to leave their party upon discovering that even the recent frightful events were not going to deter their colleagues from using a demagogic device that most certainly was effective with the masses.

The government's draft of the supplemental law suffered many modifications in the course of its consideration by the Reichstag and its committee. At the time of its third reading Stresemann declared: "The emergency character of the law no longer exists." But it still amounted to a constitutional amendment and thus required a two-thirds vote under Article 76 of the constitution. This majority was achieved through a union of parties from the *Volkspartei* on the Right to the Independents on the Left. Only isolated Populists joined the German Nationalists and Bavarian Populists in voting against the bill. The vote, on July 18, was 303 to 102. A declaration of amnesty and a law clarifying the duty of civil servants to protect the Republic were also passed. (Radbruch had declared the amnesty necessary because of "the long list of unprosecuted crimes committed against political figures on the Left.")

These laws had hardly been published on July 21 before the Bavarian government went on the warpath once again. On July 24 it published its own Decree for the Protection of the Republic which was to "replace the national law" within Bavaria. In other words, the men of Munich sought to nullify a national law by a piece of land legislation — a clear violation of the constitution (Article 13), indeed the first of this kind in the history of the united German state. Equally clear was the legal inadequacy of their case. Their argument that the national law violated the national constitution was simply absurd, for the law had been passed as an amendment and all the requirements for an amendment had been observed.

What had driven the Bavarian government to violate the constitution was primarily the decision to place all crimes against the new law, along with political murder and treason, under the jurisdiction of the Special Court in Leipzig. This decision, which was based on a slight revision of the wording of the presidential decree, meant that the national government had broken the monopoly of the Bavarian People's Courts (*Volksgerichte*). These local courts, it will be recalled, had been established on July 12, 1919, after the collapse of the Republic of Soviets. While theoretically established as provisional, in actual fact the People's Courts had kept right on functioning year in and year out. Political in their composition, these courts ignored the defendants' rights prescribed in German criminal procedure, and, what was worst of all, there were no legal means of relief from their sentence, neither appeal nor review. They provided, in other words, a medium in which could develop an entire system of special Bavarian political criminal law directed exclusively against the Left. The spirit of these courts is illustrated by the scandalous punishment meted out on October 20, 1922, by the *Volksgericht* of Munich, to Felix Fechenbach, formerly secretary to the murdered Kurt Eisner.[24] On the formal charge of high treason, but in reality for a journalistic offense of years before, he was sentenced to not less than eleven years' imprisonment. All the circumstances of this case justify the conclusion that this sentence was an act of political vengeance which had nothing at all to do with justice. It took years of legal struggle before this gross and inexcusable miscarriage of the law could be corrected by a Supreme Court decision of December 1926. Such were the People's Courts which the Bavarian Government's decree baldly substituted for the Supreme Court of Germany!

The national government naturally declared the Bavarian decree null and void. But in the actual political situation of that time this step, in itself, meant nothing. Ebert still possessed sufficient self-control to compose a friendly letter to Count Lerchenfeld, the Bavarian premier, in which he sought to prepare the way for reconciliation, but in which he also made quite clear that he would otherwise have to take more effective measures "as guardian of the national constitution and of the national interest." It took weeks of difficult negotiation before the Bavarian government finally, on August 24, retracted its unconstitutional decree. And the national government paid dearly for this retraction.

The Bavarians had demanded a Bavarian chamber of the Special Court. This was denied them, but a South German chamber was established, to which three Bavarian lay judges (*Laienrichter*) would belong. Ebert was personally responsible for effecting this compromise. He was aware that German unity was at stake, and at a time when dangers threatened from without. He was prepared to purchase this unity at the cost of splitting the Special Court, however illogical the move might be and however long Radbruch might oppose it. In practice, the fears of both experts and amateurs alike about the Special Court at Leipzig proved unfounded. Ebermayer admitted this with remarkable candor when he praised both chambers for having "remained completely free of any partisan air." [25] If by this he wished to imply that even the Rightist assassins would not have been judged differently by ordinary courts, one is certainly correct in questioning his judgment, especially in regard to the Rathenau case. For the Special Court found Ernst Techow guilty only of having been an accomplice to the murder and sentenced him to fifteen years' imprisonment. A regular court would have held the murderers' chauffeur a partner to the crime and would have punished him accordingly with death.* In any event the Special Court for the Protection of the Republic lasted for only a few years. By 1926 its criminal jurisdiction had been transferred to regular courts.

A further consequence of the excitement at Rathenau's death was the union of the two Social Democratic parties. Tendencies in this direction had existed for some time. The politically sophisticated

---

*Credible reports tell us that Ernst Techow sincerely repented of his deed and experienced a complete moral conversion. As a member of the French Foreign Legion he did all he could to assist Jewish victims of Nazi persecution.

leaders of the Independents were quick to realize that their striking success at the polls in June 1920 was no measure of their party's real strength. And many found no comfort in the prospect of being damned eternally to the more or less fruitless role of opposition. For it was clear that the chances for a purely socialist regime were becoming progressively slimmer. Both the causes and the consequences of Rathenau's murder showed how great the danger of reaction really was. And reaction would mean the fall of the Republic. The opinion consequently grew that the Social Democratic movement could no longer afford the luxury of two parties and the constant internecine warfare of their press. In September 1922 the two party groups, convening separately in Augsburg and in Gera, declared themselves in favor of union. A joint convention was then held in Nuremberg on September 24 to confirm the merger. Wels of the Majority Socialists and Dittman of the Independents were elected co-chairmen of the new, united party. At their convention only a handful of official Independent Socialist delegates had opposed the merger and refused to join. But the situation was very different among the Independent voters: most of them refused to return to the Social Democratic fold and went over to Communists. This was shown clearly in the next election.

But great as was the impact of Rathenau's death upon German domestic politics, it left an even greater mark upon the economic scene. Now the tumble of the mark could not be stopped. The dollar, still under 350 on the day of the murder, climbed to 670 by the end of July, to 2000 in August, and to 4500 by the end of October. So Helfferich had perhaps been wrong after all in blaming the fulfillment policy alone for the German inflation. In fact the foreign minister's murder had so clearly demonstrated the existence and the danger of destructive forces in the Reich that both at home and abroad the faith, already slight, in Germany's ability to achieve healthy recovery was largely lost. Or, in the words of a later Supreme Court decision: "Rathenau's murder [had] the ultimate effect . . . throughout the world of completely destroying confidence in the future recovery of our currency, so that . . . the paper mark ceased to be regarded as a generally accepted standard of value." [26]

Of course the murder was not the only cause of this accelerated devaluation. German hopes for some tolerable solution to the reparations question and especially for an international loan faded more with every month. In May and June a committee on loans of the Reparations Commission had met in Paris with the famous American banker Pierpont Morgan as one of its members. The committee adjourned without results in mid-June after Poincaré publicly announced that he would accept no diminution of the reparations. German efforts to obtain a moratorium were answered by the French Premier's demand that in case of a moratorium, Germany must furnish "productive guarantees," i.e., such industrial or similar establishments as would assure the Allies of profits in lieu of reparations. This was generally taken as a sign that Poincaré was reaching for the Ruhr, or at least for its nationalized mines.

The feelings of the French toward Germany had been especially sharpened by the Treaty of Rapallo. But what would they have said if they had seen the secret memorandum which General von Seeckt handed to his Chancellor, Dr. Wirth, in September 1922? One consequence of the Treaty of Rapallo had been the resumption of diplomatic relations between Germany and Russia, in other words, the appointment of ambassadors to Moscow and Berlin. Count Brockdorff-Rantzau, once foreign minister but idle since his resignation in July 1919, was being considered for the Moscow embassy. He was prepared to accept the post, but only on his own conditions. One of these, referring to collaboration with Rathenau, had lapsed with the latter's murder. This made all the more important his second condition, that the generals, and that meant Seeckt above all, not be permitted to interfere with his mission. He had been on bad terms with Seeckt ever since returning from Versailles, and no words were strong nor sarcastic enough to suit him when referring to men who had once crossed him. He is even supposed to have threatened that he would challenge Seeckt to a duel should the latter take it in his mind to interfere.[27]

Naturally fundamental differences of opinion underlay this simmering feud. "A German foreign policy directed exclusively to the East," Brockdorff wrote in a memorandum of July 15, 1922, "would not only be premature and dangerous at this time, but also barren and hence mistaken." [28] For such a policy would alienate not only an already hostile France, but England too. In early September Wirth forwarded this memorandum to General von Seeckt, who replied to it on September 11 with a significant memorandum. This note, from which we have already quoted passages on Poland, was written in Seeckt's best and most effective style and was full of that absolute assurance with which he set about the solution of even the most difficult political problems. But despite its imposing facade, his note remains only one more demonstration of the general's ineptitude for politics.

Seeckt makes it clear that he was blind to the dangers of the Communist threat to Germany. He also shows that he was completely wrong in his appraisal of Franco-British relations, referring with wild exaggeration to "tensions [between the Allies] which indubitably existed and had become especially acute in the Near East." He had really convinced himself that these tensions were about to produce an open rupture which would, in turn, give "England such an interest in the military strengthening of France's next-door neighbor [Germany]" that "England would simply have to accept as part of the bargain that this neighbor would look to the East for its new strength." America, he believed, was "interested in Germany's economic recovery and anything but an enemy of Russia." One is not astonished to see this man counting on new military adventures, indeed saying that they are "almost at hand today," nor to see him express the unmitigated feeling of superiority of a Prussian general with the words: "Military minds can best weigh the arguments for and against a war; the statesman's duty is to lead. *In spite of everything the German people will follow its leader into the battle for its existence.*" To the utter misfortune of the German people, this prophecy proved true.

In concrete terms Seeckt's proposal was to develop the Russian armament industry with the help of private German firms and, further, to satisfy "Russian desires for additional military assistance so far as seems feasible and advantageous." All this was, of course, to remain a secret, not only from other governments, but also from that of Germany. "Participation and indeed official knowledge on the part of the German government cannot be considered," the general dryly explained to his Chancellor. Only "agreements involving the Reich" would require "knowledge on the part of the political leadership."

Wirth was clearly satisfied with the position of silent partner which Seeckt had given him. To be sure, he went ahead with Brockdorff's nomination over Seeckt's objections, and the Count was sent to Moscow in October. On the other hand, he gave Seeckt completely free rein. Not only did Wirth close his eyes to Seeckt's military machinations with the Reds, the Chancellor even provided him with the necessary funds. For concealment of Seeckt's activity a society was invented with the innocuous name, "Society for the Encouragement of Commercial Enterprises" (GEFU), and with a trusted agent of von Seeckt's, a Major Tschunke, at its head. Its real program included the Russian manufacture of not only artillery ammunition and Junker airplanes, but also a poison gas. A large part of this program was actually carried out. Tschunke described its military aspects in a report composed in 1939: "In light of the restrictions on our munitions industry at that time, the great number of shells of outstanding quality which were produced in Russia and brought to Germany were not to be ignored, still less Russia's active role in the recreation of our air and armored forces." With these words Tschunke attested to the truth of Scheidemann's revelations before the Reichstag in December 1926.

Poincaré learned nothing about these events behind the scenes; but the reports which he was receiving from the Allied Control Commission were enough to convince him that the German generals were doing their utmost to circumvent the Versailles treaty's disarmament provisions, just as the great Scharnhorst had done after the Treaty of Tilsit. Sunday after Sunday Poincaré delivered speeches throughout his country, kindling and directing French tempers against Germany and thus exciting feelings of real alarm not only there but in England as well. Moreover, the Entente had been weakened by the Turkish victory — about which Paris and London had quite different views — over Lloyd George's protégés, the Greeks. The most important consequence of this loosening of the Entente was the English Conservatives' decision to leave the cabinet. This meant Lloyd George's resignation, which occurred on October 19.

Poincaré had every reason to be pleased. He had never learned to get along with his British counterpart, nor had he suffered any illusions about the fact that Lloyd George's flexible, fertile mind had constituted a constant threat to his own implacability. The new Prime Minister, the clever Scotsman Bonar Law, whose powers were already sapped by sickness, failed to impress Poincaré. Even though he could be expected to oppose any bold move on France's part, there was no reason to think that he could thwart one. Two weeks after Lloyd George fell, there was also a new government in Rome. This involved more than a shift of men; the entire system of government was changed. The parliamentary system had collapsed under Fascist attack. On October 30, 1922, Mussolini formed his government and initiated the Fascist rule that was to last until July 24, 1943. There was no reason to believe that the new regime would treat Germany with any more consideration than had its predecessors.

The reparations problem was approaching a crisis. It is true that progress seemed to have been made in regard to payments in kind. In August and September Hugo Stinnes and the Marquis de Lubersac, president of the Alliance of French Reconstruction Associations, had concluded a treaty providing for delivery of materials worth one and one-half billion gold marks. The treaty was the object of more criticism in Germany than in France. The Germans accused Stinnes of doing now, at considerable private profit, what he had once sharply attacked Rathenau for seeking in the Wiesbaden Agreement.[29] But what was to be done about the money payments if the plunge of the mark, and thus the ruin of the German budget, could not be stopped? Even the Reparations Commission was wandering in the dark. In early November the new chairman, Barthou, brought his commission to Berlin. The German government had invited several famous neutral experts on finance to Berlin at this time, in order that they might confer and advise on the situation, especially on how to stabilize the mark. Among these were Keynes and the Swede Cassel, neither of whom can be called Germanophobes.

The negotiations with the Reparations Commission proved fruitless, since each party challenged the other to make proposals. The experts advised the German government to make every effort to stabilize the mark. Their majority report, signed by such men as Keynes, Cassel, and the Englishman Robert H. Brand (later Lord Brand), took the position that Germany should undertake this task upon its own resources and not depend primarily on foreign aid. They pointed out that at the contemporary rate of 3500 marks to the dollar the Reichsbank's gold reserves were ·double the total currency in circulation.[30] No currency had ever collapsed with so solid a gold base readily available. The experts also found a revision of the reparations necessary, although they did *not* regard this revision as a *prerequisite* of stabilization. They did agree, however, that a temporary moratorium had to be granted. Lord d'Abernon, who concurred with the report in general, later called it the most important document to appear in the entire reparations controversy. But neither the creditors nor the debtors paid it any practical attention. It is true enough that the German government appended this report to their note of November 13, in which they once more begged the Reparations Commission for a moratorium and explained their plans, presuming such a moratorium were granted, for the stabilization of the mark. This note, which Lord d'Abernon tells us had been composed by Dr. Kastl of the Ministry of Finance, had gained the approval of the whole spectrum of parties from the People's Party through the Social Democrats. At last Wirth could breathe with relief. But twenty-four hours later he resigned.

This time it was the Social Democrats who dissolved the government. Ebert, who clearly saw the international dangers ahead, wished to set Germany's government upon a broader base in order that it might better meet the coming blows. In October an overwhelming majority of the Reichstag had extended his term of office to June 1925. He was not entirely pleased by this move; he would have preferred another election, which, at that time, he was certain he could win. But he did welcome this proof that collaboration could be achieved among the parties from his own Social Democrats to Stresemann's *Volkspartei* (for Stresemann deserved much of the credit for the move). Ebert therefore invited Wirth to enter into conversations with these parties with the aim of forming a new and broader cabinet, and Wirth accepted. The People's Party was ready to agree, and both the Center and the Democrats backed the plan. But the Social Democrats refused to collaborate with the *Volkspartei*, in whose social policies they had no faith. When no solution could be found after several days' negotiations, Wirth resigned and his Social Democratic ministers left their offices. Here it may suffice to quote the passage from Radbruch's memoirs in which he evaluates the tactics of the Social Democrats. He first criticizes Wirth's action as "superfluous," but he then goes on to say: "After these mistakes were committed by others, the Social Democrats committed a grave error when, fearful of offending the masses or their once independent party brethren, they refused to participate in a government with the People's Party, a party that had supported us three times on critical issues: the Protective Laws, Ebert's re-election, and the note of November 13." [31]

One may well doubt whether, after the excitement and strains of the preceding years, Wirth could have found the strength to carry on. But in any event and despite his differences with the Social Democrats on foreign policy (and at the moment this was the paramount issue), he would have made a good chancellor, one certainly much better than the man who took his place, the director of the Hamburg-American Line, Dr. Cuno.

VIII

OCCUPATION AND SEPARATISM
IN THE RUHR

───────

Superior Government Privy Councilor Dr. Wilhelm Cuno had
served his Emperor well in many positions of great responsibility,
particularly in the Imperial Treasury, and during the war he had
brought credit to himself as director of the National Grain Authority.
His reputation was so great and the opinion of his abilities so high
that Albert Ballin, the famous head of the Hamburg-American Line,
invited him to join the corporation's board. Cuno must have made
himself useful there as well; for in November 1918, when Ballin
died — it was generally assumed that he took his own life out of sorrow at Germany's misfortune — Cuno succeeded to his post. Regarded as one of his country's leading economic experts, he had
represented Germany repeatedly in this role at international conferences. He was a man of faultless manners and appearance, and
people said that President Ebert, who was not especially blessed
along this line, had been particularly impressed by his finesse. As
early as Genoa, Rathenau had predicted Cuno's rise to power to his
friends: "We shall have to smoke even that cigar, — if only because
of its excellent wrapper."

But the factors which directed attention to Cuno in the crisis
caused by Wirth's resignation must certainly have lain deeper than
the wrapper. Many Germans were tiring of party politics; they
blamed it for the ceaseless cabinet shifts and looked forward to a
steadier recovery if "businessmen" would assume the tasks of government. They believed that a regime headed by men "whose signatures alone assured them discount" would make a particularly good
impression abroad. Cuno seemed admirably suited for such a role

because he had had practical experience in the high civil service and thus knew the inner workings of the state. Furthermore, his commercial activities had won him good connections in America. The Reichstag leader of the Democrats, Dr. Carl Petersen, a Hamburg lawyer who knew Cuno well, seems to have pressed especially hard for his appointment.[1] Cuno was certainly no Democrat in any partisan sense. Initially a Populist, he had later joined the Centrists to whom he, as a Catholic, must have been welcome. But he had never become prominent in party politics, and it was his nonpartisan reputation which recommended him so strongly at a time when the credit of all the parties had sunk so low. Ebert, who tried, as President, to abstain as best he could from party prejudices, invited Cuno to form a cabinet.

After several days of difficult negotiations Cuno managed to fashion a regime. It was called a "business ministry" and, in fact, contained several nonpartisan members, like General Gröner (minister of transport), former State Secretary Albert (minister of state), the former ambassador to Copenhagen, Dr. von Rosenberg (foreign minister), and the mayor of Essen, Dr. Hans Luther (minister of food). But Cuno naturally had to establish firm bonds with the national parties and select most of his ministers from their ranks. His range of choice was limited to the bourgeois parties of the Middle — People's Party, Centrists, and Democrats — since the Social Democrats had refused him their support. Thus, from its inception, the new government appeared more slanted to the Right than Wirth's had been before the Social Democrats brought it down.

This difference did not at first seem important, for Cuno took care to emphasize his intention to stay on his predecessor's course. He acknowledged not only Wirth's motto, "First bread, then reparations," but also his note of November 13, on which, as Cuno stated in his inaugural address to the Reichstag on November 24, he was firmly resolved to build his program. He received the Reichstag's overwhelming support: only the Communists and the Racists, an offshoot of the German Nationalists, opposed him. Representatives of the several lands adopted this same position at a conference which the new national government held with them in December. This additional support was especially welcome since there had been an ominous change of government in Bavaria in early November. Premier Lerchenfeld, against whom nationalists and the secret societies had been howling violent protests, had been obliged to resign, for the Bavarian People's Party had concluded that Lerchenfeld's opposition to the national government was far too weak and, especially, that he had accommodated himself all too readily to the Law for the

Protection of the Republic. In Lerchenfeld's place the party put their colleague Eugen von Knilling, a former royal minister popular among the nationalists.

Important among these nationalist groups were the National Socialists, whose skillful demagogic leader, an Austrian named Adolf Hitler, had found the motto "Against Marxists and Jews" especially effective. The government of Prussia had banned the National Socialist Party; and Severing had forbidden Hitler to speak in public, threatening him with deportation as an unwelcome alien if he disobeyed. This made Hitler all the more welcome in Bavaria, and the air was full of rumors that he was plotting a putsch. But when the Social Democrats in the Bavarian Landtag made interpellations on this point, Schweyer, minister of the interior, replied coolly that the Law for the Protection of the Republic did not apply to the National Socialists, that the Bavarian government felt strong enough to counter plans for violence whether they stemmed from the National Socialists or from Socialists on the Left. On November 30 Hitler answered this official attestation of unconcern with five mass meetings in Munich, at which he stormed against any fulfillment policy, vehemently damned all the other parties for having tolerated the Revolution, and praised his movement as Germany's sole hope. This was only a few weeks after Mussolini's March on Rome. The people of Munich therefore knew what one of Hitler's followers meant when honoring his leader as the "German Mussolini." [2]

Berlin had less fear of invasion by Hitler than by Poincaré. The German note of November 13, 1922, had not had the desired effect. And Cuno had found no more success with his proposal of December 9, which went even further to satisfy the West by stating that the German government had resolved to try to stabilize the mark on its own if international loans should prove impossible. The proposal suggested, further, that reparations be financed by governmental bonds to be sold at home and abroad and to be repaid in gold. Reparations in kind would be halted for two years. The note contained a further suggestion which, at a later time and under different circumstances, was to prove significant: Germany declared itself prepared to join France and other great powers with Rhenish interests in giving some neutral great power — that is, the United States — their mutual guarantee to wage no war upon each other without the special authority of a popular referendum.

The German proposal was delivered to the new British Prime Minister, Bonar Law, in order that he might discuss it with the premiers of France, Italy, and Belgium at their London Conference of December 9 through 11. This meeting had been called in order that the reparations question could be considered in connection with the equally complex and burning issue of the Allied war debts, that is, their obligations to England and America. The fact that France had come out of the war owing millions to the two Anglo-Saxon powers was, to Poincaré, one more reason for insisting that Germany pay full reparations. He intended to press this claim so long as France's creditors did not forgive her debts. Lord Balfour's Note to Washington of August 1, 1922, had made this argument, but to no effect. Poincaré was opposed to any reconciliation with Germany now and managed at the conference to quash not only Germany's proposition but also Italian and British offers to assist a rapprochement. He continued to demand his "productive guarantees." The conference then adjourned, to meet again in Paris on January 2. But none ventured to place any hope in this new conference. Indeed, Poincaré only used the adjournment in the negotiations to take a step which brought him very much closer to his private goal.

For months the French Premier had taken pains to make it clear that he would not hesitate to use forceful measures if no other way were left for him to get his reparations. He refused to accept the argument that the collapse of the mark made fulfillment impossible, for, as he insisted to the Chamber of Deputies on November 7, he was convinced that the Germans "had intentionally devalued the mark and were going bankrupt on purpose." In his view it was the German state alone, and not the German economy, which was headed for ruin. German industry was prospering: its profits were almost scandalously high and unemployment was minimal. He referred, not without justification, to the foreign credits which the thriving German export trade had earned abroad, and he asked whether the German government did not perhaps possess the means of requiring its industrial and financial interests to bring at least some of these foreign credits home to the Reich.

Poincaré had made equally clear his decision to proceed alone, if necessary, should his allies fail to support him in his claims. One has, of course, every reason to believe he hoped to avoid this extreme step. Nevertheless on December 15, upon returning from the fruitless London meeting, he told the Chamber that France was prepared to proceed unilaterally. He emphasized that he was not considering "military expeditions of a belligerent nature"; this nevertheless proved to be another demonstration of Mephisto's truth: "Our first step sets us free; our second, into chains." For when the French undertook their expedition into unoccupied Germany, the choice whether it should be a military one or not was no longer theirs.

Before the French could demand "sanctions," a German "default" had to be established by the joint Reparations Commission. With respect to money payments this was impossible, for Germany had been granted a moratorium. Only the payments in kind could be attacked, and here the French declared they could demonstrate that the Germans had fallen behind in their deliveries. It was a matter of Germany's shipments of wood for 1922, which were supposed to include 200,000 telephone poles for France. A full one half of these had not yet arrived. The German government explained, by way of excuse, that the several lands, not the central government, were owners of the forests from which the wood was to come; that, because of the inflation, the lands declined to furnish the wood at the prices originally set; and so forth. The French refused to accept this explanation and took their complaint to the Reparations Commission, which met December 26 in Paris, with Barthou as chairman. There could be no doubt of the objective fact of Germany's delinquency in this respect; it was accepted by the Commission unanimously. Barthou's further recommendation that this delinquency be found to constitute a *punishable* violation of the Treaty of Versailles led to a bitter debate between himself and the English member, Sir John Bradsbury, who opposed this move with all his energy. History does not reveal such a use of wood since the wooden horse with which the Greeks had penetrated Troy, he exclaimed; and here, not Troy but Essen was the goal. Bradbury, however, was alone in his response; Belgium and Italy joined France. And so, by a vote of three to one, the commission found Germany guilty of defaulting in the sense of Paragraph 17 of the Second Annex to Part VIII of the Treaty of Versailles, and thus opened the way to "measures" against the Germans.

Sir John was, of course, quite right when he pointed out how slight these delinquencies in wood were in relation to the reparations shipments as a whole. But this argument had two edges. It cut not only Poincaré but the German government as well. For the men in Berlin had long known that the French Premier wanted his pound of flesh, that he was only waiting for the chance to use his knife. Under these circumstances did it not behoove them to take *every* care lest he find his chance, lest, in other words, any delay in his shipments occur? Is the government of a great power really to be thought incapable of delivering one hundred thousand telephone poles on time when so terribly much is at stake? Had a German general required them in war, they most certainly would have been delivered on time. And even if the national government had had to write off a few hundred thousand gold marks — what would that have meant compared to the untold sacrifices which the delay cost Germany?

Poincaré further strengthened his position by getting the Reparations Commission to find, on January 9, 1923, that Germany had also defaulted in its coal deliveries for 1922. Again the British delegate voted alone against the others.

Between these two decisions of the Reparations Commission lies the Paris Conference of January 2–4, 1923, at which the paths of England and of France definitively split. Poincaré submitted a French plan for the adjustment of reparations and the Allied debts; Bonar Law, a British proposal; and the Italian delegate, della Toretta, an Italian one as well. Each declared the others' programs unacceptable. None took the trouble to seek a compromise between the others' and his own. Poincaré had clearly had enough of all this talk, and Bonar Law was neither clever nor active enough to effect a reconciliation of their views. Meanwhile, State Secretary Bergmann was waiting in Paris, outside the door of the conference room, so to speak, in order to submit a new German plan.[3] He was not even heard. The time for discussion had run out. The conference had clearly failed and no one even took the trouble to pretend otherwise. On the contrary, both Poincaré and Law spoke of the unbridgeable gap between their points of view. After they both had so candidly stated that now their ways would part, the British Prime Minister, in his final address, assured the French Premier that the friendly feelings of the English government and people for France would remain unchanged, and Poincaré replied in the same tone.

This diplomatic dissension between England and France was as unfortunate as possible in every respect. That Poincaré would reach for the Ruhr was certain now, whether or not he really wanted to. He would be able to count on support from Belgium and Italy, but not from England. For the British naturally declined to take any direct part in the Ruhr operation. Had they collaborated, Poincaré would have been constantly obliged to heed their wishes. On the other hand, England's open disapproval of the operation could only serve to strengthen German opposition. But all German hopes for real British aid were doomed to prove false; despite the growing gap in the Entente, Great Britain stuck by France. England had maneuvered herself into a position where she could do much to sharpen the quarrel but nothing to settle or shorten it.

January 11, 1923, was the fateful day on which the Franco-Belgian operation in the Ruhr began. At first it all seemed rather harmless. In notes of this date France and Belgium declared to the German government that they had dispatched a technical control commission to observe the activities of the German Coal Syndicate, to ensure the strict execution of the reparations plan, and to adopt such measures as might prove necessary to maintain the shipments. The small bodies of troops which accompanied the engineers, the notes declared, had only the purpose of protecting them. Beyond this, the Allies concerned — Italy played only a symbolic role — had no intention of engaging in a military operation nor in a political occupation.

The intended surveillance of the Coal Syndicate was thwarted at the moment of invasion, for this body had moved its offices from Essen to Hamburg a few days before and had already transferred all its files there. In its other aspects, the Franco-Belgian program met with similar failures.

All Germany answered the occupation of the Ruhr with a scream of indignation. One can say without exaggerating that never since August 1914 had the spirit of the German people been so united. It was left to Adolf Hitler to shatter this solid national front. On January 12, the day after the invasion, he shouted to his followers in Munich's *Bürgerbräukeller*, the beer hall where he would later stage his abortive Beer Hall Putsch: "Not 'Down with France' but 'Down with traitors' should be our call! " [4] His paper, *Völkischer Beobachter*, declared that "all this chatter about a united front . . . is so much nonsense" and announced that "the assassins in Germany" had to be liquidated before anything could be accomplished against France. It is no wonder that in German political circles the National Socialists were thought a pack of fools whose mad demagogy was bound to fail in the face of "the sound sense of the German people."

But what was the national government to do? The Chancellor, Dr. Cuno, found himself suddenly confronted by a task which required a great and strong statesman — and even he had never taken himself for one. The capabilities which such a situation demands are acquired neither in a civil servant's office nor on a steamship company's board. Foreign Minister von Rosenberg was himself too insignificant to compensate for his Chancellor's failings, and this time even Ago von Maltzan, whom he had made his state secretary, did not prove to be a big enough man for such a complex task. One can certainly find no fault with the government's decision not to suffer this Franco-Belgian use of force but rather to meet it with what they called "passive resistance." The German people would not have tolerated a regime which yielded without protest to this attack, and even abroad a meek reaction would have evoked only disdain or possibly thoughts of more aggression. But the Germans should have been conscious from the start of the *limits* within which a passive resistance can be expected to succeed; perhaps they would have done well to recall Marx's words to the rebels of

Cologne after their collapse in 1848: passive resistance is like the struggle of a calf before its butcher. There was a host of compelling arguments against active resistance. But this fact was no reason to force passive resistance to its extreme and to expect to harvest fruits which, given its nature and the circumstances, it could never bear.

When the German government replied to the French note with the declaration that the occupation was an illegal violation of the treaty, they not only were correct but they were also reflecting the sense of justice of an overwhelming majority of the Germans, a sense shared by many foreigners as well. The logical consequence of the government's statement was that the directives of the occupation authorities were not obeyed. It could also be argued that since the occupation of the Ruhr robbed the German economy of its most important assets Germany would now need a further moratorium and for the same reason she would be unable to make deliveries in kind. It was all very well to talk like this; but before the German government forbade German industry to ship coal to France and Belgium, even for payment in cash, they should have considered the consequences of their act. They should have foreseen not only that France would reply with still stronger measures, but also that this boycott would mean the closing of the mines and thus the loss of work for hundreds of thousands. And what would all this unemployment mean? Simply this: that the German government, already going bankrupt, would have to feed the population of the Ruhr.

By ordering the German railroad workers to ignore any French commands, they were, of course, initially able to embarrass the French no little; but in the longer run this directive could only lead to the French usurpation of this lifeline of the Ruhr, not to mention the tragic dismissals of many loyal railroad men. When the German government directed national and local officials to disobey French orders, they ensured the dismissal of those officials. Thus the entire Ruhr area was stripped of the instruments of orderly government at a time when circumstances made orderly administration absolutely essential.

Berlin should have known Poincaré well enough to realize that he would never let passive resistance deter him from a policy to which he had not lightly committed himself and which enjoyed the support of the French people as well as a powerful majority of the French parliament. On January 11 the Chamber of Deputies had assured him of their confidence by a vote of 452 to 72. The German government should therefore have foreseen that he would not hesitate to answer ruthlessly each act of resistance with still more stringent measures. And German wartime experience in occupied

France should have shown them beyond any doubt who would be the victor in the struggle. Poincaré did not hesitate to extend the occupation beyond its original bounds, nor to erect a customs barrier at its edge, nor to reinforce his occupation forces, however painful the political and financial implications of this latter move must have been. The generals of these troops acted in the way generals always act when occupying foreign lands: they knew only the two words "order" and "obey" and responded brutally to any hint of disobedience. Their worst weapons were their military courts, which applied extremely heavy punishment even when the facts of the cases were quite uncertain. At the end of April the Prussian premier, Braun, reported to his Landtag that over 4000 people had been expelled from the former, left-bank, zone of occupation and over 800, mostly officials, from the newer zone. Two hundred and fifty people had been arrested, and the military tribunals had given sentences of over 87 years.

The worst violence occurred at the Krupp Works in Essen on March 31. In the course of a struggle between the workers and French troops the latter suddenly opened machine-gun fire on the crowd. Thirteen workers were killed. Even·more distressing was the fact that the French military court in Werden thereupon sentenced the head of the Krupp Corporation, von Bohlen-Halbach, to fifteen years' imprisonment, and eight of his principal aides to periods of ten to twenty years. In all of Germany there was no one who did not endorse Ebert's description of their trial: "An act of force which mocks humanity." They were reminded of the Chancellor's words in *Faust*:

> "Rape and Plunder" is the word
> When villains aid the vile.
> And "Guilty" ? — Ah, that's only heard
> Where decency's on trial.

The Germans had every right to object passionately to all this in their press and in their parliaments. But to what political avail? It is true that there were many, especially in the Anglo-Saxon nations, who shared the Germans' opinion of this rule of force and who, to some extent, expressed their thoughts. But this sympathy fell far short of an intent to intervene. Just as was to happen ten years later, when the horrors of Nazi rule in Germany shocked decent men throughout the civilized world, no government was prepared to intervene formally and forcibly against injustice. The Americans, to be sure, did withdraw their troops from the occupation of the Rhineland in protest against the French invasion. But this gesture only harmed the Germans more. For the French simply occupied the former American zone. The Germans could be thankful that the British did not also leave, for their zone remained a quiet refuge in the storms that laid waste the rest of occupied Germany.

But there were storms in unoccupied Germany, too. At this time, when the solid union of the German nation was more necessary and, one would think, more natural than ever before, the country was rocked by bitter interparty quarrels initiated almost exclusively by the radical Right. At first Hitler had stood rather alone under the banner "First against the criminals of November!" His National Socialist Party had been outlawed in Prussia, Baden, Saxony, and other lands on the strength of the Law for the Protection of the Republic. And the Supreme Court had confirmed this ban in a decision of March 14 with the argument that the party constituted a danger to the state and that its leader, Adolf Hitler, had boasted publicly of his disobedience of governmental orders. Despite these facts the Bavarian government had made no move, leaving Hitler a free field for his ever wilder agitation. To fill the gap created in non-Bavarian German politics by the banning of the National Socialists, Hitler's disciples, aided by extremists from the German National Party, founded a "German Racist Freedom Party" (*Deutschvölkische Freiheitspartei*) which, in its Centuries and Gymnastic Societies, organized whole groups of thugs for armed revolt.

But the Prussian police were alert, and on March 22 Severing ordered the ban and dissolution of the German Racist Freedom Party, too, according to the terms of the Law for the Protection of the Republic. His act loosed a storm of protest in the Landtag. A vehement speech by the German Nationalist Schlange-Schöningen failed to gather more than a few votes' support. Nevertheless he repeated his attacks on Severing in still more violent form four weeks later when the budget for the Ministry of Interior was being debated. But when he went so far as to exclaim that "every appeal to patriotic feelings bounces off of [Severing's] party-hardened heart," the disgust that the great majority of the Diet felt for these insulting remarks became so great that Schlange-Schöningen was obliged to yield the floor. It is indicative of the sickly decadence of German public life in those days that these words came from the mouth of a man who, time would show, was quite able to learn better and who subsequently came to recognize the evil of the National Socialist movement and to fight it with all his strength.

It is quite comprehensible that an event like the occupation of the Ruhr would stir a nation to its roots, setting both its best and worst elements into action. The passive resistance was carried out by the people of the Ruhr with impressive solidity and firmness. And since labor constituted the most important and most numerous element of this demonstration, it merits every credit for its accomplishment. It is unclear to what extent the workers were following their own inclinations and to what extent they were carrying out the orders from Berlin; in any event their attitude demonstrated that their hearts were in this opposition. But there were some, especially in unoccupied regions, whose temperaments or ambitions could not be satisfied with so passive a resistance. They proceeded to commit acts of sabotage, attack French sentries, blow up bridges, and the like.

Although such acts satisfied the bitter mood of many Germans, politically they were absurd, indeed suicidal. Only the politically immature could persuade themselves that these incidents would force France and Belgium to retreat. Their only consequence could be still worse sufferings for the unfortunate people of the occupied zones: arrests, expulsions, and executions. Thus, for instance, an explosion on the Rhine bridge at Duisburg that killed nine persons in a Belgian train was answered by a French military court in Mainz with seven death sentences. Severing and the whole Prussian government were only doing their clear duty when they tried to stop as best they could this playing with fire. But the harder they tried to save the Germans from themselves, the more violently were they attacked and defamed by the Racists and their agents. The national government, on the other hand, and the Chancellor in particular failed to set any clear course. Although the government made it unofficially clear, with respect to incidents of dynamiting in the Palatinate, "that it did not approve of that kind of resistance," Cuno later argued, in reply to a remonstrance of the papal nuncio, Pacelli, that these violent acts were to be taken as the angry reaction of a tormented nation. And Foreign Minister von Rosenberg could find no proper answer when the diplomatic representatives of France and Belgium accused the German government of having become a partner to this active resistance by expressing sympathy with the saboteurs.

The greatest attention was excited by the case of a certain Albert Leo Schlageter, who was arrested by the French criminal police in an Essen hotel on the night of April 7–8, tried for espionage and sabotage by a French military court in Düsseldorf, sentenced to death on May 10, and executed two weeks later.[5] That he was guilty of these deeds seems certain now. Nor can one doubt, unfortunately, that any other military court, particularly a German military court, would have pronounced and carried out the same judgment in similar circumstances. Only those who would have been equally shocked had the nationalities been reversed have any right to be indignant at Schlageter's fate. Nevertheless one can well understand why many Germans revered Schlageter as a patriotic, self-sacrificing martyr, however little his personal character seemed to merit this glorification. It is interesting that among those who joined in honoring him was the Communist Radek. On July 20 he called Schlageter "a good soldier of the Counterrevolution who deserves to be honored by the Communists, soldiers of the Revolution, as an honorable man; let their future task be to make sure that men such as he become not wanderers into a void but rather builders of a better future for the human race." This was at the time when in many German cities, like Breslau and Gleiwitz, the Communists were organizing disturbances and raids which led to real violence. The Rightist radicals displayed their full demagogic virtuosity by accusing the Prussian police and Severing personally of having aided in Schlageter's arrest and of having thwarted an attempt to set him free. Of course this accusation was untrue. But it was circulated so carefully and constantly that Severing found himself obliged to take recourse to the law. The Criminal Court in Elberfield found the libels which Severing had suffered false, but set his libeler, the editor of a Rightist newspaper, free.[6] The German courts could no longer be accused, as they had been in the past, of invariably supporting the authorities even in the most tenuous circumstances.

As so often happens in time of trouble, the Prussian police had to fight on two fronts. For the Communists would have been traitors to all their traditions had they sat still in so tense a situation. As usual, the Racists and Communists alike insisted with the same deep tones of moral indignation that they were only trying to defend the nation against the other side's attack; and each, as usual, accused the Prussian government of favoring the other. The difficulties, especially for the minister of the interior, grew ever greater. And the fact that Prussia was spared massive, truly threatening disturbances is as much a proof of Severing's cool imperturbability as it is of his neutrality.

But where did the German Army stand in all of this? Naturally General von Seeckt was too much a master of his trade even to consider the possibility of offering military resistance to the French. But it was only understandable that a man of his background and position would find it difficult to desist from the thought that perhaps, after all, some way or other could be found to strike a blow. His biographer maintains: "Without a doubt Seeckt initially desired active, not passive resistance; active resistance was his ultimate goal and passive, a provisional step along the way." [7] The reader must take this with a large grain of salt and not forget that it was written in 1940. In February 1923, when Seeckt spoke of the possibility that Germany would have to defend itself, he used quite different words: "Necessary preparations for defense will be made. This . . . will be accomplished as the national government wishes, that is, without any active interference with developments in the Ruhr."

Now if the German government had agreed to the organization of "preparations for defense," it must have been referring only to the eastern border. Indeed, the government did fear Polish attacks at that time. Experiences in Upper Silesia had shown that, if not the Polish government, at least Polish volunteers were capable of making border raids. And the German leaders knew Poincaré well enough to be sure that he would find a way to provoke such an attack if he thought it would help him reach his target that much sooner. The government, and especially Gessler, feared that the Reichswehr was in no condition to face this threat. It was generally agreed that the treaty limit of 100,000 men was utterly insufficient for a critical situation such as this. Moreover, the minister of defense had strong doubts about the military strength and reliability of his men, and particularly of the new, postwar recruits. The ruinous effects of inflation had made themselves felt here, too. Many a man had been attracted to the Army by its pay. But it was not possible to adjust the soldiers' wages to the falling mark as successfully as was done with workers' pay in profitable industries.

In these circumstances Gessler felt justified in increasing his forces beyond their treaty bounds by enlisting "temporary volunteers" (*Zeitfreiwilligen*). The necessary precondition for this step existed, for the International Military Control Commission had, in practice, abandoned its activities upon the invasion of the Ruhr. (The German government had declared that it would no longer tolerate inspection visits by French or Belgian officers, and the English officers were ordered by London to suspend their control activities for the time being.) [8] Thus Seeckt's hands were freed in this respect. He would have preferred to increase and equip his army quite openly, but the national government was not yet prepared to challenge the Allies so blatantly. [9] The forbidden recruits were consequently signed in secret, and the so-called "Black Army" (*Schwarze Reichswehr*) came into being.

Every secret plotting of this sort serves only to demonstrate again what Goethe said: "Woe, o woe to lies!" One act of treachery leads inexorably to the next, which in turn spawns more evil of its own. What originally was to be kept hidden from the (former) foe had now to be concealed from fellow Germans, and to the extent that it could not be kept completely secret, it evoked apprehension, suspicion, and rumor. It may well be that these rumors were exaggerated, but as long as no one knew anything for certain, the reports only grew in passage. (*Fama crescit eundo.*) And worse yet: those who carried on this forbidden game in the dark felt threatened by "traitors" all around and employed ever more ruthless and brutal means to fend them off. And so this clandestine, illicit rearmament brought new issues and new tensions to the already divided and excited German people. The men who enlisted in the Black Army were the same sort who had made up the Free Corps: there were many who hastened to the call out of an honest sense of patriotism, for they thought their country needed them; but there were others of freebooter mind and freebooter morals, and the Kapp Putsch had shown what they could do. Indeed, in the face of this earlier experience, it was only natural that in many republican circles suspicions should grow that the Black Army had other aims than mere defense against attacks of foreign foes, be they Frenchmen or Poles.

Could one forget concerns like these just because regular Army officers were in command? The President of Germany must have had his own worries on this score, for at a cabinet meeting he once inquired of Seeckt: "Now I should really like to know, where does the Reichswehr stand in all of this?" And Rabenau reports: "Quite coolly Seeckt replied, 'The Reichswehr stands behind me.'" [10] His answer was neither polite nor satisfactory, although it is true that at a later occasion Seeckt took care to tell his cabinet colleagues: "In Germany no one but myself can stage a putsch, and I assure you I plan none." It would not have been odd if the President or one of the ministers had thought of Wallenstein, who also wished to play the role of statesman as long as he had his army behind him, and of whom it was said: "No one knows at all what he believes in." Outside Berlin, at any rate, people could not but be disturbed when they observed the intimate relations that linked many a military unit to Rightist organizations.

When they so radically cut the German Army's size, the victorious Allies did not foresee that many discharged officers, deprived of their chosen careers and unable to bear inactivity, would seek in politics some outlet for their pent-up energies. The fact that, as a rule, the former officers knew nothing of their new profession disturbed neither them nor those they served. All that was required was enough "national sentiment" (*nationale Gesinnung*) — and what *that* meant was, to them, self-explanatory. With extraordinary readiness they placed themselves at the disposal of those Rightist-oriented associations which engaged in secret military arming under innocuous names. In these groups the former officers could put their skills to use and engage in the activities they knew. Their intimate relations with the Reichswehr made them especially welcome to the political string-pullers of these organizations. For it was only natural that still active officers should cherish a special affection for their "old comrades in arms." The Prussian police were particularly aware of this alliance, for they had the task of searching the secret caches of weapons that lay throughout the land. The provisions of the Treaty of Versailles, according to which all German arms were to be turned over to the Allies, had, of course, not been completely fulfilled. No matter how much had been delivered up or uncovered by the Allied Control Commission, enough of the immense war stocks to arm several thousand men still remained concealed. These hidden stores may well have constituted a treaty violation, but no German worried about that.

Responsible authorities did worry, however, lest the weapons fall into the wrong people's hands. To the extent that it was the Reichswehr that made use of these arms, the Prussian police were glad to leave it to the generals and the national government to settle accounts with the Allies. But to the extent that the munitions came into private hands, the police had to guard against their improper use. In February 1923 Gessler declared that he was opposed to any connection between the Reichswehr and the so-called "self-defense organizations" and that he and the Prussian minister of the interior, Severing, had taken steps to ensure that this policy was observed. But in these tormented months of 1923 Severing was to discover that many military authorities neither shared their minister's opinion nor intended to abide by his directives. Regular Army officers trained the "temporary volunteers" in the use of weapons, joining them to regular units in the barracks and on the drill field.

But the worst of all of this was that the Rightist groups with whom the officers linked themselves were much more interested in influencing Germany's domestic than its foreign policy. In May 1923, while searching some houses in Hamburg and Altona, the police discovered not only weapon stores but also records which were extremely compromising both to Rightist groups and to the Army. The Reichswehr's sensitivity to this discovery was betrayed by the shrill protest with which Major von Schleicher tried, without success, to silence Minister Severing. His angry outburst was probably not unrelated to the fact that the leader of the compromised *Heimatschutzverband* (League for Home Defense) was a former General Helferich. The general's confiscated documents made it clear, as Severing put it in his letter to Gessler on June 14, that these so-called self-defense groups were "fully supplied with money and with arms . . . and [were] in the process of erecting, within Germany, their own state which would use its instruments of power as it pleased in order to secure its private ends." Helferich, of course, had spoken darkly of "smashing treacherous opposition" at home and had claimed that his mercenaries had the right, without waiting for anyone to summon them, to take whatever action they deemed necessary.[11]

It was obvious that the Prussian police could not tolerate such dangerous activity, and even Gessler had been sufficiently impressed by Severing's documented complaint to see that "a clean breast of things" was in order. In consequence of this decision, the two men drew up a completely reasonable agreement on June 30. It was designed to avoid the most dangerous misuses of extralegal troops, and it would surely have worked had it been universally honored by the Reichswehr. The agreement was, by its very nature, highly secret and thus was never published officially. But reports of it crept into print, and news of the simple fact that Gessler had come to terms with Severing was enough for both extremes. Newspapers of the German Nationalists and Racists accused Gessler of having bowed to the "terrorist measures" of the Social Democratic minister of police while the Communists denounced him as a "traitor to the proletariat." [12] This alliance of the extremes against the middle would be used repeatedly from this point on, and it would entail even more serious consequences.

But more than all these political concerns, one all-encompassing economic problem occupied the attention of the German people: the rapid devaluation of the mark. In mid-January, on the day of the invasion of the Ruhr, the dollar was worth approximately 10,000 marks; by the end of the month it was worth almost 50,000. The rate fell back from this high point in a few weeks because the Reichsbank intervened. By buying marks in Berlin and abroad the bank succeeded in depressing the price of dollars to 20,000 in mid-February. And it managed to maintain this rate through March and into April. But then the operation collapsed. On April 19 the minister of economics, Dr. Becker, was forced to admit to the Reichstag that a further fall of the mark had just occurred for reasons of several different kinds, some reflecting economic facts and others the result of speculation. (According to Lord d'Abernon, Hugo Stinnes had just demanded £93,000 in foreign credits with which to cover the German railroads' bill for English coal.) [13] However that may be, the Reichsbank became convinced that it could not continue to purchase marks with gold. Having already used up a large part of its reserves and an even greater share of its foreign credits, the Reichsbank would clearly exhaust its funds in the near future if it were to go on supporting the mark in this artificial way. For there was no end in sight to the fighting in the Ruhr. And this meant not only that the people there had to be fed by the national government, but also that the raw materials which the region had formerly furnished to the German economy, especially coal, had to be bought abroad with foreign credits. The psychological effect of the bank's intervention, initially quite great, had vanished, for the longer it continued the less people believed in its success. Furthermore, financial circles knew that in 1922 the Reichsbank had guaranteed four Belgian reparations notes with a total of more than 200 million gold marks; these notes would become due each month from March through June and would have to be paid from the Reichsbank's gold reserves.

Thoughtful men, therefore, already realized that financial facts alone required the Ruhr dispute to be settled as soon as possible lest it lead to utter catastrophe. Thoughtful men knew, too, that this step would require Germany to yield to some extent. But this is exactly what thoughtless men most passionately opposed. They argued that Poincaré's piracy had brought little gain to France. And they were right. But they made a fundamental error when they let themselves believe that Poincaré was ready to yield just because he had not yet achieved his goal. On the contrary, the stalemate in the Ruhr gave him added incentive to hold on until the prize was finally won. For he too could calculate the limits of Germany's power to resist. In those same days when the Reichsbank's support of the mark collapsed, Poincaré declared at the dedication of a war memorial in Dunkirk: "Germany will wait in vain for us to vacillate even a moment . . . France will walk this road to its end." Nothing justified the assumption that he was not in earnest nor that the French nation would refuse to follow him on this course "to its end."

The German government was helpless in this desperate situation. Minister von Rosenberg was able, of course, to reply in the Reichstag to Poincaré's speech with more or less successful polemics of his own; but his words did not bring the end of struggle the least bit nearer. More realistic in this Reichstag debate was Stresemann, who explicitly rejected the motto adopted by the Rightist press: "We will not pay." "Nothing is more harmful to our fight for freedom along the Ruhr," he argued on April 17, "than those whose irresponsible statements afford our enemies further opportunity to attack us."

In the Wilhelmstrasse men hoped that the British government would not be content merely to disapprove in principle Poincaré's policy but would rather oppose it with at least an offer to mediate, and thus afford the Germans some way out. Lord Curzon, responsible for British foreign policy, was a man of much experience and many gifts, but lacked sufficient strength of character to cling to a chosen course. He was certainly no friend of Poincaré, with whom he had had violent personal differences the preceding October on the Turkish question. Curzon wished the quickest possible finish to this adventure in the Ruhr, which he regarded as dangerous from both economic and political points of view. On April 20 he delivered an address in the House of Lords in which he tried to point the way to settlement.

In this speech Curzon urged Germany to express again its willingness and readiness to pay its reparations under the condition that the sum be determined by a neutral authority "properly charged with the duty," and to provide at the same time clear assurance that the payments would be made. These words echoed an earlier suggestion by the American secretary of state, Hughes, in the last days of 1922. The speech that Lord Grey, former foreign secretary, made in this debate also warrants attention here. He argued that the reparations question could not fruitfully be regarded alone, for with it was connected France's need for security against future German aggression. At the moment, of course, Germany was quite helpless; but, as he added prophetically, "with a people as numerous as the Germans, and increasing, and as efficient as the Germans, the question of security in the course of ten or twenty years is a very real and anxious one for France, and must be so." [14]

The German government greeted Curzon's speech as a ray of hope. It gave them the courage to approach the Allies with a new proposal. But Lord d'Abernon quickly saw that the new proposal by no means satisfied his government's expectations. "Cuno and Rosenberg have got a phrase into their heads," he noted on April 26, "which will go far to wreck the chances of agreement about reparation. It is this: 'Germany will not make any offer she is not certain to be able to carry out.' As no one can possibly tell, in the present fluctuating circumstances, what Germany can pay, the phrase really means very little. They continually bring out this saying as a proof of their superior morality." [15] The ambassador's fears were all too justified.

When the German proposals concerning reparations were received by the Allied governments on May 2 they were summarily rejected by the French and Belgians. Even Curzon had to make the sad observation in his answer of May 13 that the German proposals corresponded neither in their content nor in their form to the expectations to which, on the strength of his suggestions, he was reasonably entitled. Instead of leaving the determination of the reparations sum to some international authority, the German note had fixed it at 30 billion gold marks, at the same time so encumbering this figure with clauses and conditions as to diminish its value even further. In only one of all these clauses was the international authority mentioned and even there in such a way as to permit it only to lower the total the Germans had proposed. The guarantees the Germans offered were not concrete, as Curzon had required; on the contrary, they were set forth only in vague generalities. Nor did the tone of the note fit the existing situation. Particularly inappropriate was the Germans' threat to continue passive resistance "until those territories which have been occupied without the authority of the Treaty of Versailles are evacuated and until conditions which are in conformity with the treaty are reestablished in the Rhineland." These words gave Poincaré an opportunity to demonstrate his cleverness as an advocate by enabling him to point out the difference between the spontaneous passive resistance the Germans had been talking about before and this present announcement of their government's power to stop or extend it at will; more important, the German government had also made it possible for Poincaré now to insist that he would consider no German proposals until and unless *the passive resistance were stopped*. He found this a welcome strengthening of his position; for it enabled him to turn aside all German moves, including those he might have found hard to debate, with a wave of his hand so long as the Germans had not taken a step which, as he well knew, would prove immensely difficult in terms both of the nation's politics and of its morale.

This fateful misstep by the German government had again been taken, for the most part, out of concern for domestic political facts. Fear of nationalist opposition at home prevented the government from admitting what it knew was inevitable. Rosenberg had conceded this quite clearly to the British ambassador, and Bergmann had been even more explicit in calling the German note "a compromise in almost each word between foreign facts and domestic considerations." [16] But even so the government did not escape the scathings of the Rightist press. And the mark plunged further. On the day of the British reply, a dollar cost 46,000; at the end of May, 70,000; at the end of June, 150,000 marks.

It was clear that time was running out for the Cuno government. It had shown itself unable to maneuver the Reich out of the blind alley in which it was clearly stuck. Foreign Minister von Rosenberg realized this fact, and upon receipt of Curzon's critical reply he recommended to his Chancellor, in confidence, that the cabinet resign.[17] But Cuno considered it his duty to hang on. The government then tried to smooth the waters they had ruffled by transmitting to the Allies, on June 7, a memorandum which accommodated the West in many respects. Most important, it accepted Curzon's suggestion that the amount and form of reparations payments be left up to some neutral, international authority. It also made more concrete allusions to the guarantees it was prepared to offer. Curzon would gladly have used this memorandum as the basis for an international conference on the subject. But Poincaré objected, pointing out especially that even now the Germans had said nothing about giving up their passive resistance.

June and July had passed while these notes were being exchanged, and Germany's situation was becoming ever more desperate. By the end of July a dollar cost more than one million marks. In other words, the German currency had ceased to exist. The government requested and the Reichstag passed new taxes, but there no longer were any realistic budgets for the Reich, for the lands, or for communities. The amount of currency in circulation had risen to 44 trillion marks. All commercial relationships had lapsed into utter confusion; all the savings accumulated over decades by an industrious, thrifty folk had disappeared. Worst hit was the once solid middle class, formerly regarded as the backbone of a healthy state. These people had absolutely no way to fight their fate. Whoever wishes to recapture the mood of those times should read Stefan Zweig's masterful tale *The Invisible Collection* (*Die unsichtbare Sammlung*). Some workers succeeded in keeping their real wages more or less constant during the devaluation. But their unions' treasuries were empty. And although it was true that industry still possessed the real value of its plants and a portion of the foreign credits that its exports gained, it too was now forced to awaken from its dreams and to regard with horror the coming of the end.

It was not astonishing that, in their desperation, men became unruly, even violent, particularly since the Communists scented here an excellent opportunity to advance the world revolution one step further. The state's instruments of power were restricted and to some extent unreliable. Its domestic enemies indulged in veritable orgies and became especially dangerous now since each was able to establish exclusive centers of power in separate lands: the Rightist radicals in Bavaria; the Leftists in Saxony and Thuringia.

The Bavarians were still convinced of their mission to save the Reich from "Marxism" even though they were unable to point to a single Marxist national law. The Bavarian atmosphere was so thick that it even overcame the Bavarian components of the national Army. As early as the fall of 1922 Seeckt had begun to experience difficulty in preserving, if only externally, the Reichswehr's unity. He traveled repeatedly to Munich for talks with General von Lossow, commander of the Bavarian divisions. When Lossow returned these visits in April 1923 he informed Seeckt, as Rabenau reports, "of the rather astounding fact that the numerous patriotic organizations in Bavaria were indispensable, because over 51 percent of all available weapons were in their hands." [18] Such was the state of things in the much-praised "quiet corner of the Reich" in spite, or perhaps because, of the State of Emergency which the men in Munich still stubbornly maintained. Seeckt had no choice but to remind Lossow that he, as a soldier, dared not become the servant of a political party, still less of armed bands. But the Reich was too weak to take any effective steps against the erosion of its powers.

Among the political parties which enjoyed this questionable relation with the Reichswehr, by far the most important was the National Socialist Workers' Party which, under the hypnotic influence of Adolf Hitler's untiring demagogy, was gathering ever greater numbers of Bavarians into its fold. Not since Ferdinand Lassalle had there been a demagogue in Germany who was so able to carry away an audience. Lassalle had loved to talk about the enthusiastic applause he received. But his audiences had numbered a few hundred at the most, whereas thousands upon thousands hung on Hitler's words. It is quite true that, by dint of their classical style and richness of thoughts, printed versions of Lassalle's speeches had an effect on later generations, while Hitler's words vanished with the day and situation whence they sprung. But no one can doubt that Hitler knew how to make the hour serve his impassioned ends. For he realized that in time of crisis nothing makes such a massive, moving effect upon one's listeners as vehement, even libelous, attacks upon others, especially upon others who seemed more fortunate. Shakespeare's Jack Cade knew this trick in his day. And it was bound to prove particularly effective when worked upon a nation like the Germans, whose capacity for envy the old Prince Chlodwig Hohenlohe had called their national vice. This was the principal reason for the immense effect of Hitler's anti-Semitic rabble-rousing. For most Germans were firmly convinced that the Jews knew some secret way to remain untouched by the economic misery that gripped the rest. At the very most, it is only true that a small number of Jewish financiers managed to keep their fortunes and to live in a style that evoked bitter criticism. The overwhelming majority of middle-class Jews — doctors, lawyers, merchants, and white-collar workers — were being robbed of their life's work by the inflation, along with their gentile colleagues. Hitler's anti-Semitism was a fruit of the Schönerer movement in Austria, which had sought to stir up German nationalism against the Czechs and Magyars, but especially against the Jews. This product of another political climate found a very fertile soil in Bavaria, and later in the Reich.

In those early years of the National Socialist movement nothing would have been easier for the Bavarian government than to kill off Nazism by deporting the Austrian Hitler as an "undesirable alien." The national government could do nothing here, for the control of aliens was part of the authority of the lands. German administrative law regards as "undesirable" that alien who "constitutes a danger to the internal or external peace, security, and order of the state." [19] Since Bismarck and his successors had employed this provision against poor Russian students who attended Social Democratic rallies, the men in Munich need have had no legalistic doubts about using it against a demagogue who took his followers out into the streets, armed them, and, with their aid, dispersed hostile assemblies by force — who, in short, appeared so dangerous that the minister of the interior warned him explicitly against arranging putsches and refused to take his word of honor in reply.

On May 1, 1923, Hitler gathered 5000 of his followers for "field exercises," arming them with weapons from Reichswehr barracks. The Bavarian government found itself obliged to summon Reichswehr units and armed police to relieve them of their weapons and thus avoid bloodshed. No government conscious of its rights and duties would have hesitated to deport such a dangerous alien, who led armed bands and disturbed the public peace. It was not respect for legal arguments that kept the men in Munich from making this obvious move, nor was it any sentimental consideration of the fact that Hitler had been born only a few kilometers from the German border. Their motive stemmed rather from the fact that in Hitler they saw a "nationalist" who could be put to good use against the

"Marxists," especially the Social Democrats of Berlin. When Severing outlawed the National Socialist Party in Prussia, he gave the Munich government one more reason to protect Hitler and give him free rein. That in the end this movement would threaten everything dear to Catholic Bavarian federalists and particularists they were not able, or did not wish, to see, even when Minister Schweyer declared to the Landtag that the National Socialists' platform was "politically questionable from the Bavarian point of view." And then there were Hitler's connections with Reichswehr circles in Munich, among which his follower and friend, Captain Röhm, was particularly influential. It remains the historic guilt of the Knilling regime that, blinded by its hatred of Social Democracy and a centralized Reich, it nourished a demagogic movement which was infinitely more dangerous than the Social Democrats and a far greater centralizing force than the Weimar constitution. To realize that this movement could only weaken German powers of resistance in the Ruhr would have required a broader understanding than was possible in Munich.

The government of Saxony was the exact opposite of that in Bavaria, especially after Minister of Justice Zeigner was elected premier by a bare majority of the Landtag. Attorney Zeigner had joined the Social Democrats after the Revolution. By no means without talents, he was, however, excitable and without restraint, a man who tried to hide his inner insecurity by playing the bully.[20] At this time, moreover, as was to become clear in 1924 at a trial which had extremely unfortunate consequences for him, he was in the hands of a blackmailer, under whose pressures he let himself be seduced into committing grave crimes. Zeigner's anti-Rightist measures were by no means unwarranted. For by the end of 1922 the government of Saxony had become aware of the bribery by means of which Rightist organizations had gained possession of secret weapons; and the longer this practice continued the more reason the government had to complain that the Reichswehr hindered rather than helped the fight against the Rightists. The Saxons had good reason to regard the Black Army with misgivings. But Zeigner so misused his weapons in this fight that even Severing felt forced to complain. Zeigner voiced his differences with the national government and the Reichswehr in violent speeches and turned more and more toward the Communists. By May the leaders of the Saxon Social Democrats had agreed to join the Communist Party in creating proletarian defense organizations. A similar movement was taking shape in Thuringia.

These opposition movements, which reflected the divergent politics of various land governments, helped to destroy the internal unity of Germany. Moreover they gave encouragement to a move-

ment that can by no means be considered harmless: separatist agitation in the occupied areas along the Rhine. Rhenish separatism had
already raised its head in the months immediately after the Empire's
collapse. Its leader was the former state's attorney, Dr. Dorten of
Wiesbaden, a wealthy fancier of horses and an extremely ambitious
man, who considered the time propitious to wrest the Rhineland
from Prussia. This was, at any rate, the announced goal of the Rhenish People's Union (*Rheinische Volksvereinigung*) which Dorten
founded. According to its announced platform the Rhenish Republic
was supposed to become simply one more land in the German Reich.
But people generally suspected that this was a false front, behind
which lurked Dorten's real goal: a Republic of the Rhine *outside*
the Reich — that neutral buffer state desired so strongly by numerous
Frenchmen, among whom Poincaré and Foch were not the least.

When, in the drafting of the Treaty of Versailles, the French had
been forced to desist from their plans for the left bank of the Rhine,
the separatist movement there had suffered a concomitant relapse.
But the occupation of the Ruhr gave it new strength.[21] New separatist associations sprang to life, like the "Rhenish Republican
People's Party" with a certain Smeets as its leader, and the "Rhenish
Independence League" headed by Matthes. There can be no doubt
that this movement never comprised more than a minority of the
people of the Rhine. All the regional leaders of the national parties,
from the German Nationalists to the Communists, refused to support it. But political leaders who opposed separatism soon felt the
power of the occupation authorities, especially their power of quick
expulsion. Thus, for instance, the Democratic delegate Pastor Korell
was driven from his Rhine-Hessian home for opposing the French
policy in a Reichstag debate. On the other hand, the French authorities let the separatists arm their followers and helped them terrorize
the populace. Only thus could the separatists hold large rallies and
proudly pretend to represent the Rhinelanders. To be sure, the
prophecy that the Rhenish Republic would be proclaimed on July
14, the national holiday of France, did not prove true. But the danger
persisted. And the further economic chaos progressed, the louder
the separatists became in stating that their real goal was secession
from the German Reich which was bound to collapse under its pressing burdens and inner dissension.

A most peculiar alliance of francophilic separatism with a
nationalist and monarchist *Putschismus* came to light in Munich. In
June 1923 the People's Court there heard, with self-assumed
authority, the trial of Professor Fuchs and his associates for high
treason.[22] Fuchs, a music critic in his fifties, had formerly been on the

staff of the *Münchner Neuesten Nachrichten,* a National Liberal
paper. He was no more fit to be a statesman or even to conduct a
putsch than is a donkey to walk a tightrope. He was one more of the
many who regarded Bavaria as the fountain of health and Berlin as
the swamp of disease, and he had convinced himself that it was
God's will that he deliver his Bavaria from Berlin. But he let an
agent of France pay for this endeavor, since he was persuaded that
France would support an independent Bavaria. His activity warranted a sentence of long imprisonment, and it was not surprising
that, while pronouncing this sentence, the court seized the occasion
to castigate France and Poincaré.

The significant aspect of the whole affair was the environment in
which it grew: the armed "self-defense units," *Oberland, Ober-
land-Treu, Blücher,* and all the rest. All these German superpatriots
were ready to make an armed attack on "Marxist and Jewish Berlin"
at any time. One must read the record of the trial — it reads like a
cross between Zane Grey and Edgar Wallace — to get an idea of the
incredible way in which the minds of these would-be statesmen
worked. They seem never to have realized that their activity was
highly treasonable, nor did the People's Court take the trouble to
point this out. It preferred to display its political sophistication instead by pronouncing "that a critical danger of the communization
of Germany has existed for some time, exists today, and will continue to exist until the authority of the German Reich and of its
several states is considerably more firmly established on its *federalist
base.*" Most interesting of all, perhaps, was the discovery that Fuchs
had spun his threads not only to the Munich Army Command but to
the Police Commission, as well. His helpers here were Frick and
Pöhner, Hitler's henchmen. The entire picture revealed by the trial
confirms the judgment Severing later made of Bavarian conditions
at that time: "There was such confusion in the Bavarian administration that it was easy for every adventurer to satisfy himself within
the white and blue borders of the land." One of these adventurers
was Captain Ehrhardt of the Kapp Putsch. He had escaped from his
Leipzig trial cell and now, aided by Bavarian gendarmes, was busy
arming the warriors of the Oberland Bund, training them, and preparing them for their victorious march against the North.

This then was the condition of Germany at the beginning of
August 1923 when the Reichstag reassembled in Berlin. The Communists tried to make this condition still more critical by calling a
general strike. And in fact disturbances did occur at various points.
In Berlin the police, aided by responsible labor leaders, succeeded in

avoiding bloodshed and in restoring peace in several days. In other places, like Hanover and Gelsenkirchen, there were dead and wounded. But after a few days these places were also quiet. The entire Communist maneuver had made no sense. However desperate the situation, and consequently men's moods, throughout the Reich, there was no reason to expect any sort of improvement through strikes and unrest.

Given the crisis that faced Germany in this summer of 1923, the reception that the Reichstag would give to Cuno's government became all the more important. The delegates approved the taxes Cuno proposed, but the continued existence of his regime clearly depended upon the Reichstag's confidence in the Chancellor's ability to steer the German ship of state to harbor. Not even the government itself had any confidence that their new leader could do so. Cuno, who suffered complete nervous collapse from time to time, scarcely inspired confidence when he assured anyone who would listen that he simply could not remain in office; and Rosenberg groaned to the British ambassador that chaos was inevitable, the position could not be held.[23] The Reichstag discussions of August 8–10 failed to illuminate an exit. The best impression was created by Stresemann, who showed how far he had developed since those days of 1919 when he had fought hard against the Weimar constitution. Now he was prepared to recognize that it had done much to pave the way for German growth; "Without putsches from Right and from Left and without all our secret armed bands we would be even further along with our stabilization." The leader of the Democrats agreed and called for a chancellor willing to be "energetic even at the cost of popularity"; his words sounded like an invitation to Stresemann. The decisive blow to Cuno's cabinet was struck on August 11, when the Social Democratic bloc decided by a large majority to withdraw their confidence from the government. Cuno immediately resigned with all his ministers. Public opinion considered Stresemann the man of the hour, and it was he whom President Ebert asked to form a cabinet.

One thing was quite clear to Stresemann: he would have to erect his government upon as broad a parliamentary base as possible, including in his cabinet every party which earnestly desired to assist in the solution of Germany's immense problems without insisting that each step along the way conform to its private party program. He saw, as he already had explained to his own bloc, three possibilities: a minority cabinet like Wirth's, a Socialist labor government, or a great coalition extending from the German People's Party to the Social Democrats. He aimed at this third possibility. It was not easy to persuade the Social Democrats. Many of their hotter heads would have much preferred to plunge into an endless debate with the People's Party on the tax and economic policies to be followed in the future. But Stresemann managed to convince them that the needs of the hour left no time for such delays, and in this he received Severing's support. The personnel of the cabinet also offered problems. The Social Democrats wanted Gessler to be dropped, while the other parties — and Ebert — wished him retained. Finally the Social Democrats desisted from this demand, and two days later Stresemann's cabinet was complete.

Besides the office of chancellor, Stresemann took the Foreign Ministry; for in the immediate future it was in foreign affairs that Germany's most important decisions would have to be made, and he was correct in believing himself better able to make these decisions than some professional diplomat unacquainted with the facts of political and parliamentary life. Just as pressing, and perhaps more difficult, tasks awaited his minister of finance; for everybody realized that the old money had lost its use and that a new currency would have to be introduced. In this post the Chancellor put a Social Democrat who had won a distinguished reputation with his studies of finance. This man was Dr. Rudolf Hilferding, a native Austrian, once a pediatrician in Vienna, but later a student of socio-economic problems. Upon becoming a citizen of Prussia he had joined the Independents, editing their Berlin paper, *Die Freiheit*. The subsequent fusion of the two Socialist parties opened to him a greater sphere of influence and prospects of career. He was a Jew and thus exposed, as a minister, to scurrilous attacks; but Schwerin-Krosigk, who worked with him while in no way sharing his political point of view, testifies that "in private life he was a kind, unprejudiced man with a sense of humor." [24] The question was whether, along with his knowledge and competence, he also possessed the force and power of decision which the German minister of finance, in this more than critical moment, needed on the grandest possible scale.

Gustav Stresemann was the first liberal statesman in the entire history of the German Reich to be asked to lead it as its chancellor.[25] To be sure, one might think of Prince Hohenlohe in these terms; but his liberalism was so dilute that in any other land but Germany he would have been called an enlightened conservative. Stresemann's liberalism was devoid of any variety of radicalism. The National Liberals, whose leader he had become after Bassermann's death in 1917, had consistently followed a policy which their friends called "flexible" and their enemies called "opportunistic." The same could be said of Stresemann's policies before the war, although he had initially pressed within his party for a greater emphasis on liberalism. During the war, however, his nationalist enthusiasm had out- weighed all else, and after the defeat he found it hard at first to readjust and form a clear idea of liberalism's role in a completely altered world. But basically he had never lost his liberal point of view, and he remained particularly conscious of its intimate connec- tion with the great classical tradition of German thought. From this tradition he drew strength and consolation throughout his life. Goethe was the special object of his admiration and constant study. The fact that Napoleon also fascinated him shows that Stresemann's intellectual horizon was not hemmed in by a nationalist bias.

One can also attribute to his liberalism that gradual conquest of his own prejudices which marks his development after 1919. In the realm of foreign policy he grew from a nationalistic war hawk to a sober realist who saw things as they actually were and not as he wished them to be. Without denying his preference for the mo- narchic form of state, he realized that, at least for some time, there could be no return in that direction and that in a republic the states- man's primary duty is to awaken in his colleagues and constituents a sense of personal political responsibility. A third fruit of his liberal heritage is to be seen in his changing attitude toward Social De- mocracy. He discovered that it was not enough to urge the workers to "shake off their red chains," that, on the contrary, the Social Democratic movement possessed powers that were both available and necessary for the reconstruction of the Reich. Although his personal relationship to Ebert had never been warm, it was im- possible for him to avoid the profound impression which Ebert's realistic thought and simple patriotism made on every unprejudiced observer.

Stresemann regarded as his first task the creation of a great coalition which would make possible the collaboration of his own party with the Social Democrats. He was, however, fully aware of the real difficulties he would have to overcome among members of his own party. In an article of July 1924 commemorating his prede- cessor, Ernst Bassermann, he later wrote: "It seems to be the fate of the National Liberals' leaders that they suffer less from contest with other parties than from psychic rot induced by intraparty quarrels." Gustav Stresemann was to experience his full measure of this disease.

His first sample came with the Reichstag's vote of confidence on August 14, when thirteen members of his own party abstained from voting. The new government nevertheless succeeded in displaying a strong majority of 240 against 76 Nationalists, Populists, and Com- munists. The Rightists had explained in the debate that they were opposing the new regime because it was under Social Democratic influence. The Bavarian People's Party was content to abstain. Thus Stresemann had a base in the Reichstag, a base which was strong and broad enough to permit him to grapple with the problem of quieting or stopping the fighting in the Ruhr.

In the midst of this change of government what seemed pleasant news came from London. A change of government had recently taken place there, too. Bonar Law, fatally ill, had resigned at the end of May. As his successor, the King appointed the former chancellor of the exchequer, Baldwin, a man who up to then was little known but who was to remain at the head of the Conservative Party for almost a decade and a half. Lord Curzon, whose life-long ambition had been thwarted by Baldwin's appointment, remained foreign minister and tried to make history in this more modest post by opposing Poincaré's policies in the Ruhr. Having sought in vain to achieve a common Allied reply to the German propositions of June 7, Curzon turned to an attack upon the French Premier, on whom he squandered little affection, in an extraordinarily detailed note on August 11 which contained no less than fifty-five paragraphs and which was couched in extremely pointed language.[26] Its most sensational section was that in which it brusquely denied the legal justification of the Franco-Belgian occupation of the Ruhr and explicitly supported the Germans' point of view. "The highest legal authorities in Great Britain have advised His Majesty's Government that the contention of the German Government is well founded, and His Majesty's Government have never concealed their view that the Franco-Belgian action . . . was not a sanction authorized by the treaty itself."

Naturally this note was received with great joy in Germany; the government took every care to have it widely distributed in the original together with a German translation. The anger of the French was correspondingly great. But Poincaré quickly showed that he could play this game, too. Within a week he replied with an equally specific note, rebutting the English arguments point by point.[27] Even the opponents of his policy have to admit that he won this paper skirmish; in particular he demonstrated to Curzon that the British government could not employ the argument that the occupation was not authorized by the treaty since they previously, by both word and deed, had taken exactly the opposite point of view. Poincaré denied that he desired the ruin of Germany; he argued that he merely wished to avoid the ruin of France: "To preserve Germany from ruin, one need not nourish it at the expense of France and her Allies on special favors which will only encourage an easy, feverish

German recovery and result in a German hegemony in trade and industry. We need not hand over to Germany the kind of domination that she was unable to win for herself in battle." At the time they were spoken, these words sounded like cynical mockery. Today they have a very different ring.

But what had this diplomatic flurry profited Germany? As quickly became apparent, nothing at all. Poincaré was perfectly content to rest in a position so favorable for him that he refused to negotiate until Germany gave up its passive resistance. And England had no leverage with which to pry him loose. Stresemann was therefore faced with a bitter choice: either to keep up the fight, although no one saw a chance for its success, or to yield, giving up the passive resistance without condition. He summoned all his energy and skill to the task of avoiding both extremes. He put an end to the absurd social boycott which the former government had applied to the French ambassador, engaging instead in extensive conversations with M. de Margerie. In these talks he sought to make perfectly clear that he did not oppose in principle giving France even the "productive guarantees" which Poincaré so passionately wished if only the liberation of the Ruhr were settled first. The ambassador seems to have shared Stresemann's desire for reconciliation, but he was obliged to transmit his Premier's unconditional refusal. Stresemann further demonstrated his realistic sense by admitting that Germany would have to be prepared to pay more than the maximum he had offered.[28]

The last German illusions of British aid were dispelled on September 20, when an official communiqué was published announcing the results of a Paris conference between Baldwin and Poincaré. The statement explained that the two men were "happy . . . to discover that on no question is there any difference of purpose or divergence of principle which could impair the cooperation of the two countries." With this Lord Curzon's attempt to oppose Poincaré's policies was publicly abandoned by his Prime Minister. This was, as the Frankfurter Zeitung pointed out, a clear warning for Germany to expect no British pressure on France toward a tolerable solution in the Ruhr.

But worst of all, there was no more time for talk. The situation was desperate and demanded a solution, not in two or three months but tomorrow. "The present costs of passive resistance," Stresemann noted on September 7, 1923, "amount to forty million gold marks every day . . . This need makes such enormous demands on our Treasury that even confiscatory taxes can no longer cover it." The ruin of the paper mark had assumed such grotesque dimensions that people no longer bothered to use it. The dollar, worth between three and four million marks in mid-August, climbed over ten million by September and then soared higher to 20, 50, 100, even 160 million before the month was out.

The Reichsbank had long since given up all hope of intervention. Its president, Dr. Havenstein, a proper civil servant of the old Prussian school who had won praises for his management of loans during the war, stood helpless before the problems of a time so out of joint. He blamed the whole affair on Germany's unfavorable balance of trade and thought he was doing his duty by printing money day and night. In August 1923 he reported to the Reichsrat with some pride that his bank was now able to issue 46 billion new marks every day. Lord d'Abernon, who understood something of economic matters, noted with indignation that no member of the Reichsrat had a word of criticism to offer against such an insane policy and exclaimed: "It appears almost impossible to hope for the recovery of a country where such things are possible." In intimate conversation he gave expression to his horror by remarking that in a country with healthy notions about its money a man like that would long since have been hanged.[29] Stresemann was no expert in the field of money and banking, but he had realized for some time that Havenstein was not big enough for his duties and now did more than merely suggest that he resign. But the Reichsbank had been made completely independent of the government — upon the insistence of the Entente — so the Chancellor was not empowered to force its president to resign. And Havenstein was not the sort of man to quit his post.

In the meantime, Hilferding was confronted by the problem of creating a new currency which would replace the utterly discredited mark and possess some guarantee of stability. For, as he explained to the executive committee of the Reichstag, without a stable currency Germany could hope for neither a foreign policy nor a budget, neither an administration nor an economic life. There was every reason to fear that the farmers would decline to exchange their new harvest for a currency which, whatever numbers might adorn it, was so much wastepaper.

This problem of a new currency was at the same time quite simple and most complex. In point of fact the inflation would be ended when the legal, but actually worthless, banknotes were officially declared invalid and withdrawn from circulation, when the money presses ceased their mad acceleration and came to final halt, and when the amount of new currency to be put into circulation was firmly set at a level which corresponded with the minimum fiscal and economic requirements of the country. With respect to the fiscal problem, this meant, of course, that the governmental budgets, national, land, and local, would actually have to be balanced. In other words, their requirements could no longer be met by borrowing from the central bank but rather through taxes, imposts, and tariffs according to the axioms of rational fiscal policy.

But there was a psychological prerequisite to this reform: the restoration of popular confidence in the nation's currency after the bitter, distressing experience of the recent past. How was the government to convince the nation that the new money would not also dwindle and disappear? Classical monetary theory knew only one certain way to assure this confidence: the erection of a currency upon a foundation of gold — the most constant standard of value and, consequently, the one most trusted by human beings. But the Reich did not have sufficient gold. The experts were therefore obliged to seek some other firm foundation on which to base the notes they were about to issue. Credit for finding an answer to this problem must be given to Karl Helfferich. Whenever his partisan passions did not blind him, he remained an expert in the field of money and finance. Helfferich proposed that a National Mortgage Bank (*Rentenbank*) be established which would receive an interest-bearing mortgage on all agricultural and industrial land in Germany and would issue interest-bearing National Mortgage Bank Notes backed by this mortgage. This national mortgage took precedence over all other encumbrances upon the property but, being universal, did not have to be registered at the land courts. It could, therefore, be regarded as "good as gold." Helfferich did not wish to link this new currency to the value of gold, but to rye instead. The "rye mark" which he proposed was to be pegged to the price of one pound of rye. His thought was that a German currency based on rye, the chief product of German agriculture, would find immediate acceptance among the German farmers and thus ensure the nation's threatened food supply.

Helfferich's plan was not the only one to be laid before the minister of finance. The decision was up to Hilferding, and now, unfortunately, it became apparent that he was far stronger as a critic than as a constructive thinker. He was sufficiently clever and well versed in the theories of finance to find the weaknesses in every proposition and to examine them with patient care. But time was running out, and a decision had to be made immediately. To the despair of his colleagues, Hilferding simply could not make up his mind. One might perhaps say that his misfortune lay in knowing too much about what was at stake. Parliamentary discontent exploded late in September during a conversation between the Reichstag leader of the People's Party, Dr. Scholz, and the leader of the Social Democratic delegation, Hermann Müller. Scholz told Müller that his delegates did not believe Hilferding satisfied the requirements of his office; Scholz thought two thirds of Müller's Social Democrats shared this opinion. Müller replied, "You might well be right," and proceeded to offer objections to the minister of economics, Dr. von Raumer of the People's Party, objections which Müller believed were likewise shared by a majority of Raumer's own party. And so, at the occasion of a cabinet shuffle on October 3, both Hilferding and Raumer had to go. The new minister of finance was the former minister of food and agriculture, Dr. Luther, who, while unable to compete with Hilferding as a theoretic scholar, exceeded him by far in his ability to take decisive action. He succeeded, as we shall see, where his predecessor had failed to make a move.

These problems of Germany's foreign and fiscal policies were by no means the only ones with which Stresemann's government had to struggle. Interparty feuds continued to obstruct the cabinet at every step. Stresemann's acceptance of Social Democrats in his regime met with an extreme opposition on the Right that even extended into the ranks of the People's Party. This opposition became particularly acute when men began to realize that Stresemann hoped to end the trouble in the Ruhr or, as the German Nationalists in the Reichstag and the Prussian Landtag said, sought "compromise at any price with spiteful, irreconcilable France." As an indication of the confusion, irresponsibility, and rabble-rousing that ruled these Rightist ranks, we may recall that the delegate Hergt, a former minister and considered one of the most enlightened of his party, exclaimed at the Nationalists' convention on September 23: "We have faith only in a solution won by force. This is not to say that we wish war with France. We believe that France would be taking a frightful risk if she were to try to advance farther into Germany. But we ought to make France at last aware of all the risks involved!" Is there any other name for this sort of wild talk than irresponsible rabble-rousing?

Meanwhile, from the Ruhr, the warnings grew more and more insistent that the power of resistance was coming to an end. On August 21 the industrial magnate Otto Wolff told Stresemann in confidence that morale was constantly deteriorating in the Rhineland and conditions there were lapsing into anarchy. Jarres, the mayor of Duisburg, a nationalist and a conservative member of the *Volkspartei*, told the Chancellor that he should not expect the Ruhr to hold out beyond September. And Stinnes in his newspaper publicly called for negotiations with the French "in order to save Germany, Europe, and the world from the catastrophe that is otherwise inevitable." [30]

Not only clear insight but also a high degree of courage would be required by any statesman who, under these circumstances, decided to give up the passive resistance in the Ruhr. Stresemann possessed this bravery as well as this vision. On September 26 a proclamation of the President and of the cabinet announced the end of the resistance in the Ruhr. "To preserve the life of the nation and the state, we are confronted now by the bitter necessity of ceasing our struggle." This was by no means a rhetorical exaggeration. It was the simple description of a frightening set of facts. All the screams of protest that these words evoked, all the rebellious stirrings that they unleashed, in no way alter the fact that at this moment Stresemann showed himself a true statesman who should be honored by his nation for having taken the right step when to do so was as difficult as it was necessary. It is quite easy to celebrate the victorious hero returning in triumph, and "the singers do not tell us of the man who met defeat." But historians, who try to raise themselves above the battles and the party strife of their day, know how rare those statesmen are who can meet this "most acid test of life" and show that they are able to control themselves. And it is precisely because, as the war years had demonstrated, Stresemann tended to let his heart direct his mind that he merits special recognition for having done what was necessary even though it was a deeply saddening, even humiliating, step. For Stresemann knew better than anyone else that with this move he conceded to Poincaré the triumph for which he had been fighting since January 11, 1923. One can find some consolation in the observation that the German people must have recognized the statesmanlike qualities which Stresemann demonstrated here, for they entrusted the direction of foreign policy to him until his death. The victorious Poincaré lost his people's confidence a few months after his triumph.

But at the time, of course, things looked quite otherwise. The proclamation of the end of passive resistance signaled into life all German forces of disturbance and destruction. Stresemann had taken careful pains to prepare the ground for his move with candid statements to the governments of the lands as well as to the leaders of political parties and of professional groups. Among all these he had been able to win great majorities to his side; but among them, too, were nationalists who continued to protest even though they could offer no clear alternative solutions. Helfferich's proposal that the passive resistance "be replaced by an open break with France" sounded heroic, but also like a suicide's last words. When, in the Reichstag debate of October 8, Count Westarp labeled surrender in the Ruhr "the result of a regime that is afraid to govern without the help of Social Democrats," the Chancellor could immediately reply: "You have said yourself that you would not wish to keep up the passive resistance any longer. A purely non-Socialist (*rein bür-gerliches*) cabinet would therefore have reached this same decision." Accusations like Westarp's could be silenced in Reichstag debate, but they spread over an excited nation with growing strength.

Again it was the Bavarians who first poured oil on the flames. Von Knilling, the Bavarian premier, had admitted in the Reichsrat that it was time to cease resistance in the Ruhr. But in the night of September 25–26 — that is, immediately before the proclamation was to be published — the members of the national government were informed by the editorial offices of the Berlin press that the government of Bavaria had, without notifying Berlin, declared a state of emergency, named von Kahr "state commissioner-general" (*General-staatskommissar*), and given him full powers of government. The cabinet, which gathered immediately, had no choice but to announce, in that same night, a state of emergency throughout the Reich. Full powers, however, were not given to General von Seeckt, who had been at the meeting, but rather to Gessler, minister of defense. This decision disappointed those militarist, nationalist groups who had looked forward to a Seeckt dictatorship now that chaos had reached a peak.

Knilling must certainly have realized that in making this abrupt move behind the back of the national government the government of Bavaria was violating the simplest rule of loyalty. For on September 27 he made a personal telephone call to Stresemann to explain the reasons for this fait accompli. Excitement in Bavaria had grown so great, he argued, that there was every reason to fear lest "one side commit a stupid act." It must be noted, however, that under the conditions then prevailing in Bavaria, this "side" could only have been the Nazis or other radical Rightist groups. For the Social Democrats could hardly have been expected to rebel against a decision made by members of their own party in the national cabinet, and Communists were practically extinct in Bavaria. In this situation one was forced to wonder why the men in Munich had ever thought of giving full powers to a man like Kahr, whose intimate relations with Rightist bands had become notorious. Knilling answered this question, even before Stresemann could ask it, by explaining that Kahr's conservative reputation would make it all the easier to influence these organizations, and he assured the Chancellor that Kahr would carry out his mission in a completely loyal way.[31] It did not take long for Herr von Kahr to show what he understood by "loyalty."

In the course of their telephone conversation Stresemann had called Knilling's attention to the exciting stimulus that the Kahr dictatorship would provide to radical Rightists in northern Germany, especially now that their Bavarian comrades had boasted in Nuremberg that Bavarian fists would be needed to restore order in Berlin. Only a few days later, on October 1, German newspapers carried the following report, as alarming as it was mysterious: "Early today *National Communist bands*, trying to seize Küstrin, succeeded in penetrating to the inner parts of the city, which were devoid of military posts. The commander of the Küstrin garrison has arrested their leader, and the garrison, which is being strengthened by nearby Army units, has been directed to use all means in restoring complete order."

Strange, most strange! Who and what were these "National Communists"? It was certainly true that Germany had a plethora of parties and subparties, but no one had ever heard of this species before. And who was the anonymous leader of these "bands" who was arrested by the local commandant but kindly spared the publicity of mention in an official report? His name was Buchrucker; he was a "Royal Prussian Major, retired" and commanded the "Labor Troops" (*Arbeitskommando*) — in other words, the Black Army — in Küstrin.[32]

Ever since 1922 Buchrucker had been organizing these "Labor Troops" within the Third Army Area, that is, in the Prussian province of Brandenburg. He had characterized these troops in the following way: they were formally considered civilian clerks and laborers, although they wore Army uniforms, lived in Army barracks, and had Army personal documents complete with military rank. Buchrucker himself had been a civilian consultant to the Army Area Command since early 1923. The Area Command (*Wehrkreis*), and hence the Reichswehr, knew what was going on but was content to close its eyes so long as Buchrucker's activity did not violate too blatantly the directives from above. What was particularly dangerous was the fact that the Reichswehr was not alone in playing this game. At least equally important were the so-called patriotic leagues, the private armies of the Rightist parties, which provided not only most of the Black Army's officers but also the necessary funds. Because of inflation it was simple for these leagues to provide whatever amounts of money were required. Naturally the authorities took care that only those men were enrolled in the Labor Troops whose political views were absolutely reliable. They managed to convince these men "that the Reichswehr, having organized this system, intends shortly to free Germany from its foreign yoke." One can therefore well imagine what sort of spirit reigned among these troops. Until the word was given to attack the foreign foe, they regarded as their principal enemy the Prussian police. Anyone suspected of having connections with the police was considered a traitor. And "Verräter verfallen der Fehme"; or, more baldly put, such men were brutally killed.

With such a crew of freebooters behind him Buchrucker was inspired to play statesman. He conceived the plan of gathering his forces in and around the fortresses of Küstrin and Spandau, marching with them upon Berlin, and there — these are his own words — "forcing the national government to carry out the strengthening of the Army that already had been planned." All this was on the assumption "that the Reichswehr approved of [Buchrucker's] design." The night of Saturday and Sunday, September 29 and 30, was selected for the assembly of his troops. But the Army refused to put up with this sort of tomfoolery. The Defense Ministry ordered the arrest of Buchrucker, then at Area Command headquarters in Berlin. An officer of the General Staff was thoughtful enough to inform Buchrucker of this order on September 30, whereupon the latter "took the next train to Küstrin." At this point, he later said, he was convinced that his planned operation was hopeless, but also that he would be unable to dismiss his restless troops. And so he used them for a "mock attack" which was supposed to end as quickly as possible with their surrender. This surrender did indeed take place quite soon, as soon as the garrison commander showed he was in earnest. Buchrucker was arrested with his officers. The Special Court in Kottbus, which unfortunately met behind closed doors, sentenced him on October 27, 1923, to ten years' imprisonment for having committed high treason. He had to suffer only a fraction of this punishment. For when the political situation seemed to have calmed down a bit, President Hindenburg granted him pardon.

Buchrucker's abortive putsch had one good consequence: the Black Army was dissolved. But its memory was kept alive in German minds by the Vehmic murder trials, which brought to light at least a part of the felonies committed by members of these troops.[33] It was a loss both to the German professional administration of justice and to the public's legal sensibilities that most of the trials for the Vehmic murders were held in secret. As a result, the trials did not have the educative, quieting effect that one might otherwise have expected of them. It was only natural that the Küstrin putsch should strengthen the suspicions of those who already had their doubts about the Army. And events in Saxony and Thuringia were about to justify these misgivings all too well.

But first there was a cabinet crisis in Berlin. The ministers were unanimous in their opinion that they had to ask the Reichstag for a special "enabling act" (*Ermächtigungsgesetz*) which would permit them to act quickly in the crisis and make the necessary regulations for the solution of the country's financial and fiscal problems. But in cabinet discussions of the steps to be proposed, important differences developed between the *Volkspartei* ministers and their Social Democratic colleagues on the question of the length of the working day in industry. During the Revolution the People's Representatives had established the eight-hour day with their decree of November 23, 1918, thus fulfilling one of the Social Democrats' oldest and most important demands. Many members of the labor movement regarded this decree as the most significant achievement of the Revolution. But now employers insisted that if Germany's chaotic economy were to be repaired a longer working day would be required. And the *Volkspartei* ministers joined in this demand.

This development severely embarrassed the Social Democratic ministers, who did not dare differ with their constituents on such a cardinal point. Their party's delegation in the Reichstag refused, though by a scant majority, to back an enabling act that dealt with socio-economic matters. As a result of this decision, the government resigned on October 3.

Ebert requested Stresemann to stay on and form another cabinet; this he accomplished within three days, owing to a compromise solution to the question of the working day. The most important cabinet changes were, as mentioned above, the departures of Hilferding and von Raumer, together with Luther's assumption of the Ministry of Finance. Then came the heavy battle in the Reichstag for the enabling act. The German Nationalists, who naturally were gravely disappointed at this renewal of the great coalition, now made every effort to overthrow the cabinet. The President was obliged to announce that he would dissolve the Reichstag if the act were not passed with the two-thirds majority required for constitutional amendments. Nevertheless the German Nationalists joined the Communists in trying to block the measure by absenting themselves from the chamber at the vote. Their plan was to make it more difficult for the other parties to obtain the presence, required by Article 76, of two thirds of the Reichstag's members. But their maneuver failed.

On October 13 the law was accepted by a vote of 316 to 24, with only 7 abstentions. Once again several members of the *Volkspartei* — like the industrial magnate, Dr. Vögler — were among those who abstained. The law was to be effective for only a limited time: it would lapse with any change in the coalition or, at the latest, on March 31, 1924.

The government immediately used its new authority to attack the most pressing problem: currency reform. As early as October 15 a decree called the German Mortgage Bank (*Rentenbank*) and its *Rentenmarks* into existence. The *Rentenbank* embodied the essence of Helfferich's program, though with one basic difference: the idea of the "rye mark" had been dropped. The new *Rentenmarks* were pegged to the price of gold, as was the national mortgage by which they were to be backed; they were to be redeemable upon demand in interest-bearing gold mortgage certificates. They were not made legal tender, and thus their provisional character was made clear from the start. The *Rentenmarks* were not yet a new currency, but they did constitute the first step toward a revival of the nation's confidence in its money. The most important way to make this confidence at all possible was, of course, to protect the public from arbitrary increases in the volume of *Rentenmarks* put into circulation. The necessary limitation was ensured by having the decree state precisely the maximum amount that could be issued and, especially, the amount that might be credited to the Reich. This meant that, upon the distribution of the *Rentenmark*, the national government would have to cease giving Treasury notes to the Reichsbank in exchange for new paper money.

November 15, 1923, was the date set for the opening of the *Rentenbank*. A few days before this date the proprietor of the Darmstadt National Bank, Dr. Hjalmar Schacht, was named national currency commissioner (*Reichswährungskommissar*). Luther realized that the creation and preservation of this new currency was a task which he could not manage in addition to his already difficult and pressing duties as minister of finance. Ordinarily this new task would have devolved upon the president of the Reichsbank, but both the cabinet and the educated public had so completely lost confidence in Havenstein that the government was obliged to invent the make-shift office of currency commissioner. It was generally agreed that Schacht possessed the requisite competence and energy, and as one of the founders of the Democratic Party he was considered a reliable supporter of the Republic.[34]

In the four weeks which separated the publication of the decree from the opening of the *Rentenbank* and the issuance of the first

Rentenmarks, many events occurred which brought the German state to the brink of chaos and which will concern us below. But in spite of everything the date was met. The *Rentenmarks* made their first appearance on November 15, and at once were avidly sought by both the commercial world and the general public. The critical question at this juncture was the rate at which *Rentenmarks* should be exchanged for the older paper money. Now, since the *Rentenmark* was supposed to bear the same relation to the dollar as had the gold mark before the war, that is, 4.2 to 1, Berlin quotations for the dollar would set the rate. But with the publication of the decree the Berlin price of the dollar, 1260 billion marks on November 14, began to rise with such speed that by November 20 it had reached 4200 billion. This price yielded the exchange rate of one *Rentenmark* for one trillion paper marks. This was the fantastic level at which the *Rentenmark* was stabilized. It signified the utter expropriation of those who still held paper marks. This was tragic, but it was a necessary move if Germany were to reach the terra firma of a stable currency and thus avoid drowning in a flood of paper marks. Yet it is quite understandable that this extremely painful remedy should only increase the excitement and distress of the German people.

Ever since cessation of passive resistance in the Ruhr, fire threatened to break out of the furnaces of political passions in Bavaria, in Saxony and Thuringia, and in the occupied areas. Kahr showed very quickly how much confidence could be placed in those soothing words with which Knilling had sought to reassure Stresemann. On October 29 he nullified the Bavarian decree which earlier had put the Law for the Protection of the Republic into effect in the land. This meant that this national measure, so hated by the guardians of Bavarian order and their armed bands, was no longer to be applied within the blue and white borders. In terms of constitutional law this act amounted to rebellion against the government in Berlin, a rebellion which was in no sense mitigated by Kahr's public espousal of a Bavarian monarchy a few days later. "Let it not be proclaimed, but rather grow and come by itself," were the great man's words of October 1 to the Munich press.

This statement naturally distressed the radical Leftist governments of Saxony and Thuringia. Factory councils called for open war and general strike. On October 5 the Communists, thinking their time had come, declared their willingness to join the governments of Saxony and of Thuringia in order "to weld labor together in the face of fascist danger." On October 10 Zeigner took the fateful step of accepting two Communists into his cabinet in order, as he explained to his Landtag, "to preclude the danger of a plutocratic military dictatorship" which, he said, was clearly and presently at hand. A few days later Thuringia followed his example. Thereupon Bavaria broke off relations with Saxony. All of these disturbers of the peace unctuously assured the nation that they were defending the integrity of the Reich "with unswerving fidelity," while each was fighting in his own way against the Reichswehr and its responsible minister, Gessler, who possessed the legitimate executive power.

Open conflict first broke out in Bavaria. Hitler saw to that. His organ, *Völkischer Beobachter*, insulted the national government and General von Seeckt in such indecent terms that Gessler ordered General von Lossow, commander of the Seventh Division, which was stationed in Bavaria, to close the paper. Since Lossow had already been named military commander of Bavaria by Gessler under his full emergency powers, Lossow had no choice but to carry out this order. But instead of doing so, Lossow asked Kahr if he approved of this ban. Unauthorized as Lossow's question was, Kahr's reply — that Lossow should ignore Gessler's command — was equally unauthorized and even illegal. But Kahr's answer was even more than that. It was a flagrant breach of the promise Knilling had made to the Chancellor. It was also proof of Kahr's utter incapability in politics, for if he had had the slightest bit of political sense he would have greeted with joy this powerful blow the national government had delivered to a movement which was pursuing ends so opposite to his own and which clearly and imminently threatened to outgrow his control. But little men who wish to play the hero have always been especially dangerous types. In Kahr's brain there burned the single, simple phrase, "To Berlin"; he dreamed of creating there something he was pleased to call "order."

Lossow was so forgetful of his duty as to refuse to carry out his order from Berlin, even going so far as to favor Gessler with the explanation that the prohibition of the *Völkischer Beobachter* would evoke great distress among the "best patriotic circles." [35] Gessler immediately relieved von Lossow of his command and replaced him with General Kress von Kressenstein. At this, Kahr and the government of Bavaria rose in open mutiny. Kahr tried to rip the Seventh Division from the Reichswehr by installing Lossow as *Landeskommandanten* for Bavaria and forcing the division's troops to enter "the loyal service" of the Bavarian government. This was, as Seeckt stated in his order to the Reichswehr that same day, "an unconstitutional invasion of the military chain of command." It was also the boldest rebellion on the part of a member state that ever occurred in the entire history of a united Germany. And the patriotic phrases with which Kahr accompanied his crime made it all the more revolting.

There can be absolutely no doubt of the illegality of the Bavarian events. Karl Rothenbücher, a brave Munich professor of constitutional law, has offered incontrovertible proof of this.[36] And Anschütz, in his commentaries on the national constitution, calls this "assumption" of the Seventh Division by the government of Bavaria simply a "blatant violation of the constitution." The governments of the other South German lands took the side of Berlin. But what could the national government do? It is quite true that all the constitutional requirements for a national operation (*Reichsexekution*) against Bavaria had been met. (See Article 48, Paragraph 1.) But force would have excited armed resistance and civil war. And there was every danger that in this event North German *Schützverbände*, the Pomeranians for example, would join their Bavarian brethren in the fray. No one could predict the effect in other countries of this sight of Germany consuming itself. But it was certain that the Separatists in the Rhineland and the Palatinate would then have won their game.

The national government was rescued from this desperate situation by the clumsy excesses of the Socialist-Communist coalitions in Saxony and Thuringia. While Zeigner was busy delivering excited speeches against the Reichswehr, his Communist ministers called for violence and resistance to the troops. Gessler decided that immediate intervention was necessary in Saxony, where the Reichswehr's position had become intolerable. (For this move he was ready to assume that personal responsibility which politically and legally was his as exerciser of full emergency powers.) [37] His advance into Saxony and Thuringia with Reichswehr regiments improved the national government's military situation vis à vis Bavaria. The march on Berlin must have seemed less enchanting to the Bavarian patriots when they knew that, if they crossed their blue-white border, they would meet not "proletarian platoons," but regular Army regiments.

In the cabinet meeting of October 27 Stresemann supported Gessler's plan with the argument that these moves would greatly strengthen the position of the Reich against Bavaria. His Social Democratic ministers took the position that the government should try to persuade Zeigner to resign before resorting to force. The cabinet then decided to entrust the Chancellor with the composition of an appropriate letter to Zeigner. In this letter, which he sent that same day, Stresemann urged Zeigner "to effect the resignation of the government of Saxony, because its inclusion of Communist members . . . [is] inconsonant with constitutional conditions." Should the cabinet not resign by October 28, the letter went on, a national commissioner would be appointed, "who would take the administration of Saxony into his own hands until constitutional conditions were restored."

As was to be expected, Zeigner did not accept this invitation. And so on October 29 Ebert, acting under Article 48 of the constitution, issued a decree giving the national Chancellor the necessary powers. Stresemann appointed his friend Heinze, People's Party delegate and former minister, the national commissioner (*Reichskommissar*) for Saxony. Heinze went energetically, perhaps too energetically, about his work. He aroused opposition particularly when Reichswehr units drew up before the Saxon ministries with fixed bayonets in order to lend emphasis to the commissioner's request that the ministers resign. But he succeeded in putting an end to the crisis in three days. On October 31 the Social Democrat Fellisch, with the help of the Democrats, was elected premier by the Saxon Landtag. Fellisch formed an exclusively Social Democratic government, and as early as November 1 Ebert was able to withdraw his decree of October 29. Shortly thereafter a similar sequence of events took place in Thuringia.

These acts by the national government excited a most lively criticism in republican circles. Men were greatly disturbed at the fact that, while vigorous steps were taken against the radicals of the Left in Saxony and Thuringia, the equally dangerous Bavarian radicals of the Right were opposed with nothing more effective than paper protests. This criticism was made not only by the Social Democrats — to say nothing of the Communists — but also by members of the Democratic Party and its press. The Social Democratic ministers suffered acute embarrassment. They despised Zeigner and his unscrupulous tactics, but how could they share responsibility for the forceful unseating of a Social Democratic premier while Herr von Kahr remained, still unenlightened, on his little throne? It is true that in the cabinet meeting of October 27 they had accepted Stresemann's letter to Zeigner.[38] And their minister of justice, Radbruch, had accompanied Hilferding, also a Social Democrat, and Dr. Gradnauer, Saxony's wise representative in Berlin, to Dresden in the vain attempt to persuade Zeigner to resign as Stresemann's letter had requested.

But at the next step, which followed necessarily from the preceding one, the Social Democratic ministers balked. Their continued collaboration with Stresemann depended upon their ability to persuade their Social Democratic colleagues in the Reichstag to

support them on this course. For obvious reasons, they were unable
to do so. Instead, the Social Democratic delegation on October 31
resolved, with only a slight minority opposed, to leave the government coalition unless three conditions were met. The most important
of these was their demand for immediate steps against the Bavarian
violators of the constitution; another was a transformation of the
military state of emergency into a civil one. Stresemann and Gessler
refused both demands. For, with respect to Bavaria, there were only
two choices: reconciliation or rupture; the national government
simply did not possess the power to force Bavaria to change its
ways. And so the three Social Democratic ministers, Radbruch, Sollmann, and Robert Schmidt, resigned on November 2. Stresemann
stayed on with a rump cabinet. The fact that the Democrats remained at his side was attributed by Stresemann to the influence of
Dr. Carl Melchior of Hamburg, who said his London sources had
told him that people there hoped Stresemann would stay. This was
certainly Lord d'Abernon's hope.

The withdrawal of the Social Democrats meant that the government not only lost therewith its special powers derived from the
Emergency Law of October 13, 1923, but also that it now represented a minority of the Reichstag. A new majority could only have
been created by the addition of the German Nationalists to the
cabinet. But they refused to participate in a government under
Stresemann. The chairman of the Nationalist delegation, Hergt,
would have been willing, but he symptomatically explained: "I am
powerless; events are rolling by me as I stand." [39] Even more
symptomatic was the fact that now a revolt broke out against
Stresemann in his own party. Here his most vehement critics were
von Lersner, formerly in the Foreign Service, and Maretzki; they
tried to stampede their party colleagues by saying that Seeckt had
told Stresemann the Reichswehr had lost confidence in him. [40]

Actually the following events had taken place. In late September
General von Seeckt had explained to the national President, in a
conversation at which the minister of defense was also present, that
the Reichswehr was too weak to carry on a war on two fronts against
both Right and Left, and that he therefore considered it necessary
for the government to conclude an armistice with one side or the
other. Ebert, who immediately comprehended what Seeckt meant,
replied by inquiring if Seeckt thought that the government should
seek a settlement with the Right — that is, submit to its conditions.
He went on to add that he refused to do this; that, if the Reichswehr
were not prepared to protect the state against its enemies, he would

prefer to "leave the house." This had not been Seeckt's intent at all, and with tears in his eyes the general told Ebert so. The real trouble, he explained, lay with the Chancellor. Mistrust of Stresemann was simply too widespread. Again Ebert replied by putting a question: Was Seeckt prepared to say this to the Chancellor in person? When the general assured him he was, Ebert called Stresemann by telephone to say that Seeckt and Gessler wished to speak with him. Seeckt was man enough to repeat his remarks bluntly to the Chancellor, whereupon Stresemann, extremely excited, responded: "In other words, you are saying that the Reichswehr refuses to obey?" Immediately Gessler interrupted to say: "Herr Reichskanzler, only I can tell you that." At this von Seeckt fell silent, and for the moment the situation was saved.[41]

We shall never know whether Seeckt had been persuaded by Rightist politicians to make this move. But we can assume that Rightist members of Stresemann's own party, who were already causing him troubles enough, quickly learned of Seeckt's statement and used it to Stresemann's disadvantage. Their source could only have been Seeckt or one of his confidants.

It is true that by means of constant personal intervention Stresemann succeeded in holding the *Volkspartei* delegation and the entire party behind him. But what sort of caricature of parliamentary government is it when the leading statesman, in the hours of severest national crisis, has to expend his valuable energies and time in putting down mutinies in his own party instead of being able to count on his party's continual and energetic support?

However much Stresemann regretted the Social Democrats' departure from his cabinet, he had hoped that their leaving would be followed by a relaxation of the tensions in Bavaria. For one of the Bavarians' rabble-rousing phrases had now become empty: there were no more "Marxists" in the national government, against which the "truly Bavarian soul" might be made to rage. That the needs of the hour called for mutual reconciliation rather than hate and civil war was the message of the leading dignitary of the Roman Catholic Church in Bavaria, Cardinal Faulhaber, Archbishop of Munich, in his thoughtful letter to the Chancellor of November 6:

How can we hope to master the economic crisis that already is so great and the miseries of the coming winter that widespread unemployment will bring unless all decent men work together, regardless of faith, position, or party? How else can we eradicate the blind, raging hatred for our Jewish fellow citizens and other ethnic groups, a hatred that flies throughout the land screaming "Guilty!" but never asking proof? And how else can we avoid a civil war, which would wreak new, untold desolation and seal the ruin of our poor nation in the blood of self-inflicted wounds?

One cannot doubt that with these words the cardinal was think-ing of the insane demagogy with which Hitler was raging through Munich and its blue-white hinterland. For Hitler would certainly have been distressed if quiet had come and the Bavarian government had sought a reconciliation with Berlin. Perhaps Kahr had some such reconciliation in mind when he called a meeting for November 8, 1923, in the *Bürgerbräukeller*, the Munich beer hall that Hitler was about to make famous. At this meeting Kahr planned to explain his program to those people who were considered respectable in Munich. We shall never know his real intentions because his speech was halted by a pistol shot.

Ever since the eruption of open conflict between Bavaria and the Reich, Hitler's thirst for action had become more and more acute. He was convinced that the revolutionary blow of which he dreamed would now succeed.[42] In late September the armed "battle groups" had placed the political leadership of their entire move-ment in his hands. These groups were not concerned with law and justice; after all, a leading role was played in them by Captain Ehrhardt, who was still wanted in Berlin for his part in the Kapp Putsch and whom the "order-loving" Bavarian government, without a twinge of conscience, continued to protect. Heavily armed troops, as strong as several regiments, stood on the Thuringian border ready for the order to advance. Kahr must have known all this. Had Hitler therefore any reason to doubt that Kahr was planning some sort of decisive action? As for himself, Hitler wallowed, albeit verbally, in the blood that was to flow. "In this battle heads will roll," he screamed as his followers roared approval, "and they will be either ours or others'." It is true that Hitler knew that Kahr, unlike him-self, hoped to establish a monarchy, specifically, a Wittelsbach monarchy. But Hitler was quite prepared to sing this song too, for the nonce, and to refer to the former Bavarian Crown Prince Rup-precht as "His Majesty the King" in conversations with the latter's supporters. Of course he intended to keep up this game only until he had succeeded in bringing Kahr to join him in precipitating armed revolt. He had no doubts whatsoever about who would direct the operation once the shooting had started.

Furthermore Hitler thought he now had an ally who shared his hopes more closely than did Bavarian Separatists and whose name was bound to be of critical importance to the Army: Ludendorff.

For some years now the general had been living in Munich, nourishing there his anger at Berlin and the national government, which to him embodied that set of forces which had elbowed him aside in 1918, and his wrath increased with every month of his enforced inactivity. He had barely escaped imprisonment after the Kapp Putsch. But his luck had made him neither more clever nor more gentle, for nothing in the world could dispel his illusion that he knew something about politics and had a mission to serve his country in that field. In the course of these weeks conversations between Hitler and Ludendorff took place repeatedly. It is hard to say what the two finally agreed upon. Ludendorff could hardly have known that Hitler had assured one of Lossow's agents he would never let Ludendorff play a political role; Hitler said he needed Ludendorff's name to win over the Army and would restrict him to purely military tasks. The "Führer" was already speaking of himself in most exalted tones; he compared himself not only to Mussolini but also to Gambetta — and Napoleon. For there is no other explanation for his remark that Napoleon had also liked to surround himself with unimportant men. But from neither Kahr nor Lossow did Hitler hear the word for which he pined. Kahr instead told the leaders of the armed bands that he forbade any putsch which he did not himself prepare and that he alone would give the signal to begin.

Hitler had not the slightest intention of waiting that long. He was preparing a "massive night exercise outside of Munich" for the night of November 10–11 which was to end with an invasion of the city by his troops and his violent assumption of power. Suddenly the meeting Kahr had called for the evening of November 8 seemed to offer him a better opportunity. With a few quickly gathered "storm troopers" he broke into the gathering just as the worthy state commissioner-general was ponderously unwinding the thread of his statesmanlike rhetoric. Like a mad man Hitler jumped upon a chair and fired a shot at the ceiling. Kahr broke off. The audience was absolutely still. At this moment Hitler announced: "The national revolution has begun." He claimed that the barracks of the Army units and of the gendarmes had already been seized and that the Seventh Division and the police were marching upon Munich under the swastika. At pistol point he ordered Kahr and the gentlemen sitting at his side, General von Lossow and Police Chief Seisser, to follow him into the next room under escort of his troops. There he pressed them to accept his program. One would be forced to call his the program of a man with delusions of grandeur, had it not ten years later been realized in part: "The Bavarian government is deposed. Pöhner becomes premier with dictatorial powers; Kahr is regent;

Hitler takes over the national government; Ludendorff commands the national army; Seisser is minister of police." When his three prisoners failed to agree immediately, Hitler, who had been brandishing his pistol wildly until then, now turned the weapon to his own temple, screaming, "If by tomorrow afternoon I have not won, I will be a dead man." While the future German Führer was pacing furiously about the room, the three Bavarians quickly and secretly agreed to humor him for the moment, although they clearly wanted no part in all this folly.

At this point Hitler seemed to be in command of the situation. He ran back into the hall, where, proclaiming his program and giving the false impression that the three Bavarians had decided to support him, he delivered an impassioned speech against "the criminals who are ruining Germany today." His address had an enormous effect. We shall never know to what extent its success was due to his fascinating fluency or to his false portrayal of the facts. But for the moment Hitler seemed to have won over Kahr and his followers.

In the meantime, Ludendorff had appeared, having been summoned by one of Hitler's henchmen. (He most likely had been waiting for the call.) Kahr, Lossow, and Seisser surrendered, with Kahr insisting once more that he was a monarchist. But such petty details did not deter Hitler now. He assured Kahr that he, too, wanted to right the wrongs which the "November criminals" had inflicted on the "kingdom" and especially upon "His Majesty's most blessed father."

And so the five men, in what seemed to be a firm and sincere alliance, stepped before the jubilant assembly. Hitler promised "to take neither food nor rest until the November criminals have been thrown to the ground, until, upon the ruins of today's miserable Germany, there will rise, resurrected, a Germany of might and grandeur, of freedom and of glory." Contrasted to these confident tones, Kahr's careful words, audible only to the unprejudiced and diligent listener, seemed rather strange. He called himself the "protector of the monarchy" and confessed that he had joined these men only "with a heavy heart." Ludendorff, who certainly must have been displeased by the office allotted him by Hitler, made clear in one short sentence that, while he was with these men, he did not intend to take orders from any one, even if that man be the leader of the National Socialists. By virtue of his rights as a free German, "seized by the grandeur of the moment, and astonished," he placed himself at the disposal of this new German government.

Did this mean then that Hitler's putsch had really succeeded and that he, if only in Munich, was at the head of a new German national government? No, it was only an illusion that was shattered in less than a day. Kahr had no sooner regained his freedom (the Bavarian ministers were still held by Hitler's forces) than he tore up the promise that had been extorted from him at pistol point and, with posters on all the Munich streets, opened a counteroffensive against the "treachery and deceit of ambitious scoundrels," the National Socialist Party, and the other battle groups, all of which he now declared disbanded. The Army gave him its support. Its higher officers boiled over with rage to think that a foreign agitator, a mere corporal, dared order them about. They, like most members of the German upper classes, who remembered Bismarck's dark words for demagogues — sly Loki and blind Hodur — had only the most violent disdain for rabble-rousers and did not distinguish between the nationalist and other species. Lossow, probably disturbed a bit at having disobeyed an official order, had only the desire to repay Hitler for the dishonor he had brought him. At this point word came from Berlin that full powers throughout Germany had been given to General von Seeckt, chief of the army command (*Chef der Heeresleitung*).

The national Chancellor, taken completely by surprise at the news of the Munich putsch, called a meeting of the cabinet with the President that very night. The Prussian minister of the interior also attended. In the face of such immense, acute danger they decided that it was necessary to concentrate all emergency authority in a military hand. And so a presidential decree of November 8 transferred Gessler's powers to von Seeckt. Necessary as this step might well have been, it was hardly calculated to reassure devoted supporters of the existing state. Severing asked the general how the Berlin garrison would behave if the Bavarian division really made its way that far. Seeckt, after a short silence, repeated his dire reply of the night of the Kapp Putsch: "Reichswehr does not fire on the Reichswehr." Severing rose, told the President, "In that case I have no more business here," and left the meeting to mobilize the Berlin security police and to occupy the government district with strong units.[43] He could depend on his police. Furthermore, he thought it wise to remind von Seeckt that the Republic would still have armed forces at its disposal even if the Reichswehr were to fail it. Given the general's mysterious character and uncertain political views, one finds it hard to say whether Severing's step was necessary. At any rate Seeckt carried out his duty and immediately published the following proclamation: "Unauthorized interference with the order of the Reich and its lands will be energetically suppressed by the Reichswehr under my command no matter from what side this attack may come."

After the defection of Kahr and Lossow the putsch was hopeless. But a rabid man like Hitler could not give up the battle before some blood had flowed, and Ludendorff had too high an opinion of himself to withdraw his assistance now. And so, on the morning of November 9, their march, as senseless as it was sanguinary, proceeded through Munich to the *Feldherrnhalle* on the Odeonsplatz, where it pathetically collapsed. A police unit was drawn up there, much weaker in numbers than the armed band led by Hitler and Ludendorff. But the discipline of the police carried the day. After the first shots the attackers fell to the pavement or ran away. Hitler threw himself — or was pulled — down. When the firing had ceased, he fled in a waiting auto to the villa of his friend Hanfstaengel, called "Putzi," where he was arrested two days later. Ludendorff, certain that no one would dare shoot at the *"Feldherr* of the World War," kept marching right into the ranks of the police, who arrested him. Fourteen of Hitler's men lay dead upon the street, three of them his best-known followers. One of these was a high provincial judge; his presence showed how far the National Socialist intoxication had spread even among those groups whose professional training and responsibilities should have secured them most against it. Another disturbing fact was the presence in Hitler's traitorous band of cadets from the Munich Infantry School, members of the Reichswehr. The soldier of fortune Rossbach had persuaded them to join.

The few hours during which Hitler thought he was in power were enough to show what National Socialist rule would mean. "Jewish private homes were looted and two dozen hostages were seized, the names having been selected from the telephone directory simply because of their Jewish sounds." [44] An armed horde swept into the chambers of the municipal council and dragged out the Social Democratic members. These magistrates, as one of them later testified under oath in court, were subjected to mockery, spittle, blows, and threats of death. Fortunately the Nazis' time of glory collapsed so quickly that these prisoners escaped with their lives — if not with their clothing. Such incidents should have sufficed to open the eyes of every reasonable German. But the people of Munich were still as enthusiastic about their Hitler as ever.

Their affection, of course, did not alter the fact that not Hitler but rather State Commissioner-General von Kahr had won. What if things had turned out otherwise — if Hitler, along with Ludendorff, had been victorious in Munich? Whatever the ultimate military developments might have been, one is certainly justified in assuming that the regular Army units stationed in Thuringia and Saxony would have made the march on Berlin a good bit more difficult than the enthusiastic Bavarian patriots had ever imagined as they sat behind their steins. The practical result of such a march would have been the end of the Reich. All of Hitler's subsequent successes cannot erase the fact that at that time he would have conjured up an immediate German catastrophe against which he would have been absolutely helpless. Not only would the French have refused to tolerate his national government for one single day, but the other Allies would have joined them in their ban. Poincaré's policy of force would have been justified to all the world and Rhenish separatism would have found success. Under the leadership of the Social Democrat Hoffmann, formerly the Bavarian premier, a separatist movement had developed in the Palatinate; it failed only for lack of Social Democratic support. But would the Socialists have preserved their opposition to Hoffmann's plans if Hitler had come to power in Munich? One need only recall the infinitely complex economic problems, especially the currency reform then just in progress, in order to realize that the abortive Munich putsch had been as devoid of prospects as of reason. But the tragedy remains that in the Germany of that day such an absurd and violent act did not end a man's political career so long as he had at his command a sufficient supply of "national feeling" and of nationalistic cant.

At a time when those who boasted of their patriotic sentiments were making ruthless use of the national emergency to further their private cause, it would have been a real miracle if the separatists had let this especially favorable moment pass without trying to satisfy their wishes, too, by force. The cessation of passive resistance had shown them that in the occupied areas the national government's powers were at a new low. Poincaré's continued severity and his absolute refusal to make a conciliatory gesture to the retreating Reich gave these separatists every reason to believe that they would find in him a strong protector of their cause if they could once succeed in presenting him with an accomplished fact. And so one armed putsch followed another. On Sunday, September 30, 1923, the Düsseldorf separatists staged an armed demonstration that ended in bloodshed. An overwhelming majority of the population made clear their rejection of this separatist treason. Equally clear was the

278 THE WEIMAR REPUBLIC

partisanship of the French occupation forces, who arrested and disarmed the Prussian police when they tried dutifully to protect the citizenry from the separatist bands.

But the severe moral defeat they suffered here did not restrain the separatists from new misdeeds. Their next move took place in the Belgian zone of occupation, where, on October 21, they seized the city hall of Aachen and proclaimed a "Rhineland Republic." At this same time a series of putsches were exploding in the French zone: in Bonn and in Coblenz, the seat of the Allied Rhineland Commission (October 21–26); Wiesbaden and Trier (October 22); and Mainz (October 23). On October 25 in Coblenz the separatist leader Matthes proclaimed his own version of the Rhineland Republic and announced its first cabinet. On October 29 Messrs. Matthes and Dorten announced that this self-styled government had given them full powers, a grant which did not keep the two gentlemen from falling immediately into a violent quarrel.

While the Belgian occupation authorities, after some hesitation, assumed a properly neutral attitude, the French in many places gave the appearance of favoring the separatists. They displayed their sympathies most openly in the Bavarian Palatinate, where the French General de Metz was in command. He not only urged the provincial Landtag to proclaim the Palatinate's autonomous independence of Bavaria (October 24), but also went so far as to tell the representative of the Bavarian government to his face that "the sovereign authority of the Bavarian government no longer exists in the Palatinate." In substantiation of his argument the general referred to Munich's conflict with Berlin, by which, he argued, Bavaria had broken the constitution and set itself outside the law. No matter how just were the protests of the national government against this French general's intervention in a domestic German affair, it was only natural that the Frenchman should play the trumps which Kahr and the other men in Munich had negligently placed in his hand. Thus it became clear that the effect, if not the purpose, of the Bavarian adventure favored Germany's enemies strongly and that a victory for Hitler would have been as fatal to the Reich as to Bavaria.

The national government sent sharp notes to Paris protesting the illegitimate behavior of the French occupation authorities, and Poincaré, in equally sharp replies, denied that they had at any time exceeded their lawful duty to preserve peace and order. But whoever studies this exchange of notes in hopes of arriving at a disinterested judgment is forced to conclude that the German objections were basically well founded. Such a distinguished advocate as

Poincaré finally found no other way out than to break off the correspondence with the declaration that he had no reason to join the German government in a discussion of the separatist movement. His statement amounted to an open admission of defeat. Moreover, the Germans were by no means alone in their conviction that Poincaré wished at least to see whether, with the separatists' help, it might be possible to achieve that amputation of the left bank of the Rhine which had been his goal as early as Versailles. Clemenceau, who quite clearly takes this position,[45] may have been influenced by his personal hostility to Poincaré. But public opinion in England also accepted this interpretation of Poincaré's motivation, as is shown clearly in Professor Toynbee's *Survey of International Affairs* for 1924; and we shall see below that the foreign secretary, Lord Curzon, shared this conviction.

There can be no doubt that Poincaré had absolutely no use for the old proverb that one should build golden bridges toward a defeated foe. In abandoning passive resistance Stresemann had fulfilled the condition which Poincaré had set to any resumption of detailed negotiations. But when the German government now sought to discuss with him ways to revive the economy of the occupied areas, it was met with his brusque refusal. The occupying powers had of course just as great an interest in this economic revival as did Berlin, for it was they who would have to fight the chaos which inevitably would follow further work stoppage. But the French Premier was counting on the Ruhr magnates' being far too interested in the revival of their businesses to let things come to such a pass; he also counted on being able to dictate to them the terms of their revival.

Nor had he reckoned wrong. As early as October 8 the Phoenix Trust, under the leadership of Otto Wolff, accepted the terms imposed by the *Mission Interallié de Contrôle des Usines et des Mines* (Micum). In return for its confiscated metal goods and the grant of export licenses, the trust resumed the delivery of coal to the Entente and also pledged itself to pay taxes on the coal sent to the Allies. This agreement constituted a hard blow to the German government, and Stresemann took care to let Wolff know that he had sorely wounded the government's authority with his move.[46] But to what avail? The nation's distress was so great that the Berlin government had to let events take their course, seeking at best to take care lest, in these negotiations between Micum and the magnates of the Ruhr, the national interest be completely ignored. This task was by no means easy. And it was only after hard fighting, which almost brought the negotiations to a halt, that the Berlin government was able to get Micum to agree that surplus deliveries made under these arrangements were to be credited to the Reich as reparations. On November 23, 1923, representatives of heavy industry signed an agreement with Micum which was to last until April 15, 1924. The agreement set very heavy conditions upon Ruhr industries. Approximately 30 percent of their anticipated coal production was to be delivered to the West or to its occupation authorities; in addition, heavy payments were to be made to cover taxes on coal already delivered as well as on coal to be sold in the future. Poincaré at last possessed the productive guarantees he had been demanding for so long.

This agreement was beyond a doubt severe. Its severity struck German industry directly; but indirectly and ultimately it hurt the state, which had promised to make good to the Ruhr firms whatever of their tribute was credited to the Reich as reparations. (The Chancellor's letters of November 1 and 21 said these payments to the firms would be made when the finances of the Reich were again in order.) The Ruhr industrialists insisted that it would be utterly impossible for them to observe this oppressive agreement all the way to its planned end in mid-April 1924. And all the experts of Europe agreed. But they were wrong. For in fact the agreement, with a few modifications, survived and functioned until the final adoption of the Dawes Plan in early October 1924.[47] One must conclude that Micum had estimated the industrial capabilities of the Ruhr better than the Ruhr industrialists themselves. Of course this result was possible only because of the successful German currency reform, in which an equal number of experts had not believed.

In judging the attitude of the French one dare not overlook the fact that Stresemann himself had aroused the distrust of even moderate Frenchmen once again by granting the former crown prince of Prussia permission to return to Germany. Many people outside of Germany — and not only in France — with good reason considered the crown prince to be an outspoken representative of German nationalism and thoughts of revenge. Those Germans who argued that he could not be banned from his fatherland forever should have stopped to ask themselves whether, after all, this was the proper time for his return, when the nation's passions were already so aroused. This was Severing's reaction in conversations with the crown prince's representative. But Stresemann, who had been in repeated personal contact with the prince, seems indeed to have wished to help effect his return. He even found a way to interest in the idea the Social Democratic members of his cabinet together with the representative there of the Prussian Ministry. Stresemann considered the crown prince politically safe. He told d'Abernon, the

British ambassador, that the prince was primarily a fancier of women and horses and was by no means popular among the nationalists. Perhaps the ambassador was correct in guessing that Stresemann wished to use the prince as a welcome counterweight to the Bavarians' propaganda for the Wittelsbachs.

Crown Prince William was naturally required to promise he would refrain from all political activity, and he seems initially to have intended to keep his word. He could not, of course, withstand the temptation forever, but he was too unimportant as a person and enjoyed too little popularity to become dangerous. And even the foreign dangers which his return had conjured up were quick to pass. The French had tried to make this a matter of formal Allied concern; for, after all, the prince still was on the list of war criminals and, at least in theory, the Allies' rights of prosecution still existed. But once more it became apparent that the mood of 1920 had dissolved. In the West there was neither an inclination to take further steps against the "criminals" nor a desire to revive the wartime alliance. England in particular energetically opposed the French, and the Conference of Ambassadors contented itself with a resolution which found its way into the files.[48]

The same day the Conference of Ambassadors passed their resolution, November 21, 1923, the German Reichstag was assembling at Berlin to decide the fate of Stresemann's regime. Upon the withdrawal of the Social Democrats on November 2 Stresemann's regime had become a rump government, for only one of the posts thus made empty had been filled — the Ministry of the Interior by the mayor of Duisburg, Jarres, a right-wing member of the People's Party. The Reichstag was so composed at this time as to place the cabinet's fate in the hands of the Social Democrats and the German Nationalists. If neither of these two parties supported Stresemann, his government would fall. The German Nationalists declined unconditionally to assist a chancellor who had called off passive resistance in the Ruhr; instead they proposed a motion of no confidence. Their spokesman, Hergt, even went so far as to express his admiration for "Bavaria, the land of order." And so the responsibility fell principally upon the Social Democrats.

Their position was truly difficult. Their restless constituents and the threatening attitude of the Communists forced them to deploy their heaviest parliamentary artillery against the government's operations in Saxony and Thuringia and its seeming protection of the rebels in Bavaria. On the other hand, at least the wiser of its leading delegates realized that if Stresemann's cabinet were to fall no better one would follow. They sought to escape from this dilemma by

proposing a resolution of no confidence which was expressly directed
at the government's actions in Saxony in order to make certain that
the Rightists would reject it. Having thus safely displayed to their
constituents their lack of confidence in a regime they did not wish
to fell, they might have been able to vote safely against the Nationalists' resolution. But Stresemann declined to "execute the nation's
affairs on the strength of a decision based on such political arithme-
tic." He demanded an explicit vote of confidence, which was immediately moved by the parties of his government coalition.

Now the Social Democrats were forced to show their colors: they
voted no. Thus they unseated Stresemann, a man whom, at the
bottom of their hearts, they had wanted to retain. This action ensured their absence from the government for years. President Ebert,
who had risen from their ranks, saw this most clearly, reproaching
his friends with these words: "Your reason for unseating the Chancellor will be forgotten in six weeks. But you will still be suffering
the consequences of your stupidity after ten years have passed.[49]
This was the judgment of a statesman, and history proved him right.
It remains a heavy debit in the accounts of the Social Democratic
Party that it unseated a chancellor whose foreign policy conformed
to their wishes and who, at the same time, was helping more than
any other to strengthen Germany internally. The same Hermann
Müller who in November 1923 moved the Social Democrats' resolution of no confidence against Stresemann's regime begged the delegate Stresemann in June 1928 to join, as foreign minister, the cabinet
over which he, Müller, presided.

Yet one must not forget how difficult for the Social Democrats
their decision was. For the Stresemann-Gessler-Seeckt policies
against Saxony and Thuringia on the one hand and against Bavaria
upon the other seemed inconsistent and highly partisan. In hindsight
it is much easier to see these policies in their full light and to realize
that they were, in fact, correct, indeed, that they may well have been
the only way to preserve the German Reich. For even without
moving into Bavaria, the Reichswehr, by simple virtue of its advance to the borders of Saxony and Thuringia, effectively blocked
the Bavarian traitors' march upon Berlin. And the fact that this was
accomplished without bloodshed (one might perhaps say, without a
second Langensalza *) was certainly to Germany's good fortune.
The other half of their objection was the refusal of the national

* The Battle of Langensalza (June 27–29, 1866, near Erfurt) was an important
engagement fought during the Austro-Prussian War. In it Prussian forces succeeded
in intercepting and, after considerable struggle, capturing the entire Hanovarian army
on its way south to its Bavarian allies. TRANSLATORS.

government to tolerate Communist-influenced regimes in the heart of Germany at this critical time; but after the experience which men have since had with Communist governments and Socialist Unity parties one is obliged to judge Stresemann's decisions a bit more realistically.

On November 23, immediately after the Reichstag had rejected the coalition's motion of confidence 231 to 156, Stresemann went to the President to tender his own and his cabinet's resignations. Ebert had previously declined to dissolve the Reichstag because an election was impossible so long as such great parts of Germany were under the burden of occupation; and Stresemann had agreed. Stresemann, fully cognizant of this situation, had deliberately contributed to his own overthrow because he wished to retain direction of German policy only if he were supported by a Reichstag majority upon which he could depend and which would assure him all the authority he needed in foreign and domestic affairs. He was proud to have fallen in open parliamentary battle, and of all those involved, he had the least cause to be ashamed of the result. For everywhere there was but one reaction to his fall: headaches. On November 25 Lord d'Abernon found the confusion in the political world "indescribable," and in the Reichstag corridors the delegates made fun of themselves with the observation that the Chancellor should ask reporters why he fell, for none of the delegates knew.[50] Even the German Nationalists were afforded only a short triumph at the thought that once again they had brought a "fulfiller" to a fall, for they were shortly obliged to observe that their "triumph" brought them no closer to their goal.

Stresemann was chancellor of Germany for only three months. But these three months were not only packed with extremely stirring and important events; they also served to assure Gustav Stresemann his place in German history and his stature among European statesmen. In the hours of its deepest defeat he had led the German nation with a spirit that prepared the way for its revival. The cessation of the futile battle in the Ruhr, for which he was thanked then with passionate hate, is today considered his clearest claim to fame; and it was his regime which made the *"Rentenmark* Miracle" possible. One need only compare him with his German Nationalist critics of the time — Helfferich, Hergt, Westarp, and the rest — to see how responsible statesmanship differs from partisan sniping. Furthermore, these critics, unlike the Social Democrats, did not have the excuse of having learned their political trade under circumstances which had damned them to eternal opposition. One need only ask oneself what would have become of Germany if its direction had been entrusted to the hands of the German Nationalists, as they had requested of Ebert. The question answers itself: either they would have plunged the country into a new catastrophe or they would have found themselves obliged to burn the idols they had formerly revered.

Fortunately neither the President nor a majority of the Reichstag was ready for such adventurous experiments. When the dust of the crisis had settled it became apparent that things were still rather as they had been before and that the new government would be obliged to pick up the burden where the former regime had had to lay it down. Stresemann, to be sure, was no longer chancellor, but he stayed on as foreign minister, and his mere presence served to reassure both Germany and the West. The leader of the Center's Reichstag delegation, Dr. Wilhelm Marx, became chancellor. Although by no means an outstanding man, he combined reliability and flexibility in a fruitful way. He was an older Rhenish jurist, formally a member of the *Kammergericht* by virtue of his being president of the Senate. Immediately after Stresemann's fall, Marx had expressed to him the thanks of the Center Party for his self-sacrificing devotion to duty and, simultaneously, the wish that he would join the new regime as foreign minister. Gessler, Luther, and Jarres kept their former posts. The only change of significance to party politics was the addition to the cabinet of Emminger, a member of the Bavarian People's Party, as minister of justice. His presence gave men reason to believe that his party wished to escape the purely negative role to which it had been relegated by Bavarian politics.

Thus, in the partisan sense, the new government was also a minority regime; it could hold out against the opposition of the Right only with assistance from the Left. And this assistance was forthcoming. The Social Democrats went even further: they supported an enabling act (*Ermächtigungsgesetz*) which, until February 15, 1924, permitted the Marx government to carry out, without the Reichstag consent ordinarily required by the constitution, those measures "which it deemed necessary and useful in alleviating the distress of *Volk und Reich*." This was an extraordinarily broad grant of emergency power, limited only by the right of the Reichstag and the Reichsrat to request the withdrawal of such measures after their imposition. But the act was justified by the pressing needs of the moment, needs which simply did not leave enough time for parliamentary debate and decision. At the request of the Social Democrats, a fifteen-man parliamentary commission was established to be consulted in confidence by the cabinet before it resolved on any new decree. Since this enabling act amounted to an amendment to the constitution, it required a two-thirds majority vote. This was achieved, 313 to 18, with the help of the Social Democrats, who went so far as to enforce party discipline on the measure. The German Nationalists abstained from voting.

If one is to measure such emergency legislation by the quality of its results, then one's judgment of the law of December 8, 1923, must be very favorable. No less than sixty-six decrees were issued under its authority, most of them in February 1924, just before it went out of effect. One can honestly doubt, however, whether many of these decrees were necessary to alleviate "the distress of the people and state" in the sense of the authorizing legislation. For the leaders of the national bureaucracy seized eagerly upon this opportunity to carry out pet projects which, under normal conditions, would have faced insuperable opposition in the Reichstag. Especially in the Ministry of Justice, authors of certain dust-covered proposals seized this new opportunity and used all their energy and influence to revive their moribund proposals as "emergency decrees." Such activity prompted Dr. Kohlrausch, a professor of criminal law at the University of Berlin, to coin the phrase, "bureaucrats' fascism" (*Geheimrats-Mussolinismus*).

In point of fact the enabling act was used to effect sweeping changes in the composition of German courts and in both criminal and civil procedure, ostensibly to lessen the unquestionably high costs of the administration of justice. The alterations in civil procedure were of too technical a nature to warrant discussion here. But in the field of criminal procedure an institution of immense political significance was banished by decree: the jury. The jury bench, occupied exclusively by laymen who, instructed on points of law by the presiding judge, had the responsibility of deciding guilt or innocence, vanished. In its place appeared the so-called *Schöffengericht*, in which lay members sat together with trained professional jurists to debate and pass judgment. It is quite true that good arguments can be made for and against both kinds of court. But the striking political fact is that, through the stroke of a pen, the German nation suffered the loss of an institution so important, both in theory and in history, as the jury without reacting in any way. In the history of England, the principle has been repeatedly maintained that a people is truly free only when a man's guilt is determined by *judicium parium*, by the judgment of his peers, that the responsibility for seeking and finding a verdict rests solely on the judgment of his fellow citizens. The German state had become a republic, but the

German people still lacked a sense of the importance of their own individual civic responsibility. This deficiency was manifested here in an area that had nothing whatever to do with party politics.

The proper field of activity for the emergency decrees was, of course, the German economy, especially currency and tax matters. The success of the currency reform was by no means assured when Stresemann's government fell, although the distribution of *Rentenmarks* had begun as promised on November 15. From this day on the government was no longer able to acquire more money conveniently by unrestricted borrowing from the Reichsbank. Schacht's *Rentenbank* allotted it only 900 million *Rentenmarks* for purposes of state, along with 300 million to cover the national debt at the Reichsbank. These were critical days for the national minister of finance, who was obliged to make repeated use of the emergency law to open up new sources of revenue or to facilitate the speedier collection of taxes already due. But at the same time he was forced to concern himself with a new problem which was closely connected to the currency reform: the question of revaluation. Here a sudden shift in policy by the Supreme Court drove him to quick action.

It is the nature of inflation to favor the debtor at the creditor's expense. For the debtor can repay the money he received with funds of lesser value and thus is made all the richer by the currency's decline in value, while his creditor becomes proportionately poorer. This state of affairs became constantly less tolerable as the inflation increased. A mortgage which had helped the debtor build his house, for instance, could be repaid in inflated marks which would scarcely buy the creditor a new pair of shoes. But insufferable as this situation was, it was hard for the courts to find relief. The Reichsbank notes and treasury certificates were in fact marks and, as such, legal tender which every creditor was required by law to honor at face value. This principle, which stemmed from the time when paper money was redeemable upon demand in gold, had not been altered when, at the beginning of the war, the obligation to redeem was abrogated. The law of August 4, 1914, had made this point explicit. Consequently, when the judiciary clung tenaciously to the principle "a mark is a mark," it was merely engaging in a conscientious observation of the law. At any rate this was the opinion of the Supreme Court up to November 28, 1923. On this day, after the new currency had already been introduced, the Supreme Court suddenly discovered that the axiom, "a mark is a mark," was contrary to faith and credit, and the Court therefore granted the creditor a right, under Paragraph 242 of the Code of Civil Law, to a "revaluation upwards" of his claim. The judgment did not undertake to set clear lines for the determination of this revaluation, nor, for that matter, did it even begin to solve the many problems involved.[51]

Naturally this decision evoked a storm of enthusiasm among those persons who had lost their fortunes in the inflation. And these people were not only numerous but also, for the most part, influential. What this decision had really done was to open a legal war of each against the others. For if every creditor could hale his debtor into court in order that the judge might revalue their contract upwards to a greater or lesser degree, as he saw fit, the consequences were infinite. It was therefore the legislator's clear duty at least to limit this threatening flood of litigation by having standard revaluations promulgated for typical kinds of debts. And people quickly learned that the minister of finance planned to make just such a ruling on the strength of the enabling act. But at this point something occurred which had never happened before: the judges rose against the legislators. In January 1924 the executive committee of the Association of Supreme Court Justices passed and immediately published a resolution. Just as though they were on constitutional authority superior to the cabinet and the Reichstag, these gentlemen warned the national government not to let the precedents of the Supreme Court "be upset by legislative fiat." They not only announced that the Supreme Court had learned "with displeasure" of projected legislative steps, but they even went so far as to point to the "serious danger"; in other words, they threatened that the Supreme Court would find the expected laws unreasonable and hence void.

The strikingly revolutionary character of this declaration must have been apparent to everyone familiar with the traditions of the German bench. For more than a century German judges had been trained to honor unconditionally "the positive law." Nothing had been more bitterly condemned than the notion that a judge should test the law against his private sense of right and wrong. His duty was to apply the laws whether or not he personally approved of them. The Prussian constitution had even expressly forbidden him to pass on the legality of "properly published royal ordinances." (Article 106, Paragraph 2.) To cite natural law now against legislative acts was not only contrary to duty but even absurd in the eyes of all informed jurists. Ever since Savigny the natural law had been considered dead and buried; now the proponents of revaluation had suddenly hoisted natural law as their battle flag. Indeed, German university professors actually mouthed the obsolete phrase or even preached: "Not the law, but only justice, is sacred." This sort of thing had never occurred so long as Germany was a monarchy; the revolt of an association of judges against the government of the King of Prussia would have struck every German justice or professor as utterly inconceivable. But against the Republic they dared to do so without even stopping to realize that the judges, who after all were among those hardest hit by inflation, might appear to have something other than the public at stake in their sensational revolt. Nor were they restrained by the consideration that at this juncture the government already had superhuman obstacles to contend with, the willful increase of which should have given every German patriot good cause to stop and think. So little could the German Republic trust its own institutions of government!

No government, regardless of its political orientation, could have afforded to yield to this piece of juridical blackmail. None could have ignored the necessity of limiting revaluation to some degree, if only because the state, with its 144 billion marks of war debts, was the debtor most favored by the inflation. Nor could any government have ignored the extremely deleterious effect which the judges' action would have on the whole judicial process. One of the wisest experts was to write: "As a result of this attitude of the Supreme Court, political authorities found themselves faced by millions upon millions of legal claims which had been confirmed by the Supreme Court in the strongest conceivable way. Thus what might have been an equitable act of grace was called 'dispossession.' Nothing could have a more distressing effect upon the population than this." [52]

It is not at all astonishing that the revenue decree of February 14, 1924 (the third such measure to be taken under the emergency law), which included an attempted solution to the revaluation problem, evoked a storm of popular indignation. Several courts even went so far as to void the provision, declaring it illegal. Now one can certainly debate the correctness of the rate of 15 percent by which debts were to be increased. For this figure was later raised to 25 percent in the revaluation law of July 16, 1925. But one cannot ignore the fact that one of the major psychological components of the revaluation frenzy was the blind faith of many Germans that everything would remain the same — insofar as their interests were concerned — as it had been before the war; in other words, they believed that they could avoid the destructive effects of the war and treated the defeat as if it all had never happened. And when this illusion was destroyed, the disenchanted blamed the cabinet at the time, or the Republic in general, but not the unpleasant events of 1914–1918, which they preferred to forget. It is illustrative of the Germans' lack of political instinct and their fatal pursuit of special interests that a special Revaluation Party was formed, with a former chief justice of the Supreme Court at its head.

Another problem remains to be discussed in reference to inflation: that of urban real estate. The inflation had benefited home owners with mortgages, particularly those who had been able to pay off their mortgages with worthless marks. Those, however, who depended for income on rents from their property suffered considerable loss. It has been mentioned above that the so-called rent control measures had already frozen rents at prewar levels. These laws were not peculiar to Germany alone, but rather exemplified a legislative trend common among all the belligerent states. The rent increases which were allowed as the mark began to fall failed to keep pace with the general tempo of inflation and of higher prices, so that the building which had formerly furnished income to one or more owners became now a constant consumer of their capital, to be sold off at any price. But in making the sale they encountered yet another problem: the capital gains tax which the municipal authorities had levied. Now of course no capital gain had actually accrued; for the sale price, if reckoned in gold marks, generally fell far short of the prewar cost of purchase. But the local authorities found it to their advantage to insist that "a mark is a mark" and attributed to the seller completely fictitious gains, which they duly taxed. The inevitable consequence was that the parties entered a false, lower price in the sale contract, while the rest was slipped "under the counter" to the seller. The former owner, who had profited by this duplicity, was quite content. Later, however, after the currency had been reformed and stabilized and after he had had a chance to compare, in terms of gold marks, the selling price of his property with its present, stable value, he was understandably pained at the memory of the sale. So he used the duplicity, from which he had previously profited, as grounds for suit against the purchaser in an attempt to regain his property. Thousands of such "false purchase" suits were filed in the next few years; their victims were principally foreigners, whose harder money had been quite attractive to German property owners during the inflation. The legal questions that applied cannot be treated here. But these trials, in which the plaintiff based his case upon his own trickery, certainly contributed nothing to the Germans' respect for the law.

Let us turn now from the consequences of the stabilization of the mark to the achievement itself and the events that made it possible. Of critical importance for the sequence of these events was the fact that the presidency of the Reichsbank fell vacant through Havenstein's death on November 20, 1923, in the last days of Stresemann's regime. At last it was possible to call a man to this post who was equal to the problems of the time. The appointment was formally in the hands of the national President, but the Reichsrat could propose names and the Reichsbank's Board of Directors could express its recommendations. The directors' candidate was Helfferich, whom Havenstein had evidently also wished to see his successor. No objection could be made to Helfferich's professional capacities for the post, but politically it was utterly impossible to entrust an office so important for the entire national economic program to a man who stood in such sharp and outspoken opposition not only to the present cabinet, but to the very concept of republican government.

His leading competitor for the post was the national currency commissioner, Dr. Schacht, whose technical qualifications were equally apparent and whose task of stabilizing the mark would clearly be eased if he were named president of the national bank as well. According to everything that anyone knew of him at that time, there was no reason to doubt that he was a sincere supporter of the Republic and a reliable Democrat. These words sound strange today, now that we know his subsequent development and his collaboration with Hitler. But there was nothing in Schacht's early career to prepare the observer in the autumn of 1923 for such a metamorphosis, and perhaps one may even assume that Schacht himself had no such notions at that time. He sought to further his candidacy by strengthening his relations with politicians on the Left, especially with the Social Democrats. Otto Braun and Severing have both told how they were invited, to their surprise, by a friend of Schacht's to a dinner where Schacht had an opportunity to expound his principles and program. There would be no need to go into such detail if, in 1948, Schacht had not been bold enough to boast that "nothing other than a Social Democratic regime" had called upon him, "a well-known proponent of laissez-faire economics, for help." [53] In actual fact there was not one single Social Democrat in Marx's cabinet, which was then in power. Furthermore, the Socialist members of the Prussian government — whose votes would be critically important in determining the Reichsrat's advice to the President — had been solicited by Schacht himself. And with success. For since both the Reichsrat and the national cabinet supported Schacht, Ebert appointed him president of the Reichsbank on December 22, 1923.

The hopes which men had placed in Schacht's ability to carry out the currency reform were realized. He possessed the necessary expertise and ruthlessness to see it through during the next critical months. He dealt successfully with both the speculation, which threatened first, and the understandable, yet extremely dangerous, attempts within the commercial economy to accumulate huge stocks of foreign credits to meet any emergency. He also frustrated the desire of industry in the occupied areas to establish a Rhenish-Westphalian bank of issue. He owed much of his success to his having assured himself, from the start, of the sympathy of British financial circles. Even before he took office he traveled to London in order to establish contacts there, especially with Montagu Norman, governor of the Bank of England. The opinions of London financiers, among whom Norman enjoyed an unusually strong influence, were quite in favor of German economic recovery and reconstruction and vigorously opposed to the French policy of extracting reparations by sheer force. Schacht's declaration that he firmly intended to return to the gold standard received the complete approval of Montagu Norman and the other English bankers with whom he dealt. These men were not content to let their expressions of sympathy remain platonic, but rather took care to make clear their readiness, in principle, to support the Reichsbank with credits during its transitional difficulties. This was a promise of supreme value.

Of course this promise was based on the presumption that the reparations problem would be solved in such a way as to preclude the continual recurrence of crises under which Germany and the whole world economy had been suffering for the past few years. Now the first great, decisive step in that direction was taken: the calling of an international commission of experts, in which representatives of the United States would also take part.

The first encouragement for such a commission came from the United States. Charles E. Hughes, secretary of state to the Republican President Harding, realized that the American politicians who had destroyed Wilson's plan for peace were cherishing an illusion when they thought that they could maintain an ostrichlike policy with respect to Europe, avoiding its postwar problems by turning their backs to the scene. "We cannot dispose of these problems by calling them European, for they are world problems, and we cannot escape the injurious consequences of a failure to settle them." These were his words to the American Historical Association on December 29, 1922, where he made the important proposal that financial authorities of international reputation should join forces to find the answer which had eluded the politicians: What can Germany pay and what form should these payments take? At that moment, just before the occupation of the Ruhr, the time was hardly ripe for such a meeting, and France remained opposed to negotiations while the passive resistance continued. But as soon as Stresemann had abandoned this, the British government, which had just assembled representatives of the entire empire in London, decided the proper time had come to pursue Hughes's proposal further in the hope of finding some way out of the blind alley. And so in a note of October 12, 1923, the government of the United Kingdom asked whether the United States would agree to join with England and its allies, if they in turn agreed, in such an investigation of the problem. The United States agreed. Now it was up to France, or better, Poincaré.

At last history had presented Poincaré with an opportunity to gain the fame of a great statesman. In his Ruhr adventure he had conquered the Germans as completely as even he could have wished. As a result of the Micum contracts he had his productive guarantees firmly in his hands. In France he was at the acme of popularity. He could truly have afforded to be magnanimous now and prove to the world that it was not hunger for revenge that had motivated him, but rather a concern for the just interests of his country and for the preservation of peace. Instead, he showed that he was less of a statesman than he was a lawyer. He also showed that he lacked all those humane qualities without which men of even the keenest intelligence and the most resolute energy must labor in vain. He was clever enough not to decline, but he was too small a man to accept with honest joy. He invented formal difficulties, pranced about on the paragraphs of the Versailles treaty, and played the grand defender of the Reparations Commission. By this means he forced the British to make several formal modifications in their plan. Thus the Reparations Commission had to be included in the new approach. But the members of the commission had wrestled with the hard facts of this almost insoluble problem long enough now to have become free of political prejudices and to welcome any actual progress. And so on November 30, 1923, they agreed unanimously (that is, with French approval) to establish two subcommittees of experts. One of these committees was to investigate ways of balancing the German budget and stabilizing the mark. The committees were explicitly directed to listen to the testimony of German representatives before formulating their recommendations. And even more important, American experts were to be invited to participate in the committees' work.

Formally this sounded quite different from the original plan. Even Poincaré had to admit to himself that experts asked to find a way to balance the German budget would have to examine *all* aspects of the reparations problem. Nevertheless he now agreed.

And the committees, including their American members, were appointed before the year was out. The significance attached to this collaboration by Americans was clearly expressed by the fact that they were put at the head of the first and politically decisive committee. Its chairman was Charles Dawes of Chicago, who, although he bore the title "General," was president of a trust company. Though not especially rich in constructive ideas, he was certainly a man of sound political instincts, well versed in both the practice and the theory of finance; and he possessed the ability, inestimably valuable in his present task, to awaken confidence on every side. A far greater reputation as a master of finance was enjoyed by Owen Young of New York, the committee's vice-chairman, who, along with the two British delegates, Lord Stamp and Sir Robert Kindersley, exercised the most influence upon the committee. The second committee, which was to consider the flight of capital from Germany, was headed by a first-rate English expert, Reginald McKenna, formerly chancellor of the exchequer and now director of the largest private bank in England.

In the middle of January, while the experts were beginning their work, Poincaré's policy of sanctions received a second setback. At the end of 1923 the separatist movement, which had collapsed in most places, was still holding out in the Bavarian Palatinate, where the so-called Government of the Autonomous Palatinate enjoyed the special protection of the French General de Metz. The French even succeeded, against British opposition, in having the Interallied Rhineland Commission officially register a decree of this regime and thus recognize its legitimacy. But the French insistence that the separatists truly represented the attitude of the populace was shattered by a frightful act of violence. On January 9, members of the autonomous government, among them their President Heinz, a landowner in Orbig, were murdered by unknown agents in Speyer. Although a reward of 50,000 francs was offered, the occupation authorities were unable to find the murderers. Even people in no wise disposed to sympathize with lawlessness must conclude that the deaths did, in some measure, enjoy the local population's approval.

But it was Lord Curzon who delivered the decisive blow to Poincaré's policies by directing Clive, the British consul general in Munich, to proceed immediately to the Palatinate in order to inspect conditions there in person. The French authorities, who could not afford an open conflict with England, could do nothing against this move. Clive's report, which was immediately delivered to Parliament, stated that the overwhelming majority of the population

had no use for the "autonomous government," which owed its existence solely to the favor of the French.[54] This report pulled the
carpet out from under Poincaré. He had no choice but to put up a
flurry of resistance and then retreat. In the first part of February the
entire separatist movement was dissolved and the legal German authorities restored to power. This was a success with which the Germans had every reason to be content. But now it became apparent
that among the Germans there were elements at work who were
ready to spoil the best prospects. In a completely superfluous way
they resorted to violence in Pirmasens and Dürkheim, not only killing dozens of separatists but also indulging in horrors and brutali-
ties which had heretofore been regarded as impossible in Germany.

With the end of inflation a gradual consolidation began to take
place in the unoccupied areas of Germany. The clearest sign of this
improvement was the abrogation of the military state of emergency
on February 28, 1924. A presidential decree, however, still armed
the national minister of the interior with several extraordinary
powers with which to combat subversive activities. And so General
von Seeckt's regime had reached its end, to the relief of many and
the severe disappointment of others. For nationalist and militarist
circles had cherished the hope that Seeckt would keep his extraordinary powers, using them either to hoist himself into position of
dictator or even to play the role of General Monk for the Hohen-
zollerns. And such thoughts were not entirely foreign to Seeckt's
mind. A few days after he had been given extraordinary powers for
the defense of the Republic and its constitution, he wrote to his
sister: "I see no other solution than some form of dictatorship. I
should be happy if someone else would take this step. I do not desire
such a development for myself but rather for the nation." [55]
He may or may not have meant what he said. At any rate Seeckt
was clever enough to realize quickly that as dictator he would have
assumed responsibilities beyond his personal powers. No matter
how sarcastically he made fun of Stresemann's policy of fulfillment in
private, Seeckt could not avoid concluding that his proclamation of
a military dictatorship would have united all the great powers against
Germany, destroying every last chance for rapprochement. And
even if the coup had proved successful, he would have faced an
inevitable bankruptcy. Along with these considerations he also toyed
with the idea that he might even succeed Ebert when the President's
term expired in 1925. With this end in view, he was obliged to maintain at least the external appearances of loyalty to the constitution.
Seeckt naturally sought to extend his personal powers as far as

possible; but when met by presidential resistance, he was forced to yield. When, on November 25, 1923, he outlawed all projects and organizations of the Communist, National Socialist, and Racist parties, he was certainly acting according to his general directive. But many of his subordinate generals, such as General von Lossberg, commandant in Münster, misused their powers in a manner which disclosed both their minuscule respect for the law and their massive political clumsiness. Lossberg went so far that, as Gessler put it to Severing, he had to be "properly chewed out" (*gehörig zusammengestaucht*) by Seeckt. But Severing assures us that General Seeckt was personally determined to avoid friction with the civil authorities.[56]

When the state of emergency was ended, the national government had good reason to believe that one of the worst causes of unrest had just been removed through the compromise arrived at with Bavaria on February 18. The Bavarians were obliged to desist from their attempt to enlist in the service of the land those Army troops which were stationed there. In return, the form of the military oath was changed somewhat and the Bavarian government was assured that, in the future, the military authorities would relieve the *Landeskommandanten* only "after consultation" with Munich. Von Lossow, on whose behalf the Bavarian government addressed a fruitless petition to Gessler, was dismissed. The once glorious State Commissioner-General von Kahr vanished from the scene. The Republic, whose interests he had so thoughtlessly and clumsily endangered, did not disturb his *otium sine dignitate* (dishonorable ease). Ten years later, however, Hitler had the old man killed.

On February 26, 1924, Hitler was obliged to face the Munich People's Court. In its settlement with the national government Bavaria had agreed to abolish its illegal People's Courts — but not until April 1, 1924! Thus in their great farewell performance of the Hitler trial, the men of Munich could show the world just how their court would wield the self-appropriated sword of justice to maintain order and advance the public good.[57]

The defendants included Hitler and his henchmen Pöhner, Frick, and Röhm — and General Ludendorff. For Ludendorff had been caught red-handed and put under arrest. His indictment could therefore not be avoided. But the grand jury found its task most distasteful, and their spokesman sweetened their recommendation of two years' fortress arrest with so many bows and words of praise that anyone could see how satisfied he would be with an acquittal. The general was acquitted promptly on the strength of an argument which must have enraged not only every jurist but every thinking person. The judges had clearly forgotten the words in the Second Part of *Faust*:

> And the judge who cannot punish
> Finally joins the criminals.

Ludendorff alone is to be thanked for the fact that their verdict did not lead to immediate political disaster; for he used the trial to display his utter political incapability to all the world. To be sure, his stupid rantings about "international Jewry" did not lower him in German estimation at that time. But his violent stream of anti-Catholic venom was more than even the militarist politicians could bear. His attack on the attitude of the Vatican during the war, which he baldly labeled "anti-German," impelled even the German Nationalists to lose enthusiasm for him.[58] Stresemann did no more than his simple duty as foreign minister when he called Ludendorff's statement "completely unjustified in fact and offensive in form" and rejected it "most emphatically."

Hitler's case was altogether different. He knew, of course, that the prima-facie evidence of his high treason could not be obscured. Nor could he deny his traitorous activities, about which thousands of people had been told. And so he decided to reverse the argument; he blatantly acknowledged his deeds, and demanded that he be publicly honored for them. He knew that he had here a rich opportunity to address all Germany — so long as the court permitted him to use its chambers as a platform. Because this requirement was amply met, Hitler was able to make free use of the twenty-four days of his trial (for the verdict was not given until April 1) to defame not only Kahr and company, who had turned their backs on him, but also the constitutional government, its organs and its personnel. His impassioned finale disclosed his aims:

> The army we have organized is growing ever faster, day by day, hour by hour. I cherish the proud hope that precisely in these days the hour will finally come, that the scattered bands will become battalions; the battalions, regiments; the regiments, divisions; that the old cockade will be rescued from the filth; and that the old banners will be unfurled again.

These were words which the Bavarians around their beer tables could recite to each other in triumphant tones. For they knew exactly what was meant by this struggle in which the old banners were to be unfurled again: the war of revenge to restore the old regime, a war particularly against France, toward which hatred had been growing ever greater. Many of them lived to see the war for which they yearned. But since the frightful awakening that it would bring was still hidden in the future, their enthusiasm was boundless. This mood filled the entire courtroom and engulfed the bench. Although the professional jurists could not bring themselves to ignore their duty to find Hitler guilty, the lay judges balked at the thought of even the minimal legal sentence: five years' fortress arrest. Only after their professional colleagues assured them that Hitler would have to serve only a small part of his formal sentence, and after they had been permitted to specify, as part of Hitler's sentence, his eligibility for release on probation after six months' arrest, did the people's judges agree to the verdict. Probation for a traitor who had declared as loudly as possible how proud he was of his high treason! Stripped of all its circumlocution this meant that the court regarded six months' fortress arrest as sufficient punishment for a potently treasonable undertaking against the existing state, an undertaking that had cost many men their lives. One might well compare this extremely mild punishment to the sentence that this same Munich People's Court had already given to twenty-five-year-old Fechenbach: eleven years' imprisonment (with an explicit denial of later relief) for the publication of an old telegram which was probably no longer secret and certainly no longer either important or relevant. But Fechenbach was a radical of the Left and Hitler, of the Right!

The court's master stroke, however, consisted in its decision to ignore the law which clearly required the deportation of an alien convicted of high treason (Law for the Protection of the Republic, Paragraph 9, Section 2) with an argument which Hitler, under any other circumstances, would have labeled "rabbinical refinement."

But even before the Hitler trial reached its shameful end, the German Reichstag had suffered dissolution. On February 26 a major debate had begun in which the government had to defend its policies and, in particular, the emergency decrees it had issued under the enabling act. On March 6 its foreign policy became the subject of a verbal duel between Helfferich and Foreign Minister Stresemann. The minister was supported by good reasons and sound logic; the speaker for the opposition, by the passions of the nation.[59] The actual issue at hand was the government's attempt to arrive at an understanding with the Allies on the basis of the recommendations which Stresemann expected to be made by the international experts. Helfferich objected most violently to this plan — even before the recommendations had been made. But when Koch-Weser, leader of the Democratic Party, interrupted him to ask what other policy he would propose with regard to the French, Helfferich could offer no reply. Certainly his final acquiescence to Koch-Weser's repeated demands for satisfaction can scarcely be regarded as an adequate answer: Helfferich said he would "draw the most extreme consequences from the continued violation of the treaty by the French."

In debating these questions the opposition had only a minority of the Reichstag on its side, for the 170 Social Democrats supported the government. But it was these same Social Democrats who, by insisting on some changes in the emergency decrees, forced the government to dissolve the Reichstag. Now, there undoubtedly was every reason to take exception to many of the decrees, and there was probably no one in the German political world who was satisfied with each and every order. But the government was able, and indeed obliged, to reply that the sum of these decrees comprised an interconnected whole which found its justification in the great objectives of coping with a crisis of incomparable severity and of maintaining the stability of the mark, without which all would be lost. There were certainly many Social Democrats who accepted this argument. As a result of the fusion with the Independents, however, these calmer minds were outweighed in their party by those who regarded only the most immediate interests of the working man and who sought to persuade themselves and their constituents that this hour of greatest national need required no sacrifice from them — for instance, in relation to the number of hours in a working day. Consequently, they insisted on referring the emergency decrees to a Reichstag committee even though Chancellor Marx made clear to them in advance that, in anticipation of this eventuality, he had already obtained a presidential decree dissolving the Reichstag. This policy of the Social Democrats, who, to be sure, had supported the enabling legislation but who now hoped "in this way to escape responsibility for the unpopular decrees," has never been criticized more sharply than by Otto Braun in his memoirs.[60] The policy crowned all the mistakes which had commenced with the departure of the Social Democratic ministers from Stresemann's cabinet.

The Reichstag was dissolved on March 13, 1924. New elections were set for May 4. The campaign was strongly influenced by the report which the international commission of experts made to the Reparations Commission in early April and by the German government's declaration on April 16 of its intent to cooperate with the experts' recommendations. The Rightist opposition naturally seized upon these documents to launch an attack on what Helfferich was pleased to call "the fulfillment policy which is now officially rechristened liberation policy." This former minister of William II now spoke in maudlin tones about the "curse of sinning against the spirit of national self-preservation" and prophesied darkly that the German nation would be "lost beyond redemption" if it were to "burden itself anew with this foul curse" by accepting the experts' proposals. The government replied in vain that it hoped in this way "to effect a solution to the reparations question and the liberation of our brothers in the Rhineland and in the Ruhr" and that the experts' proposals promised to replace "oppressive military force with principles and claims based upon economic reason." In vain the government reminded its electorate that the severe sacrifices to which it had been driven had saved Germany from utter ruin. In vain it beseeched the electorate to show a sense of responsibility. The polls were to show how slightly this sense of political responsibility was developed among German men and women.

More than 7.5 million votes supported the opposition parties on the Right: 5.7 for the German Nationalists and 1.9 for the National Socialists. This meant the German Nationalists had won 96 district seats in the Reichstag. And since the workings of German proportional representation had netted them 10 additional delegates on the strength of surplus votes, they were now the strongest group in the Reichstag and had every claim upon its chair. The Social Democrats had dropped from 171 delegates to only 100, demonstrating clearly that, as Otto Braun put it, "the voters had sympathy neither for their flight from responsibility nor for their consequently ambiguous policy." Braun goes on to add, as a further explanation of the Socialists' losses, his belief that the former Independent voters had refused to follow their leaders into union with the Social Democrats. This interpretation might well be true; it would help account for the growth of the Communist vote from 500,000 to 3,700,000. They now had 62 delegates, only 3 less than the Centrists. In the liberal middle the Democrats lost 11 seats and the People's Party 20. The fact that Stresemann's party suffered such severe losses in spite of his quite energetic participation in the campaign shows not only that he was no longer at his height of personal popularity but also that internal strife was weakening his group. The bloc's right wing — von Lersner, Maretzki, Quaatz, and the industrial magnates Klönne and Vögler — seceded to form the German National Liberal Party (*Nationalliberale Reichspartei*); most of them eventually found their way to the German Nationalists. Stinnes, with whom Stresemann had come to differ sharply, died in the course of the campaign (April 10, 1924). Evidently a large part of his party could not keep pace with Stresemann's development into a practical statesman.

Thus the elections of May 1924 exemplified in a clearer manner the tendency already apparent in June 1920: the voters' massive desertion from the responsible center, which supported the Republic, to the two extremes on left and right, which threatened it. True, the German People's Party had furnished a temporary parliamentary reinforcement of the middle when it joined the great coalition; but even this aid was more than canceled by countercurrents among the electorate. The German Nationalists' victory at the polls encouraged them to demand a completely new cabinet, with their party in principal power. But, just a few days before the election, a terrible misfortune had robbed them of the man whom they had hoped to see their chancellor: Karl Helfferich had been killed on April 23 in a train wreck at Bellinzona. He was only fifty-one years old. Even his opponents were quick to point out that, with his death, German political life had lost a man of extraordinary talents and outstanding knowledge. But no one can tell with any certainty whether he would have had the necessary skill and will to lead the German Nationalist Party out of the sterile and purely negative position into which it had fallen under Hugenberg's leadership.

The election returns led many members of the People's Party to desire the admission of the German Nationalists to the government. For if the voters, especially the voters on whom the People's Party counted, really preferred, as seemed to be the case, the parties in the opposition to those in the government, then they could keep their own party from sinking under the burden of unpopular responsibility only by sharing the load of government with their political neighbors. This was Stresemann's opinion, even though collaboration with the Nationalists would demand a very great personal sacrifice on his part. For the Nationalists had directed their campaign particularly against him, indulging in gross accusations and slander. The fact that a university professor and teacher of law had been among the most conspicuous of these slanderers is illustrative of the moral and intellectual state of Germany at that time.[61] Stresemann knew that he had to suffer this Rightist calumny because as foreign minister he was forced to emphasize the primacy of foreign policy and he could hold that policy in its course only on the condition that he collaborate with the Nationalists. The crucial question in this respect was his government's reaction to the Dawes Report, which is discussed below. Another problem was the international situation which had been radically altered by changes in the governments of England and of France. In both these countries new parliaments had been chosen; and the leaders of both countries, Baldwin and Poincaré, had met defeat.

The British elections (December 1923) had been occasioned not by foreign affairs but rather by the Conservative Prime Minister's attempts to institute protective tariffs. This policy had cost his party one hundred seats and its parliamentary majority. The Liberal Party was once more returned in considerable strength, although it remained weaker than the Labour Party. According to parliamentary tradition, the responsibility for forming a new government seemed to fall on the Labour Party. But since Labour by no means enjoyed a majority of the House, it was up to the Liberals to decide if they would adhere to the rules of the tradition. The Liberal leader, Asquith, acquiesced and allowed Labour to form a new government even though this decision was probably to the serious disadvantage of his own party, which from this time on suffered a steadily accelerating decline. Thus in January 1924 the direction of the English cabinet was assumed by the Socialist Ramsay MacDonald, a man whose name suggested a new course in British foreign policy. For in 1914 he had belonged to that small minority opposed to England's entry in the war. Although that was all history now, people did know that he still harbored pacifist tendencies and was eager to arrive at a general international understanding which should include Germany and even Russia. He immediately set about clearing the smoky international air by sending a personal letter to Poincaré (January 26) in which he expressed his desire to clarify and settle Franco-British differences in candid, amicable conversations conducted on the basis of mutual good will. Poincaré replied in the same spirit, and their further correspondence led to a practical rapprochement and to an agreement to use the recommendations of the Dawes Commission as the foundation of their future reparations policy.

But in the French elections of May 11, 1924, Poincaré suffered heavy losses. His defeat undoubtedly had domestic causes, too, but it also made unmistakably clear that a large part of the French electorate had lost its enthusiasm for Poincaré's adventures in the Ruhr. And, in fact, Poincaré's defeat marks the end of a major, critical chapter in European political history.

It would be superficial to conclude, solely on a basis of the results of the French elections that Poincaré's policy was in fundamental error. And the juridical question whether the occupation of the Ruhr was in accordance with the Versailles treaty may properly be ignored here; jurists were and still are divided on this issue, and there is no supreme court of final decision. But the historian must decide if Poincaré's policy was *politically* right. And his judgment of that policy will not be determined simply by computing mathematically whether occupational costs exceeded or fell short of the amount France was able to extract from Germany as a result of the occupation. Far more important is this question: did the occupation of the Ruhr help or hinder the solution of the reparations problem?

On the one hand, it can be argued that since the occupation was followed by an international settlement on the basis of the Dawes report, it indirectly produced a settlement which led to at least four years of relative calm. Would this stability have been attained if Poincaré had not taken his final, fateful step of occupying the Ruhr? The facts of the historical developments outlined above give one no reason for answering in the affirmative. On the contrary, they force one to conclude that neither the German currency reform nor the general settlement of the reparations question would have come about had they not been forced by Poincaré's brutal intervention. The pressures exerted by German nationalism on Berlin were much too strong to have permitted any German government to reach such a solution without external aid.

But even if one agrees to this extent that Poincaré's occupation of the Ruhr achieved a type of success, one must still insist that it was a political error, an error for which no one was to pay more dearly than the French. For the occupation evoked a bitterness among the German people which could only aid those who were busy inciting their countrymen to hatred against the "ancestral foe," and this bitterness would finally prove stronger than the skills of all the statesmen who tried to build a bridge of understanding from each side of the Rhine.[62] Furthermore, the occupation meant the utter ruin of precisely those Germans whose intellectual and economic backgrounds made them the natural opponents of the bloodthirsty war hawks. This tragic expropriation of the educated German middle classes was not just a heavy loss for Germany. It was a European disaster.

The man whom the French had raised to Poincaré's place had a sensitive feeling for these darker aspects of the Ruhr adventure. Edouard Herriot, leader of the Radical Party, was a well-educated man of liberal opinions and a "good European," aware even of German intellectual affairs. No one can doubt Herriot's sincere desire to help fashion a Europe in which each nation might enjoy its due rights. But, like every French political figure, he too was forced to insist on German reparations for France; and he too was obliged to respect the general opinions of his constituents who, in spite of the shifts reflected at the recent polls, continued to regard with skepticism the Germans' professed intent to fulfill the conditions of Versailles, and to ponder with alarm the Germans' growing numerical and economic superiority. And so Herriot, too, saw in a general acceptance of the Dawes Report the best way out of the torments of the times and the dangers of the future.

IX

THE DAWES REPORT AND
THE LONDON CONFERENCE

THE members of General Dawes's commission had devoted enormous energy to their task. They had held innumerable meetings, had spent two weeks in making immediate surveys of the situation in Berlin, and had tapped every available source of information. But most important, they had had the courage to conceive of their mission in dimensions appropriate to its nature, without regard to the political restrictions which the French government, in particular, had wished to set. The Reparations Commission, in its resolution of November 30, 1923, had simply charged the experts to "seek ways and means to balance the German budget and measures to stabilize her currency." The experts, as they emphatically explained, had not approached their task as politicians, but rather as men of practical economic experience, and as such they had seen clearly from the start that Germany's budget and currency depended absolutely upon the "obligations which the Treaty of Versailles had imposed upon Germany." Consequently, the experts attacked the reparations problem straight on and sought practical ways for Germany to make her required payments. They entertained no doubts whatsoever concerning Germany's obligations in this respect. "Germany," they declared at the beginning of their report, "suffered inappreciable damage; her primary moral obligation is to those who have suffered so severely through the war." They were convinced that no constructive proposal could be effective unless the parties involved had the desire to carry it out in good faith. Thus armed with impressive knowledge and with a marked sense of justice, they sought a way to ensure both creditors and debtors their rights.[1]

In this respect it proved most fruitful that they made a sharp distinction between two different questions. The first was: what amount of revenue can Germany *raise*, by virtue of its economic capabilities, through taxes, profits of nationalized operations, and the like? The second, entirely separate question was: how much of these internal revenues can Germany *transfer* to foreign creditors without again ruining its currency and the value of the mark? With the second problem in mind, the experts adopted the ruling axiom that the German government would meet its obligations fully upon depositing the stipulated amount of gold marks in the designated German bank to the account of the "reparations agent." The transfer of these funds to foreign creditors was not the responsibility of the German government, but rather of the reparations agent and his international committee. This arrangement constituted a real relief for the German government and was also clearly consonant with the considered interests of the creditor nations.

In answering the first question the Dawes Committee examined Germany's recent financial policy in great detail. They found several opportunities — the management of the national railways, among others — for justifiable criticism. The result of this expert appraisal was the estimate that, in a normal year, Germany could raise approximately two and one-half billion gold marks in surplus revenue. But they were by no means inclined to regard contemporary conditions as normal. It was therefore proposed that the full regular annuity be reached only after four years of gradually increasing payments. On the other hand, the creditor countries were expected to share, though perhaps to a lesser extent, in the anticipated upswing in the German economy, a careful schedule of which was worked out. German reparations deliveries of every kind were to be included in this annuity, so that there would be no further need for treaty payments of any sort. This principle, too, was designed to help nurture economic and political stability. The experts declined with good reason to set a figure for the total German reparations debt. They were afraid of the hot iron that had so often burned the fingers of debtors and creditors alike.

In determining Germany's capacity to pay, the experts had made an assumption which was of critical significance at the time — and under the conditions — of the Franco-Belgian occupation of the Ruhr: "Our proposal," they emphasized, "is based on the assumption that the fiscal and economic unity of Germany will be restored." This meant that, if the Dawes report were to go into effect, the occupying powers would have to rescind all the regulations that created a customs barrier between occupied and unoccupied Germany and relinquish the authority they had seized in the administration and operation of the region's rail system. Although this portion of the report was directed against Poincaré's recent policies, he was able to note with satisfaction that the experts accepted one demand for which he had fought so stubbornly: the productive guarantees. Of these the German rail system was most important. The experts proposed the transfer of the railways from the government to a corporation which would have a capital of twenty-six billion gold marks and a board of eighteen directors. Half of the directors were to be named by the German government; the other nine by the creditors' trustee. The entire board would elect a German as general manager. The corporation was to issue eleven billion gold marks' worth of bonds secured by a first mortgage on the railways' fixed plant. These bonds would yield five percent interest in normal years and were to be transferred to the trustee of the Reparations Commission for reparations purposes. A second guarantee was to consist of five billion gold marks' worth of industrial debentures, bearing five percent interest and to be retired at the rate of one percent per year. These bonds, the individual obligations of German concerns, were to be secured by first mortgages on the plant and property of the respective concerns. The German government had proposed much the same idea in its note of June 7, 1923; and the burden was all the more justifiable since, as the report made clear, former obligations on these properties had been repayable in paper marks during the inflation. Finally, the creditors were to be given a certain degree of control over the national revenues from import and excise taxes on tobacco, sugar, beer, and alcohol. Of these annual revenues, 1,250,-000,000 gold marks were to serve as further security for reparations payments.

In defense of these productive guarantees the experts were able to use one argument that had not been at Poincaré's disposal: the assurance of a loan of 800,000,000 gold marks which they proposed be made to Germany from abroad, that is principally from the United States, to help her over initial difficulties. The special purpose of this loan was the establishment of the necessary gold reserve for the central bank which, since it was equipped with the sole power to issue notes, was to have the mission of preserving and defending the stability of the mark. The administration of this bank was to be entrusted to a general board consisting, again, half of Germans and half of foreigners. One foreign member of the general board was to be "commissioner," with the duty of supervising the issuance of notes and the maintenance of reserves.

With this plan the experts hoped they had removed reparations payments from the effects of German political strife. They saw that the best security for the payments lay in the realization by the German government and the German people that it was to their own interest "to accept in good faith a burden which the world is satisfied is within their capacity to bear, and to liquidate as soon as possible a burden which is and should be onerous."

Such words show that the experts did not let themselves be misled by any sentimental sympathy for the Germans' plight; they cleaved strictly to facts and to economic considerations. But what else could the Germans expect? They could hardly complain at being forced to bear the consequences of having lost a war even as so many other conquered nations had done in the course of history, so long as this burden remained within the limits of economic feasibility and did not deny them the possibility of continuing their life as a nation and of attaining future prosperity. Now, where these limits lay could not, of course, be defined with mathematical precision. But no one who knows how many billions of marks the Germans furnished Hitler for rearmament can accuse Dawes and his colleagues of having saddled Germany with an intolerable task.*

The Marx-Stresemann government realized that the Dawes Report offered them a way out of the desperate situation into which the occupation of the Ruhr, passive resistance, and inflation had put Germany, and that some form of international rapprochement was the absolute precondition for the preservation of the new currency. They had therefore, as was mentioned above, announced in their note of April 16 their readiness to cooperate in the execution of the experts' plan. For this reason Stresemann and, especially, Ebert were particularly concerned that the new government to be formed after the recent elections, regardless of which parties were concerned, pledge itself to an acceptance of the plan. This question affected the German Nationalists most of all. They were demanding the leading role in the new cabinet and had already proposed their new delegate, Grand Admiral von Tirpitz, as chancellor. The Nationalists required a considerable lack of political tact to suggest at this

---

* Schwerin-Krosigk, Hitler's minister of finance, offers the following table of Hitler's military expenditures in his book *Es geschah in Deutschland*, p. 188 (amounts in billions of reichsmarks).

	1934	1935	1936	1937	1938	1939	Total
From taxes and loans	2.0	2.8	5.8	8.3	17.2	11.9	48
From *Mefo* notes	2.1	2.7	4.5	2.7	. .	. .	12
Annual Totals	4.1	5.5	10.3	11.0	17.2	11.9	60

[*Mefo* notes were a form of script issued by the *Metallurgische Forschungsgesellschaft* — which had only this function — to contractors for public works including, of course, rearmament.]

time, when Germany was so extremely dependent upon foreign sympathies, the former naval minister to William II, a man who in England, at least, was regarded as one of the principal authors of the war. The London *Times* correctly labeled Tirpitz' candidacy a demonstration of the Germans' political rashness and of their failure to comprehend the sensitivity of the British on this matter.

The hopes of the Nationalists, however, did not founder on personalities but rather on the question of policy. Having fought the recent campaign largely with declamations against reparations and with attacks upon the Dawes Report, they could not bring themselves to accept the report as a part of their platform. On the other hand, not only the parties in the former cabinet — People's Party, Centrists, and Democrats — but the Social Democrats and the Bavarian People's Party as well all shared Stresemann's convictions on this point. In consequence of this split, the extended negotiations failed, though the People's Party in particular had taken pains to accommodate the Nationalists, with Stresemann even offering his cabinet post to them. The end was the same as the start. Marx's cabinet, which had resigned on May 26, resumed their governmental responsibilities on June 2 with no essential changes. The important thing was that Stresemann was still foreign minister. But the events of these weeks gave Ebert reason to exclaim: "It is tragic the way a man like Stresemann is treated by his own party."

The Reichstag debates which followed the formation of Marx's new cabinet showed that he could reckon on a parliamentary majority in support of a positive reparations policy. The Nationalists' resolution of no confidence was rejected by a vote of 239 to 194 on June 6, while a government motion to return to the agenda of the day was accepted by the same majority. Now the cabinet could devote their efforts to preparations for negotiations with the Allies. They assumed that the Dawes Report would constitute the subject of an international conference. At the moment there were considerable difficulties in the way of such a meeting, since the two leading Allied powers, England and France, were by no means agreed on the agenda of such a conference. French public opinion was firm in the belief that the Dawes Plan alone was to be discussed and no other matters at all — especially not the matter that naturally concerned Germany the most: French evacuation of the Ruhr. Repeated meetings of the two premiers were required before, finally, on July 9 at a visit of MacDonald's to Paris, an agreement was reached which set the conference for July 16 in London and established a mutually satisfactory agenda. This agenda corresponded to the wishes of the French insofar as it mentioned only the Dawes Plan and emphasized the enforcement of the Treaty of Versailles. But more important than all these questions of detail was the basic fact that American participation in the conference was assured.

While German participation was not expressly mentioned in the Franco-British agreement, it grew out of the nature of the problem at hand. For if, as the agreement emphasized, the Allies wished to inaugurate an era of understanding, they could no longer depend upon ultimata as their tools, but would rather have to consult with Germany in free negotiations about the steps required to carry out the Dawes Plan. It lay also in the nature of the problem that these negotiations with Germany would have to be preceded by inter-allied discussions. The creditors had first to agree among themselves on several matters of policy as well as of procedure and definition before they could face their common debtor. But even this initial part of the conference showed that the meeting was truly blessed with a spirit of reconciliation and a desire for understanding. This good omen became particularly apparent in the discussion of a question which had become quite sensitive during the earlier debate on ad-mitting the occupation of the Ruhr to the agenda: Did a creditor nation enjoy the right to apply sanctions *unilaterally* if Germany violated its treaty obligations? After long discussions, in which the French firmly held their ground, a compromise was finally reached, establishing a court of arbitration consisting of three neutrals, with an American presiding. Since the Dawes Report had already pro-posed that sanctions be applied only after a "flagrant" default on Germany's part had been established, this compromise could be ex-pected to satisfy the Germans. And the decision to restore the eco-nomic and financial unity of Germany — that is, to end the economic and financial exploitation of the Ruhr — demonstrated the Allies' desire to accommodate the Germans' wishes.

On August 2, 1924, an invitation was issued to the Germans, whose delegates arrived in London on August 5. At their head stood the Chancellor, Dr. Marx; the minister of foreign affairs, Dr. Strese-mann; and the minister of finance, Dr. Luther.[2] Stresemann had spent the summer persuading the German nation to accept the Dawes Plan, while explaining to the Allies that this acceptance would require several concessions to German public opinion. Most important among these was the promise of the military evacuation of the Ruhr as soon as possible. To be sure, this issue had been ex-cluded from the official agenda, but Stresemann hoped that this meeting of all the principal statesmen of Europe would neverthe-less give him an opportunity to raise the question, especially since he was certain of MacDonald's friendly support.

The reception the Germans received in London almost exaggerated an expression of the fact that the time of dictation had
passed and that, as MacDonald put it in his welcoming address, the
Allies looked forward to conversations in which each party would
find sympathetic listeners. But at the same time the opening of the
talks was marked by an incident which might well have had unfortunate consequences. In transmitting the initial German reply to
the Allies' joint decisions, the Chancellor, mindful of German opinion, thought it necessary to allude briefly to the need for a rapid
military evacuation of the Ruhr. Since he spoke in German, his
speech had to be translated. Now the German delegation enjoyed the
services of a first-class linguist, a Dr. Michaelis, who had mastered
seven tongues to absolute perfection and fluency, a veritable virtuoso of the interpreter's art. Unfortunately he also possessed a
virtuoso's vanity, and now, at this historic moment, when he was
called upon to mount the diplomatic stage, he thought he could best
play his assigned role by hurling the words — which the Chancellor
spoke with careful calm — with such emphasis and pathos into the
faces of the West that they sounded like a declaration of war. The
result, naturally enough, was indignation among the Allies, especially
the French, and deep dejection among the Germans. The chairman,
MacDonald, succeeded tactfully in calming the ruffled waters to
some extent, and the German delegates quickly replaced their
passionate interpreter with a paler model who limited himself
strictly to his professional task. This was Dr. Paul Schmidt, who went
on to serve steadily into Hitler's times as "the extra on the diplomatic stage."[3]

This is not the place in which to pursue the details of the lengthy,
trying negotiations. In several minor questions the Germans succeeded in winning still further concessions with the valuable help
of the American bankers who were charged with the granting of
the loan and who thus sought to keep Germany's economy as free as
possible of the effects of political strife. The concept of a "flagrant
default," which was to be the precondition for any sanction, was defined more sharply as the Germans had desired. Both sides met in
a mutual policy of amnesty for all Germans and all members of the
occupation. In this way, as their protocol read, the statesmen hoped
"to wipe out the past to the utmost possible extent." The only exceptions to this general amnesty were those crimes committed
against the life of persons and resulting in death.

But the most difficult and sensitive issue remained the one which
the conference was not authorized to treat: the evacuation of the
Ruhr by the French and Belgian troops. Here German and French

public opinion were diametrically opposed, and the representatives of both nations knew that their parliaments and people were watching them most sharply on this single point. Herriot had expressly assured his parliament that he would *not* concede to the evacuation at the London conference. It is a credit not only to MacDonald's energy and desire for peace, but also to the conciliatory spirit of the entire meeting, that the English Prime Minister finally succeeded in persuading Herriot to have a secret, informal talk with Stresemann. The secrecy of their meeting had to be most carefully preserved, lest an outbreak of national passions be caused by an indiscrete word to the press, whose representatives, of course, were gathered from the entire world in London and hung upon every word of the assembled statesmen. Herriot had every reason to practice caution, for he could not forget the fate of Briand, felled by his parliament during the conference at Cannes. Nor can one criticize him for failing to have complete confidence in the alleged honest desire of the German nation for reconciliation while strong and arrogant German nationalists were busy singing another song. Furthermore, there were difficulties with respect to the disarmament controls, which had lapsed with the occupation of the Ruhr.

But in spite of all this Herriot finally promised to withdraw all the forces from the Ruhr within one year and to evacuate Dortmund immediately. This concession was a great achievement on Stresemann's part, of which he had every reason to be proud. But the real credit is due the man who had to make these concessions. And not only did Herriot manage to avoid the fate of Briand, he also succeeded in actually winning the support of both houses of his parliament, even after an extended Senate address by Poincaré in opposition. In the course of these efforts Herriot had even gone so far as to declare that an entire nation could not be suppressed and had pointed to the warning example of Napoleon, who, by ignoring this truth, became its victim. "If the old militaristic Germany is to be destroyed, *we who favor a republic must support democratic Germans so that a new Germany can arise.*" This was a platform to which at least those Germans who took seriously their Republic and reconciliation among nations had to agree.

But to what extent were these Germans able to make their way forward through the flames of nationalist agitation? Even the final meeting of the conference had almost resulted in an explosion because the German delegates had tried to satisfy a desire of the Right. Chancellor Marx had the duty of responding for the German delegation to Chairman MacDonald's extremely friendly closing words. He intended to reply in this same warm manner, but he also wished to include in his response a renewed protest against the so-called "war-guilt lie." The wording of this protest had been settled in advance between the Chancellor and his foreign minister.[4] They had fortunately decided that, before Marx delivered his address, he would first consult with MacDonald. When, in the pressure of the last day's business, no time was found for such a meeting, the Chancellor was wise enough to omit the words of protest from his speech. His decision was doubtlessly to Germany's advantage; for such a protest would not have remained unanswered. It would have united all the Allies in a common front against Germany; and the bad feeling with which the conference would have closed would have destroyed in one blow all the spirit of reconciliation which the meeting so successfully had served.

Domestic politics prohibited Stresemann from displaying Marx's statesmanlike restraint. Upon their return from London, the German delegates were welcomed home with the customary cries of nationalist wrath. The so-called Patriots' Leagues adopted a resolution condemning the London Accord, with the touching naïveté of the irresponsible, as "Germany's enslavement." The German Nationalists in the Reichstag renewed the seven demands they had made before the conference and which they claimed had not been fulfilled. Their complaints were, of course, only partly just, but it was true that agreement on the "immediate . . . military evacuation of the area of invasion and sanctions" had not been entirely achieved. Yet to any unprejudiced observer it was clear that partly because of MacDonald's help and Herriot's good will, more had been accomplished on these lines than Germany had had any reason to expect. The seventh demand of the German National Party read: "Formal revocation of the false accusation of war guilt."

Now in certain diplomatic situations it is often no disadvantage at all to have the domestic opposition demanding more of the foreign party than the government itself desires to ask; reference to these strong internal pressures can actually serve to strengthen the negotiator's hand. But once the negotiations are over, any responsible domestic politician will weigh the pros and cons of the agreement and arrive at his decision accordingly. The fact that the advantages of the London Accord far outweighed the disadvantages must have been as apparent at that time as was later proved beyond doubt by the course of events. It was extremely fortunate for Germany that for a few years some form of order was established with respect to the reparations issue. It was a great step forward from not only the economic, but also the moral point of view that the unity of Germany was immediately restored through the nullification of Franco-

Belgian measures in the Ruhr; that part of the occupation was with-drawn; and that expelled residents of the region were permitted to return. And it was a great success to have won assurance that the occupation forces in the Ruhr would be evacuated within a space of time that most certainly was infinitesimal in the life of a nation. When the opposition affected disbelief in the French intent to honor this promise, they acted in part against their better knowledge and most assuredly in a politically stupid manner, for they thereby aroused suspicion and alarm among those very statesmen of the West who were eager to achieve conciliation and who, indeed, had already given practical proof of this desire.

Any international revival of the war-guilt question was bound to have this same unfortunate effect — and none other. From any realistic point of view it was clearly irrelevant for the German government, or any other government, to make a flat declaration about the origins of the war or to decide who or what had caused it. This question could be answered, if at all, only through objective, scientific research; and Germany had already taken a major step in this direction by opening the archives of its Foreign Ministry and making its documents available to international scholarship in the pioneering publication *Die Grosse Politik der europäischen Kab-inette*.[5] It was with justice that Hans Delbrück, Count Max Mont-gelas, and Paul Rohrbach referred to these volumes in their joint declaration. It was obvious that neither German nor Allied histo-rians were swayed by what the German government had been re-quired to acknowledge in Article 231 of the Versailles treaty. And one could safely presume that such men as MacDonald and Herriot did not regard as the acme of political wisdom a policy which forced a conquered foe to confess in writing a crime which he passionately felt he had not committed. But it was something quite different to challenge these men to debate openly this question on which Allied public opinion was almost unanimously opposed to Germany. Furthermore, public opinion in the West would have become even more embittered if people there had realized the truth. Precisely those Germans who before the war had spoken arrogantly of German world hegemony and of a "gay and glorious war" (*fri-schen, fröhlichen Krieg*) were acting now as though Germany were the innocent victim of a war which others had contrived. And the same Germans who found Article 231 an unprecedented insult burst into jubilant enthusiasm at the cinema when a film showed Frederick the Great giving the order to invade Maria Theresa's Austria in time of peace. It was fortunate that the public did not know that William II, considered the chief villain by the West, was insisting that the real authors of the war had been the Jewish Free-masons of France and Italy.

Now whatever one may think of a protest against the war-guilt clause, its omission was hardly any reason to reject the London Accord that granted Germany such considerable advantages. And this was the question that the Reichstag now faced. For Annex I to the Protocol of August 9 had explicitly stated that the experts' report would not take effect until Germany had taken "the necessary measures to promulgate and enforce the laws required to carry out the Dawes Plan in the form approved by the Reparations Commission." Immediately after the close of the conference, the Marx government submitted drafts of such laws to the appropriate legislative bodies. These laws concerned principally the national bank and the national railways, the five-billion-mark mortgage on industrial properties, and the liquidation of the *Rentenbank* notes. These proposals represented in sum the entire burden which the German nation would have to assume under the Dawes Plan and the reparation terms set forth therein. They also included the granting of certain rights of control to the creditor nations, especially in the management of the national railways and bank. The burden was heavy, but only to be expected after an unsuccessful war; and even the control rights, however much they might have pained German national pride, were not only justified by the facts, but also designed to preclude the sort of political squabbling that had so weakened Germany's international position in the recent past.

In favor of the necessary legislation were the government parties and the Social Democrats, as well as the newly founded Economic Party and the Bavarian People's Party. Against the laws were the German Nationalists, the National Socialists, and the Communists. Thus the government was confident of a simple majority, while the Nationalists were in the same comfortable position they had enjoyed at the ratification of the Treaty of Versailles: once again they could stridently oppose what they knew would pass and thus at no risk gain the reputation of being champions of the national honor. They made even fuller use than before of the tactical advantage that belongs to the irresponsible opposition. But the existing situation could have given a resolute and ruthless opponent of this dangerous demagoguery an incomparable opportunity of striking a telling blow.

If the national government had dissolved the Reichstag and appealed to the nation for a vote of confidence, it not only would have won a major victory against the Rightists, but also would have driven home to the German people the lesson that democratic government requires responsible government. Faced with the question of whether they preferred to accept the Dawes Plan or to heap upon themselves a repetition of the recent past, the German voters would have had no choice but to accept, by electing such delegates as were prepared to ratify the London Accord. An overwhelming majority of the leaders of all the great economic interest groups had declared themselves in favor of acceptance. Among these was even the powerful Federation of German Industry (*Reichsverband der Deutschen Industrie*), to which belonged the most important contributors to the parties of the Right. The entire domestic and foreign situation would have been clarified by a new election at this juncture. But, although numerous voices in favor of such a move were raised upon the Left, the cabinet remained unpersuaded. Opposition to this step emanated principally from the German People's Party and its leader, Stresemann. This party was even more determined than before to bring the Nationalists into the government in order to thrust a sense of responsibility upon them; and a strengthening of the Social Democrats, as could be expected from an election at this time, would not have served this purpose.

And so this great opportunity of furthering the political education of the German people was missed. In its stead the German Nationalist demagogues were given a chance to engage in a grotesque display of their irresponsibility. For it turned out that they had erred in their design. One of the proposed laws — concerning the new national railway company — implied, in the opinion of the relevant authority in the Ministry of Justice, an alteration in that part of the national constitution which concerned the railroads. Thus such legislation, constituting an amendment to the constitution, would require a two-thirds majority in the Reichstag (Article 76 of the Weimar constitution). But a two-thirds majority was not to be had if the Nationalists remained solidly opposed. On August 27, upon the second reading of the draft, 248 votes were cast in its favor to 174 votes of Nationalists, Racists, and Communists against it. The measure had been rejected, and with it, if the vote was permitted to stand, the entire Dawes Plan; for, as was pointed out above, the plan was to go into effect only after Germany had passed *all* the necessary laws.

Later this same day an official announcement of the German government declared that President Ebert had decided to dissolve the Reichstag if the Dawes Plan were not ratified in whole. Now, it would seem, the German Nationalists would finally have a chance to prove their prowess at the polls. But lo! They fled the opportunity as though with fear. When the votes were gathered after the third reading of the law, it became apparent that only 52 Nationalists had stuck fast to their no, while 48 decent men and women of the German National Party had voted yes, thus helping the National Railroad Law to a two-thirds majority (311 to 127) and the Dawes Plan into execution. In vain did Ludendorff cry: "This is a disgrace to Germany. Ten years ago I won at Tannenberg. Today they have won a *Jewish Tannenberg.*" In the minds of the Nationalists the main thing was that a national vote of confidence on the Dawes Plan had been avoided. For this prize they were prepared to suffer a few coarse words of abuse from Ludendorff. A letter which Seeckt wrote to his wife a few hours after this vote grants us a peek behind the scenery. Here he not only expresses his delight at having escaped the elections that the Leftists had desired, but also attributes the principal credit for this stroke to his most intimate colleague, General von Schleicher, "who was at his post in the Reichstag today from nine until four-thirty." Even more revealing is this statement: "In the final analysis it was a battle between two parties, neither of which was on the stage: on the one side, Ebert; on the other, someone else, of whom fortunately the papers do not yet speak." He referred, of course, to himself.[6]

The most tragic part of this mean maneuver was that, in great measure, it succeeded. The Nationalists avoided an election which would have made the German voters aware of their own responsibility for their future. In the elections which were held a few months later, when the Dawes Plan had already taken effect and the electorate could rest assured that their ballots would bring no new catastrophe over Germany, the German National Party was able once again to play successfully the role of the sturdy defender of the national honor and the determined foe of international socialism, international finance, and, of course, international Jewry. The party's industrial benefactors, for whom the defeat of the Dawes Plan would have meant ruin, reached into their pockets again, once the danger had passed, to finance the party as its trustworthy aid in the common struggle against trade unions and Social Democrats. But worst of all, even after the Nationalists had so clearly failed this test of their political responsibility, their neighbors in the cabinet still clung to the hope of bringing them into the government. The director of this political phantasy was again the People's Party. According to Seeckt's letter, mentioned above, Stresemann had "won his party's assent on domestic issues" the very day of the Reichstag vote. Stresemann probably had a hand, therefore, in the September declaration of the People's Party in the Reichstag which expressed their wish that the Nationalists be invited to join the government in accordance with the illusory but high-sounding principle "that a limitation of unavoidable partisan strife to a tolerable degree and the restoration of the nonpartisan foreign policy required for any success is to be achieved only through the reunion of six million German Nationalist voters with the German body politic and through assurance of their cooperation."

Before the Reichstag vote the Chancellor had promised the Nationalists an invitation to join his cabinet in the event that they should accept the Dawes Plan. Whether this condition was met when the delegation split in two became a problem with which mathematicians and logicians could concern themselves for days. In the final analysis, the decision depended upon the direction in which the German National Party chose to move, and there was no doubt that the negative component proved dominant. Hergt, the party's chairman, was blamed for the 48 votes which had ensured the Dawes Report and was forced to resign. On September 8 Stresemann himself wrote to a party colleague: "Hergt and Westarp are playing an utterly false game. They discussed with us privately the admission of Nationalists to the cabinet if the Dawes Plan were accepted, and now they accept congratulations for having voted against it." [7] But in spite of this insight Stresemann and Marx let the German Nationalists lead them by the nose to such an extent that they finally made the statement concerning the war-guilt question which the Nationalists had so vehemently demanded. Not only did they declare that they did not accept the verdict of the Versailles treaty, as had been said often enough before, but they went on to demand that the German nation "be relieved of the burden of this false accusation," for otherwise "no true reconciliation and spirit of understanding among nations" could be achieved.

That this declaration was made one day before the official signing of the London Accord (August 30, 1924) suggested in itself a certain lack of diplomatic tact. But so long as the statement merely appeared in German newspapers, the Allied governments were able to ignore it, even though their press, with greater or less vehemence, criticized the peculiar methods of the Germans. The declaration closed, however, with the assurance that the German government would call it to the attention of the Allied governments. Stresemann seems to have been completely serious in this matter; not even the warnings of well-intentioned foreign statesmen could divert him from his plan. MacDonald sent word that everything which had heretofore been done to make Germany's situation more favorable would be destroyed if the War-Guilt Note were formally transmitted.[8]

Fortunately Stresemann had left Berlin for a rest immediately after the close of the Reichstag debates, leaving Under-Secretary von Maltzan in charge of the Foreign Ministry. Maltzan saw quite clearly that the German government was about to commit a grave error of immeasurable consequence. Stresemann's domestic concerns were of no relevance to him. Indeed, Lord d'Abernon thought he perceived that, while Stresemann was tending toward the Right, his assistant was moving the opposite way. Maltzan decided to offer passive resistance to his superior on this issue. Having first assured himself of the British ambassador's support, he simply failed to send the note. Naturally Stresemann was beside himself on his return, but he could not counter the sound arguments of Maltzan and d'Abernon. Could he justify, all for the sake of an empty gesture, endangering the 800,000,000-mark loan which was about to be made and which was of such critical importance to Germany? And so the transmission of the note was postponed indefinitely. But Maltzan's days on the Wilhelmstrasse were numbered.[9] At the end of the year he was appointed ambassador to Washington. In his place Stresemann put the former chief of ministry von Schubert, with whom he felt more in harmony. Maltzan's life was prematurely ended by an airplane accident on September 23, 1927.

One cannot doubt that Stresemann's attitude in this affair was based principally upon domestic considerations or, to put it more precisely, upon his need to win the support of German Rightist circles for his foreign policy. For he must have realized that a bitter debate with the Allied powers on the question of war guilt would yield no practical results but would rather conjure up new difficulties in dealing with questions yet to be settled. There was especially the matter of German disarmament according to the requirements of the peace treaty. The Interallied Military Control Commission wished to resume its activities, which had ceased in every practical sense at the beginning of the occupation of the Ruhr. In late 1923 this issue had become the subject of a month-long exchange of notes between the Allied Conference of Ambassadors in Paris and the German Foreign Office. With all the tools of logic and with references to German honor on the one hand and to European hopes for friendly conciliation on the other, Stresemann sought to obstruct or at least to delay the resumption of control activities. But the Allies were particularly intent upon reinstituting the surveillance after events in 1923 — events such as the Buchrucker Putsch and the Bavarian disturbances — had clearly shown that the actual number of weapons and of armed troops exceeded the treaty limits by far, and that "nationalist and militarist organizations" were engaging in "uninterrupted and increasing activity" even after the cessation of hostilities in the Ruhr.

This charge was the subject of a joint letter which MacDonald and Herriot sent to the Chancellor, Dr. Marx, from Chequers on June 22. Experts who were personally acquainted with the facts of German disarmament were unanimously agreed that in no sense had it been completely carried out. This sentiment found expression, among other places, in an article published by an English member of the Control Commission in the *Quarterly Review* for October 1924. The author was Brigadier General J. H. Morgan, a distinguished jurist, a man who was familiar with Germany and with German literature and whom no one could accuse of having any kind of anti-German feelings. In his article he described in detail how the German military authorities had, at every step, kept the Control Commission from penetrating to the heart of affairs; and he came to the conclusion that General von Seeckt, whom he regarded as the organizing center of this resistance, had at his disposal at least 500,000 men who had received military training since 1921. At the time this article was almost unanimously condemned by the German press as a violent distortion of fact;[10] but later, under Hitler, the German generals were proud to boast of all the tricks which Morgan had ascribed to them in his article. That the Army's active forces slowly became greater than they should have been was a "fact of which Seeckt was naturally aware," according to Seeckt's biographer. "Here began that process," he goes on to say, "which was not to bear fruit for another decade, but which, in 1924, Seeckt was determined to preserve at all costs from destruction at the hands of the enemy."[11] To be sure, Morgan exaggerated when he closed his article with the prophecy that, if the military controls were removed, the peace of Europe would last little more than one year. But he exaggerated only with respect to the speed with which war would come; in all essentials Morgan was, unfortunately, all too right.

The exchange of notes centered principally on the Allies' insistence on the "general inspection," which they thought necessary after the long hiatus in order that they might determine what sort of progress or retrogression the German disarmament had made in the meantime. It is in no way astonishing that Seeckt opposed this proposition with all his might and main; for there was much that he wished to keep hidden from the Allies at all costs. He even threatened to resign if the German government were to accept the Allies' demand.[12] It is certain that Stresemann joined Seeckt in these efforts so long as he possibly could. But finally, on the eve of the London Conference, he had no choice but to yield to necessity and accept the general inspection (June 30, 1924). He tried, of course, to mask his retreat by feigning an understanding that this general inspection would automatically mark the finish of control. But in their note of July 9 the Allies countered this maneuver with the firm statement that the withdrawal of the Control Commission would depend not only upon the results of the forthcoming inspection, but also upon the settlement of five explicit complaints which they had raised before and repeatedly renewed. And so the general inspection, against which Seeckt had fought so hard, came to pass. But he did not resign after all. The execution of the inspection consumed the rest of the year. And it did not result in a confirmation of the German government's official assurance that the required disarmament had been carried out.[13] The Allied inspection was of considerable political significance, as the German people learned at the beginning of 1925, when the Allies, with reference to the search, refused to withdraw their occupation forces from the so-called Cologne Zone in the Rhineland. We will return to this below.

Still another diplomatic issue of major importance came into the foreground with the acceptance of the Dawes Report: the admission of Germany to the League of Nations. In Germany as well as other countries opinions on this question had undergone remarkable change. The great powers, which had originally refused Germany admission to the League, now earnestly desired such a move; at Geneva in September 1924, at the fifth meeting of the League, Mac-Donald gave an almost enthusiastic expression to this wish, and Herriot joined him, if with cooler words. In Germany a small but active group had long been convinced that both in the national interest and in that of world peace Germany should have a seat at Geneva; for only there, by way of example, could the German government successfully press for the rights of German minority groups in other countries. Count Bernstorff, formerly ambassador to Washington and now a Democratic member of the Reichstag and leader of the Alliance for the League of Nations, was a prominent proponent of this point of view. But at the moment this opinion was held by only a minority, to which belonged — apart from convinced pacifists — Social Democrats, Democrats, and Centrists. General German opinion was originally against joining the League, for it was regarded as an instrument for maintaining the new, post-Versailles status quo. This was naturally the view of the Nationalists in particular, who were strongly prejudiced against international organizations of any form. But outside these Rightist circles moods gradually changed, until the German government, and Stresemann in particular, came to view admission to the League as the logical consequence of the new course taken with the acceptance of the Dawes Plan and the London Accord. It was, however, significant that Stresemann approached this matter with great care and many doubts. His public utterances were directed principally against those who tried to press him into hasty action on this point, and his consideration of the Nationalists' opinions became evident when, in his note of September 29, he linked the war-guilt question to even this topic by expressing his government's concern lest joining the League of Nations be misconstrued as the concomitant acceptance of the Versailles treaty's war-guilt clause. This thought had, of course, never occurred to the Entente powers; hence they could, with good conscience, reply that such an interpretation was farthest from their minds.

On the other hand, the German government was completely correct when it requested assurance in advance that Germany would be granted a permanent seat in the Council of the League immediately upon admission. It had every claim to this position; for even in defeat it remained a great power. All ten powers which belonged to the Council of the League of Nations, and to which the memorandum had been sent, gave their consent. A further problem, which lay hidden here, became apparent later, when Germany submitted its formal request for admission to the League. The Germans used this occasion to make a further stipulation which caused even more concern: they argued that Germany's enforced disarmament meant that she ought to be freed from the obligations set forth in Article 16 of the League Charter. This article required every member of the League to apply sanctions against any country that undertook aggressive warfare, outlawed by the charter. These sanctions were not necessarily to be merely economic, an interruption of commercial and financial relationships; they could also consist of military participation in a common exercise of force under the aegis of the League. Now it was self-evident that a disarmed nation like Germany could — indeed was obliged to — ask for special treatment; but whether its special circumstances also extended to a release from sanctions of every kind was another question altogether, one which the French immediately rejected.

This reference to the problems Stresemann faced in foreign policy shows how much more he could count upon the Left than on the Right for his support and, thus, how much he complicated his task by trying to accommodate the German Nationalists. Nevertheless, he and his party still continued to press for their admission to the cabinet. In this effort he received support from the Chancellor and the greater part of the Centrist delegation. The resistance within the government parties stemmed principally from a majority of the Democrats, particularly their leader, Reichstag representative Koch-Weser (previously Koch-Kassel after a former constituency). Koch, who had taken the place of Carl Petersen, now mayor of Hamburg, had by no means that superior force of personality which marks the natural party leader; but he was an intelligent man, with great experience, broad knowledge, and an extraordinary ability to grasp problems quickly. He had no illusions about the German Nationalists' basic aversion to the Republic and its conciliatory foreign policy, and he therefore considered their admission to the government a mistake. In any event he was convinced that the Democratic Party would deny its very essence if it were to form a coalition with the Nationalists. A minority of the Democratic delegates, among them the former minister Eugen Schiffer, did not share this view. This difference soon led to a formal division of the party.

The negotiations concerning the formation of a new government filled most of September and October. They involved feelers sent out not only to the Right, but also to the Left toward the Social Democrats. But in neither direction could an agreement among the parties be reached. The Social Democrats found now how accurate Ebert had been in calling their dismissal of Stresemann's cabinet a fateful stupidity. One cannot criticize Stresemann for calling attention to their error in a speech at Frankfurt-am-Main. Here he emphasized that in overthrowing his government they had struck a hard blow at precisely those elements in the German People's Party "which, even at the cost of severe sacrifice, had fought for the Great Coalition not only in the national government, but also in the lands." He was referring, of course, to Prussia, where the cabinet was still based upon the Great Coalition.

On October 20, 1924, Marx realized that his efforts were in vain, and so, with the unanimous consent of his cabinet, he requested the President to dissolve the Reichstag. Ebert acceded to this request and new elections were set for December 7, also the date of elections for the Prussian Landtag. Those who had hoped that the elections would provide the clear and certain basis for the formation of a new government were disillusioned. Some changes were apparent, but their meaning was not sufficiently clear to indicate what sort of government the German nation really wished. Only one fact was evident: the nation was returning from the two extremes of Left and Right. Both the National Socialists and the Communists had lost about one million votes, dropping to 14 and 45 delegates, respectively. It was, of course, a help in the formation of any cabinet to have the number of eternal naysayers lessened in this way. On the other hand, both the German Nationalists and the Social Democrats increased their Reichstag seats, the former to 131, the latter to 103. The moderate parties, the Centrists, the People's Party, and the Democrats, all won a few seats, but not enough to give them a parliamentary majority. The problem, therefore, remained the same as before: the necessity of extension to either the Right or the Left.

When Marx gave up his attempts to form a new cabinet in January 1925, Ebert entrusted the task to Dr. Luther, the former minister of finance. Luther executed a turn to the Right by inviting four Nationalists to join his government. To be sure, he had required of these men quite significant conditions, on which the Centrists in particular had insisted. They had to pledge allegiance to the Republic and its flag of black, red, and gold, and to the maintenance of former foreign policy — in other words to Stresemann's course. All this was rather clearly the opposite of all those propositions with which they had wooed votes; but they, too, found Paris worth a Mass. Their party leader, Schiele, received the politically critical Ministry of Interior; two other German Nationalists were given the ministries of Economics and of Food. The new minister of finance, von Schlieben, had previously been director of the Ministry and thus, as a civil servant, nonpartisan; but now he counted himself among the German Nationalists. The Center furnished two ministers to the new government; the Bavarian People's Party, one. Gessler remained in the Ministry of Defense as a "technical expert." Stresemann's presence in the Foreign Ministry guaranteed the continuation of the former foreign policy. The Democratic Party did not regard itself bound to the new government by Gessler's participation.

The new Chancellor had no specific party affiliation, although his views came closest to those of the People's Party. Like so many ministers of this period, he had been trained in municipal administration, and even as a young man had won the reputation of being especially expert in the fields of administration and economics. He had, even increased this fame in the administration of his several ministries, particularly that of Finance. But he had never been a parliamentarian, and one does him no injustice in saying that he had little use either for parliamentarians or for the often quite complex processes of parliaments. Such an attitude is all too understandable on the part of a man who was concerned throughout his life with the technical aspects of administration and legislation, but it can become fatal if such a man is called to be the political leader of a nation.

In Prussia, where the last Landtag elections had been held four years before, the new elections showed a movement to the Right. The German National Party rose to 109 delegates, almost reaching the strength of the Social Democrats, who had dropped to 114. Nevertheless, the former government coalition still enjoyed a majority, however weak. Consequently, the Prussian cabinet could have stayed, had the German People's Party not broken the coalition. It is true that their ministers had found it possible to collaborate to their own satisfaction with those of other parties, even the Social Democrats, and showed no personal inclinations to resign. But their Landtag delegation, whose sympathies were with the Right, passed a resolution on January 6, 1925, expressing the desire to ally with the German Nationalists rather than the Social Democrats. This resolution obliged the ministers of the People's Party to resign.

The ensuing crisis lasted a full month, in the course of which it became apparent that a new government was possible only upon the base of the Weimar Coalition. Since the Social Democrats were prepared to see a Centrist in the chair, Marx was made premier of Prussia. But on February 20, to everyone's astonishment, the Landtag's vote of confidence in the new regime was lost by a vote of 221 to 218. The plotters of this defeat were Franz von Papen and several other conservative Centrists who, despite their delegation's resolution, had sought to destroy the Weimar Coalition by abstaining from the vote. This was Papen's first appearance on the domestic political scene. And it was no more successful than were his later efforts, for the final result was that a Weimar Coalition cabinet was organized anew under the direction of the Social Democrat Otto Braun. This fact, of course, did not keep Papen from boasting of this heroic deed in his memoirs. Not until April 3 was the crisis settled with the acceptance of Braun as premier. Besides Braun only one other Social Democrat belonged to the cabinet: Severing, the minister of interior. The Center was represented by Minister of Justice Am Zehnhoff, as well as by Hirtsiefer and Steiger; the Democratic Party, by Finance Minister Höpker-Aschoff and Trade Minister Schreiber; while Becker, formerly undersecretary and now the minister of culture, was the close ally of the Social Democrats.

It took a long time to form this government. It lasted, however, with only a few changes in personnel, until 1932 — longer than any other government in Germany. It was not until that year that Franz von Papen, who had become Chancellor of the Republic, succeeded in overthrowing the Prussian government. He did so through a misuse of the extraordinary powers granted him by the President. By that time, of course, the President of Germany was no longer named Ebert. His name was Hindenburg.

X

EBERT'S DEATH AND
HINDENBURG'S ELECTION

Aᴛᴇʀ the London Accord which adopted the Dawes Plan had
been signed on August 30, 1924, its provisions were set in motion
and the various stipulated organizations brought into being. On
September 3 an American, Parker Gilbert, was installed as reparations agent. The Franco-Belgian customs border that had separated
occupied and unoccupied Germany was abolished shortly thereafter. On October 10 the Dawes Loan of 800 million gold marks was
extended, the greatest part being supplied by American under-
writers. That the public quickly oversubscribed the loan was evidence of Western confidence in Germany's economic power and
capabilities now that a stable currency and peaceful growth were
in prospect. On October 28 the Micum was dissolved, and on October 29 the Reparations Commission formally reported that the economic and financial unity of Germany had been restored. Most of
those residents of the region who had been expelled returned to the
Ruhr in the course of the year, and political prisoners were given
freedom. In carrying out this latter action the French government
went out of its way to make clear, through a generous interpretation
of the accord's provisions for amnesty, that it now was pursuing a
"policy of reconciliation" (*politique d'apaisement*). Dortmund was
evacuated on October 20; in other regions the Franco-Belgian forces
were reduced and made as "invisible" as possible.

The German laws relative to the Dawes Plan were executed with
equal dispatch. On September 27 the German Railroad Company
came into being. Carl Friedrich von Siemens, a descendant of the

great inventor Werner von Siemens, became chairman of its board of directors; president of the company was Oeser, the national minister of transport. Both men were members of the Democratic Party. In obedience to the law Siemens resigned as Reichstag representative for Berlin; and four weeks before the deadline set at London, the Franco-Belgian authorities transferred the railways formerly under their control to the new German company. The Bank for German Industrial Debentures was founded on September 30. On October 4 the Reichsbank was reorganized: the former directors were all re-elected, and Schacht remained as chairman of the board.

All these changes took place smoothly, thereby giving, in conformance with the spirit of the Dawes Plan, a more friendly and peaceful cast to Germany's relations with the rest of the world. But on January 5, 1925, the German nation experienced an unpleasant surprise when the occupation authorities declared that they did not intend to evacuate the so-called Cologne Zone by January 10. Now, with respect to the withdrawal of the occupation of the left bank of the Rhine and of the bridgeheads, the Treaty of Versailles had stipulated that the bridgehead at Cologne and the related area should be evacuated five years after the treaty had taken effect. Since the treaty had gone into force on January 11, 1920, the deadline would have been reached on January 10, 1925. But Article 429, which contained this stipulation, began with the condition: "If the conditions of the present treaty are faithfully carried out by Germany . . ." The Allies now claimed that this prerequisite had not been met. They referred, of course, to the treaty's provisions for German disarmament. Stresemann protested immediately, and an extended exchange of notes ensued, lasting into November. In the course of this correspondence the Parisian press published an extract from the Control Commission's report on the general inspection which noted a large number of violations, particularly with respect to the so-called Five Points which had been an object of discussion since 1923. That these complaints were well founded can no longer be disputed today. But the discussion had gradually lost its vigor in the face of the diplomatic developments which led to the Treaty of Locarno. And the cessation of the Control Commission's activities had been one of this treaty's results.

The debate concerning the evacuation of the Cologne Zone was a cloud upon the political horizon. But the execution of the London Accord had strengthened world confidence in peaceful development to such an extent that the German economy experienced a brisk revival. Not only self-confidence returned, but also the confidence of foreign economic circles. This assurance had already been demonstrated in the striking success of the Dawes Loan; now the willingness of foreign bankers, especially the Americans, to grant loans to German industrial enterprises was about to give lasting proof of this faith. These men knew the enthusiasm and skill with which the German people work, and they had no doubt that the nation would quickly recover from the unfortunate plight in which it had been put by its military and political defeats and by inflation.

But the transition from a period of inflation to a state of sound currency and scarce money also entailed a number of serious problems. Many an entrepreneur and merchant who had become accustomed to enjoying unlimited credit and trifling debts had to alter his methods, indeed, even his attitude, in order to adjust to the new situation; and not everyone could make this change. Firms which had expanded recklessly during the inflation saw the bases of their existence melt away and therefore had to contract by selling off portions of their operations. If they did not make this decision soon enough, they found themselves in extremely desperate straits. The history of the once-so-envied Stinnes holdings best illustrates these dangers. Hugo Stinnes did not live to see these newer times; he had died in the spring of 1924. His heirs, who at first had carried on the family's policies of expansion, suffered enormous losses and found themselves, as early as June 1925, forced to undertake an extensive liquidation of their overextended empire. Indeed, as Stresemann noted in his diary at the time, it even appeared for a while that the family had lost all it had ever possessed.

The same causes led to the collapse of another concern, Barmat Enterprises, a company whose economic importance cannot be likened to the Stinnes holdings, but one whose fate, if only for political reasons, excited the public imagination to a much greater degree. Barmat, originally a Russian Jew, had emigrated as early as 1907 to Holland, from which place he had established close relations with several leaders of the German Social Democrats. During the war and immediately thereafter he had forwarded large quantities of food stuffs to Germany. In this enterprise he profited from the actions of political figures who were responsible for feeding the German people after the military collapse. The politicians could certainly justify their collaboration on the grounds that it was to the vital interest of their nation to import food. But the relations continued after the food imports had ceased and Barmat had turned his attention to new endeavors. Like many others, during the inflation he sought to finance his new enterprises with loans. These credits, to the extent of millions of marks, were furnished by the Bank of Prussia [*Preussische Staatsbank (Seehandlung)*] and later, indirectly, by the German Postal System from its money-order funds. Barmat was able to satisfy his creditors through early autumn 1924. But then difficulties arose with which he was less and less able to cope. The creditors refused to extend their loans; public attention was brought to the events; and official investigation was undertaken; and on December 31, 1924, Barmat and the other principals of his firm were arrested. At this, the company collapsed under a debt of something like ten million marks.

Irresponsible figures in the opposition, who, since autumn 1924, had been trying to find profit in this affair, claimed that Barmat had received these loans with the help of bribes and of pressure exerted by political friends on his behalf. Among those most severely compromised was the Centrist minister of the post, Dr. Höfle, who was responsible for the careless use to which postal funds were put. He was obliged not only to resign his office, but also to suffer imprisonment pending trial. He died in prison on April 20, 1925, under circumstances so extraordinary that the Prussian Landtag established a special committee to investigate the matter. The committee's findings cast an unflattering light upon the proceedings of the attorney general's office. The Social Democrats Bauer and Richter were compromised most severely. Bauer, who had once been Chancellor, was required by his party to resign his seat in the Reichstag for having "failed to distinguish politics from business." Richter, a former metal worker who had become an excellent commissioner of the Berlin police, was removed from his office by Severing for having lost, in his dealings with Barmat, "that sense of perspective necessary for the recognition of proper limits." [1]

So far, at any rate, one could scarcely accuse the Social Democratic Party of lacking a sense of the proprieties of public life. But opponents of the party thought they had found here an opportunity for a war of annihilation. They succeeded in having the Prussian Landtag name a committee to investigate the Barmat affair. Such investigatory committees had been introduced into German public law by the makers of the Weimar constitution in imitation of the English model. But while in England the members of a parliamentary committee generally are guided by a sense of the objective need for information, a large number of their German counterparts regarded such a committee as an instrument of demagogy and valued its open proceedings as a convenient place for casting suspicion upon their political opponents and, under the safe cover of parliamentary immunity, for impugning their reputations.

In the Barmat Committee the main target of the German Nationalists' attack was Ernst Heilmann, leader of the Social Democratic delegation in the Landtag. Heilmann was an intelligent man and an effective speaker with extraordinary rhetorical talents, but he had a challenging, almost arrogant manner of speech that irritated his opponents to the extreme — especially since they hated him already for being a Jew. He was also a brave man, ready to accept with courage the consequences of his deeds. He declined to flee to safety when Hitler assumed power; later he was tortured to death in a concentration camp by racist heroes. Heilmann was a friend of Barmat's, had advised him in business affairs, and had aided him with personal recommendations. These latter activities offended even liberal circles. Nevertheless, it could not be proved, nor is it probable, that Heilmann profited personally from these connections. Thus he was able to weather the storm that was directed against him.

But the German Nationalist demagogues had a much larger target: the President of Germany. They tried to exploit the fact that in 1919 Ebert had recommended Barmat be given a permanent visa for his many trips to Germany. Since Barmat was at that time engaged in supplying Germany with food supplies, the President clearly had every good reason to make such a recommendation. At any rate, neither this affair nor any of Barmat's activities connected with foodstuffs bore the slightest relation to the offenses of which Barmat had been accused. But the German Nationalists on the committee continually sought, by means of unfounded statements and pettifogging questions, to create suspicion against the President. This was one part of a systematic persecution which will be discussed below.

The whole Barmat affair found its denouement in a criminal case almost unique in the annals of German jurisprudence. The public trial before a jury in Central Berlin lasted well over a year. Under the direction of a judge who was as intelligent as he was impartial, all the diffuse and complex affairs of the Barmat Enterprises were examined and, so far as possible, illumined in detail. Not until March 30, 1927, was the verdict ready. Its argument, which was distinguished by its careful clarity, and which may be considered a valuable contribution to the economic history of inflation and recovery, required no less than 545 large printed pages. The formal findings bore little relationship to the popular indignation with which the proceedings had begun. The principal defendant, Julius Barmat, was found guilty of two acts of bribery and was sentenced to eleven months' imprisonment; half of the sentence had been served while awaiting trial. He was found innocent of all the other charges. This result is not to be regarded as Barmat's moral rehabilitation; on the contrary, the court made quite clear that it disapproved of many of his commercial acts. But all sense of the gross villainy with which the Barmats had been depicted for years is certainly absent from this judgment.[2]

The persecution of Ebert, which played a part in the Barmat scandal, reached its climax near the end of 1924. Both the intensity and the range of this campaign are illustrated by the fact that the President was obliged to lodge almost one hundred and fifty formal complaints of abusive and offensive language or slander. Unlike Bismarck, who boasted that he "filed these suits with practiced ease"[3] and who kept a supply of printed complaint forms ready for this very purpose, Ebert took these steps with greatest reluctance. Bismarck had used them as a weapon in his campaign of terror against political opponents, even against men like Theodor Mommsen; but to Ebert they were means of self-defense against unscrupulous persecutors and journalistic mercenaries who were deliberately trying to debase the President in the public's mind.

A certain Dr. Gansser belonged in this category. When Ebert arrived in Munich for a visit in 1922 Gansser screamed the insult "traitor" to his face. What other choice had Ebert but to file a formal complaint against the churl? In the resulting trial before the Munich court the defendant tried to justify his slander by referring to Ebert's role in the Berlin general strike of 1918. Now, this strike had been fomented by radical extremists. The Social Democratic workers, who could not escape involvement in the strike, had begged their party leaders to join the leaders of the operation. Ebert acceded to this wish only after considerable resistance on his part and only after the Social Democratic workers had insisted that the national interest required that he help lead the strike because only in this way could it be brought to a speedy close. It was in this sense, then, that Ebert served among directors of the strike. All these facts were determined in the course of the trial. But now the Munich court subpoenaed the President in order that he might give public testimony and be cross-examined by Gansser's counsel, a fevered National Socialist. Whether there was any legal basis for this affront to the President's dignity was a debated issue at that time. Shortly thereafter a law was passed according to which the President's testimony was to be taken at his office. The President's legal counsel, Wolfgang Heine, drew from the attitude of the Munich court the conclusion that Ebert would be the object of insulting attacks if he were to go there and would be deprived of the protection due his person and his rank; he had good reason for so thinking. But whether he was right in deducing further that Ebert should therefore withdraw his complaint is another question. For this decision encouraged Gansser to publish an even bolder open letter to the President, in which he accused the latter of accepting the accusation of traitor and demanded that he resign his office. When another complaint was filed against Gansser for this latest offense, he disappeared over the border. Shortly thereafter, in May 1924, the Bavarian National Socialists sent their courageous colleague to the Reichstag, thus enabling him to return to Germany under parliamentary immunity.

Gansser's triumphs served as inspiration to a certain Rothardt, who edited a Racist sheet, the *Mitteldeutsche Presse*, in Stassfurt, south of Magdeburg in Prussian Saxony. Not only did he reprint Gansser's open letter under the headline, "A Bitter Pill for Fritz Ebert," but he also added observations which corresponded to his own intellectual level, like the sentence: "Come on now, Mr. Ebert, prove that you really are not a traitor." Again the President had to lodge complaint. And again a trial had to be undertaken, this time before the *Schöffengericht* of Magdeburg.[4]

It took from December 9 to 23, 1924, to try the case. Extensive testimony was taken concerning the strike of January 1918, and depositions were made reflecting Ebert's attitude to the strike in particular as well as his position on the whole question of national defense. Any impartial evaluation can lead only to the conclusion that Ebert's position was fully justified. Nor did the court — which sentenced Rothardt to three months' imprisonment — fail to see that truth. But the court went on to find that, according to the criminal code, Ebert had committed treason in joining the strike, even though, as it hastened to add, his actions might well be judged otherwise from a political, historical, or moral point of view.

This sentence was a juridical absurdity. To argue its madness again, after all the devastating criticism which the best legal minds in Germany have directed at it, would be to carry owls to Athens. The whole idea of isolating the legal decision from political and moral considerations was an example of the worst and most unrealistic kind of conceptual jurisprudence, the kind that might well be appropriate in the "jurists' seventh heaven" at which Rudolph von Ihering liked to poke fun, but one which had no place in a political trial. After all, the defendant had not written a juridical dissertation, but rather a political pamphlet designed to ruin the President's career. The question of whether the judge who heard the case let himself be influenced by his political prejudices need not be treated here. But there can be no doubt of the fact that he was in no way master of his task. It was unfortunate that a shortcoming of German law brought cases of this sort before judges hardly qualified for such a task and who only in exceptional cases possessed the force of character and breadth of vision demanded by such a situation. No bar examination, however brilliantly passed, can guarantee such special qualities.

That Ebert was no traitor, that he had done his full, patriotic duty in the war which cost him two sons — these were truths no serious man, whatever his political shading, could doubt so long as he retained any trace of a sense of responsibility. But because the local judge in Magdeburg had ruled that Ebert was a traitor, every unscrupulous Nationalist orator and journalist could repeat the insult with impunity. The German Nationalist deputy who had been elected vice-president of the Reichstag, Gräf-Thüringen, even went so far as to excuse himself with a reference to the Magdeburg decision from the customary call of the Reichstag leaders upon the President.

On the other hand, there was also something approaching an organized force of decent men. On December 24, the day after the verdict had been given, the national cabinet took the unusual step of calling upon Ebert in order to deliver to him a formal statement expressing their common conviction, without regard to party, that his activities had always been designed to advance the interests of the German fatherland. Numerous state and municipal governments expressed the same conviction. A declaration was published at Heidelberg over the signatures of such eminent scholars as Wilhelm Kahl, Heinrich Herkner, Gerhart Anschütz, and Friedrich Meinecke. In an open letter to the President, Hans Delbrück and such friends as Walter Goetz, Theodor Heuss, and Helene Lange expressed their satisfaction at "seeing a person to whom our nation owes so much still at its head."

Such expressions of sympathy from the best sort of Germans served to soften the blow which Ebert felt. But he suffered, nonetheless, indescribable pain. Day and night he was tortured by thoughts of the bitter injustice that had been done him. He had, of course, immediately appealed the Magdeburg verdict. But months would pass before the higher court could speak. Meanwhile, all the attacks and taunts in the Barmat Committee continued. Noske tells us that "Friedrich Ebert was literally scourged to death by the shameful persecution which, during his final illness, he was forced to suffer at the hands of an egregiously vulgar press . . . [He was] forced to fight for his honor. Ebert was unable to follow soon enough the emphatic advice of his physicians that he submit to clinical treatment. Exposed every day to further attacks in the Barmat Committee, he remained, racked with pain, at his post." [5] In mid-February, when he finally accepted the demands of his physicians and submitted to an operation, it was too late. The appendicitis and peritonitis had progressed too far. Ebert, only fifty-four years old, died a few days after the operation.

Thus died the first President of the Weimar Republic, a man who had led his nation through six bitter years of threats and pressures from abroad and fratricidal politics at home. Even though one cannot count him among those great statesmen who will always be remembered in history, one may certainly give him credit for accomplishing, as well as was humanly possible, the infinitely difficult task that was placed before him. He had been required to resurrect a state from utter collapse, to lead a people back to peace and order after five years of war and months of civil strife, and to preserve the unity of the nation against self-seeking centrifugal forces. After the revolutionary events that took place in the winter of 1918–1919, this task could fall only to a Social Democrat; and the entire German people should have thanked Providence for giving them in Ebert a Social Democrat who, without ever betraying the ideals of his youth, aimed his official actions at one goal alone: the service of all Germany and all Germans. But how devoid of such a sense of gratitude were his fellow countrymen! Journalists who called themselves nationalists exercised their dull wit on the former "saddlemaker" or "barkeeper"; and many members of the middle class, having overcome their first fears of revolution, enjoyed these boorish jests instead of taking pride in their nation's ability to produce from the ranks of common people a man with so much political perspective, ripe wisdom, and moral decency. In Ebert's unassuming dignity they had missed the brilliant glory of the Empire without considering what that glitter had cost the German people and without thinking how much greater and stronger a man's character must be if he is to stand at the head of a nation which has lost all hope of triumph and which can look forward, at best, only to escaping or softening grave humiliations at the conquerors' hands.

Nor were bourgeois circles by any means the only groups offended by Ebert's humble background and simple manner. Such attitudes became evident even in labor groups. The dissident workers were not just those radicals who hated Ebert the "socialistic patriot" or even "the traitor to his class." Many ordinary workers had no special respect for this man who, after all, had once been one of them. Their attitude is illustrated in a painful incident recorded by Severing in his memoirs. Ebert had come to Wilhelms-haven to watch the launching of one of Stinnes' ships which was to be named in honor of the old labor leader, Karl Legien. Severing recalls regretfully that the shipyard workers, instead of hailing their President with cheers, greeted him with stony silence and ignored him as he passed along their ranks. Stresemann probably diagnosed this apathy correctly in a later conversation with Lord d'Abernon, in which he argued that "the ordinary people have no affection for Ebert; only the intellectuals are for him. In these latter circles, whenever I mention his name it is met with universal approval . . . The truth is, the Germans do not want a president in a top hat . . . He has to wear a uniform and chestful of medals. When they see as their leader a man who wears a top hat and who looks as though he might have been a neighbor, then each thinks to himself: 'I could do that too.'" [6] Men of truly democratic heart were rare in the German Republic.

The officers of the Reichswehr were, of course, even less pleased at having, as the commander-in-chief of the German Army, a mere civilian who was too short to qualify for private in the imperial guards. But mention must also be made here of the fact that those officers whose duties put them in closer contact with the President came to honor him highly. This was particularly true of General von Seeckt, whose haughty, critical spirit found few it could respect.

It is not merely sad, it is disgusting, that a man like Ebert was made the object of a systematic persecution by certain Germans who sought to blacken his character and rob him of his fellow citizens' respect. This campaign of hate had a single, transparent aim: the persecutors wished to make Ebert's re-election impossible. They therefore tried to make people believe that Ebert was hanging onto his office, seeking ways to avoid the popular election required by the constitution. In truth it had been Ebert who constantly had pressed for such a vote while the parties, for perfectly honorable reasons, had extended his term of office by law to July 1, 1925, a day he did not live to see. There can be no doubt that his chances for re-election, formerly quite good, were hurt by this postponement. One can even assume that Ebert himself stopped counting on a second term. He probably planned, instead, to devote himself to leading and reorganizing the Social Democratic Party, educating it from a passive attitude in the face of popular trends to a more purposeful and realistic political program. When death struck this task from his hands, the loss was not his party's alone, but all Germany's.

The realization that Germany had suffered a heavy loss dawned upon large portions of the nation immediately after Ebert's death. All whose hearts were not hardened by political prejudice were impressed by the funeral ceremonies, at which Chancellor Luther, Prussian Premier Marx, and Reichstag President Löbe found fitting, moving words. His mortal remains were buried in his native city, Heidelberg, and the president of Baden, Dr. Hellpach, prophesied at the interment that the moving finger on the wall would write flaming warnings to any successor who should leave the path that Ebert had set.

Having buried its first president, the German people faced the task of ensuring that he would not also be the last to be directed by an inner sense of identification with the Republic. For the Weimar constitution had given the nation as a whole the mission of choosing its president through direct, universal, and equal suffrage. Between the death of Ebert and the new election the functions of the president were carried out by the chief justice of the Supreme Court, Dr. Walter Simons, former minister of foreign affairs.

Those, like Max Weber, who had succeeded in instituting the popular election of the president had imagined that outstanding public figures would stand for the office, men whose names would have a national ring far beyond the limits of any single party. But now, when their theory was to be put to the test, it became apparent that German public life was extraordinarily devoid of men of such stature. This poverty afflicted the Social Democrats as much as the so-called bourgeois parties. For a few days Gessler was considered as a common candidate of several moderate parties. The minister of defense could count on sympathy in Rightist circles, for he had defended the interests of the Army with great skill. On the other hand, he was a member of the Democratic Party, and therefore, in spite of the attacks he suffered from members of his own party, there was no reason to doubt his sincere acceptance of the Republic. He was acceptable to the Center because he was a Catholic; to the liberals, because he was liberal. He had, moreover, personal qualities which would have made him a strong candidate, particularly the ability to attract and inspire followers. But the candidacy ran aground on Stresemann's misgivings.[7] He reminded the Centrist deputy Fehrenbach that according to Hoesch, the German ambassador to Paris, Gessler would meet with even stronger objections there than would some Rightist figure. Subsequent events give good reason to believe that Gessler's disadvantages were not as great as Stresemann believed. But at that time his doubts were respected, and Gessler's candidacy was not proposed.

The several parties, therefore, had no choice but to propose their separate candidates. The Social Democrats nominated Otto Braun; the Center, Wilhelm Marx; the Rightists, Dr. Jarres, mayor of Duisburg, minister of interior under Stresemann and Marx, and a member of the People's Party. But even Jarres' joint candidacy was supported only by the People's Party and the German Nationalists, since the Bavarian People's Party had nominated their premier, Heinrich Held; and the National Socialists, Ludendorff. The Democratic Party proposed the president of Baden, Dr. Hellpach. An extraordinarily brilliant orator, he could stir the impressionable while satisfying the sophisticated. But in other respects, as his memoirs show, he lacked many of the qualities demanded by such a high position. And lastly there was the Communists' candidate, Reichstag delegate Ernst Thälmann. Thus the German people had seven men from which to choose. As was to be expected, no candidate achieved the required majority on the first ballot: Braun received 7.8 million votes; Marx, almost 4; Hellpach, 1.5; while Jarres succeeded in gathering 10.7. The Communist won 1.8 million; Held, almost 1 million; and Ludendorff, only 200,000. And so another round of voting was required.

The law (of May 4, 1920) for the election of the president contained two provisions — both borrowed from the French — concerning the second ballot: the majority, necessary for a first-ballot victory, was lessened to a simple plurality; and new nominations could be made. The second ballot was, therefore, by no means a run-off election in the sense of the prewar Reichstag campaigns. It was designed, rather, to force compromise among the parties. The moderates responded to the exigencies of the situation by withdrawing the candidacies of Braun and Hellpach and concentrated their support behind Marx as the single candidate of the *Volksblock*. If they could succeed in transferring all of Braun's and Hellpach's support to Marx, the latter's victory was assured. The Rightists realized that Jarres had no chance against this alliance, for the mayor of Duisburg was in no sense a national figure. In their quest for a national figure the leaders of the Right hit upon Field Marshal von Hindenburg, then living in retirement in Hanover. To be sure, he was almost 78 years old by this time; he had never concerned himself with politics; and he was no better acquainted with the realities of political process than was any other retired officer. His ideas belonged to a world that had irrevocably disappeared, and he considered himself utterly unfitted for the office of president. But he possessed a great name, one that was connected with the most glorious German memories of the World War. And this was the only consideration in the minds of the architects of his candidacy. Their principal spokesman was Admiral von Tirpitz, who succeeded in overcoming Hindenburg's initial resistance and in wresting from him, in a conversation on April 7, 1925, a formal agreement to run.

What did the foreign minister say to all this? Did not the doubts which he had raised concerning Gessler as a candidate apply even more strongly to Hindenburg? Did he not have every reason to have far more fear for the prospects of his conciliatory policy toward France if Germany were to be led not by its republican minister of defense but by a royalist general whom the whole world regarded as the embodiment of Prussian militarism? Stresemann's personal papers indicate that he certainly was not delighted by the choice. His ambassadors reported truthfully that Hindenburg's candidacy had made a "catastrophic" impression in other countries; a "very disturbing" cable from Maltzan in Washington troubled him especially. And he noted with evident relief that the candidacy had been received quite coolly, if not critically, by important groups of moderates.[8] Nevertheless, he could not bring himself to oppose the candidacy, and thus ruin it, by showing, with all the authority of his office, how Hindenburg's election would injure Germany's relations to the world. In an article for his newspaper Stresemann veritably danced on eggs trying to demonstrate that the choice of president would determine neither Germany's form of government nor its foreign policy. In the literal sense this was, of course, quite true. But it is equally true that Hindenburg's election was certain to encourage and strengthen those Germans who opposed both the Republic and international amity.

At any rate, Hindenburg was elected president on April 26, 1925. He received 14.6 million votes; Marx, 13.7; while Thälmann had to content himself with 1.9. Hindenburg had been unable to win an absolute majority; but the law did not require one. It is at once both ironic and fitting that it was the Communists who, because of their hopeless insistence on Thälmann's candidacy, put Hindenburg into office. If only half the Communists had voted for Marx, Hindenburg would have lost. It may well be that the Communist dialectic contains a formula which dissolves every distinction between a republican judge and a royalist general. But subsequent historical developments have shown that the difference was truly great, even when regarded solely from the worker's point of view.

Another partial explanation for the astonishing result of the election was the Protestant prejudice against a representative of the Catholic, clerical Center Party. In many parts of Germany there were numerous Protestant voters who, although otherwise quite liberal, wished under no circumstances to see an outspoken Catholic at their head. This is one of the undercurrents of popular feeling which confront coalition candidates of different parties in any popular election. The counterparts to these liberal Protestants were the devout Bavarian voters, who were quite united with their fellow Catholic Marx on all issues related to the Church, but who could not bring themselves to support a man linked to the hated Socialists of Berlin. And even that reactionary wolf in Centrist clothing, Franz von Papen, who suffered this same fear of Socialists, boasts in his memoirs, without blushing, that he betrayed his party in favor of the general — without, of course, resigning the seat in the Prussian diet which he owed to the Center.

But these are mere details. The important result of this election was the discovery that republicans comprised a minority in the German Republic. It was clearly of vital necessity to the new state that it have at its head a man who believed in it. The German people, however, had just elected to this post a man without the slightest bond to this new state, a man who, on the contrary, had always been proud to be a loyal servant of his king, who clung with all his heart to the monarchy of old, and who would have counted that day the happiest of his life on which he might return his powers to the hands of some Hohenzollern monarch. For Hindenburg was tortured by a fact known only to his intimates: on November 9, 1918, he had urged his Emperor and King to flee to Holland. Neither the loyal Prussian monarchists nor William II himself could forgive him that. This is the reason that Hindenburg had taken such great pains to cast a heavy veil around his activities that fateful day, so as to hide them from the German people. The faithful Gröner was, of course, prepared to take all responsibility upon himself. But this was no help in Hindenburg's private struggle with his conscience. And the memory of that hour continued to occupy and to disturb his mind without cease, even, if we are to believe Professor Sauerbruch, to the last days of his life.

All this, of course, is not to say that Hindenburg would have been willing to misuse his office to help effect a restoration of the monarchy. He was kept from doing so by his reverence for the oath which he had sworn as President to uphold and defend the constitution and to which he, as a God-fearing man, considered himself bound. Nevertheless, it could only hurt the Republic to have as its chief of state a man who was politically, socially, and emotionally linked to its bitterest enemies and who found personal insult in its very flag. A new form of government needs time and careful cultivation if it is to take firm root in the minds and habits of the people. It needs this special care all the more if it is born in defeat and is obliged to forswear fame for many years. But how could this care be given the German Republic if its new mentor and leader did not believe in it?

There is, to be sure, no reason to assume that all the men and women who voted for Hindenburg wished thereby to express their preference for the monarchy over the Republic. What really helped the former field marshal of the Emperor was the yearning of countless thousands for the return of a time when they had felt happy and which they could not bring themselves to admit had passed away. The present was so unpleasant, while the past, with its peace, its prosperity, and its feeling of security, appeared in restrospect even more glittering and attractive than it really had been. The voters gave expression to this longing by electing a man who belonged completely to this golden yesterday. Theirs was a feeling stronger than all the logical arguments that one could bring against it. And to this extent this German presidential election formed an exact parallel to the French election of December 10, 1848, from which Louis Napoleon emerged as victor, to the astonishment and horror of all who had convinced themselves that people are guided by reason.

On the other hand, one dare not overlook the fact that a vigorous and powerful reactionary movement in political writings had arisen and was sympathetically received by literate Germans. Oswald Spengler can serve as the best-known representative of this school. In his *Decline of the West*, the first volume of which appeared in 1918, the year of Germany's defeat, he had made the grand attempt to construct a morphology of cultures that would span all human history.[9] And, because of the brilliance of his style and the dazzling boldness of his theories, he had achieved significant success, despite the many errors and distortions the experts were able to point out. The very title of the book had helped its sales; the title had, of course, been hit upon before the war, but it corresponded perfectly to the mood of many Germans after catastrophe had struck. Now Spengler was not just a philosopher of history; he was also a politician. And the fame which he had won with his *Decline of the West* accrued to his political tracts as well, however clearly — as Ernst Troeltsch remarked at the time — they may have shown "the danger of interpretive reporting" (*die Gefahr des Feuilletonismus*).[10] These tracts are in truth full of the most arbitrary statements, the most bizarre constructions, and the most reckless generalities, all of which, however, impressed the uninformed reader, who found all the more comfort in the burden of their message. When a man like Spengler labeled the Revolution of 1918 the work of "freed convicts, writers, deserters, who wandered about . . . roaring and thieving, deposing, ruling, beating, writing" (in the tract *Prussianism and Socialism*, which he composed in 1919); when he described it, in short, as "the most stupid and cowardly revolution in world history, the one most devoid of honor and ideas," he impressed at least those Germans who were dissatisfied with their new rulers. And thus they became all the more receptive to his dithyrambs in honor of Prussianism, which he celebrated as Germany's only constructive force, indeed, as its true socialism. How well must such a message have set the stage for Hindenburg, the symbolic embodiment of Prussian spirit!

But Spengler is only one of the many who later were understood to have fought for the "conservative revolution." [11] Among the others, at least Arthur Möller van den Bruck warrants mention here, if only because the title of his publication in 1923, "The Third Reich," has become a familiar phrase. This entire school was more given to criticism than to positive help with the reconstruction of Germany. But in this situation negative criticism was both effective and successful.

The presidential election was also a triumph of revived militarism. Hindenburg was not only the field marshal of the World War; he was also one of the inventors and the first effective propagator of the legend of the undefeated Germany Army and of the "stab in the back" which had betrayed it to the foe. With his election this myth was made an official dogma of the German state. Millions of his supporters hoped thus to rehabilitate the field-grey army and to pronounce their repentance for having temporarily strayed from time-honored ideals. Thus it was that many a German voted for Hindenburg, not although, but rather because, the world could see in him the symbol of the old Germany that "in glittering armor" had shouted defiance to the world. And if the French wished to see in this forebodings of a future war of revenge, many a Hindenburg supporter would have answered that the Germans had as much right to plan on one as had the French after their defeat of 1870.

But was not Hindenburg also the symbol of Germany's defeat in 1918? Had he not hoisted the white flag on September 29, when, along with Ludendorff, he demanded the immediate conclusion of an armistice? Ah, but he had not signed the formal armistice at Compiègne; Erzberger had done that, and Erzberger had been murdered by German nationalists. So there was no more point in worrying about such details as the telegram of November 10, in which Hindenburg had told Erzberger that even if the Germans could not gain their conditions, they would have to accept an armistice anyway. And who was now to know that at Spa the field marshal, with tears in his eyes, had begged Erzberger to undertake the trip to Compiègne for the sake of the fatherland? [12]

Now those Germans were satisfied who, to quote Stresemann

again, had been yearning for "a man in uniform . . . with a chest-ful of medals." They had a man with the build of Roland, the giant before the Bremen town hall; a man whose wooden statue in the Königsplatz in Berlin had been studded with good-luck nails by countless admirers during the war; a man whose face seemed immune to joy and pain alike and whose deep voice reminded one of a Wagnerian hero. Now the Army, perhaps not to General von Seeck's delight, had a commander-in-chief whom it could regard as one of its own. What did it matter to them if the President of Germany were totally unfamiliar with the civilian problems of politics that he was obliged to face? Or if, as Stresemann was soon to discover, he were too old and too lethargic to concern himself with these problems? Such things were the business of the Reichstag politicians. And the politicians were respected very little by the Hindenburg supporters — when, indeed, they were not explicitly damned as "lackeys of the Barmat brothers." The wave of filth stirred up by the German nationalist and racist demagogues had achieved its purpose.

No matter how Hindenburg might comport himself in the immediate future, his election as president of Germany was a triumph of nationalism and militarism and a heavy defeat for the Republic and parliamentary government.

SUMMARY OF THE REICH GOVERNMENTS
1919—1925

1. *Scheidemann* (Social Democrats): February 13, 1919, to June 21, 1919.
   Social Democrats: Landsberg, Bauer, Noske, David, and others.
   Center: Erzberger, Giesberts, Bell.
   Democrats: Preuss, Schiffer, Gothein, Dernberg.
   In addition: von Brockdorff-Rantzau (Foreign Office).

2. *Bauer* (Social Democrats): to March 27, 1920.
   Social Democrats: H. Müller, David, Noske, and others.
   Center: Erzberger (Finance), Giesberts, Bell, Meyer-Kaufbeuren.
   Democrats, from November 2, 1919: Koch (Interior), Schiffer (Justice),
      Gessler (Reconstruction).

3. *Hermann Müller* (Social Democrats): to June 21, 1920.
   Social Democrats: David, Robert Schmidt, Schlicke, Bauer, Köster (For-
      eign Office).
   Center: Wirth (Finance), Giesberts, Bell, Hermes.
   Democrats: Koch, Gessler (Defense), Blunck.

4. *Fehrenbach* (Center): to May 10, 1921.
   Center: Wirth, Giesberts, Hermes.
   Democrats: Koch, Gessler.
   People's Party: Heinze, Scholz, von Raumer.
   In addition: Simons (Foreign Office), Gröner (Transport).

5. *Wirth* (Center): First cabinet, to October 26, 1921.
   Center: Brauns, Giesberts, Hermes.
   Social Democrats: Bauer, Gradnauer (Interior), R. Schmidt.
   Democrats: Schiffer, Gessler, Rathenau (Reconstruction).
   In addition: Rosen (Foreign Office), Gröner.

6. *Wirth* (Center): Second cabinet, to November 22, 1922.
   Center: Brauns, Giesberts, Hermes.
   Social Democrats: Bauer, Köster (Interior), Radbruch (Justice), R.
      Schmidt.
   Democrats: Gessler, Rathenau (Foreign Office, from January 31, 1922,
      to July 24, 1922).
   In addition: Gröner.

7. *Cuno*: to August 13, 1923.
   Center: Hermes, Brauns.
   Democrats: Oeser (Interior), Gessler.
   People's Party: Becker (Economics), Heinze.
   Bavarian People's Party: Stingl.
   In addition: Gröner, Luther (Food), Albert, Rosenberg (Foreign Office).

8. *Stresemann* (People's Party): First cabinet, to October 6, 1923.
   People's Party: von Raumer (Economics).
   Center: Brauns, Höfle, Fuchs.
   Social Democrats: R. Schmidt, Sollmann (Interior), Hilferding (Finance), Radbruch.
   Democrats: Oeser, Gessler.
   In addition: Luther.

9. *Stresemann* (People's Party): Second cabinet, to November 30, 1923.
   People's Party: Jarres (Interior, from November 11).
   Social Democrats: R. Schmidt, Sollmann, Radbruch to November 3.
   Center: Brauns, Höfle, Fuchs.
   Democrats: Oeser, Gessler.
   In addition: Luther (Finance), Koeth, von Kanitz.

10. *Marx* (Center): First cabinet, to June 3, 1924.
    Center: Brauns, Höfle.
    People's Party: Stresemann (Foreign Office), Jarres.
    Democrats: Oeser, Gessler, Hamm (Economics).
    Bavarian People's Party: Emminger (Justice).
    In addition: Luther (Finance), von Kanitz.

11. *Marx* (Center): Second cabinet, to January 15, 1925.
    Center: Brauns, Höfle (to January 9, 1925).
    People's Party: Stresemann, Jarres.
    Democrats: Oeser, Gessler, Hamm.
    In addition: Luther, von Kanitz.

12. *Luther*: First cabinet, to January 20, 1926.
    German Nationalists: Schiele (Interior), von Schlieben (Finance), Neuhaus to October 20, 1925.
    People's Party: Stresemann, Krohne.
    Center: Brauns, Frenken (Justice, to November 21, 1925).
    Bavarian People's Party: Stingl.
    Democrats: Gessler.
    In addition: von Kanitz.

NOTES

Bibliographical Note

The best survey of the literature for this period is given in the catalogue of the Wiener Library in London, 19, Manchester Square: "From Weimar to Hitler, Germany 1918–1933." Later additions are published in the literature surveys in the quarterly bulletin of the library. I welcome this opportunity to thank Dr. Alfred Wiener and his colleagues for their constant cooperation. Of general accounts of the period I cite the following:

Ferdinand Friedensburg, *Die Weimarer Republik* (Berlin, 1946).

Arthur Rosenberg, *Geschichte der Deutschen Republik* (Karlsbad, 1935). English translation: *A History of the German Republic* (London, 1936).

Friedrich Stampfer, *Die ersten 14 Jahre der Deutschen Republik* (Offenbach-Main, 1936).

Paul Merker, *Deutschland — Sein oder Nicht Sein?* (Mexico, 1944).

S. William Halperin, *Germany Tried Democracy* (New York, 1946).

Godfrey Scheele, *The Weimar Republic, Overture to the Third Reich* (London, 1946).

Carl Misch, *Deutsche Geschichte im Zeitalter der Massen von des Französischen Revolution bis zur Gegenwart* (Stuttgart, 1952), chapters vi through viii.

Abundant material is offered in Cuno Horkenbach, ed., *Das Deutsche Reich von 1918 bis Heute* (Berlin, 1930), with supplements for 1931 and 1932.

NOTES

In the following citations, in most cases in which both British and American editions are given the pagination is that of the British edition.

CHAPTER I: The Collapse of the Monarchy

1. Bernard Schwertfeger, ed., *Rudolf von Valentini: Kaiser und Kabinettschef* (Oldenburg, 1931), p. 226.
2. Eugen Schiffer, *Ein Leben für den Liberalismus* (Berlin-Grunewald, 1951), p. 129.
3. Germany, Official Documents. *Untersuchungsausschuss über die Weltkriegsverantwortlichkeit. 4. Unterausschuss, Die Ursachen des Deutschen Zusammenbruches im Jahre 1918. Vierte Reihe im Werk des Untersuchungsausschusses. Unter Mitwirkung von Dr. Eugen Fischer . . . Dr. Walter Bloch . . . im Auftrage des Vierten Unterausschusses hrsg. von Dr. Albrecht Phillip . . .* (12 vols. in 15 pts., Berlin, 1925–1929), vol. II, pt. 1, p. 105 (Hobohm). Hereafter cited as *UDZ*. English abridged translation: Ralph H. Lutz, ed., *The Causes of the German Collapse in 1918* (Stanford, Calif.–London, 1934).
4. *Ibid.*, p. 107, note 1.
5. Erich Eyck, *Bismarck: Leben und Werk* (3 vols., Zürich, 1941–1944), I, 369. English abridged translation: *Bismarck and the German Empire* (London, 1950).
6. Karl von Wiegand, *Frankfurter Zeitung*, November 14, 1926.
7. Schwertfeger, *Valentini*, p. 245.
8. Theobald von Bethmann Hollweg, *Betrachtungen zum Weltkrieg* (2 vols., Berlin, 1919–1921), II, 128. English translation: *Reflections on the World War* (1 vol. in 2 pts., London, 1920). Gothein *UDZ*, vol. VII, pt. 2, p. 313.
9. Germany, Official Documents. *Untersuchungsausschuss über die Weltkriegsverantwortlichkeit. Zweiter Unterausschuss des Untersuchungsausschusses der Nationalversammlung* (Berlin, 1920). Enclosure 3, p. 186. English translation: *Official German Documents Relating to the World War: The Reports of the First and Second Subcommittees of the Committee Appointed by the National Constituent Assembly To Inquire into the Responsibility for the War, together with the Stenographic Minutes of the Second Subcommittee and Supplements Thereto* (2 vols., New York–London, 1923).
10. Ottokar Czernin, *Im Weltkrieg* (Berlin–Wien, 1919), p. 163.
11. *Zweiter Unterausschuss* (see note 9), p. 213.
12. *Ibid.*, p. 214.
13. Bethmann Hollweg, *Betrachtungen*, II, 131.
14. Friedrich Meinecke, *Strassburg, Freiburg, Berlin, 1901–1919; Erinnerungen* (Stuttgart, 1949), p. 247.
15. *UDZ*, vol. VII, pt. 1, p. 233.
16. Bethmann Hollweg, *Betrachtungen*, II, 191.

17. *UDZ*, VI, 232.

18. Karl Helfferich, *Der Weltkrieg* (3 vols., Berlin, 1919), III, 111. *Der Erzberger-Prozess. Stenographischer Bericht über die Verhandlung im Beleidigungsprozess des Reichsfinanzministers gegen den Staatsminister, a. D. Dr. Karl Helfferich* (Berlin, 1920), p. 703.

19. Richard von Kühlmann, *Erinnerungen* (Heidelberg, 1948), p. 492. *UDZ*, vol. VII, pt. 2, p. 92.

20. *UDZ*, vol. VII, pt. 1, p. 384; vol. VII, pt. 2, 167.

21. Conrad Haussmann, *Schlaglichter; Reichstagbriefe und Aufzeichnungen* (Frankfurt am Main, 1924), p. 102.

22. *Erzberger-Prozess*, p. 727.

23. *Ibid.*, p. 712.

24. Bethmann Hollweg, *Betrachtungen*, II, 226.

25. (Oberst) Bauer, *Der Grosse Krieg in Feld und Heimat* (Tübingen, 1921), p. 184.

26. *UDZ*, I, 153.

27. Erich Ludendorff, *Meine Kriegserinnerungen, 1914–1918* (Berlin, 1919), p. 363. English translation: *My War Memoirs, 1914–1918* (London, 1919) or *Ludendorff's Own Story, August 1914–November 1918* (New York, 1919). *UDZ*, II, 31.

28. Kühlmann, *Erinnerungen*, p. 502.

29. Haussmann, *Schlaglichter*, p. 129.

30. *UDZ*, vol. VII, pt. 2, p. 390.

31. Friedrich Meinecke, "Kühlmann und die päpstliche Friedensaktion von 1917," *Preussische Akademie der Wissenschaften*, 1928, XVII.

32. Kühlmann, *Erinnerungen*, p. 475.

33. *UDZ*, vol. IV, pt. 2, p. 125.

34. Erich Ludendorff, ed., *Urkunden der Obersten Heeresleitung, über ihre Tätigkeit, 1916–1918* (Berlin, 1920), p. 428.

35. *Ibid.*, p. 434. *UDZ*, VIII, 139 (Bredt).

36. *Ibid.*, p. 140.

37. *UDZ*, vol. IV, pt. 2, p. 131. Kühlmann, *Erinnerungen*, p. 483.

38. *UDZ*, vol. VII, pt. 2, pp. 28, 94.

39. *UDZ*, VIII, 135. *Urkunden OHL*, p. 425.

40. *UDZ*, VIII, 76.

41. *UDZ*, vol. VII, pt. 2, pp. 127, 129.

42. John W. Wheeler-Bennett, *Brest Litovsk: The Forgotten Peace* (New York–London, 1938), p. 37.

43. *UDZ*, II, 46, 70.

44. Schwertfeger, *Valentini*, pp. 185, 187, 190.

45. Kühlmann, *Erinnerungen*, p. 516.

46. Haussmann, *Schlaglichter*, pp. 184, 185.

47. *UDZ*, II, 136.

48. *Ibid.*, p. 92.

49. *Ibid.*, p. 142.

50. *Ibid.*, p. 337.

51. *Ibid.*, p. 184.

52. General Max Hoffmann, *Die Aufzeichnungen des General-Majors Max Hoffmann* (2 vols, Berlin, 1929–1930), II, 226. *UDZ*, III, 309 (Delbrück).

53. *UDZ*, II, 191.

54. *Ibid.*, p. 339.

55. *Ibid.*, p. 387.
56. David Lloyd George, *War Memoirs* (6 vols., Boston–London, 1933–1937), VI, 3382, 3423.
57. *UDZ*, II, 223.
58. *Ibid.*, p. 225.
59. *Ibid.*, p. 390.
60. *UDZ*, VIII, 285.
61. Karl von Hertling, *Ein Jahr in der Reichskanzlei; Erinnerungen an die Kanzlerschaft meines Vaters* (Freiburg im Breisgau-Berlin, 1919), p. 176. Friedrich Payer, *Von Bethmann Hollweg bis Ebert* (Frankfurt am Main, 1923), p. 82.
62. *UDZ*, II, 400, 405.
63. Max von Baden, *Erinnerungen und Dokumente* (Stuttgart, 1927), pp. 331, 336. English translation: *Memoirs* (2 vols., New York, 1928).
64. *Ibid.*, pp. 338, 346.
65. *Amtliche Urkunden zur Vorgeschichte des Waffenstillstandes* (Berlin, 1919), pp. 194, 199.
66. Max von Baden, *Erinnerungen*, p. 500.
67. *Urkunden . . . des Waffenstillstandes*, pp. 137, 147.
68. *Ibid.*, p. 196.
69. *UDZ*, vol. XI, pts. 1 and 2.
70. Max von Baden, *Erinnerungen*, p. 499.
71. *Ibid.*, p. 518.
72. *Ibid.*, p. 573 ff.
73. *UDZ*, VI, 247.
74. Max von Baden, *Erinnerungen*, p. 592.
75. Haussmann, *Schlaglichter*, p. 267.
76. Max von Baden, *Erinnerungen*, pp. 619, 626.
77. *Urkunden . . . des Waffenstillstandes*, p. 263.

CHAPTER II: From the Revolution to the National Assembly

1. Abraham J. Berlau, *The German Social Democratic Party, 1914–1921* (New York, 1949).
2. Friedrich Stampfer, *Die ersten 14 Jahre der Deutschen Republik* (Offenbach-Main, 1936), p. 61.
3. Friedrich Meinecke, "Die Revolution. Ursachen und Tatsachen," in *Handbuch des deutschen Staatsrechts*, edited by Gerhard Anschütz and Richard Thoma (Tübingen, 1930), p. 113. Gustav Noske, *Erlebtes aus Aufstieg und Niedergang einer Demokratie* (Offenbach-Main, 1947), p. 81.
4. *Ibid.* Gustav Noske, *Von Kiel bis Kapp; zur Geschichte der deutschen Revolution* (Berlin, 1920). Albrecht Mendelssohn-Bartholdy, *The War and German Society; the Testament of a Liberal* (New Haven, Conn.–London, 1937).
5. Noske, *Kiel bis Kapp*, p. 68.
6. Winston S. Churchill, *The Aftermath* (New York–London, 1929), p. 200.
7. Noske, *Kiel bis Kapp*, p. 72.
8. Hugo Preuss, *Staat, Recht und Freiheit; aus 40 Jahren Deutscher Politik und Geschichte* (Tübingen, 1926). Walter Simons, *Hugo Preuss* (Berlin,

1930). Carl Schmitt, *Hugo Preuss* (Tübingen, 1930). Erich Eyck, "Zum Gedächtnis von Hugo Preuss," *Hilfe* (1926), p. 430.

9. Friedrich Purlitz and Sigfrid Steinberg, eds., *Deutscher Geschichtskalender 1919* (Leipzig, n.d.), pp. 259–261.

10. Lujo Brentano, *Mein Leben in Kampf um die soziale Entwicklung Deutschlands* (Jena, 1931), p. 332.

11. Eyck, *Bismarck*, II, 423.

12. Pius Dirr, *Bayrische Dokumente zum Kriegsausbruch und zum Versailler Schuldspruch* (München-Berlin, 1922). "Kriegsschuld-Lüge vor Gericht," *Süddeutsche Monatschefte* (München), XIX J., vol. II (May 1922).

13. Anton Erkelenz, ed., *Zehn Jahre Deutscher Republik; ein Handbuch für republikanische Politik* (Berlin, 1928), p. 25 ff.

Chapter III: The Weimar Constitution

1. Germany, Official Documents. *Bericht und Protokolle des 8. Ausschusses über den Entwurf einer Verfassung des Deutschen Reiches* (Berlin, No. 21 der Berichte der Nationalversammlung). Hereafter cited as *VA*.

2. *VA*, p. 275.

3. Haussmann, *Schlaglichter*, p. 292.

4. *VA*, p. 242.

5. Carl Severing, *Mein Lebensweg* (2 vols., Köln, 1950), II, 374.

6. *VA*, p. 242.

7. Friedrich Meinecke in *Liberaler Tag* (Dresden), July 1, 1928, p. 21.

8. Max Weber, *Gesammelte Politische Schriften* (München, 1921), p. 485. Karl Jaspers, *Max Weber: Deutsches Wesen im politischen Denken, im Forschen und Philosophieren* (Oldenburg, 1932), p. 30.

9. Ludwig Bamberger, *Erinnerungen* (Berlin, 1899), p. 147.

10. Willibald Apelt, *Geschichte der Weimarer Verfassung* (München, 1946), p. 377.

11. *VA*, p. 315.

12. Apelt, *Verfassung*, pp. 381, 408.

13. *VA*, p. 369.

14. Apelt, *Verfassung*, p. 298.

15. *VA*, p. 402 (Kahl).

16. Josef Hofmiller, *Revolutionstagebuch, 1918–1919* (Leipzig, 1938).

Chapter IV: The Treaty of Versailles

1. All the documents referring to the Peace Conference have been published by the American Department of State in the *Papers Relating to the Foreign Relations of the United States* (13 vols., Washington, 1942–1947) under the title of *1919, The Paris Peace Conference*. Hereafter cited as *PC*. In addition see: Harold W. G. Temperley, ed., *A History of the Peace Conference of Paris* (6 vols., London, 1920–1924). André Tardieu, *La Paix* (Paris, 1921). English translation: *The Truth about the Treaty* (Indianapolis, Ind.,– London, 1921). Ronald B. McCallum, *Public Opinion and the Last Peace* (New York–London, 1944). Thomas E. Jessop, *The Treaty of Versailles, Was it Just?* (New York–London, 1942). Alfred Cobban, *National Self-Determination* (New York–London, 1945). Geoffrey M. Gathorne-Hardy, *A Short History of International Affairs, 1920–1939* (4th ed., London, 1950), p. 17 ff.

2. Ray S. Baker, *Woodrow Wilson and World Settlement* (3 vols., Garden City, N. Y., 1922). Thomas A. Bailey, *Wilson and the Peacemakers* (2 vols., New York, 1947).

3. Georges Suarez, *Soixante années d'histoire francaise; Clemenceau* (Paris, 1932).

4. David Lloyd George, *The Truth about the Peace Treaties* (2 vols., London, 1938). Lloyd George, *The Truth about Reparations and War Debts* (Garden City, N.Y.–London, 1932). Thomas Jones, *Lloyd George* (Cambridge, Mass.–London, 1951). Arthur Salter, *Personality in Politics; Studies in Contemporary Statesmen* (London, 1947), p. 38.

5. Stephen Bonsal, *Unfinished Business* (Garden City, N.Y., 1944), p. 27 ff.

6. Suda L. Bane and Ralph Lutz, *The Blockade of Germany after the Armistice, 1918–1919* (Stanford, Calif.–London, 1942). John Maynard Keynes, "Dr. Melchior, a Defeated Enemy," in *Two Memoirs* (New York–London, 1949). Robert G. Vansittart, *Lessons of My Life* (New York–London, 1943), p. 39.

7. Edgar Stern-Rubarth, *Graf Brockdorff-Rantzau, Wanderer zwischen zwei Welten* (Berlin, 1929). Ulrich Graf von Brockdorff-Rantzau, *Dokumente und Gedanken um Versailles* (Berlin, 1925). Hajo Holborn, "Diplomats and Diplomacy in the Early Weimar Republic," in *The Diplomats*, edited by Gordon Craig and Felix Gilbert (Princeton, 1953), p. 132. Eugen Schiffer, *Ein Leben für den Liberalismus* (Berlin-Grunewald, 1951), p. 222. Moritz J. Bonn, *Wandering Scholar* (New York, 1948), p. 228.

8. Brockdorff-Rantzau, *Dokumente und Gedanken*, p. 31.

9. Wipert von Blücher, *Deutschlands Weg nach Rapallo; Erinnerungen eines Mannes aus dem zweiten Gliede* (Wiesbaden, 1951), p. 43.

10. Alma M. Luckau, *The German Delegation at the Paris Peace Conference* (New York, 1941), p. 115.

11. Heinrich von Treitschke, *Deutsche Geschichte im neunzehnten Jahrhundert* (5 vols., Leipzig, many editions), I, 621. English translation: *History of Germany in the Nineteenth Century* (6 vols., New York, 1915–1919).

12. Luckau, *German Delegation*, p. 119.

13. Lord George Riddell, *Intimate Diary of the Peace Conference and After, 1918–1923* (New York, 1934), p. 76.

14. Baker, *Wilson and World Settlement*, II, 506.

15. Gathorne-Hardy, *Short History of International Affairs*, p. 32.

16. Matthias Erzberger, *Erlebnisse im Weltkrieg* (Stuttgart, 1920), p. 369.

17. Lloyd George, *Peace Treaties*, I, 408.

18. Baker, *Wilson and World Settlement*, III, 458, 466.

19. *Ibid.*, 503.

20. Lloyd George, *Peace Treaties*, I, 711, 717.

21. Philipp Scheidemann, *Memoiren eines Sozialdemokraten* (2 vols., Dresden, 1928), II, 371. English translation: *The Making of New Germany; The Memoirs of Philipp Scheidemann* (2 vols., New York, 1929).

22. Erzberger, *Erlebnisse*, p. 371. Holborne in *Diplomats*, p. 146.

23. Scheidemann, *Memoiren*, II, 371.

24. Friedrich Payer, *Von Bethmann Hollweg bis Ebert* (Frankfurt am Main, 1923), p. 229. Erzberger, *Erlebnisse*, p. 375. *Erzberger Prozess*, p. 743. Incorrectly cited in Keynes, *Two Memoirs*, p. 69.

25. Theodor Heuss, *Friedrich Naumann; der Mann, das Werk, die Zeit* (Stuttgart, 1937), p. 694.

26. *PC*, VI, 605, 613.

27. Erzberger, *Erlebnisse*, p. 380. Payer, *Bethmann bis Ebert*, p. 300.

28. Reginald Phelps, "Aus den Groener-Dokumenten," *Deutsche Rundschau* (Gelsenkirchen), 76 J. (July 1950). Gordon Craig, "Reichswehr and National Socialism: The Policy of Groener," *Political Science Quarterly*, LXIII (June 1948).

29. Heinrich Brüning, *Deutsche Rundschau*, 70 J. (July 1947).

30. Noske, *Erlebtes aus Aufstieg und Niedergang*, p. 107.

31. Friedrich von Rabenau, ed., *Seeckt. Aus seinem Leben, 1918–1936* (Leipzig, 1940), p. 185.

32. Erzberger, *Erlebnisse*, p. 382.

33. Payer, *Bethmann bis Ebert*, p. 303.

34. Lloyd George, *Peace Treaties*, I, 690.

35. Bernard W. von Bülow, *Der Versailler Völkerbund, eine vorläufige Bilanz* (Stuttgart, 1923), p. 431.

36. Lloyd George, *Peace Treaties*, I, 705.

37. *Ibid.*, pp. 542, 521, 515.

38. *Ibid.*, p. 514.

39. Philip M. Burnett, *Reparations at the Paris Peace Conference, from the Standpoint of the American Delegation* (2 vols., New York, 1940).

40. Tardieu, *La Paix*, p. 319.

41. *Ibid.*, p. 309.

42. Etienne Mantoux, *The Carthaginian Peace or the Economic Consequences of Mr. Keynes* (New York–London, 1946), p. 105.

43. Karl Helfferich in *Neue Preussische (Kreuz-) Zeitung* (Berlin) June 2, 1919.

44. Tardieu, *La Paix*, p. 323.

45. Lloyd George, *Peace Treaties*, I, 496.

46. Baker, *Wilson and World Settlement*, II, 494.

47. *PC*, V, 27.

48. Arthur Nussbaum, *Das Ausgleichsverfahren; ein Beitrag zur Kritik des Versailler Vertrages und seiner Durchführung* (Tübingen, 1923).

49. Bülow, *Versailler Völkerbund*.

50. Eyck, *Bismarck*, I, 276.

51. *Schulthess' Europäischer Geschichtskalender*, 1919, edited by Wilhelm Stahl (2 vols, München, 1923), I, 239.

52. John Maynard Keynes, *The Economic Consequences of the Peace* (New York–London, 1920). Keynes, *A Revision of the Treaty* (New York–London, 1922). Roy F. Harrod, *The Life of John Maynard Keynes* (New York–London, 1951). Mantoux, *Carthaginian Peace*. McCallum, *Public Opinion*. Jones, *Lloyd George*, p. 177. Salter, "Keynes the Artist-Economist," in *Personality in Politics*, p. 144.

53. Keynes, *Economic Consequences*, p. 59. Mantoux, *Carthaginian Peace*, p. 102.

54. Winston S. Churchill, *World Crisis*, IV, 156.

55. Harrod, *Keynes*, p. 259.

56. Bailey, *Wilson and the Peacemakers*, vol. II.

57. James T. Shotwell, *At the Paris Peace Conference* (New York, 1937), p. 26.

58. Lloyd George, *Reparations*, p. 26.

CHAPTER V: From the Treaty to the Kapp Putsch

1. W. Prion, "Die Finanzen des Reiches," in *Handbuch der Politik*, edited by Gerhard Anschütz, Fritz Berolzheimer, and others (6 vols., Berlin–Leipzig, 1920-1926), IV, 4.

2. Karl Helfferich, *Deutschlands Volkswohlstand, 1888–1913* (Berlin, 1914), pp. 99, 141.

3. Richard Lewisohn, *Die Umschichtung der europäischen Vermögen* (Berlin, 1925), p. 10.

4. Gerhard Anschütz and Richard Thoma, eds., *Handbuch des Deutschen Staatsrechts* (2 vols., Tübingen, 1930–1932), I, 324.

5. Noske, *Kiel bis Kapp*, p. 192.

6. Germany, Official Documents. *Stenographische Berichte über die öffentliche Verhandlung des Untersuchungsausschusses. Zweiter Unterausschuss* (see Chap. I, note 9).

7. Hergt's testimony in the Jagow case: see Karl Brammer, *Verfassungsgrundlagen und Hochverrat. Nach stenographischen Verhandlungsberichten und amtlichen Urkunden des Jagow-Prozesses* (Berlin, 1922), p. 20.

8. Great Britain, Official Documents. *Documents on British Foreign Policy, 1919–1939*, edited by E. L. Woodward and R. Butler (First Series, London, 1946–), vol. III, chap. V. (Hereafter cited as *DBFP*.)

9. Josef Bischoff, *Die letzte Front* (Berlin, 1935).

10. *DBFP*, III, 245, 256.

11. Blücher, *Weg nach Rapallo*, p. 81.

12. *DBFP*, III, 213, 230, 254, 231, 253, 255.

13. Handbill of *Der Tag* (Berlin), 1919.

14. *Der Erzberger Prozess* (see Chap. I, note 18). Siegfried Löwenstein, *Der Prozess Erzberger-Helfferich; ein Rechtsgutachten* (Ulm, 1921).

15. Compare Theodor Birt's remark about Erzberger in his essay about Aristophanes, *Von Homer bis Sokrates; ein Buch über die alten Griechen* (4. Aufl., Leipzig, 1929), p. 367.

16. Brammer, *Verfassungsgrundlagen und Hochverrat*, p. 75.

17. Jacques Benoist-Méchin, *Histoire de l'Armée Allemande* (2 vols., Paris, 1936–1938), II, 80–122. English translation of Vol. I: *History of the German Army since the Armistice* (Zürich, 1939).

18. Noske, *Kiel bis Kapp*, p. 207.

19. Rabenau, *Seeckt*, p. 222.

20. Brammer, *Verfassungsgrundlagen und Hochverrat*, p. 78.

21. *Ibid.*, p. 62.

22. Rabenau, *Seeckt*, p. 219, note 3.

23. Severing, *Mein Lebensweg*, I, 258.

24. John H. Morgan, *Assize of Arms, Being the Story of the Disarmament of Germany and Her Rearmament, 1919–1939* (London, 1945; New York, 1946), p. 74.

25. Walter Frank, *Ritter von Epp; der Weg eines deutschen Soldaten* (Hamburg, 1934).

26. Walther von Lüttwitz, *Im Kampf gegen die November-Revolution* (Berlin, 1934).

27. Severing, *Mein Lebensweg*, I, 280.

28. August Winnig, *400 Tage Ostpreussen* (Dresden, 1927), p. 78.

29. Severing, *Mein Lebensweg*, I, 260, 269. Morgan, *Assize of Arms*, p. 149.

30. Arnold J. Toynbee, *Survey of International Affairs, 1920–1923* (London, 1925), p. 91.

31. Severing, *Mein Lebensweg*, I, 256.

32. Rabenau, *Seeckt*.

33. Severing, *Mein Lebensweg*, I, 262.

34. Brammer, *Verfassungsgrundlagen und Hochverrat*, p. 84.

35. Ludwig Schemann, *Wolfgang Kapp und das Märzunternehmen vom Jahre 1920, ein Wort der Sühne* (München, 1937).

CHAPTER VI: Weakness at Home and Threats from Abroad

1. Severing, *Mein Lebensweg*, I, 293.

2. Toynbee, *Survey, 1920–1923*, pp. 13, 104.

3. Karl Bergmann, *Der Weg der Reparation* (Frankfurt am Main, 1926), p. 62. English translation: *The History of Reparations* (Boston–New York–London, 1927).

4. Viscount Edgar V. d'Abernon, *An Ambassador of Peace* (3 vols., Garden City, N.Y.–London, 1929), I, 64.

5. Bonn, *Wandering Scholar*, p. 255.

6. Severing, *Mein Lebensweg*, I, 301. Rabenau, *Seeckt*, p. 249.

7. Rabenau, *Seeckt*, p. 252.

8. Bergmann, *Weg der Reparation*, p. 57.

9. G. Borsky, *The Greatest Swindle in the World. The Story of German Reparations* (London, 1942), p. 48.

10. Severing, *Mein Lebensweg*, I, 295.

11. Lloyd George speech of March 3, 1921, quoted in *International Conciliation Pamphlets*, May 1931, no. 162, p. 171.

12. d'Abernon, *Ambassador*, I, 134.

13. Bergmann, *Weg der Reparation*, p. 89.

14. d'Abernon, *Ambassador*, I, 132.

15. Severing, *Mein Lebensweg*, I, 322.

16. Francis P. Walters, *A History of the League of Nations* (2 vols., London, 1952) I, 153.

17. Benoist-Méchin, *l'Armée Allemande*, II, 182. (See Chapter V, note 17.)

18. Rabenau, *Seeckt*, p. 300.

19. Bergmann, *Weg der Reparation*, p. 104.

20. d'Abernon, *Ambassador*, I, 164, 169.

21. d'Abernon, *Ambassador*, II, 39.

22. Harry Kessler, *Walter Rathenau; sein Leben und sein Werk* (Berlin–Grunewald, 1928). Alfred Kerr, *Walter Rathenau; Erinnerungen eines Freundes* (Amsterdam, 1935). Etta (Federn–) Kohlhaas, *Walter Rathenau; sein Leben und Wirken* (Dresden, 1927). Gerhart Hauptmann, "Walter Rathenau," in *Vossische Zeitung*, September 30, 1927. Eugen Fischer-Baling, *Walter Rathenau, ein Experiment Gottes* (Berlin, 1952). Mendelssohn-Bartholdy, *The War and German Society*, p. 223. Walter Rathenau, *Gesammelte Reden* (Berlin, 1924).

23. Kessler, *Rathenau*, p. 310.

24. Gustav Radbruch, *Der innere Weg; Aufriss meines Leben* (Stuttgart, 1951), p. 159.

25. Bergmann, *Weg der Reparation*, p. 122. Keynes, *Revision of the Treaty*, p. 85.

26. Toynbee, *Survey, 1920–1923*, p. 98. Morgan, *Assize of Arms*, p. 139. *American Journal of International Law*, XIV (1920), 95; XVI (1922), 268, 674. Claud Mullins, *The Leipzig Trials* (London, 1921).

27. *Der Erzberger Mord. Dokumente menschlicher und politischer Verkommenheit* (Brühl, 1921), p. 44.

28. *Schulthess' Europäischer Geschichtskalender, 1921*, ed. by Ulrich Thürauf (2 vols., München, 1926), I, 273.

29. Walters, *League of Nations*, I, 153.

30. Schiffer, *Leben für den Liberalismus*, p. 232.

31. d'Abernon, *Ambassador*, I, 216.

32. Georges Kaeckenbeck, *The International Experiment of Upper Silesia. Study in the Working of the Upper Silesian Settlement, 1922–1937* (New York–London, 1942).

33. Severing, *Mein Lebensweg*, I, 333.

34. *Ibid.*, p. 336.

CHAPTER VII: The Murder of Rathenau and the Fall of Wirth

1. Bergmann, *Weg der Reparation*, p. 112. d'Abernon, *Ambassador*, I, 226.

2. Lloyd George, *Truth about Reparations*, 65 ff. Jacques Chastenet, *Raymond Poincaré* (Paris, 1948). Albert Lebrun, "Poincaré." *Hommes et Mondes; Revue mensuelle*, No. 42 (January 1950). Arthur Salter, *Personality in Politics*, p. 193 ff.

3. Kessler, *Rathenau*, p. 323.

4. Rathenau, *Reden*, p. 377. Jones, *Lloyd George*, p. 184.

5. d'Abernon, *Ambassador*, I, 279.

6. Rabenau, *Seeckt*, p. 316.

7. Edward Hallett Carr, *German-Soviet Relations between the Two World Wars* (Baltimore, 1951), pp. 18, 40, 55.

8. Rabenau, *Seeckt*, p. 308.

9. *Ibid.*, p. 309.

10. Blücher, *Weg nach Rapallo*, p. 149.

11. *Ibid.*, p. 161.

12. Bonn, *Wandering Scholar*, p. 269. Melchior's letter is given in Max Warburg, *Aus meinen Aufzeichnungen* (New York, 1952), p. 105.

13. Blücher, *Weg nach Rapallo*, p. 164, note.

14. Carr, *German-Soviet Relations*, p. 60.

15. Blücher, *Weg nach Rapallo*, p. 159.

16. Rabenau, *Seeckt*, p. 312 f.

17. Warburg, *Aufzeichnungen*, p. 100.

18. Bergmann, *Weg nach Rapallo*, p. 164.

19. Rathenau, *Reden*, pp. 423–437.

20. Kessler, *Rathenau*, p. 362.

21. d'Abernon, *Ambassador*, II, 46. Kessler, *Rathenau*, p. 363.

22. Karl Brammer, *Das politische Ergebnis des Rathenau-Prozesses* (Berlin, 1922).

23. Radbruch, *Der innere Weg*, p. 161.

24. Max Hirschberg and Friedrich Thimme, eds., *Der Fall Fechenbach, juristische Gutachten* (Tübingen, 1924). See also *Acht Jahre politischer Justiz; das Zuchthaus, die politische Waffe* (Berlin, 1927), p. 193.

25. Ludwig Ebermayer, *Fünfzig Jahre Dienst am Recht* (Leipzig–Zürich, 1930), p. 177.

26. Germany, Official Documents. *Entscheidungen des Reichgerichts in Zivilsachen* (Leipzig, 1880–) CXIII, 138 (April 20, 1926).

27. Blücher, *Weg nach Rapallo*, p. 168.

28. *Der Monat* (München), I (November 1948).

29. Lewinsohn, *Umschichtung der europäischen Vermögen*, p. 99.

30. Bergmann, *Weg der Reparation*, p. 195. d'Abernon, *Ambassador*, II, 127. Toynbee, *Survey, 1920–1923*, p. 185.

31. Radbruch, *Der innere Weg*, p. 168.

CHAPTER VIII: Occupation and Separatism in the Ruhr

1. Severing, *Mein Lebensweg*, I, 377. Johannes Fischart (Erich Dombrowski), *Neue Köpfe* (Berlin, 1925), p. 116. (Vol. IV of his *Das alte und das neue System.*)

2. Konrad Heiden, *Geschichte des Nationalsozialismus, die Karriere einer Idee* (Berlin, 1933), p. 108. English abridged translation: *A History of National Socialism* (New York, 1935).

3. Bergmann, *Weg der Reparation*, p. 206.

4. Heiden, *Nationalsozialismus*, p. 113.

5. Severing, *Mein Lebensweg*, I, 402.

6. *Ibid.*, I, 408.

7. Rabenau, *Seeckt*, 324.

8. Morgan, *Assize of Arms*, p. 213.

9. Rabenau, *Seeckt*, p. 324.

10. *Ibid.*, p. 342.

11. Severing, *Mein Lebensweg*, II, 117.

12. *Ibid.*, II, 130. Paul Merker, *Von Weimar zu Hitler* (Mexico City, 1944), p. 79.

13. d'Abernon, *Ambassador*, II, 305. Seydoux, *De Versailles au Plan Young* (Paris, 1932), p. 122.

14. Great Britain, Parliamentary Debates. 53 H.L.Deb. 5s. col. 804. Harold Nicolson, *Curzon: The Last Phase, 1919–1925, A Study in Post-War Diplomacy* (Boston–New York–London, 1934), p. 363.

15. d'Abernon, *Ambassador*, II, 203.

16. Bergmann, *Weg der Reparation*, p. 240.

17. d'Abernon, *Ambassador*, II, 219.

18. Rabenau, *Seeckt*, p. 348.

19. *Handbuch der deutschen Staatsrechts*, I, 280. (See Chapter V, note 4.)

20. Radbruch, *Der innere Weg*, p. 171. Severing, *Mein Lebensweg*, I, 430.

21. Max Springer, *Loslösungsbestrebungen am Rhein, 1918–1924* (Berlin, 1924). *Die separatistischen Umtriebe in den besetzen Gebieten* (Berlin, 1924). Germany, Official Documents. *Urkunden über die Machenschaften zur Abtrennungen des Rheinlands* (Berlin, 1924). (Collected by the National Ministry for the Occupied Districts.)

22. *Bayerisch-Deutsch oder Bayerisch-Französisch?* (München, 1923).

23. d'Abernon, *Ambassador*, II, 227.

24. Lutz von Schwerin-Krosigk, *Es geschah in Deutschland; Menschenbilder unseres Jahrhunderts* (Tübingen, 1951), p. 80.

25. Gustav Stresemann, *Vermächtnis, der Nachlass*, edited by Henry Bernhard, Wolfgang Goetz and Paul Wiegler (3 vols., Berlin, 1932). Hereafter cited

as Stresemann, *Vermächtnis*. English translation: *Diaries, Letters and Papers* (3 vols., New York, 1935–1940). Rudolf Olden, *Stresemann* (Berlin, 1929). English translation: *Stresemann* (New York, 1930). Antonia Vallentin, *Stresemann; vom Werden einer Staatsidee* (Leipzig, 1930; reference below is to the 1948 edition). English translation, *Stresemann* (New York, 1931). F. G. Hirsch, "Stresemann in Historical Perspective," *Review of Politics*, XV (July 1953).

26. Great Britain, Official Documents. *Parliamentary Papers, 1923. Miscellaneous No. 5, Cmd. 1943.* "Correspondence with the Allied Governments respecting Reparations Payments by Germany," XXV, 319 f.

27. France, Official Documents (Ministère des affaires étrangères). *Documents diplomatiques. Réponse du gouvernement français à la lettre du gouvernement britannique du 11 août 1923 sur les réparations* (Paris, 1923). Issued as a Yellow Book.

28. Stresemann, *Vermächtnis*, I, 101, 112.

29. d'Abernon, *Ambassador*, II, 240; III, 110.

30. Stresemann, *Vermächtnis*, I, 95, 116, 115.

31. *Ibid.*, p. 132.

32. Bruno Buchrucker, *Im Schatten Seeckts; die Geschichte der "Schwarzen Reichswehr"* (Berlin, 1928).

33. Carl Mertens, *Verschwörer und Fememörder* (Charlottenburg, 1926).

34. Hjalmar Schacht, *Die Stabilisierung der Mark* (Stuttgart, 1927).

35. Stresemann, *Vermächtnis*, I, 169.

36. *Archiv des öffentliches Recht* (Tübingen), Neue Folge VII (1924), 11.

37. Stresemann, *Vermächtnis*, I, 184, 185.

38. *Ibid.*, p. 187. Radbruch, *Der innere Weg*, p. 171.

39. Stresemann, *Vermächtnis*, I, 195.

40. *Ibid.*, p. 200.

41. Information from Gessler.

42. Heiden, *Nationalsozialismus*, chap. v. Alan Bullock, *Hitler. A Study in Tyranny* (New York–London, 1952), p. 90 ff.

43. Severing, *Mein Lebensweg*, I, 447.

44. Rudolf Pechel, *Deutsche Gegenwart* (Darmstadt, 1952), p. 235.

45. Georges Clemenceau, *Grandeur et Misères d'une Victoire* (Paris, 1930), p. 190. English translation: *Grandeur and Misery of Victory* (New York, 1930).

46. Stresemann, *Vermächtnis*, I, 159, 161.

47. Bergmann, *Weg der Reparation*, p. 266.

48. Stresemann, *Vermächtnis*, I, 266. d'Abernon, *Ambassador*, II, 269, 277. Severing, *Mein Lebensweg*, I, 434. Arnold J. Toynbee, *Survey of International Affairs, 1924* (London, 1926), p. 400.

49. Stresemann, *Vermächtnis*, I, 244 f. Stampfer, *Vierzehn Jahre Republik*, p. 354.

50. d'Abernon, *Ambassador*, II, 275. Stresemann, *Vermächtnis*, I, 245.

51. *Entscheidungen des Reichsgerichts*, CVII, 76.

52. Arthur Nussbaum, *Die Bilanz der Aufwertungstheorie* (Tübingen, 1929), p. 14. Erich Eyck, *Krisis der deutschen Rechtspflege* (Berlin, 1926), p. 4.

53. Hjalmar Schacht, *Abrechnung mit Hitler* (Hamburg, 1948), p. 2.

54. Nicolson, *Curzon*, p. 375. Toynbee, *Survey, 1924*, p. 313.

55. Rabenau, *Seeckt*, p. 384.

56. Severing, *Mein Lebensweg*, II, 3.

57. R. Breuer, *Der Hitler-Ludendorff Prozess* (Berlin, 1924). *Der Hitler-Prozess, Auszug aus den Verhandlungsberichten* (München, 1924).

58. Karl Helfferich, *Reichstagreden* (2 vols., Berlin, 1922–1925), II, 221.

59. *Ibid.*, p. 218. Stresemann, *Vermächtnis*, I, 338.

60. Otto Braun, *Von Weimar zu Hitler* (New York, 1940), p. 147.

61. Stresemann, *Vermächtnis*, I, 408, 324.

62. Compare Paul von Schwabach, *Aus meinen Akten* (Berlin, 1927), p. 429, letter to Eyre Crowe.

CHAPTER IX: The Dawes Report and the London Conference

1. *Das Sachverständigen-Gutachten. Der Dawes- und McKenna-Bericht, nach dem Originaltext* (Frankfurt, 1924). Bergmann, *Weg der Reparation*, p. 275 ff.

2. Germany, Official Documents. *Die Londoner Konferenz Juli–August 1924* (Berlin, 1924; Reichstag Pamphlet No. 263 of that year).

3. Paul Schmidt, *Statist auf diplomatischer Bühne, 1923–1945* (Bonn, 1949). English translation: *Hitler's Interpreter* (New York–London, 1951).

4. Stresemann, *Vermächtnis*, I, 499, 564.

5. For the importance which the editors of *Die Grosse Politik* ascribe to political considerations, compare the correspondence in *The Times Literary Supplement* of August, September, and October 1953, especially the letters of Miss Isabella Massey (September 11, October 16) and James Joll (September 25).

6. Rabenau, *Seeckt*, p. 405.

7. Stresemann, *Vermächtnis*, I, 559.

8. *Ibid.*, p. 562.

9. Vallentin, *Stresemann*, p. 150.

10. Morgan, *Assize of Arms*, p. 266.

11. Rabenau, *Seeckt*, p. 401.

12. *Ibid.*, p. 452.

13. Benoist-Méchin, *l'Armée Allemande*, II, 346.

CHAPTER X: Ebert's Death and Hindenburg's Election

1. Severing, *Mein Lebensweg*, II, 50.

2. Germany, Official Documents. *Urteil des Schöffengerichts Berlin Mitte in der Strafsache gegen Barmat und Genossen* (Berlin, 1929). Kaufhold, *Der Barmat-Sumpf* (Berlin, 1925).

3. Eyck, *Bismarck*, III, 188.

4. Karl Brammer, *Der Prozess des Reichspräsidenten* (Berlin, 1925).

5. Friedrich Ebert, *Kämpfe und Ziele* (Dresden, 1927), p. 376.

6. d'Abernon, *Ambassador*, II, 115.

7. Stresemann, *Vermächtnis*, II, 44.

8. Great Britain, Public Record Office. "Nachlass des Reichministers Dr. Gustav Stresemann," 1925, for April 15, 16, 18, 1925, under Serial #7129 H. The letter to Maltzan of April 7 is under Serial #7135 H. (Also available at the United States National Archives under Germany, Auswärtiges Amt, Politisches Archiv.)

9. Ernst Troeltsch, *Historische Zeitschrift*, CXX (1919), 383 f. Heinrich Srbik, *Geist und Geschichte vom deutschen Humanismus bis zur Gegenwart* (2 vols., München, 1950–1951), II, 318. Robert Drill, "Spengleriana," *Aus der*

Philosophen-Ecke; kritische Glossen zu den geistigen Strömungen unserer Zeit (Frankfurt am Main, 1923), p. 37.

10. Ernst Troeltsch, *Der Historismus und seine Probleme* (Tübingen, 1922), p. 507, note.

11. Armin Mohler, *Die Konservative Revolution in Deutschland 1918 bis 1932* (Stuttgart, 1950).

12. John W. Wheeler-Bennett, *The Nemesis of Power: The German Army in Politics* (New York–London, 1953), p. 23.

INDEX

African colonies, 112–113, 114
Agrarian League, 160
Albedyll, von, 5
Albert, 228
Allenstein, 107
Alliance for the League of Nations, 319
Alsace-Lorraine, 33–34, 40, 125; in Franco-Prussian War, 83; in Treaty of Versailles, 86–87, 108–109
Alsberg, Dr. Max (1877–1933), 144, 147
Amnesty Law (August 4, 1920), 159–160
Annexationism, 2, 4, 37, 48, 59, 123, 125, 142; and Stresemann, 14; and Supreme Command, 22, 23; and Treaty of Brest-Litovsk, 26
Anschütz, Gerhart (1867–1948), 268, 331
Anti-Semitism, 151, 251, 271, 313; in Army, 4; Ludendorff and, 15, 31, 296, 315; and Preuss, 54; and Eisner, 57; and Cohn, 135; and Alsberg, 147; and Rathenau, 185, 201, 211, 214, 215; German Nationalists and, 190; Helfferich and, 212; Hitler and, 229, 248, 276; and Hilferding, 253; and Heilman, 328
Arco-Valley, Count, 78
Armistice, 32–46, 50, 94, 95, 100, 103, 105, 106, 116, 121, 122, 126, 144
Army, 5, 15–17, 25, 39, 134, 138, 247, 267, 333; Rightists in, 2–4; and Revolution, 44–45, 51–53, 136; in constitution, 74; in Treaty of Versailles, 86, 109, 110–112, 147; and Treaty of Versailles, 103; and Baltic States, 140–142; and Kapp Putsch, 148–150, 153–154, 157–158; and Spa Conference, 164–166; in Saxony, 179, 268; and Upper Silesia, 191; and Ruhr occupation, 238–242; in Bavaria, 249, 261–264, 267; and Munich putsch, 272, 273, 275–276, 277; and disarmament, 318–319; and election of Hindenburg, 339, 340
Asquith, H. H. (1852–1928), British Prime Minister (1908–16), 83, 301
Auer, Erhard (1874–1945), member of the Bavarian cabinet, 58, 78
Australia, 30, 112
Austria-Hungary: in First World War, 8, 12, 18, 26, 32, 37; and Bismarck, 68, 87–88; union with Germany, 77, 109; in Treaty of Versailles, 106
Austro-Serbian War, 58

Baden, 78, 236
Baldwin, Stanley, later Lord (1867–1947), British Prime Minister (1923–24, 1924–29, 1935–37), 255, 256, 300–301
Balfour, Lord (1848–1930), 230
Ballin, Albert, 227
Baltic Barons, 140
Baltic States, 108, 139–142
Baltic Volunteers, 148
Bamberger, Ludwig, 72
Bank for German Industrial Debentures, 325
Bank for Maritime Reconstruction, 175
Barmat, Julius (b. 1889), 326–329, 331–332, 340
Barth, Emil (b. 1879), 49, 59
Barth, Theodor, 54
Barthou, Louis (1862–1935), French politician, 203, 225, 231
Basserman, Ernst, 253, 254
Bauer, Gustav (1870–1944), Chancellor (1919–20), 102, 159, 327
Bauer, Colonel Max (1869–1929), 15–16, 18, 149
Bavaria, 62, 189–190, 236, 281, 295; abdiction of William II, 38; and constitution, 57–59, 73–74; and Revolution, 78–79; Kapp Putsch, 152–153, 160; Home Guard, 165, 175–176, 179, 188; and Decree for Protection of Republic, 218, 219–220, 228–229; and Hitler, 247–249; separatism, 250–251, 278, 293; and Stresemann, 261–264, 266–268, 270, 271; Munich putsch, 272–277
Bavarian Patriots, 58
Bavarian People's Party, 58, 62, 79, 152, 176, 190, 218, 228–229; and Stresemann, 255; in Marx's cabinet, 284; and Dawes Report, 307, 313; in Luther's cabinet, 322; and 1925 election, 335
Beer Hall Putsch, see Munich putsch
Becker, Dr. Carl (1876–1933), minister of culture (1921, 1925–30), 242, 323

102–103, 104–105; National Emergency Contribution, 133; dissolution demanded, 143, 149
National Defense Forces, 103
National Economic Council, 76–77
National Emergency Contribution, 132–133, 162
Nationalism, 2, 141, 248, 302; and Factory Council Law, 134; and Investigating Committee, 139; and Kapp Putsch, 147, 148; and Ruhr occupation, 156, 245; and June 1920 election, 162; and Spa Conference, 168; in Bavaria, 228; and separatism, 250; and Crown Prince William, 280; and London Conference (1924), 310, 311; and 1925 election, 340
Nationalists, *see* German National People's Party
National Liberals, 24, 253, 254; and Army, 3; and annexationism, 4; and Peace Resolution, 13, 14; and Bauer, 16; and Democrats, 60, 61
National Mortgage Bank, see *Rentenbank*
National Railroad Law, 314–315
National Socialist League, 3n
National Socialists, *see* Nazis
Naumann, Dr. Friedrich (1860–1919), Reichstag representative, 3n, 52, 162; and Peace Resolution, 13, 27; and constitution, 70, 76
Naval Affairs, Committee on, 11
Navy, 3, 6, 121; submarine warfare, 7–11; sailors' mutiny, 41–42, 52; Scapa Flow incident, 103, 110, 169, 179; Treaty of Versailles provisions, 109
Nazis, 80, 147, 157, 233, 295; in Bavaria, 229, 247–249; outlawed in Prussia, 236, 249; stage Munich putsch, 275, 276; in May 1924 election, 299; and Dawes Report, 313; in December 1924 election, 321; and Ebert, 329–330; in 1925 election, 335
New Zealand, 113
Norman, Montagu, governor of the Bank of England (1920–44), 291
Noske, Gustav (1868–1946), Reichstag representative (1906–20), minister of defense (1919–20), governor of Hanover (1920–33), 70–71, 78, 110; and abdication of Emperor, 37–38; and Revolution, 52, 53; in Weimar Coalition, 65; and Treaty of Versailles, 101, 103–104; and colonies, 113; and Baltic problems, 142; and Kapp Putsch, 149–150, 153; fall of, 156–158

Oeser, Rudolf (1858–1926), Prussian minister of the Reich, 74, 151, 325
Organization Consul, 189
Orgesch, see Home Guards
Otto, King of Bavaria, 57

Pabst, Captain, 148, 149
Pacelli, Eugenio, Monsignor, later Pope Pius XII (b. 1876), papal nuncio (1918–30): and negotiations for peace, 12–13, 20, 22; and Ruhr occupation, 237
Pan-German League, 142–143
Papen, Franz von (b. 1879), Chancellor (1932), 323, 337
Paris Conference (1923), 232
Particularism, 38, 57, 79, 100, 152, 177, 249
Passive resistance, 233–234, 237, 239, 245, 246, 256, 259–261, 266, 277, 279, 281, 292, 306
Patriots' Leagues, 311
Patriots' Party, 59
Payer, Friedrich von (1847–1931), Reichstag representative, vice chancellor (1917–18): and Peace Resolution, 13, 14; and Bethmann-Hollweg, 16; as vice chancellor, 24, 26, 30, 34; and Treaty of Versailles, 103, 105, 162
Peace Resolution, 13–14, 15, 19–21, 23, 26, 28, 143, 144, 145
Pensions, 118–119, 124
People's Party, *see* German People's Party
Petersen, Dr. Carl (1868–1933), Reichstag representative (1919–24), mayor of Hamburg (1924–33), 3, 228, 321
Philipp, 154
Plumer, General, 89
Pöhner, Ernst (1870–1925), 152, 190, 251, 273, 295
Poincaré, Raymond (1860–1934), French Premier (1922–24, 1926–29): his character, 199–200, 224, 239; and reparations, 201, 202, 221–222, 229–232, 246, 280; at Genoa Conference, 203, 208–209; and Ruhr occupation, 232, 234, 235, 243, 244, 245, 255, 256, 260, 277, 292, 301, 302, 304, 310; and separatism, 250, 251, 278–279, 293–294; and Dawes Committee, 291–292; defeated, 300, 301
Poland, 4, 148, 204, 222, 239; and Treaty of Versailles, 87, 99, 106–107, 109; war with Russia, 169–170; alliance with France, 173; and Upper Silesia, 180–181, 191, 192, 193